Starting and Operating a Business in Georgia

A Step-by-Step Guide

By Michael D. Jenkins,
Thomas J. Harrold, Jr., and Betsy Birns McCall

The Oasis Press® / PSI Research
Grants Pass, Oregon

92 AA

D1225361

Published by The Oasis Press®
© 1984, 1992 by Michael D. Jenkins, Thomas J. Harrold, Jr., and Betsy Birns McCall.

This publication is designed to provide accurate and authoritative information
in regard to the subject matter covered. It is sold with the understanding that the
publisher is not engaged in rendering legal, accounting, or other professional
service. If legal advice or other expert assistance is required, the services of a
competent professional person should be sought.

> *—from a declaration of principles jointly adopted by a committee of*
> *the American Bar Association and a committee of publishers.*

The author of chapters 1–10 of the *Starting and Operating a Business* series is
Michael D. Jenkins. The authors of the state chapter of *Starting and Operating
a Business in Georgia* are Thomas J. Harrold, Jr. and Betsy Birns McCall.

Managing Editor: Vickie Reierson
Editorial Assistance: Melody Joachims and Debbie Johnson
Format Design & Typography: Constance C. Dickinson
Assistant Typographer: Jan Olsson
Administrative Editor: Rosanno Alejandro

Please direct any comments, questions, or suggestions regarding this book to
The Oasis Press®/PSI Research:

Editorial Department
300 North Valley Drive
Grants Pass, OR 97526
(503) 479-9464
(800) 228-2275

The Oasis Press® is a Registered Trademark of Publishing Services, Inc.,
an Oregon corporation doing business as PSI Research.

Library of Congress Catalog Card Number: 80-83053

ISBN 1-55571-134-0 (paperback)
ISBN 0-916378-37-3 (binder)

Printed in the United States of America
Third edition   10 9 8 7 6 5 4 3 2 1 0   Revision Code: 92AA

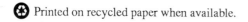 Printed on recycled paper when available.

Table of Contents

Part IV – State Laws & Related Resources

Notes to the State Chapter: What's New

Chapter 11. State Laws and Taxes

Index

Related Resources

Forms and Worksheets in this Book

Notes to Chapters 1–10

This new update of chapters 1–10 features a number of major additions, including a new section on the Family and Medical Leave Act of 1993. You will also find changes in current federal tax rates, legislation, and credits. To help you identify the most significant changes and additions to the text, review the list below. This list gives you the chapter–section number where you will find the specific discussions.

- New tax break for investing in stock of small business corporations, other than S corporations – 2.4
- S corporations less advantageous after Congress raises top tax rates on individual income from 31% top rate to 39.6% – 2.5
- New study at New Jersey Institute of Technology indicates that failure rate of new businesses is much lower than previously believed – 1.10
- Changes in tax rules for individual and corporate estimated taxes for 1994 – 4.6
- Write offs available for goodwill and other intangible assets when purchasing assets of a business – 3.5
- Business meals and entertainment expenses are only 50% deductible, starting in 1994 – 8.6
- Congress extends tax deduction for health insurance of self-employed persons, employer educational assistance plans, and the targeted jobs tax credit retroactively to June 30, 1992 – 2.2, 8.3, and 8.11
- Computer software now generally deductible over three years under the new tax law – 3.5
- Medicare portion of Social Security taxes (FICA and self-employment taxes) will apply to all of your earned income after 1993, not just the first $135,000 – 4.12
- Federal excise taxes on gasoline and diesel fuels increased by 4.3 cents per gallon – 7.3
- Luxury taxes on boats, airplanes, furs, and jewelry all repealed, retroactive to January 1, 1993. Tax on luxury autos remains, but will be indexed for inflation in 1994 – 7.3
- Tax rate increase for C corporations will only affect large corporations with over ten million dollars taxable income – 2.4
- No tax deduction allowed for compensation of more than one million dollars a year paid to certain executives – 8.9
- New section added on limited liability companies (LLCs) – 2.6
- SEC issues new rules making it easier for small firms to sell stock in public offerings – 4.14

The author of chapters 1–10 of the entire Starting and Operating a Business series, is Michael D. Jenkins. Mr. Jenkins, an attorney at law and a certified public accountant, is a graduate of Harvard Law School. He has worked in Los Angeles and San Francisco as an accountant and as an attorney with a prominent San Francisco firm well-known in the venture capital arena. He is a member of the State Bar of California, the American Bar Association, the American Institute of Certified Public Accountants, and the California Society of Certified Public Accountants.

How to Use this Book

0.1 Getting the Most Out of this Book

To most effectively use this book, become acquainted with the many helpful features it provides. Remember that each edition is updated annually to provide you with the most current information available. To find the most recent changes made to federal laws in chapters 1–10, refer to the What's New page. For similar state information, refer to the Notes page, which immediately precedes Chapter 11.

0.2 Numbered Section Heads Correspond to Table of Contents and Index

Text

Discussions range from explaining how to start and operate your business to examining such practical issues as insurance, marketing, cashflow management, internal financial controls, and much more. This book also explains federal and state government requirements and tax laws, as well as a number of emerging trends and issues your business may face.

Topics Noted in Margins

To make the information in this workbook easily accessible to busy people, the primary topics discussed within each numbered section are identified by "sideheads" in the margin beside the text.

Smaller Heads for Subtopics

When subsections of primary topics are discussed, the sideheads are slightly smaller.

Lists

- This small bullet helps you easily locate lists of requirements, things to do, and aspects of a particular subject or law.

Checklists

☐ Small boxes encourage you to enter a check, so that you can clearly see those items you've considered and dealt with—and those left to do.

Where the Action Begins

A number of worksheets are provided for you to answer questions and fill in numbers that form the basis for action plans, self-evaluation, budgeting, personnel policies, marketing feasibility studies, and the like.

The worksheets are set apart by boxes to clearly show where your interaction is required, to focus your thoughts, to record information, and to create the plans and reports that will help you establish and guide your business.

Worksheets

Sources and Data   Resources are set in tabular form to highlight the many agencies and companies listed to assist you.   **Contacts** Addresses Phone Numbers (listed in directory style)   **Resources**

The detailed Table of Contents will help you quickly find any specific section of the book you wish to refer to. The first digit of the chapter–section number indicates the chapter, followed by a period and the section number.

Table of Contents

The endnotes follow each chapter and are provided to assist you in accessing specific statutes, cases, regulations, and publications and to use this book as a starting place for legal research.

Endnotes

The subject-matter index, organized alphabetically with cross-referenced entries, provides an exhaustive list of the topics, indexed not only by the terms actually used in the entries but also by various other terms you might think of instead. The Index is referenced by the chapter–section number, not by page number, to help you find the corresponding discussion in the text.

Index

At the back of this book, you'll find a compendium of additional resources that will save you valuable research time and money.

Related Resources

The Appendix features a checklist of tax and various other major requirements for most businesses and a checklist of official government posters and notices required to be displayed by a business.

Appendix

Since many business requirements depend on submitting specific forms to various government agencies, some samples of these forms are included for your reference and listed in the Table of Contents.

Forms

At the back of this book, you will also find post cards preaddressed to government agencies and other sources so you can request additional information, posters, and forms.

Post Cards

Preface

Anyone who runs a small business today, or who is thinking about starting one, knows that he or she faces serious and growing challenges. The hurdles one must get over to start or continue to operate a business seem to have grown a little higher each year since this series of books was first introduced in 1981. In particular, the government has shifted more and more responsibilities onto the shoulders of employers in recent years, a trend that seems likely to continue. As a result, many large and small firms are currently putting off expansion and hiring plans until the new Clinton universal health care proposals are finalized, since mandated health care benefits could well become the biggest financial responsibility ever thrust upon the nation's businesses — especially upon smaller businesses.

Despite the growing complexities of running a business, the slow-growth economy, and the fact that according to Dun & Bradstreet, more than 420,000 businesses failed in the last decade, small businesspeople have not been deterred. Quite to the contrary — business start ups are flourishing in this tough environment. According to an August 1993 article in *Investor's Business Daily*, for every business that failed in the "wave of creative destruction" in the 1980s, at least 15 new businesses sprang up to take its place. While many in the mass media have bemoaned the rash of takeovers, leveraged buyouts, mass layoffs, downsizing, corporate restructuring, and other wrenching changes in the 1980s and early 1990s, all this ferment seems to have provided fertile ground for new, small, and nimble businesses.

In fact, according to Dun & Bradstreet, the number of "total concerns in business" almost tripled in the 1980s to more than eight million by 1990. That compares very favorably to the 1970s, when the total number of businesses increased by just 13.8%, to 2.8 million by the end of that decade. The desire of Americans, especially many recent immigrants from all corners of the world, to start and run their own businesses seems indomitable, obstacles or no.

The publisher and I would like to think this 51-book *Starting and Operating a Business* series — which features a book for each state and the District of Columbia — might have played a significant part in empowering many of the millions of people who have started their own businesses since our first edition in 1981. A more modest view, however, would suggest that we were merely on the leading edge of change, part of a huge expansion in the resources that have arisen in recent years to provide help to new and small firms.

At the time we introduced this series, there were only a few useful small business self-help books available, and relatively few government resources devoted to helping new enterprises get off the ground.

Today, however, there are books and software programs offering assistance on almost every aspect of running a large, small or medium-sized business. In fact, this book series is now only part of a much larger series of business self-help books on a wide array of subjects offered by the publisher, The Oasis Press. In addition, there are now Small Business Development Centers (SBDCs) and "one-stop" business permit offices in almost every state, and while state governments are cutting services left and right, most are expected to maintain or even increase their business services and economic development and other assistance to small businesses.

Why the turnaround? State governments recognize that new and existing small businesses are the backbone of their economies and the only sector of the economy that is currently providing growth in jobs for their residents. Thus, it should not be surprising that the states are doing as much as possible to encourage business growth, expansion, and relocation.

I became involved in this trend after advising small and large businesses over the years — first as an economic and management consultant, then later as a tax attorney and more recently as a certified public accountant. After years of helping many small businesses and venture capital start ups get off the ground, I had become increasingly aware of the need for a single, authoritative, and practical guide that would serve people starting and operating a business in a particular state — and acutely aware that no such guides existed, except in a very few states.

Thus, in 1980, I was particularly receptive when my neighbor and publisher, Emmett Ramey, approached me with the idea of writing a nuts-and-bolts guidebook for the state of California that would guide a small business person or entrepreneur through the maze of red tape at both the federal and state levels of government, as well as provide the basic steps and advice needed to get a new business off the ground.

We decided to create an operating manual that would draw together — in a readable, usable, and nontechnical format — the practical facts of life a person needed to know when establishing a business in California. Since first publishing that California edition, we have enlisted local experts in each of the other states to work with us and coauthor the books for those states.

By and large, tax, legal, and business information is useless when it is out of date. As a result, we update each state chapter (Chapter 11) and the federal section (chapters 1–10) in this series approximately every twelve months.

So, if you want an up-to-date guide to the basic financial, legal, and tax ground rules that apply to most businesses operating in your state, the *Starting and Operating a Business* series has been designed with you in mind as a self-help tool. It is also intended to be a useful (and footnoted) reference source to the attorney who has only a limited knowledge of business taxation and the basic regulatory requirements of a large number of federal, state, and local government agencies. Accountants will also find this series a useful resource for understanding the broad scope of government regulations that affect their small business clients.

While the *Starting and Operating a Business* books provide an authoritative discussion of many legal and tax matters regarding small business, they are not intended to be a substitute for professional legal or tax advice. On the contrary, they are designed to help you focus on key points to explore in greater depth with your attorney, accountant, benefits consultant, or other adviser. By being better informed, you can use your professional advisers' time more efficiently.

Many of the items covered in this book have been added at the request of readers who have written to us with their suggestions. This series is not a "finished" project, but is under constant revision. Accordingly, as the principal author, I invite and welcome your feedback or suggestions as to improvements we might make. Your letters should be addressed either to me or my coauthor for the state chapter of this edition, in care of the publisher.

Michael D. Jenkins
January 1994

Dedication

To America's entrepreneurs — tenacious, courageous men and women — whose contribution to the variety, richness, and quality of our lives is immeasurable.

Preliminary Considerations

Part I

Chapter 1

Making the Decision to Go into Business

Entrepreneurship is the last refuge of the troublemaking individual.

— James K. Glassman

1.1 Introduction

Neither this book nor any other book can tell you whether or not you should take the plunge and go into business for yourself. You alone must make that difficult decision. Before you make the decision, carefully consider some of the key points discussed in this chapter. Some of the points discussed you may not have considered yet, while others may assist you in dealing successfully with some initial problems you may face.

One of the first points to consider when starting your business is the major financial risk you will be taking. Once you have committed yourself financially, it will not be a simple or easy thing to change your mind and back out.

In addition, be aware there is a high failure rate among new businesses. Don't assume just because you are an expert in your field, you will be an automatic success. You will need to have strengths in other areas as well. In fact, statistics show that a very high percentage of those business failures result from poor management. Poor or ineffective management is usually a lack of balanced experience and competence in three areas:

- Marketing strategies — Know what kind of product or service to sell, how to target and reach your customers, and how to sell your product or service at a price that maximizes your profits.

- Technical ability — Be able to get the work done and do it right, so you will have satisfied customers. If you are going into the auto repair business, for example, you better know a lot about how to keep autos running right, or you will not be in business very long.

- Financial knowledge — While you do not necessarily have to be a financial wizard, you do need to know how to plan and control your business' cash flow, raise or borrow the money you will need to start your business, and get through tight periods without being caught short of cash. A certain amount of financial sophistication is becoming more and more important in today's increasingly complex financial world, even for the small business owner.

If you are lacking experience or knowledge in one or more of these three critical areas, the odds of your business succeeding are greatly reduced.

This chapter engages you in the process of realistically evaluating your entrepreneurial strengths and weaknesses. It is also intended to cause you to focus on some of the typical start-up problems and choices you are likely to face, as well as assist you in dealing effectively and rationally with those issues.

Worksheets are provided at the end of the chapter. While reading the text, pick up a pencil and write in your responses when appropriate. Often, the simple process of writing down your thoughts on specific problem areas may provide significant new insights.

1.2 Advantages and Disadvantages of Owning Your Own Business

Have you realistically considered both the advantages and the disadvantages of owning and operating your own business? If not, the time to do so is before, not after, you have committed yourself.

Advantages

If you are actively considering going into business for yourself, you most likely have already thought about the potential advantages, such as:

- Being your own boss and not having to report to a superior;
- Having the independence and authority to make your own business decisions;
- Direct contact with customers, employees, suppliers, and others;
- The personal satisfaction and sense of achievement that comes with being a success, plus the recognition that goes with it;
- The opportunity to create substantial wealth and job security for yourself;
- The opportunity to be creative and to develop your own idea, product, or service;
- The chance to make a living doing something you truly enjoy; and

- Doing something that contributes to others, whether it be providing an excellent product or service, providing employment, paying dividends to stockholders, or doing something else that is useful or that creates value.

If you are like most people, you may not have thought much about the downside of going into business; however, awareness of the potential disadvantages should not discourage you from your goal of going into business for yourself, if you have a strong commitment to that goal.

Disadvantages

Seriously consider whether you and your family are prepared to handle the disadvantages that often come with being an entrepreneur:

- In many ways, you are still not your own boss. Instead of having one boss, you will have many — your customers, the government agencies to whom you must report, and in some cases, your key suppliers.

- There is a large financial risk. The failure rate is high in new businesses, and you may lose not only your own money but also that of your friends and relatives who may have bankrolled you.

- The hours are long and hard. When you start your business, you will no longer be working 9 to 5. Count on working 10- to 12- or even 15-hour days, often six or seven days a week.

- You will not have much spare time for family or social life. And you can forget about taking any long vacations for the first few years since the business is unlikely to run itself without your presence for any long length of time.

- Your income may not be steady like a salary. You may make more or less than you could working for someone else, but in either case, your income may fluctuate up and down from month to month.

- The buck stops with you. If a problem arises, there is no boss you can take it to and say: "What do we do about this?" You are the boss and all the responsibility is yours. If anything goes wrong, the cost comes out of your pocket.

- You may be stuck for years doing work you do not like. Unlike an employee, you cannot simply quit and look for a better job. It may take you years to sell the business or find some other way to get out of it without a major financial loss.

- As a business grows, the amount of activity not associated with the primary business objective will increase. You will spend more time on personnel, administrative, and legal matters and less doing what you may have wanted most to do in your business.

- Increasing legislation and litigation make owning a business very risky. You can work a lifetime to build a business only to have it lost because of a lawsuit or a new law or regulation.

1.3 Typical Characteristics of the Successful Entrepreneur

A good deal is known about what it takes to be a successful entrepreneur. For the most part, it seems the one overriding factor is a tremendous need to achieve. In short, attitude seems to have almost everything to do with success in business, while factors, such as intelligence, education, physical appearance, and a pleasing personality, are much less important. Characteristics of typical successful entrepreneurs include:

- An overpowering need to achieve, as opposed to a need to be liked or to exercise power; the form in which different individuals measure their achievement varies widely, ranging from amassing wealth to building a larger organization to creating a better mousetrap than anyone else;
- The trait of following through on a commitment, not quitting halfway through when the going gets tough: in short, perseverance;
- A positive mental attitude or the ability to remain optimistic in new and unfamiliar situations, which essentially grows out of being self-confident about one's abilities;
- Objectivity — the ability to accurately weigh and assess risks associated with a particular course of action, as well as being realistic about one's own abilities and limitations;
- A respectful attitude toward money, but a tendency to look upon money as a means for accomplishing things, or a way of keeping score in the game of business, rather than as a thing to be sought as an end in itself;
- The tendency to anticipate developments and to make things happen rather than constantly reacting to problems as they arise;
- Resourcefulness — the ability to solve unique problems in unique ways and to be able to handle things that come up for which the entrepreneur has no previous experience to rely on as a guide;
- Strong personal relations skills — the characteristics of being cheerful and cooperative, and usually getting along well with, without necessarily being close to, employees and associates;
- Well-developed communication skills, both in oral and written presentations; and
- Well-rounded technical knowledge with emphasis on the knowledge about the physical process of producing goods and services.

How do your personal characteristics stack up against the foregoing profile of the typical successful entrepreneur? If that profile doesn't sound very much like you, maybe you had better give some long, hard thought as to whether you are cut out for making it as a business owner.

Running a business is not like working for someone else. No one is there to tell you what to do when something goes wrong. You are responsible for everything.

Are you capable of handling that kind of total responsibility? Are you a self-starter, capable of planning, organizing, and carrying out projects on your own? If not, you may find that starting and running a successful business is not for you.

Running a business demands a great deal in the way of initiative, hard work, self-discipline, and resourcefulness. On the other hand, solving the problems that arise from day to day and making it all work out can be a source of immense satisfaction, as well as be financially rewarding.

Before reading further, get a pencil and complete Worksheet 1, which is a useful questionnaire that may help you to get a better idea of your suitability for playing the role of entrepreneur in the real world. Worksheet 1 is located at the end of this chapter.

1.4 Knowing Your Market

One of the most important questions you should ask yourself is whether you feel that you know and understand the market for the particular kind of products or services you intend to sell. Do you know who your competition is and whether the particular market you intend to appeal to is large enough for both you and the existing competition? Also, how will your products or services measure up against those of your competitors in terms of quality and price?

If your product or service is something new or unusual, you need to have a sense of whether you will be selling an item that is wanted and needed in the marketplace. Or, even if you intend to sell a product or service that you know there is a need for, you should be satisfied in your own mind that you are going to be making it available at the right place at the right time.

Few sights are sadder than the boarded-up mom-and-pop store or restaurant — in which the owners have sunk their life savings — that never got off the ground for some obvious reason, such as lack of visibility from the street, lack of substantial foot traffic by its doors, or some other fatal flaw the inexperienced owners overlooked.

To succeed, you must find the right business opportunity. If you do not have a clear idea of what business you want to go into and where you want to operate it, you will need to do some intelligent investigation of all possible opportunities that might be suitable for you.

If you already have a concept of what you want to do, you will still need to do a great deal of investigating to make sure it is as good an opportunity as it appears to be. In either case, a lot of initial research and footwork is going to be advisable, unless you want to close your eyes and indulge in wishful thinking.

Determining Market Feasibility

In other words, to quote a well-known brokerage firm: "Investigate before you invest." This often entails doing your own marketing feasibility study before committing yourself to opening a new business.

A marketing feasibility study is simply a systematic analysis of any information you can obtain about the potential market for your product or service. This information can include the competition you face, the amount of sales you can reasonably expect to obtain in that particular market, and whether that level of sales will be adequate for your business to operate at a reasonable profit. For example, if you are planning to build homes in a small community where there is only a demand for five homes a year, and you need to build and sell ten homes a year to survive, doing a marketing feasibility study might help you realize your proposed business venture is not feasible, even if you were to capture 100% of the local housing market. Investigate first, then invest.

Alternatively, if you have several thousand dollars to spend and a well-defined idea of what it is you want to do, you can hire a professional economist or marketing consultant to do a feasibility study. In every major city, there are several firms that can do a thorough marketing and demographic study for you. Such a feasibility study can be quite valuable, but it will also be fairly expensive. Most people starting a new business tend to do their own marketing feasibility study, which is usually done very informally, if at all. The exception would be for people who create a formal, written business plan. A thorough analysis of the market for a new business' product or service is always a key portion of any such business plan. The Oasis Press publishes books and software that can assist you in creating a written business plan. See the list of publications in the back of this book for ordering information.

Before doing a marketing feasibility study, you obviously need to know what business you want to go into. When choosing your type of business, keep these thoughts in mind:

- If you see that a particular business is doing quite well and you want to go in and compete head-to-head with it, don't make the mistake of adopting a me-too approach and going in with the assumption that you can take away a lot of their business by competing on a price basis. Other than price, you better have a lot of good reasons why you think another business' customers will switch over to you. Other good reasons could include a distinctly better product, service, or location.

- Keep your eyes open for developing social, economic, and technological trends that will create new markets that you can move into at an early stage. It will help if you are a voracious reader of magazines such as *Time*, *Newsweek* (social trends); *Forbes*, *Business Week* (economic trends); or *Omni* or *Discover* (technological innovations).

An example of how observing social trends can translate into profits — in this instance stock market profits — is the case of an investment analyst in the 60s who noticed the trend toward mini-skirts and correctly anticipated that the spread of mini-skirts among women would create a boom market for panty hose. The analyst made a killing by buying stocks of panty hose makers.

So how do you go about analyzing the market for your product or service once you have focused on a particular business you might want to start? Worksheet 2 will help you pinpoint the kind of information you need to develop to satisfy yourself that a good market exists for whatever it is you are planning to sell. Before you read any further, take out a pencil and spend some time writing down your responses to each of the items on Worksheet 2.

Market Data Resources

Once you have identified your most likely potential customers, find out how to locate your business or structure and to direct your advertising and promotional efforts to most efficiently reach them. Fortunately, there is a great deal of published data you can use if you need to do this type of research. One of the best sources is *Sales and Marketing Management Magazine*, which publishes *Survey of Buying Power* each year. This survey provides breakdowns in population, households, retail sales by type of business, and total purchasing dollars for each county in the United States and for cities with a population of more than 10,000. To request information on *Survey of Buying Power*, see Statistical Information in Section 10.4.

Some of the printed sources of market information you can use in your research are:

- A.C. Nielsen market studies
- McGraw-Hill research studies from McGraw-Hill Publishing
- *National Trade and Professional Association (NTPA) Directory*
- Newspapers
- Statistical abstracts
- Trade magazines

Many of these items can be found in your local business or university library. The *NTPA Directory* can be ordered from:

National Trade and Professional Association Directory
Columbia Books
Washington, DC
(201) 898-0662

Various industry and government sources of information to consider are:

- Trade associations
- U.S. Chamber of Commerce
- U.S. Department of Commerce
- U.S. Small Business Administration

Another excellent source is the 1990 U.S. census data, which gives vast amounts of detailed information on the U.S. population and its buying habits by individual census tract. You may want to obtain a couple of useful pamphlets from your nearest U.S. Small Business Administration field office. Ask for the pamphlet entitled, *Researching Your Market*, for guidance on how to do your own market research.

Finding the Optimum Site

Even more important in your local community may be studies and future projections as to population and income trends that have been done by local groups, such as your local chamber of commerce or, in some areas, the local planning commission. If finding the optimum site to locate is important to your marketing effort, do the following:

- Talk to a knowledgeable person at your local chamber of commerce about business and other trends in the area where you intend to locate.
- Talk to a staff person at your local planning commission about census tract projections of future population growth, income trends, and economic development in the area you are considering. Also, they (or some other local agency, such as a traffic or streets department) will usually have done traffic counts showing how many cars pass certain points every day. This information can be very useful if you are opening a retail business. Also, consult any trade association, which serves your business and may have available information tailored exactly to your needs.
- Obtain a copy of the Small Business Administration's publication, *Choosing a Retail Location.*

For a complete guide to specifying, ranking, and evaluating the factors you must consider when choosing an optimum site for your new or relocating business, obtain a copy of *Company Relocation Handbook.* This handbook features a list of related reference publications and economic development organizations. Get your copy through your local book source or:

The Oasis Press
(800) 228-2275

1.5 Knowing the Business

Do you have any experience in the area of business in which you will be engaged? Of course, it is possible to learn while doing, but it helps a great deal to know a business before you start. Often, the most successful businesses are started by people who have worked in a particular line of business for years and who finally decide that they know the ropes well enough to leave their employer and start their own similar operation.

It helps to have experience in the particular business you propose to enter, but in most cases, your experience working in some other line of business will also have considerable carryover value. If you have neither type of experience, you may find you have a lot to learn once you begin the business.

A major management weakness that causes businesses to fail is the inability to get the job done and to do it right, on time, and efficiently enough to charge a competitive price for your product or service and still make a profit. For example, with the tremendous proliferation of personal computers, you may have decided to go into business repairing small computers. You may be absolutely right, but unless you have the technical capability to do such repairs, or the ability to properly select and hire employees who can do the job, you had better look for some other kind of business.

In many cases, if you know you lack the technical experience you need to open a particular kind of business, your best approach will be to get a job in that industry and work for someone else for a few years until you learn what you need to know. This may require a lot of patience, but it is definitely preferable than getting into a business you do not know well and losing your shirt in the process.

1.6 Knowing How Much Money It Will Take to Succeed

Can you afford to start a full-time business, if it will mean giving up your current employment and income? Many small businesses never really have a chance to succeed because the owners run out of money before the business becomes a viable operation. As a result, the owners often wind up having to go back to work for someone else again, disappointed and broke.

Carefully calculating and scheduling out, in as much detail as possible, the income and expenses you can reasonably expect for at least the first year of operation, as well as your living expenses and a reserve for emergencies, is a helpful step when determining how much money it will take to start and maintain your business.

You want to have enough money to last until the business reaches the point where you expect to make enough profit to live on. Remember a lot of expenses are involved in starting up almost any kind of business, and most businesses start out operating in the red for a time.

Completing worksheets 3 through 5 will help you plan your cash flow for the crucial first year of business. Worksheet 3 will help you to project your monthly sales revenue in terms of actual cash to be received. Worksheet 4 projects your monthly operating expenses for the first year of business, plus one-time, start-up expenses. Worksheet 5 is a schedule of your estimated personal living expenses during the first year.

Once you have completed worksheets 3 through 5, enter the monthly totals from the bottom line of each onto Worksheet 6, which is a summary of your cash needs. This will show you how much cash you will have to put into the business each month — and on a cumulative basis — during the first year of business. Once you have completed Worksheet 6, you will have a pretty good handle on how much money it is going to take to get your business started and approximately when you will need it.

If, under your most realistic projections, you are still running a deficit in cash flow each month at the end of the first year, you may want to do a similar projection out into the second year of operation.

If it appears you will need to borrow or raise money to keep the business operating until it gets into the black, find out well in advance how much you will be able to raise and whether or not you will be able to get that amount. If you plan to borrow, do you know how to put together a strong presentation to demonstrate to the prospective lender how you will be able to repay the loan? If not, see Section 9.7 and Chapter 10 for sources of information and help in obtaining financing for a small business.

For help in putting together an impressive loan application package, you may want to obtain a copy of *The Loan Package*, which will help you identify essential financial information for a loan, analyze your cash needs, and focus on the direction of your company. *The Loan Package* is available through your local book source or the toll-free number below.

Affordable and easy-to-use software programs that are helpful for small businesses have been developed by The Oasis Press. Many of the programs, such as *Small Business Expert* and *Start A Business*, complement this *Starting and Operating a Business* book.

The Oasis Press
(800) 228-2275

1.7 Signing a Lease

If you will need to lease space for your business location, have you located a suitable place that is available? If so, there are a number of critical points you need to consider before you sign a lease with a landlord.

Remember that a lease is a binding legal contract, and if you agree to pay rent of $1,000 a month for two years, you are on the hook for $24,000, unless you can sublease or assign the lease to someone else, which could be difficult or impossible to do, depending on the terms of the lease. Key points to consider when signing a lease agreement include:

- What are the terms of the lease? Most businesses tend to start off by either growing rapidly or folding quickly. Thus, except in a retail or service business, you will probably be better off initially leasing on a month-to-month basis or for as short a lease term as you can get, such as three or six months, even if the monthly rent is higher than for a longer lease. You will already have enough financial problems if your business fails, without being saddled with a long-term lease obligation.

- Can you put up the kind of sign you must have on the building? A business like a restaurant can be devastated if the landlord doesn't permit a sign that is sufficiently visible to passersby.

- Will the landlord permit you to make necessary improvements and alterations to the leased premises?

- Will the local health department, fire and police departments, air pollution control authorities, and zoning rules permit operation of your particular type of business at the location you have chosen?

- Is your location in a high-crime area that will require expensive burglary insurance and security precautions?

- Is there enough parking nearby or good public transit access for customers?

- Is the location appropriate to the kind of business you will conduct? There is usually no need to locate a manufacturing operation in a busy, high-traffic area. On the other hand, retail businesses are usually heavily dependent on the number of people passing nearby on foot or by car. For example, the Pillsbury Company reportedly selects its sites for Burger King fast food restaurants by looking for locations that have at least 16,000 cars passing by each day at an average speed of about 30 miles per hour.[1]

- Does the lease provide you with an option to renew — and at what rental price — after the initial term expires?

- If the lease is for more than just a few months, do you have the right to sublease or assign the lease? If so, under what conditions or restrictions?

1.8 Will You Hire Employees?

In certain kinds of businesses, during the initial start-up phases — and perhaps even afterwards — you may be able to operate without employees by either doing all your work yourself, with the help of family members, or by contracting out certain functions to independent, outside contractors. To the extent you can do so, you may find your life is much simpler by doing it yourself or with independent contractors.

Once you hire even one employee, you take on a great many responsibilities as an employer, over and above meeting a payroll every week or two. These responsibilities include paying and filing tax returns for federal and state unemployment taxes, Social Security taxes, and income tax withholding from wages. In addition, you will need to comply with workers' compensation laws, employee health and safety laws, anti-discrimination laws, U.S. immigration law restrictions on hiring, and a variety of other federal and state labor laws and regulations that may apply once you hire employees. These and other employer requirements are discussed in Chapter 5.

This section reviews some of the legal restrictions on your hiring practices and provides you with a working outline of what you will need to consider in the way of personnel policies once your business reaches the point where you will have to hire employees.

Hiring Practices

Hiring personnel can be complicated because of the broad array of state and federal laws designed to prevent an employer from hiring on the basis of discriminatory factors, such as age, sex, race, or religion. Most of these laws affect all but the smallest employers, so you will have to be alert to most of these rules to avoid even the appearance of discrimination in your hiring practices.

While anti-discrimination rules apply to promotions, job assignments, firing, and other aspects of the employment relationship as well as to hiring, the focus here is mainly on hiring practices. This is the area where most small business owners are likely to stumble into trouble, even when they have no intention to discriminate.

Things Not to Do

All questions or information you express should relate to job qualifications only and not to extraneous factors, such as age, race, sex, or physical size or condition.

If there are special occupational requirements — for example, hard physical labor that might preclude hiring certain handicapped individuals — be sure to carefully document such unusual situations or requirements.

Help Wanted Ads

Use the list below to guide you when writing a help wanted advertisement.

- Do not mention race or national origin or any attribute of national origin, such as native language.
- Do not refer to sex classifications, such as "girl wanted."
- Avoid any type of reference to age, such as "young boy" or "recent high school graduate."

Job Application Forms

Your employment application forms should avoid any questions or information on these topics:

- Arrest record;
- Whether the applicant has ever filed for unemployment benefits;
- Place of birth or where parents were born;

- Physical characteristics, such as height or weight;
- Social Security number;
- Marital status;
- Labor union affiliation;
- Request for photograph;
- Religious affiliation;
- Mode of transportation to work;
- Sex;
- Race or national origin;
- Clubs or organizations, unless you instruct the applicant not to list organizations that indicate race or national origin; and
- Native language or how the applicant learned a foreign language.

A sample employment application form is provided for your review on page 30. If you wish to add additional questions to it, be careful not to indirectly request anything that would reflect on the applicant's race, religion, sex, age, marital status, national origin, or physical condition. Because state laws differ, check with your legal adviser or state employment department before preparing your employment application.

Employment Interviews

During interviews with potential employees, refrain from asking questions, such as:

- Are you a U.S. citizen?
- When did you attend grade school, high school, or college?
- Do you have children, and who will care for them while you are working?
- Do you have any physical or mental handicap?
- What does your spouse do for a living, and are you likely to move elsewhere?
- Would your religion prevent you from working on holidays or certain days of the week?

Federal law generally bans the use of any kind of lie detector tests in most private employment situations, except for drug manufacturers and distributors and certain security firms.[2] Many state laws are even more stringent.

In addition, questions on possible felony convictions, previous military service, and drug or alcohol addiction are not necessarily illegal in all cases, but they may entail difficulties and probably should be avoided.

Checking References

As a general rule, former employers have no legal obligation to give you any information about a former employee. As a practical matter, however, most former employers will at least verify the former employee's employment and the date of employment. Since a former employer can get into trouble for giving you negative information that they cannot substantiate, don't expect them to volunteer much information or to put anything negative in writing. For that reason, you should generally do reference checks by phone. Acceptable questions would include those on:

- Verifying information given by the applicant;
- Asking about the applicant's principal strong points, weak points, and degree of supervision needed;
- Asking about the applicant's attitude;
- Asking how the applicant's performance compared with others; and
- Asking if the applicant would be rehired.

Personnel Policies

Even before you hire your first employee, you will need to outline some basic personnel policies. Better yet, if you write down your policies on matters such as hours, vacation time, and sick leave and can give such a written summary to new employees, it will greatly help to clarify the employment relationship. Perhaps it will even prevent a misunderstanding that could lead to legal action against you by an employee.

Worksheet 7 provides a series of questions that will help you focus on different personnel policies that are typical in a small to medium-sized business. For a more thorough treatment of this area, and if you wish to develop a personnel policy manual for your business, you may want to obtain a copy of *A Company Policy and Personnel Workbook* from The Oasis Press.

Related Information

To supplement the information you have just read in this chapter, you may want to read the following sections which discuss more related information:

- Employee or Independent Contractor? — Section 9.11
- Fair Employment Practices — Section 5.8
- Sexual Harassment — Section 5.8
- Immigration Law Restrictions on Hiring — Section 5.9
- Hiring a Spouse as an Employee — Section 8.12
- Employee Wage-Hour and Child Labor Laws — Section 5.7
- New Civil Rights Act — Section 9.14
- The Americans with Disabilities Act — Section 5.11
- Mandatory Family and Medical Leave Requirements — Section 5.12

In addition, to get an overview of other legal obligations that come with the territory when you have employees, scan through Chapter 5.

1.9 Other Questions You Need to Ask

- Will or should you advertise? If you do, you need to decide what kind of advertising will be the most cost-effective for your business, whether it be newspaper ads, direct mail, radio, posters, handbills, or other forms of advertising and promotion.
- Do you understand what will be involved in purchasing, managing, and restocking your inventory of goods?
- How will you go about selling? Will you hire sales clerks or outside salespeople, or will you do most of the selling yourself?
- Will you sell to customers on credit? If so, how will you protect yourself from bad credit risks and outright deadbeats?
- How much of your personal savings are you putting at risk by going into business? Are you willing to risk losing all of it if the business is a failure?
- Can you run the business alone — or with help from family members — or would you do better with one or more partners or business associates to provide additional capital and skills and to divide up some of the responsibilities of running the business?

Again, the questions posed in this chapter are not intended to discourage you from going ahead with starting your business. Chances are you have already considered most of the points raised in this chapter and are reasonably confident that you will be able to do what is necessary to make your business work. If so, many of the questions raised above probably seem rather elementary and obvious to you, as they will to most individuals seriously considering going into business, and you will now want to proceed to the discussions in the remainder of this book.

If you have not previously given serious thought to most of the above points that are relevant to the type of business you are planning to start, now is the time to take a long, hard look at whether you are adequately prepared to embark upon such a venture.

1.10 How Likely Are You to Succeed?

One of the chief deterrents to starting your own business is the fear of failure. This fear has long been enforced by scary statistics that state approximately four out of five new businesses fail after only a short period of time. Given those kinds of frightening odds, it is surprising that anyone is brave enough to start a business.

However, a recent in-depth study of business failure rates done at the New Jersey Institute of Technology (NJIT) suggests the grim statistics on new firm failures may be little more than myth. According to the study, no more than 18% of new firms fail during the first eight years of being in business. Over half (54%) of all start ups survive over eight years with either their original owners (28%) or with a change in ownership (26%). The other 28% of new firms voluntarily terminate operations without losses to creditors.

The author of the study, Bruce A. Kirchoff, professor of entrepreneurship at NJIT and former chief economist for the U.S. Small Business Administration, states, "I suspect entrepreneurs have known the truth about survival and success for some time. While economists argue that entrepreneurs are foolish to start new businesses because the risk of failure is so high, 400,000 or more new firms are formed every year in the U.S. All these entrepreneurs cannot be stupid; they look around and talk to others and realize that their chances of survival and success are far better than academic economists have estimated. It's the economists that look foolish."[3]

According to Kirchoff, the greater survival rate is consistent with the evidence that small firms are the primary job creators in the U.S. economy. The Kirchoff study is not a reason to become foolhardy or overconfident about your prospects for success. On the other hand, it does indicate that starting your own business may not be the five-to-one long shot gamble you may have been told it was.

Endnotes

1. San Francisco *Chronicle*, Aug. 3, 1980.
2. The Employee Polygraph Protection Act, 29 U.S.C. 2001.
3. Kirchoff, Bruce A., Ph.D. *Assessing Firm Failure Fictions*. New Jersey Institute of Technology, 1993.

Worksheet 1 – Self-evaluation Checklist for Going into Business

Under each question, check the answer that says what you feel or comes closest to it. Be honest with yourself.

Are you a self-starter?

☐ I do things on my own. Nobody has to tell me to get going.

☐ If someone gets me started, I keep going all right.

☐ Easy does it. I don't put myself out until I have to.

How do you feel about other people?

☐ I like people. I can get along with just about anybody.

☐ I have plenty of friends; I don't need anyone else.

☐ Most people irritate me.

Can you lead others?

☐ I can get most people to go along when I start something.

☐ I can give the orders if someone tells me what we should do.

☐ I let someone else get things moving; then I go along if I feel like it.

Can you take responsibility?

☐ I like to take charge of things and see them through.

☐ I'll take over if I have to, but I'd rather let someone else be responsible.

☐ There's always some eager beavers around wanting to show how smart they are. I say let them take the responsibility.

How good of an organizer are you?

☐ I like to have a plan before I start. I'm usually the one to get things lined up when the group wants to do something.

☐ I do all right unless things get too confusing; then I quit.

☐ Just when I'm all set, something comes along and presents too many problems, so I just take things as they come.

How good of a worker are you?

☐ I can keep going as long as I need to. I don't mind working hard for something I want.

☐ I'll work hard for a while, but when I've had enough, that's it.

☐ I can't see that hard work gets me anywhere.

☐ If I make up my mind to do something, I don't let anything stop me.

☐ I usually finish what I start if it goes well.

☐ If it doesn't go right away, I quit. Why beat my brains out?

Worksheet 1 – Self-evaluation Checklist for Going into Business (continued)

How good is your health?

☐   I never get run down.

☐   I have enough energy for most things I want to do.

☐   I run out of energy sooner than most of my friends seem to.

Count the checks you made.

How many checks are there beside the first answer to each question? _____

How many checks are there beside the second answer to each question? _____

How many checks are there beside the third answer to each question? _____

If most of your checks are beside the first answers, you probably have what it takes to run a business. If not, you're likely to have more trouble than you can handle by yourself. Better find a partner who is strong on the points you're weak on. If many checks are beside the third answer, not even a good partner will be able to shore you up.

Source: U.S. Small Business Administration.

Worksheet 2 – Marketing Feasibility Study Checklist for Your Product or Service

Your Product

Briefly describe the nature of the product or service you will offer:

_____

_____

_____

Most products or services have a life cycle, beginning with very rapid growth in the introductory stage, which slows down in the maturity stage, flattens out in the saturation stage, and finally begins shrinking in the declining stage. Which stage of its market cycle do you believe your product or service is in?

☐ introductory (high growth)   ☐ saturation (little or no growth)

☐ maturity (slower growth)   ☐ declining (negative growth in demand)

If you believe your product is in one of the earlier, faster growing stages of its life cycle, what edge do you believe your product will have over similar products that may be introduced by new competitors who may come into the field?

_____

_____

_____

If you are entering at a fairly late stage of the product marketing cycle, why is it you believe that you can succeed in taking away others' market share with your product or service?

_____

_____

_____

How is your product or service different in terms of quality and price from what is already on the market?

_____

_____

_____

Is there good reason to believe that your customers will recognize the difference? _____ If so, why?

_____

_____

_____

What is different about your marketing strategy or distribution strategy that will enable your product or service to succeed in a market where there is little, if any, growth?

_____

_____

_____

Worksheet 2 – Marketing Feasibility Study Checklist for Your Product or Service (continued)

Your Potential Customers

Not everyone is a potential customer. Certain age groups, income levels, geographic areas, ethnic groups, and educational levels will be more likely than others to be your customers. You need to focus on who will need your product and be most likely to buy it and then where to locate your business or how to structure your marketing approach to reach those segments of the market that you are most interested in reaching. Spell out below, as clearly as you can, who your customers are most likely to be.

The particular area from which I will be able to draw most of my customers is:

_____

_____

_____

_____

In addition, I should draw a significant number of customers from the following area or areas:

_____

_____

_____

My plan or strategy for reaching potential customers in the above areas can be summarized as follows:

_____

_____

_____

_____

The target market for my product or service, in terms of demographics, should be among the following persons (Describe your ideal customer's age, gender, educational level, and geographical location.):

_____

_____

_____

_____

In terms of income groups, my particular product or service should appeal primarily to people in the following income levels:

- ☐ Under $25,000 a year household income
- ☐ $25,000 – $35,000 a year
- ☐ $35,000 – $50,000 a year
- ☐ $50,000 – $75,000 a year
- ☐ $75,000 – $100,000 a year
- ☐ More than $100,000 a year

My product or service is likely to be more in demand by certain social, cultural, and ethnic groups than others. The groups that are most likely to be customers, if any, are:

_____

_____

_____

_____

_____

_____

_____

The groups that are least likely to be customers are:

_____

_____

_____

_____

_____

_____

_____

Your Competition

Even though you may have done a great job in pinpointing and studying your market segment, the job isn't done until you have considered your competition.

Main competitors in my market area are (list firms by name):

1. _____

_____

2. _____

_____

3. _____

_____

4. _____

_____

5. _____

_____

6. _____

Worksheet 2 – Marketing Feasibility Study Checklist for Your Product or Service (continued)

Based on my market research of statistical data, such as *Sales Marketing and Management Magazine*, the amount of buying power per business represented in my area is $ _____.

If I can generate that amount of sales, it: will ☐, will not ☐ be sufficient for me to operate successfully.

Five reasons why customers would buy from me rather than my competitors are:

1. _____
2. _____
3. _____
4. _____
5. _____

Five weaknesses my business will have when compared to my competitors are:

1. _____
2. _____
3. _____
4. _____
5. _____

To overcome these weaknesses, I will:

_____
_____
_____
_____
_____
_____
_____
_____
_____
_____
_____
_____
_____
_____
_____

Worksheet 3 – Estimated Cash Inflow from Sales for Year _____

	Jan.	Feb.	Mar.	Apr.	4-month Total
Gross Sales for Month					
Less: Credit Sales Made					
Subtotal: Cash Sales					
Plus: Collections on Prior Credit Sales					
Less: Bad Debts*					
Total: Net Cash Flow from Monthly Sales					

	May	June	July	Aug.	4-month Total
Gross Sales for Month					
Less: Credit Sales Made					
Subtotal: Cash Sales					
Plus: Collections on Prior Credit Sales					
Less: Bad Debts*					
Total: Net Cash Flow from Monthly Sales					

	Sept.	Oct.	Nov.	Dec.	4-month Total
Gross Sales for Month					
Less: Credit Sales Made					
Subtotal: Cash Sales					
Plus: Collections on Prior Credit Sales					
Less: Bad Debts*					
Total: Net Cash Flow from Monthly Sales					

Total Net Cash Flow from Monthly Sales for Year $ _____

* Consider using some percentage, say 1 or 2% of credit sale collections, to estimate your uncollectible debts.

Worksheet 4 – Estimated Business Cash Outlays for Year _____

	Jan.	Feb.	Mar.	Apr.	May
Monthly Expenses					
Rent					
Salaries and wages (except owner)					
Payroll taxes					
Advertising and promotion					
Insurance					
Federal estimated income tax					
State estimated income tax					
Owner's FICA or SE tax					
Telephone and utilities					
Inventory replacement purchase					
Interest on loans					
Maintenance					
Legal and accounting fees					
Office supplies					
Delivery expense					
Miscellaneous					
One-time Expenses					
Fixtures and equipment					
Decorating and remodeling					
Initial stock of inventory					
Utility and lease deposits					
Licenses and permits					
Other					
Total Expenses for Month					
Plus: Loan principal payment					
Less: Purchases on credit					
Plus: Payment on prior credit					
Net Monthly Cash Outlay					

June	July	Aug.	Sept.	Oct.	Nov.	Dec.	Annual Totals

Worksheet 5 – Estimated Personal and Living Expenses for Year _____

	Jan.	Feb.	Mar.	Apr.	May
Regular Payments					
Rent or house payment					
Property taxes					
Condo owner's dues					
Car payments					
Furniture and appliance payments					
Loan payments					
Health insurance					
Other insurance					
Household Expenses					
Food – restaurants					
Food – at home					
Telephone and utilities					
Water					
Personal Expenses					
Clothing and laundry					
Medical, dental, and drugs					
Education					
Dues and subscriptions					
Gifts and charity					
Gasoline and auto					
Entertainment and travel					
Miscellaneous spending					
Total Personal Expenses (Draw Required)					

June	July	Aug.	Sept.	Oct.	Nov.	Dec.	Annual Totals

Worksheet 6 – Summary of Estimated Cash Requirements for Year _____

	Jan.	Feb.	Mar.	Apr.	4-month Total
Net cash for month from sales – Worksheet 3					
Less: Net monthly cash outlay – Worksheet 4					
Subtotal: Net operating cash flow (or deficit)					
Less: Owner's draw for living & personal expenses – Worksheet 5					
Add: Money borrowed					
Add (or subtract): Equity capital paid in (or withdrawn) from the business					
Total: Net cash flow (or deficit) for month					
Cumulative* cash flow (or deficit)					

	May	June	July	Aug.	4-month Total
Net cash for month from sales – Worksheet 3					
Less: Net monthly cash outlay – Worksheet 4					
Subtotal: Net operating cash flow (or deficit)					
Less: Owner's draw for living & personal expenses – Worksheet 5					
Add: Money borrowed					
Add (or subtract): Equity capital paid in (or withdrawn) from the business					
Total: Net cash flow (or deficit) for month					
Cumulative* cash flow (or deficit)					

	Sept.	Oct.	Nov.	Dec.	4-month Total
Net cash for month from sales – Worksheet 3					
Less: Net monthly cash outlay – Worksheet 4					
Subtotal: Net operating cash flow (or deficit)					
Less: Owner's draw for living & personal expenses – Worksheet 5					
Add: Money borrowed					
Add (or subtract): Equity capital paid in (or withdrawn) from the business					
Total: Net cash flow (or deficit) for month					
Cumulative* cash flow (or deficit)					

* Add this month's net cash flow to the previous month's cumulative total.

Annual Totals: To get your total figures for the list below, add the three, four-month totals together for each item.

Net cash for month from sales – Worksheet 3 _____

Less: Net monthly cash outlay – Worksheet 4 _____

Subtotal: Net operating cash flow (or deficit) _____

Less: Owner's draw for living & personal
expenses – Worksheet 5 _____

Add: Money borrowed _____

Add (or subtract): Equity capital paid in (or
withdrawn) from the business _____

Annual cumulative cash flow (or deficit) _____

Sample Employment Application Form

Employment Application

Personal Data

Name: _____
　　　　　　(last)　　　　　　　　　　　　　(first)　　　　　　　　　　　　(middle)

Present address: _____
　　　　　　　　　(street address)　　　　　　　　　　(city)　　　　　(state)　　(zip)

Telephone numbers: _____　　_____
　　　　　　　　　　　(home)　　　　　　　(work)

Education

High School: _____　Graduated? Yes ☐ No ☐　Location: _____

College or University: _____　Graduated? Yes ☐ No ☐　Degree(s): _____

Other (specify type): _____　Graduated? Yes ☐ No ☐　Certificate(s): _____

　　　　　　　　　　　_____　Graduated? Yes ☐ No ☐　Certificate(s): _____

Work Experience

List below all present and previous employment, starting with the most recent.

Company name: _____　From (mo/yr): _____　Type of work: _____

Address: _____　To (mo/yr): _____　Name of Supervisor: _____

　　　　　_____　Reason you left: _____

Company name: _____　From (mo/yr): _____　Type of work: _____

Address: _____　To (mo/yr): _____　Name of Supervisor: _____

　　　　　_____　Reason you left: _____

Company name: _____　From (mo/yr): _____　Type of work: _____

Address: _____　To (mo/yr): _____　Name of Supervisor: _____

　　　　　_____　Reason you left: _____

Company name: _____　From (mo/yr): _____　Type of work: _____

Address: _____　To (mo/yr): _____　Name of Supervisor: _____

　　　　　_____　Reason you left: _____

May we contact the employers above?　Yes ☐　No ☐　If yes, list any employers you do not wish us to contact:

_____

_____

Remarks: _____

_____

_____

Worksheet 7 – Defining Your Company's Personnel Policies

Working Hours

Describe briefly the policy you will set for working hours, including:

Starting time? _____

_____

How much time will be allowed for lunch? _____

_____

Quitting time? _____

_____

Which days of the week employees will be expected to work? _____

_____

If, like many companies these days, you will adopt some kind of "flex-time" system, spell out how it will work.

_____

_____

_____

_____

Overtime

Outline your policy on overtime work. Refer to Section 5.7 of this book for legal requirements for paying overtime premiums. See also Section 11.5 regarding state wage laws. Points to consider here include:

Will you pay exempt employees (administrative or professional) overtime if they work extra hours? _____

_____

Will you require employees to obtain permission to work overtime? _____

_____

Compensation

Make a list of the job positions in the company other than your own and the compensation level for each. On a separate piece of paper, write out a specific job description for each position, outlining duties and responsibilities. Refer to sections 5.7 and 11.5 of this book for a description of hourly minimum wage requirements.

Position	Hourly wage	Salary	Total monthly pay
_____	_____	_____	_____
_____	_____	_____	_____
_____	_____	_____	_____
_____	_____	_____	_____
_____	_____	_____	_____

Worksheet 7 – Defining Your Company's Personnel Policies (continued)

Vacation Policy

Describe how much paid vacation employees will have and how this may increase after a certain number of years of service. _____

_____

Will vacation time and sick leave time off be combined into a single category for employees (as some companies now do to reward employees who do not abuse sick leave and to discourage others from using sick leave as additional vacation by playing hooky)? _____

_____

Will you pay employees, who terminate, for unused vacation? (The laws of many states require you to do so.)

_____

_____

Sick Leave Policy

Outline your policy for both paid sick leave and unpaid sick leave, or whichever you choose to provide, if not both.

Sick leave: _____

_____

Unpaid sick leave: _____

_____

Leaves of Absence

What will your policy be towards employees who request unpaid leaves of absence? _____

_____

_____

Time Off with Pay

Will you provide other time off with pay for such eventualities as funerals or emergencies in an employee's immediate family?

Funerals or family emergencies? _____

_____

Jury duty? _____

_____

Birth of a child? _____

_____

Attend work-related seminars and training sessions? _____

_____

Promotions and Evaluations

Outline your policy for evaluating employees' performance and determining when promotions will be made.

_____

_____

_____

_____

_____

Fringe Benefits

Consider which employee fringe benefits you will provide and specify your policy for each.

Medical insurance: _____

_____

Long-term disability insurance: _____

_____

Life insurance: _____

_____

Dental insurance: _____

_____

Medical expense reimbursement: _____

_____

Child care benefits: _____

_____

Maternity benefits: _____

_____

Pension or profit-sharing plans: _____

_____

Paid holidays: _____

_____

Automobiles or allowances: _____

_____

Expense accounts: _____

_____

Worksheet 7 – Defining Your Company's Personnel Policies (continued)

Fringe Benefits (continued)

Education assistance programs: _____

_____

_____

_____

Employee discounts on purchases: _____

_____

Stock options (if incorporated): _____

_____

Incentive bonus plan: _____

_____

Other: _____

_____

_____

_____

Placement Fees

If you hire employees through a personnel agency or "headhunting" firm, will you pay the placement fee?

_____

_____

Other Company Policies

_____

_____

_____

_____

_____

_____

_____

_____

_____

_____

_____

_____

Chapter 2

Choosing the Legal Form of the Business

The hardest thing in the world to understand is Income Tax.

— Albert Einstein

2.1 General Considerations

A business venture can be structured in several ways; however, the law classifies businesses so that most fall into one of three legal forms — the sole proprietorship, the partnership, or the corporation. There are also certain variations on some of these basic legal forms, such as the S corporation and the limited partnership. In addition, the limited liability company (LLC), a relatively new form of business organization, has gained legal status in a majority of states. See Section 2.6 for more on LLCs.

If you are planning to start a business, consider the following questions when deciding your business' legal form:

- Will someone else share in ownership of the business? If so, it will not be a sole proprietorship. The choice will be between a partnership arrangement and a corporation, or possibly a limited liability company.

- How important is it to limit personal liability for debts or claims against the business? If this is a major consideration, incorporating the business would generally be the best means of limiting your liability.

- Which form of business organization will result in the least taxes? While there is no universal answer to this question, the rest of this chapter explains when it is and isn't beneficial to incorporate for tax reasons.

Before choosing the legal form of your business, it is important to realize that you may need to change to a different form at some time in the

Changing Legal Forms

future. Changing legal forms is easier to do with some forms of business than with others. As a broad generalization, it is usually a simpler matter to change from a sole proprietorship to a partnership, or to change from a sole proprietorship or partnership to a corporation, than it is to move in the opposite direction.

For example, converting a corporation into a sole proprietorship or partnership may result in substantial individual and corporate-level taxes when the corporation is liquidated. This would occur if the value of the business, when transferred to the stockholders of the corporation, was greater than the cost or tax basis for their stock, resulting in taxable gains to the stockholders. If some of the corporate assets have value in excess of their tax basis, the corporation will also have taxable gains and will pay a corporate tax on such gains when it transfers the assets to its stockholders.

While there are almost always some expenses and complications in changing the legal form of a business, such changes are quite routine transactions. Many businesses start off as sole proprietorships, develop into partnerships, and later incorporate, if tax and other considerations indicate that it no longer makes good business sense not to be incorporated. Thus, the choice of one legal form when starting a business should not be considered a final choice.

2.2 Advantages and Disadvantages of Sole Proprietorships

The great advantage of operating a new business as a sole proprietorship is that it is simple and does not require any formal action to set it up. You can start your business today as a sole proprietorship — there is no need to wait for an attorney to draft and file documents or for the government to approve them.

Of course, you will need a business license, and a few states require you to register to do business. As a sole proprietor, you are the sole owner of your business. If married, however, your spouse will usually have a one-half interest in the business in a state which has community property laws.

Personal Liability

As the owner of the sole proprietorship, you will be personally liable for any debts or taxes of the business or other claims, such as legal damages resulting from a lawsuit. This is one reason why many entrepreneurs prefer to use a corporation rather than a sole proprietorship. Unlimited personal liability is perhaps the major disadvantage of operating a business in the form of a sole proprietorship.

Profit (or Loss) Is Yours

All of the profit or loss from your business belongs to you and must be reported on your federal income tax return, *Schedule C, Income (or Loss) from a Business or Profession,* on *Form 1040.* This can either be an advantage or a disadvantage for income tax purposes, depending on the circumstances.

If operating the business results in losses or significant tax credits, you may be able to use the tax losses or tax credits to reduce taxes on income from other sources. Or, if your sole proprietorship generates modest profits — but not more than about $60,000 to $75,000 a year — overall taxes may be less than if incorporated, assuming you need most of the income to live on.

As a sole proprietor, you are not considered an employee of your business. As a result, you will avoid having to pay unemployment taxes on your earnings from the business. Both the state and federal governments impose unemployment taxes on wages or salaries, but not on self-employment income. Note that a corporation would normally get an income tax deduction for the unemployment tax it paid on your salary, so that the actual after-tax savings from operating as a sole proprietorship would be somewhat less than the unemployment taxes you would avoid paying. Refer to sections 5.3 and 11.5 regarding the unemployment taxes you must pay for each employee.

Unemployment Tax Savings

Another advantage of a sole proprietorship is that you can shift funds in and out of your business account or withdraw assets from the business with few tax, legal, or other limitations. In a partnership, you can generally withdraw funds only by agreement and, in the case of a corporation, a withdrawal of funds or property will usually be taxable as a dividend or capital gain and may violate some states' corporation laws.

Withdraw Assets Tax-Free

A major disadvantage of sole proprietorships and partnerships is they cannot obtain a number of significant tax benefits regarding group-term life insurance benefits, long-term disability insurance coverage, and medical insurance or medical expense reimbursements. To qualify for favorable tax treatment regarding such fringe benefit plans, it is necessary to incorporate. A self-employed individual is allowed to deduct 25% of his or her health insurance in computing adjusted gross income.[1] This deduction will expire after December 31, 1993 unless Congress extends it again.

Limited Tax Savings for Fringe Benefits

The special advantages of corporate pension and profit-sharing plans have largely been eliminated since 1984. As of now, there are virtually no differences in the tax treatment of self-employed (Keogh) plans of sole proprietorships and partnerships, as compared with corporate retirement plans. See Section 8.3.

See the table at the end of this chapter which summarizes the key characteristics of sole proprietorships, partnerships, and corporations.

2.3 Advantages and Disadvantages of Partnerships

General Partnerships

In general, any two or more individuals or entities who agree to contribute money, labor, property, or skill to a business and who agree to share in its profits, losses, and management are considered to have a partnership. You can choose to have a general partnership or a limited partnership.

Creating a partnership can be a very simple matter since the law does not require any formal written documents or other formalities for most partnerships. As a practical matter, however, it is much sounder business practice for partners in a business to have a written partnership agreement that, at a minimum, spells out their agreement on such basic issues as:

- How much and what kind of property each partner will contribute to the venture;
- What value will be placed on the contributed property;
- How profits and losses will be divided among the partners;
- When and how profits will be withdrawn;
- Whether or how certain partners will be compensated for their services to the partnership or for making capital available to the partnership; and
- How changes in ownership of interests in the partnership will be handled.

A written partnership agreement should be prepared by an attorney and, if possible, should be reviewed by a tax accountant before it is put into effect. Partnerships are a bit like marriages; they usually start out with a great deal of trust but have a high break-up rate. Be advised that partnerships are easy to get into, require a lot of patience and understanding to live with, and are often costly and painful to get out of.

Liability of Partners

As a partner, you are an agent for the partnership and can do anything necessary to operate the business, such as hire employees, borrow money, or enter into contracts on behalf of the partnership. You and each of your partners — except for a limited partner in a limited partnership — have personal liability for the debts, taxes, and other claims against the partnership.

If the partnership's assets are not sufficient to pay creditors, the creditors can satisfy their claims out of your personal assets. In addition, when any partner fails to pay personal debts, the partnership's business may be disrupted if his or her creditors proceed to satisfy their claims out of his or her interest in the partnership by seeking what is called a charging order against partnership assets.

State and Federal Tax Requirements

While a partnership must file federal and usually state information returns — *Form 1065* is the federal form — it generally pays no income tax. Instead, the partnership reports each partner's share of income or loss on the information return, and each partner reports the income or loss on *Schedule E* of his or her individual income tax return, *Form 1040*.

Certain partnerships are allowed to use a fiscal year, rather than the calendar year, for tax filing purposes; however, these partnerships may have to report and pay income taxes directly if the use of a fiscal year results in a tax-deferral benefit to their partners.[2] The exceptionally complex accounting required to determine this tax is part of the price a partnership must pay if it elects to have a fiscal tax year.

In addition, partnerships are required to file a special report, *Form 8308*, with the IRS each time a sale or exchange of an interest in the partnership occurs.[3]

Like a sole proprietor, a partner is not generally considered an employee of the partnership for income tax and payroll tax purposes. The income tax advantages and disadvantages of a sole proprietorship are equally applicable to a partnership since a partner's share of income from a partnership is treated essentially the same as income from a sole proprietorship. For example, your income from a partnership may be subject to federal self-employment tax but not to federal and state unemployment taxes as discussed in Section 2.2.

Dissolution

Unless a partnership agreement provides otherwise, a partnership usually terminates when any partner dies or withdraws from the partnership. This is in contrast to a corporation which, theoretically, has perpetual existence. Under the laws of most states, bankruptcy of a partner or the partnership itself will cause the dissolution of the partnership, regardless of any agreement.

Limited Partnerships

The law provides for a special kind of partnership in which partners have limited personal liability: the limited partnership. The limited partnership is more regulated than the more common general partnership, but it allows investors who will not be actively involved in the partnership's operations to become partners without being exposed to unlimited liability of the business' debts, if it should go out of business.

A limited partner risks only his or her investment but must allow one or more general partners to exercise control over the business. In fact, if the limited partner becomes involved in the partnership's operations, he or she may lose his or her protected status as a limited partner. The general partners in a limited partnership are fully liable for the partnership's debts. Every limited partnership must have one or more general partners as well as one or more limited partners.

State law requires certain formalities in the case of a limited partnership that are not required for other partnerships. To qualify for their special status, limited partnerships must usually file a *Certificate of Limited Partnership* with the secretary of state or other state and county offices. Establishing a limited partnership also requires a written partnership agreement. See Section 11.2 regarding special filing requirements for partnerships under state law.

2.4 Advantages and Disadvantages of Corporations

A corporation is an artificial legal entity that exists separately from the people who own, manage, control, and operate it. It can make contracts, pay taxes, and is liable for debts. Corporations exist only because state statutory laws allow them to be created.

A business corporation issues shares of its stock, as evidence of ownership, to the person or persons who contribute the money or business assets which the corporation will use to conduct its business. Thus, the stockholders or shareholders are the owners of the corporation, and they are entitled to any dividends the corporation pays and to all corporation assets — after all creditors have been paid — if the corporation is liquidated.

Limited Personal Liability

The main reason most businesses incorporate is to limit owner liability to the amount invested in the business. Generally, stockholders in a corporation are not personally liable for claims against the corporation and are, therefore, at risk only to the extent of their investment in the corporation. Likewise, the officers and directors of a corporation are not normally liable for the corporation's debts, although in some cases an officer whose duty it is to withhold federal income tax from employees' wages may be liable to the IRS if the taxes are not withheld and paid over to the IRS as required.

Potential Loss of Limited Personal Liability

The advantage of limited liability is not always completely available through incorporation. For example, don't start a corporation on a shoestring. If your corporation is capitalized too thinly with equity capital (your money) as compared to debt capital (borrowed money), the courts may determine that your corporation is a thin corporation and hold you and your stockholders directly liable to creditors.

Failure to observe corporate formalities and the separate legal existence of the corporation can have a similar result. This is called "piercing the corporate veil" by the courts, and means if a corporation is not adequately capitalized and properly operated to protect the interests of creditors, the courts can take away the veil of limited liability that normally protects the stockholders.

Piercing the corporate veil is relatively uncommon. A much more frequent problem is that many banks and other lenders will not loan money to a small incorporated business unless someone, usually the stockholders of the corporation, personally guarantees repayment of the loan.

Despite this common business practice, the limited liability feature can still be an important protection from personal liability for other debts, such as accounts payable to suppliers and others who sell goods or services to the corporation on credit, typically without requiring any personal guarantee of payment by the owners.

Even this partial protection is a significant advantage of incorporating for most small business owners. Being incorporated can also protect you from personal liability regarding lawsuit damages not covered by your corporation's liability insurance policies; for example, someone slips on a banana peel in your store and sues the corporation for ten million dollars. To help you avoid personal liability for corporate acts, consult your attorney and keep thorough and specific records of your corporation's operations, policies, and meetings.

Unlike a sole proprietorship or partnership, a corporation has continuous existence and does not terminate upon the death of a stockholder or a change of ownership of some or all of its stock. Creditors, suppliers, and customers, therefore, often prefer to deal with an incorporated business because of this greater continuity.

Continuous Existence

Naturally, a corporation can be terminated by mutual consent of the owners or even by one stockholder in some instances.

To set up a corporation, you must file articles of incorporation with the state office that grants and approves corporate charters. See Section 11.2 for more information on state incorporating requirements.

Cost of Incorporating

Legal fees usually run between $500 and $1,000, even for a simple incorporation, and if it is necessary to obtain a permit from the state to issue stock or securities, legal fees can be much more.

Thus, it should be apparent that one of the disadvantages of incorporating is the cost involved, which will be substantial even for the simplest incorporation. In addition to the costs of establishing a corporation, there will be recurring costs, often including annual franchise or corporate income taxes.

Corporations filing their income tax returns on *Form 1120-A* or *Form 1120* will be taxed at different rates depending on the amount of their taxable income. The following table lists the current federal corporate income tax rates, which are 39% in the highest bracket.

Federal Corporate Income Taxes

Taxable Income	Tax Rate	
Not over $50,000	15%	**Corporate Tax Rate Table**
$50,000 to $75,000	25%	
$75,000 to $100,000	34%	
$100,000 to $335,000	39%	
$335,000 to 10 million	34%	
$10 million to $15 million	35%	
$15 million to $18,333,333	38%	
More than $18,333,333	35%	

As an owner, you will most likely draw a salary from your corporation. This salary will be subject to FICA (Social Security) taxes and state and federal unemployment taxes. These unemployment taxes, however, are not imposed on your income when you own a sole proprietorship or partnership. FICA taxes are generally the same (in total) on the wages of a corporate employee/owner as would be the self-employment tax on the same amount of business income if you were a sole proprietor or a partner.

For certain types of unincorporated businesses, however, such as a firm whose income is from interest or real estate rentals, or both, there is no self-employment tax on the income. By incorporating such a firm, you would unnecessarily incur FICA (Social Security) taxes of 15.3% on your earnings from the business.

Personal Service Corporations

Certain kinds of corporations called qualified personal service corporations (QPSCs) are taxed at a flat rate of 35%, instead of the graduated tax rates listed above.[4] While it may not always be clear whether an incorporated service business is a QPSC, the IRS defines a QPSC by these characteristics:

- At least 95% of the value of its stock is held by employees or their estates or beneficiaries; and
- The employees perform services at least 95% of the time in the following fields: health, law, engineering, architecture, accounting, actuarial science, performing arts, or consulting.

Double Taxation of Corporate Earnings

Regular corporations, which are also called C corporations, have one major potential disadvantage that usually does not exist for other legal forms of doing business — the problem of potential double taxation of the earnings of the corporation. This problem arises because a C corporation must pay corporate income taxes on its taxable income. Then, the after-tax earnings may be subject to a second tax on either the individual stockholders, if the earnings are distributed as dividends, or as a corporate penalty tax, if the earnings are not distributed as dividends.

The main ways in which a corporation's earnings can be subject to double taxation are:

- Payment of taxable dividends — Shareholders will be taxed when the corporation pays dividends to them out of earnings that have already been taxed once at the corporate level. In this case, the shareholders would pay individual federal income taxes (plus state tax, in most states) on the dividends they receive. If, for example, the corporation has already paid tax at a marginal rate of 34% on its income, and individual federal income tax of roughly 40% is paid by the stockholders on the remaining 66% of corporate income that is distributed to them as dividends, then less than 40% of the profit earned by the corporation will end up in the owners' bank accounts after taxes. Even less would remain after taxes in a state that has corporate or individual income taxes, or both.

- Corporate accumulated earnings tax — Corporations that retain too much of their after-tax earnings, instead of paying out the earnings as dividends, risk being hit by the accumulated earnings tax. This tax rate can be up to 39.6% of the accumulated income.

- Certain other C corporations that are considered to be "personal holding companies" under the federal tax law are exempt from the accumulated earnings tax; however, they may instead be subject to a 39.6% personal holding company tax on their undistributed income that is derived from certain sources, such as rents, royalties, and interest or dividends received from stock investments.

- Even if a corporation avoids all of the above double taxation problems during its existence, double taxation may yet arise if the corporation is liquidated or if the value of its stock has increased above the price paid for it by the stockholders. In that case, the stock holders will usually have to pay capital gains taxes if the amount they receive in liquidation exceeds the tax basis of their shares of stock.

As a practical matter, few small incorporated businesses ever encounter actual double taxation, except when the corporation is liquidated. Most small corporations do not pay dividends, and there are many tax-planning approaches that will enable a company and its shareholders to avoid the accumulated earnings tax or personal holding company tax on their undistributed earnings.

See Section 8.9 for a discussion of various tax planning techniques that will permit you to avoid the problems of potential double taxation listed above.

Income Splitting

By using a corporation, it may be possible to split your overall profit between two or more taxpayers so that none of the income gets taxed in the highest tax brackets. Thus, the total tax paid by the two taxpayers — you and your corporation — may be less than if all of the income were taxed to you, as in a sole proprietorship.

See Section 8.2 for a more detailed discussion of how income splitting can help reduce your income and estate taxes.

Fringe Benefit Plans

Federal and state tax laws permit you, as a corporate employer, to provide a number of different fringe benefits to employees on a tax-favored basis. These tax-favored fringe benefits include medical insurance plans, self-insured medical reimbursement plans, disability insurance, and group-term life insurance. An unincorporated business receives the same tax treatment for its employees, but not for its owners. In an unincorporated business, the payments made on behalf of the sole proprietor or partners for these fringe benefits are generally not deductible as expenses of the business, in contrast to fringe benefits paid for by a corporation for its shareholders/employees. So the tax benefits of employee fringe benefits, such as those listed above, are another reason for incorporating your business and becoming an employee of the corporation.

Note, however, that if your corporation is an S corporation, it will be treated much like a partnership for fringe benefit purposes, with regard to its shareholders who own 2% or more of its stock.[5] An exception to this partnership treatment of S corporation shareholders is for medical insurance premiums paid on their behalf, which can be deducted by the S corporation. However, the amount deducted by the corporation for medical insurance must be reported as taxable compensation income on the shareholder/employee's *Form W-2*, for income tax purposes,[6] but not for FICA (Social Security) tax purposes if the insurance plan covers employees generally.[7]

Unlike an unincorporated business, a corporation — other than an S corporation — can generally deduct the insurance premiums or other fringe benefit payments it makes on behalf of an employee who is an owner of the business, while the employee is not taxed on the value of the benefit provided. This is far more favorable than payments of salary to an employee, which are fully taxable.

The major types of fringe benefit plans, other than retirement plans, that allow for tax deductions to the corporation and no taxable income to the employee are discussed in more detail in Section 8.3.

Tax Break for Dividends Received by a Corporation

Another important tax advantage of a C corporation is that, in general, it can deduct 70% of the dividends it receives from stock investments from its federal taxable income.[8] This tax benefit, called the dividends received deduction, is discussed in more detail in Section 8.2.

Tax Break for Investing in Small Business Stock

The Clinton tax package that was enacted in August 1993 provides a major new tax incentive for investing in the stock of certain small corporations. This incentive is not available for investments in unincorporated businesses or in stock of S corporations.

A noncorporate investor who purchases "qualified small business stock" after August 10, 1993 and holds it for five years or more will be allowed to exclude from his or her taxable income up to 50% of any capital gain reported on the sale of stock.[9] If the current maximum tax rate on capital gains remains at 28%, this would translate into a very low effective tax rate of only 14% on gains from qualified small business stock.

Qualified small business stock is stock of a C corporation that meets an active business test during the period the stock is held. Stock in a special entity, such as a Domestic International Sales Corporation (DISC), regulated investment company, or a real estate investment trust, is ineligible. In addition, the corporation must not have more than $50 million in gross assets before or immediately after the stock is issued to the investor.

To meet the active business test, a corporation must use at least 80% of its assets in the conduct of one or more qualified trades or businesses. Personal service firms, banks, finance or investment businesses, insurance companies, and farming businesses are not considered qualified trades or businesses; neither are companies in certain extractive industries, or in the hotel, motel, or restaurant businesses.

While this section has outlined a number of important tax advantages of incorporating a business, the picture is not all that one-sided. Some of the potential tax disadvantages of corporations are discussed in more detail in Section 8.9. Most of those disadvantages are not applicable if you elect S corporation status. Deciding whether to incorporate in this state or elsewhere is discussed in Section 9.12.

Corporate Income Tax Disadvantages

2.5 Advantages and Disadvantages of S Corporations

The first thing to understand about S corporations — formerly referred to as Subchapter S corporations — is they are just like any other corporation in terms of corporate law requirements, limited liability of shareholders, and all other corporate aspects, except regarding tax treatment. An S corporation is simply a regular corporation that meets certain requirements and which has elected to be treated somewhat like a partnership for federal income tax purposes. Most, but not all, states also allow this special tax treatment for S corporations. See Section 11.2 for a discussion of how S corporations are treated for tax purposes in this state.

Once a corporation has made an election with the IRS to be treated as an S corporation, its shareholders will generally report their share of the corporation's taxable income or loss on their individual tax returns. That is, the corporation "passes through" its income or loss and tax credits to the shareholders in proportion to their stock holdings in the corporation, much like a partnership.

The S corporation does not usually pay tax on any of its income.[10] Any domestic S corporation, however, must file *Form 1120S, U.S. Income Tax Return for an S Corporation*, regardless of any tax due. *Form 1120S* must be filed by March 15, if filing under a calendar-year basis, or the 15th day of the third month following the close of a fiscal year.

An S corporation must furnish a copy of *Schedule K-1, Shareholder's Share of Income, Credits, Deductions* to each shareholder. By not providing *Schedule K-1* before filing *Form 1120S*, the S corporation could incur penalties.

In certain instances, an S corporation may be subject to tax on "built-in gains." Built-in gains are untaxed gains on the assets of a corporation that would have been recognized as taxable if the assets had been sold at fair market value on the day a corporation became an S corporation.

Profits are deemed to be distributed to the shareholders on the last day of the corporation's tax year, whether or not the profits are actually distributed.[11] Thus, if profits of an S corporation are distributed as dividends, the distribution itself is ordinarily not taxable, so there is no double taxation of distributed profits.

The Clinton Deficit Reduction tax package enacted in August 1993 has made S corporations somewhat less attractive because it raised individual tax rates to a new maximum rate of 39.6%, up from 31%. In addition, the top corporate rate remains at 34%, except for corporations with more than ten million dollars of taxable income. These corporations now pay 35%. Shareholders of an S corporation may now pay individual income tax at a higher rate than would a C corporation in some income brackets and at a lower rate in other brackets. Thus, from a tax-rate standpoint, S corporations no longer enjoy a clear advantage over C corporations.

In addition, capital gains on sale of the stock of an S corporation will not qualify for the new 50% capital gain exclusion that is discussed in Section 2.4.

S Corporation Requirements

To qualify for S corporation treatment, your corporation must meet the following requirements:

- It must be a domestic corporation — that is, incorporated in the United States.[12]
- No shareholder can be a nonresident alien individual.[13]
- All of its shareholders must generally be individuals, although certain trusts, called Qualified Subchapter S Trusts and Grantor Trusts, may hold stock under certain circumstances. No shareholder can be a corporation or a partnership.[14]
- The corporation can have only one class of common stock and no preferred stock.[15]
- There cannot be more than 35 shareholders.[16] For this purpose, a husband and wife who are both stockholders will be counted as only one stockholder, whether or not they hold the stock in joint ownership.[17]
- The corporation cannot be a member of an affiliated group of corporations.[18] If it owns stock in a subsidiary that is considered an affiliate, it may not be able to qualify under the S corporation provisions.
- Less than 25% of the corporation's gross receipts during three successive tax years must be from passive sources, such as interest income, dividends, rent, royalties, or proceeds from the sale of securities.[19] The passive income limit does not apply at all for a brand new corporation or an existing corporation that has no accumulated earnings and profits when it elects S corporation status.[20]

Electing S Corporation Status

To become an S corporation, your company must meet the above requirements and file an election on *Form 2553* with the IRS. The election must be signed by all of the corporation's shareholders,[21] including your spouse, who may have a community property interest in stock that is in your name. The S corporation election must be filed during the first two months and 15 days of the corporation's tax year for which the election is to go into effect or at any time during the preceding tax year.[22]

Since a newly formed corporation that wants to start out as an S corporation does not have a preceding tax year, it has to file an election in the two-month and 15-day period after it is considered to have begun its first tax year. Its first tax year is considered to start when it issues stock to shareholders, acquires assets, or begins to do business, whichever occurs first. Filing of articles of incorporation with the secretary of state usually does not begin the first taxable year.

Care must be taken to file the election at the right time, which can be tricky, since it is sometimes difficult to determine when a corporation first begins to do business. There can be some horrendous tax consequences if you operate the corporation as though it were an S corporation, and the election is later determined to have been filed too early or too late.

Extreme care must also be taken if a regular C corporation elects to change over to S corporation status; this should not be done without consulting a competent tax adviser. A regular corporation that elects to become an S corporation will generally be subject to an eventual corporate-level tax on any built-in gains on its assets — assets with a value greater than their tax basis — if assets are sold for a gain within ten years.

Terminating an S Corporation Election

If it becomes desirable to revoke or terminate S corporation status after a few years, as is often the case, this can be done if shareholders owning more than half the stock sign and file a revocation form.[23] A revocation is effective for the tax year it is filed, if it is filed during the first two months and 15 days of that tax year.[24] If it is filed later in the year, it does not become effective until the next tax year.[25]

Doing anything, however, that causes the corporation to cease to qualify as an S corporation — such as selling stock to a corporate shareholder — will also terminate the election, effective on the first day after the corporation ceases to qualify as an S corporation. In that case, the company must file two short-period tax returns for the year, the first — up to the date it ceased to qualify — as an S corporation, the second as a regular taxable corporation.

Once a corporation terminates an S corporation election, it cannot re-elect S corporation status for five years, unless it obtains the consent of the IRS.[26]

Reasons for Electing S Corporation Status

For a corporation, electing S corporation status can be very advantageous in some instances, and less so, or even disadvantageous in other situations. An S corporation election should not be made without the advice and assistance of a tax professional, since it is a very complex and technical area of the tax law.

Electing S corporation treatment for a corporation is usually most favorable in these types of situations:

- Where it is expected that the corporation will experience losses for the initial year or years of doing business and where the shareholders will have income from other sources that the "passed through" losses can shelter from tax. If S corporation losses are passive losses — such as losses from real estate investments — they can only be used to offset other passive activity income, except for certain shareholders who are real estate professionals.

- Where, because of the low tax brackets the shareholders are in, there will be tax savings if the anticipated profits of the corporation are passed through to them rather than being taxed at corporate tax rates.

- Where the nature of the corporation's business is such that the corporation does not need to retain a major portion of profits in the business. In this case, all or most of the profits can be distributed as dividends without the double taxation that would occur if no S corporation election were in effect.

- Where a corporation is in danger of incurring an accumulated earnings penalty tax for failure to pay out its profits as dividends.

It will often be advantageous for your corporation to operate as an S corporation in its early years, when losses can be passed through to shareholders, or when income is not so great as to push the shareholders into higher tax brackets. Also, the nontax advantage of being incorporated and protected from personal liability if the business fails is generally most important during the early years of operation, when the risk of failure is highest.

Many businesses initially start off as S corporations, obtaining the advantage of limited liability while being taxed much like an unincorporated business. Later, when or if the profit from the business becomes very substantial, the S corporation election can be terminated, and the C corporation can be used to split income between the corporation and its stockholder/employees.

Disadvantages of S Corporation Election

While there are some significant advantages to operating as an S corporation, the S corporation election is frequently not advisable under some circumstances. Some of the possible disadvantages of operating your business in the form of an S corporation are:

- The change to S corporation status may eventually result in a large corporate-level tax on built-in gains or an immediate LIFO recapture tax.

- The tax law regarding S corporations is very complex and you should expect to pay fairly substantial additional legal or accounting fees to your tax adviser, compared to what would be necessary with a regular corporation.

- S corporations are now treated almost exactly like regular corporations with respect to pension and profit-sharing plans. One important difference remains; any employee who owns 5% or more of the stock and participates in the S corporation's pension or profit-sharing plan is prohibited from borrowing from the plan, unlike a participant in a regular corporation's retirement plan.[27]

- Certain built-in gains of an S corporation may be taxed to the corporation and the shareholder for federal tax purposes.[28]

- Fringe benefit payments for medical, disability, and group-term life insurance for 2% shareholders are deductible, to the corporation, but are taxable to the shareholder/employee.[29]

- Unlike many regular corporations, very few newly electing S corporations may now have a fiscal tax year that ends earlier than September.[30]

For your convenience, a sample of *Form 2553, Election by a Small Business Corporation*, and a summary of key characteristics regarding business organization forms are provided at the end of this chapter.

2.6 Advantages and Disadvantages of Limited Liability Companies

In addition to the three traditional forms of business organization discussed above, many states have created, by statute, a new type of entity called a limited liability company (LLC). An LLC closely resembles and is taxed as a partnership, and it offers the benefit of limited liability like corporations.

In 1988, the IRS concluded in Revenue Ruling 88-76 that a Wyoming limited liability company could be classified as a partnership for federal income tax purposes, despite its limited liability, because it lacked continuity of life. Under Wyoming law, LLCs have to terminate in a specified period of years, usually 30 years or less.

Another reason for this classification is because interests in the LLC were not freely transferable. This ruling was highly favorable, from a taxpayer's standpoint, because LLCs offer the corporate benefits of limited liability, while retaining the flexible flow-through tax treatment of a partnership. This is generally preferable even to an S corporation for income tax purposes.

Because this favorable IRS ruling opened the floodgates, more than two-thirds of the states have followed Wyoming's lead in adopting similar LLC laws, and several other states are currently considering doing so.

Despite the obvious advantages of LLCs, do not be in a rush to set one up, even if you are located in one of the states that has adopted a limited liability company law. At present, if you set up an LLC in State X that allows LLCs and you do business in State Y, which does not, your LLC may not provide any limited liability protection from creditors in State Y. This is a severe risk, and one you won't face if your business is incorporated. Another potential drawback is that a subcommittee of the U.S. House Ways and Means Committee is already looking into the possibility of enacting federal legislation that would cause LLCs to be taxed as corporations in order to prevent the loss of significant federal tax revenues.

Such legislation, if enacted, would defeat the whole purpose of setting up an LLC and could even leave you in a considerable tax predicament if you put your business into an LLC and the law changed subsequently. You might even have to pay a large capital gains tax if you then decided to liquidate the LLC. Extreme caution is advised before adopting LLC status. Consult a good tax adviser before you even consider setting up an LLC. See Chapter 11 for more specific information on LLCs in this state.

Endnotes

1. I.R.C. §162(l).
2. I.R.C. §§444 and 7519.
3. I.R.C. §6050K.
4. I.R.C. §11(b)(2).
5. I.R.C. §1372(a).
6. Rev. Rul. 91-26, 1991-1 C.B. 184.
7. I.R.S. Ann. 92-16, 1992-5 I.R.B. 53.
8. I.R.C. §243(a).
9. I.R.C. §1202.
10. I.R.C. §1374.
11. I.R.C. §1366.
12. I.R.C. §1361(b).
13. I.R.C. §1361(b)(1)(C).
14. I.R.C. §1361(b)(1)(B).
15. I.R.C. §1361(b)(1)(D).
16. I.R.C. §1361(b)(1)(A).
17. I.R.C. §1361(c).
18. I.R.C. §1361(b)(2)(A).
19. I.R.C. §1362(d)(3).
20. I.R.C. §1362(d)(3)(B).
21. I.R.C. §1362(a)(2).
22. I.R.C. §1362(b).
23. I.R.C. §1362(d)(1)(B).
24. I.R.C. §1362(d)(1)(C)(i).
25. I.R.C. §1362(d)(i)(C)(ii).
26. I.R.C. §1362(g).
27. I.R.C. §4975(d).
28. I.R.C. §1374(a).
29. Rev. Rul. 91-26, 1991-1 C.B. 184.
30. I.R.C. §1378(a).
31. I.R.C. §162(1).

Notes

Key Characteristics of the Various Legal Forms of Business Organization – Summary

	Proprietorship	General or Limited Partnership
Simplicity in Operation and Formation	Simplest to establish and operate.	Relatively simple and informal, except that a limited partnership must have a written agreement.
Liability for Debts, Taxes, and Other Claims	Owner has unlimited personal liability.	General partners have unlimited personal liability; limited partners are only at risk to the extent of their investment.
Federal Income Taxation of Business Profits	Taxed to the owner at individual tax rates of up to 39.6% or more, depending on exemptions and deductions which may phase out.	Taxed to partners at their individual tax rates.
Double Taxation if Profits Withdrawn from Business	No.	No.
Deduction of Losses by Owners	Yes. May be subject to "passive loss" restrictions.	Yes. But limited partner's deductions cannot exceed amount invested as a limited partner — except for real estate, in some instances. Losses are generally restricted by the "passive loss" rules.
Social Security Tax on Earnings of Owner from Business	15.3% of owner's self-employment earnings in 1994 on first $60,600 of income, plus 2.9% on earnings of more than $60,600, half of which is now deductible for income tax purposes.	15.3% of each partner's share of self-employment earnings from the business in 1994 on up to $60,600 in earnings are taxed, plus 2.9% tax on earnings over $60,600. Half of tax is deductible for income tax.
Unemployment Taxes on Earnings of Owner from Business	None.	None.
Retirement Plans	Keogh plan. Deductions, other features now generally the same as for corporate pension and profit-sharing plans. But proprietor cannot borrow from Keogh Plan.	Keogh plan. Same as for proprietorships. A 10% partner cannot borrow from Keogh Plan.
Tax Treatment of Medical, Disability, and Group-Term Life Insurance on Owners	Not deductible, except part of medical expenses may be an itemized deduction on owner's tax return, including medical insurance premiums. However, 25% of medical insurance on an owner is allowed as a deduction from adjusted gross income — at least until December 31, 1993.[31]	Not deductible, except part of medical expenses may be an itemized deduction on owner's tax return, including medical insurance premiums. However, 25% of medical insurance on an owner is allowed as a deduction from adjusted gross income — at least until December 31, 1993.
Taxation of Dividends Received on Investments	Dividends received on stock investments are fully taxable to owner.	Dividends taxable to individual partners. See proprietorship.

Limited Liability Company	Regular Corporation	S Corporation
Generally similar to a partnership, but required to file articles of organization.	Requires most formality in establishment and operation.	Same as a regular corporation but requires close oversight by a tax adviser (an additional cost).
Members are generally not liable for an LLC's debts, but they often have to guarantee loans, as a practical matter, which is similar to a corporation.	Stockholders are not generally liable for corporate debts, but often have to guarantee loans, as a practical matter, if the corporation borrows money. Also, corporate officers may be liable to the IRS for failure to withhold and pay withholding taxes on employees' wages.	Stockholders are not generally liable for corporate debts, but often have to guarantee loans, as a practical matter, if the corporation borrows money. Also, corporate officers may be liable to the IRS for failure to withhold and pay withholding taxes on employees' wages.
Taxed to owners at their individual tax rates, unless the IRS treats the LLC as a corporation.	Taxed to the corporation, at rates higher than those of individuals — maximum of 34% or 39% in 1993, except for very large corporations.	Taxed to individual owners at their individual rates — certain gains are taxable to the corporation as well.
No, unless the LLC is treated as a corporation.	Yes, but not on reasonable compensation paid to owners who are employees of the corporation.	No, in general.
Yes, generally, if treated as a partnership by IRS. No, if treated as a corporation by IRS.	No. Corporation must carry over initial losses to offset future profits, if any.	Yes, in general, for federal tax purposes. But not for state tax purposes in all states. Loss for a shareholder limited to investment in stock plus amount loaned to the corporation. Losses may be subject to "passive loss" restrictions.
Not clear yet. Probably same as for a partnership, if treated as partnership by IRS. Same as a corporation, if the LLC is treated as a corporation.	Owner/employee of corporation pays 7.65% on his or her salary and corporation pays 7.65%. Total Social Security (FICA) tax on employer and employee is 15.3% of employee's first $60,600 of wages (in 1994). Employee and corporation each pay 1.45% on wages above $60,600.	Owner/employee of corporation pays 7.65% on his or her salary and corporation pays 7.65%. Total Social Security (FICA) tax on employer and employee is 15.3% of employee's first $60,600 of wages (in 1994). Employee and corporation each pay 1.45% on wages above $60,600.
Not clear yet, but probably none, if treated as a partnership for income tax purposes by IRS.	Yes. State and federal unemployment taxes apply to salaries paid to owners.	Yes. State and federal unemployment taxes apply to salaries paid to owners.
Not clear yet, but probably same as a partnership, if treated as a partnership by IRS.	Corporate retirement plans are no longer significantly better than Keogh plans. Deduction limits are same now as for Keogh, but participants can borrow from plan.	Plans now essentially identical to regular corporate retirement plans, except that shareholder/employee (5% shareholder) of S corporation cannot borrow from plan.
Not clear yet, but probably same as a partnership, if treated as a partnership by IRS.	Corporations may be allowed to deduct corporation medical insurance premium or reimbursements paid under medical reimbursement plan. Generally not taxable to the employee, even if employee is an owner. Similar treatment for disability and group-term life insurance plans.	Fringe benefits for 2% shareholders are deductible by corporation, but must be included in income of the shareholder who may be allowed to deduct 25% of medical insurance from adjusted gross income.
Dividends taxable to individual members, if the LLC is treated as a partnership.	Dividends are taxable to the corporation. However, 70% of the dividends received are generally free of federal income tax (unless stock is purchased with borrowed money), an important tax advantage.	Dividends taxable to individual shareholders of the S corporation, as in the case of a partnership.

Instructions for Form 2553: Sample

 Department of the Treasury
Internal Revenue Service

Instructions for Form 2553

(Revised December 1990)

Election by a Small Business Corporation

(Section references are to the Internal Revenue Code unless otherwise noted.)

Paperwork Reduction Act Notice.—We ask for the information on this form to carry out the Internal Revenue laws of the United States. You are required to give us the information. We need it to ensure that you are complying with these laws and to allow us to figure and collect the right amount of tax.

The time needed to complete and file this form will vary depending on individual circumstances. The estimated average time is:

Recordkeeping . . . . .6 hrs., 28 min.
**Learning about the
law or the form** . . . . .3 hrs., 16 min.
**Preparing, copying,
assembling, and sending
the form to IRS** . . . .3 hrs., 31 min.

If you have comments concerning the accuracy of these time estimates or suggestions for making this form more simple, we would be happy to hear from you. You can write to both the **Internal Revenue Service,** Washington, DC 20224, Attention: IRS Reports Clearance Officer, T:FP, and the **Office of Management and Budget,** Paperwork Reduction Project (1545-0146), Washington, DC 20503. **DO NOT** send the tax form to either of these offices. Instead, see the instructions below for information on where to file.

General Instructions

A. Purpose.—To elect to be treated as an "S Corporation," a corporation must file Form 2553. The election permits the income of the S corporation to be taxed to the shareholders of the corporation rather than to the corporation itself, except as provided in Subchapter S of the Code. For more information, see **Publication 589,** Tax Information on S Corporations.

B. Who May Elect.—Your corporation may make the election to be treated as an S corporation only if it meets **all** of the following tests:

1. It is a domestic corporation.

2. It has no more than 35 shareholders. A husband and wife (and their estates) are treated as one shareholder for this requirement. All other persons are treated as separate shareholders.

3. It has only individuals, estates, or certain trusts as shareholders. See the instructions for Part III regarding qualified subchapter S trusts.

4. It has no nonresident alien shareholders.

5. It has only one class of stock. See sections 1361(c)(4) and (5) for additional details.

6. It is not one of the following ineligible corporations:

(a) a corporation that owns 80% or more of the stock of another corporation, unless the other corporation has not begun business and has no gross income;

(b) a bank or thrift institution;

(c) an insurance company subject to tax under the special rules of Subchapter L of the Code;

(d) a corporation that has elected to be treated as a possessions corporation under section 936; or

(e) a domestic international sales corporation (DISC) or former DISC.

See section 1361(b)(2) for details.

7. It has a permitted tax year as required by section 1378 or makes a section 444 election to have a tax year other than a permitted tax year. Section 1378 defines a permitted tax year as a tax year ending December 31, or any other tax year for which the corporation establishes a business purpose to the satisfaction of the IRS. See Part II for details on requesting a fiscal tax year based on a business purpose or on making a section 444 election.

8. Each shareholder consents as explained in the instructions for Column K.

See sections 1361, 1362, and 1378 for additional information on the above tests.

C. Where To File.—File this election with the Internal Revenue Service Center listed below.

If the corporation's principal business, office, or agency is located in ▼	Use the following Internal Revenue Service Center address ▼
New Jersey, New York (New York City and counties of Nassau, Rockland, Suffolk, and Westchester)	Holtsville, NY 00501
New York (all other counties), Connecticut, Maine, Massachusetts, New Hampshire, Rhode Island, Vermont	Andover, MA 05501
Florida, Georgia, South Carolina	Atlanta, GA 39901
Indiana, Kentucky, Michigan, Ohio, West Virginia	Cincinnati, OH 45999
Kansas, New Mexico, Oklahoma, Texas	Austin, TX 73301
Alaska, Arizona, California (counties of Alpine, Amador, Butte, Calaveras, Colusa, Contra Costa, Del Norte, El Dorado, Glenn, Humboldt, Lake, Lassen, Marin, Mendocino, Modoc, Napa, Nevada, Placer, Plumas, Sacramento, San Joaquin, Shasta, Sierra, Siskiyou, Solano, Sonoma, Sutter, Tehama, Trinity, Yolo, and Yuba), Colorado, Idaho, Montana, Nebraska, Nevada, North Dakota, Oregon, South Dakota, Utah, Washington, Wyoming	Ogden, UT 84201
California (all other counties), Hawaii	Fresno, CA 93888
Illinois, Iowa, Minnesota, Missouri, Wisconsin	Kansas City, MO 64999
Alabama, Arkansas, Louisiana, Mississippi, North Carolina, Tennessee	Memphis, TN 37501
Delaware, District of Columbia, Maryland, Pennsylvania, Virginia	Philadelphia, PA 19255

D. When To Make the Election.—Complete Form 2553 and file it either: **(1)** at any time during that portion of the first tax year the election is to take effect which occurs before the 16th day of the third month of that tax year (if the tax year has 2½ months or less, and the election is made not later than 2 months and 15 days after the first day of the tax year, it shall be treated as timely made during such year), or **(2)** in the tax year before the first tax year it is to take effect. An election made by a small business corporation after the 15th day of the third month but before the end of the tax year is treated as made for the next year. For example, if a calendar tax year corporation makes the election in April 1991, it is effective for the corporation's 1992 calendar tax year. See section 1362(b) for more information.

E. Acceptance or Non-Acceptance of Election.—The Service Center will notify you if your election is accepted and when it will take effect. You will also be notified if your election is not accepted. You should generally receive a determination on your election within 60 days after you have filed Form 2553. If the Q1 box in Part II is checked on page 2, the corporation will receive a ruling letter from IRS in Washington, DC, which approves or denies the selected tax year. When Item Q1 is checked, it will generally take an additional 90 days for the Form 2553 to be accepted.

Do not file Form 1120S until you are notified that your election is accepted. If you are now required to file **Form 1120,** U.S. Corporation Income Tax Return, or any other applicable tax return, continue filing it until your election takes effect.

Care should be exercised to ensure that the election is received by the Internal Revenue Service. If you are not notified of acceptance or nonacceptance of your election within 3 months of date of filing (date mailed), or within 6 months if Part II, Item Q1, is checked, you should take follow-up action by corresponding with the Service Center where the election was filed. If filing of Form 2553 is questioned by IRS, an acceptable proof of filing is: **(1)** certified receipt (timely filed); **(2)** Form 2553 with accepted stamp; **(3)** Form 2553 with stamped IRS received date; or **(4)** IRS letter stating that Form 2553 had been accepted.

F. End of Election.—Once the election is made, it stays in effect for all years until it is terminated. During the 5 years after the

Instructions for Form 2553: Sample (continued)

election is terminated under section 1362(d), the corporation can make another election on Form 2553 only with IRS consent.

Specific Instructions
Part I

Part I must be completed by all corporations.

Name and Address of Corporation.— Enter the true corporate name as set forth in the corporate charter or other legal document creating it. If the corporation's mailing address is the same as someone else's, such as a shareholder's, please enter this person's name below the name of the corporation. Include the suite, room, or other unit number after the street address. If the Post Office does not deliver to the street address and the corporation has a P.O. box, show the P.O. box number instead of the street address. If the corporation has changed its name or address since applying for its EIN (filing Form SS-4), be sure to check the box in item F of Part I.

A. Employer Identification Number.—If you have applied for an employer identification number (EIN) but have not received it, enter "applied for." If the corporation does not have an EIN, you should apply for one on **Form SS-4**, Application for Employer Identification Number, available from most IRS and Social Security Administration offices.

C. Effective Date of Election.—Enter the beginning effective date (month, day, year) of the tax year that you have requested for the S corporation. Generally, this will be the beginning date of the tax year for which the ending effective date is required to be shown in item I, Part I. For a new corporation (first year the corporation exists) it will generally be the date required to be shown in item H, Part I. The tax year of a new corporation starts on the date that it has shareholders, acquires assets, or begins doing business, whichever happens first. If the effective date for item C for a newly formed corporation is later than the date in item H, the corporation should file Form 1120 or Form 1120-A, for the tax period between these dates.

Column K. Shareholders' Consent Statement.—Each shareholder who owns (or is deemed to own) stock at the time the election is made must consent to the election. If the election is made during the corporation's first tax year for which it is effective, any person who held stock at any time during the portion of that year which occurs before the time the election is made, must consent to the election although the person may have sold or transferred his or her stock before the election is made. Each shareholder consents by signing and dating in column K or signing and dating a separate consent statement described below. If stock is owned by a trust that is a qualified shareholder, the deemed owner of the trust must consent. See section 1361(c)(2) for details regarding qualified trusts that may be shareholders and rules on determining who is the deemed owner of the trust.

An election made during the first 2½ months of the tax year is considered made for the following tax year if one or more of the persons who held stock in the corporation during such tax year and before the election was made did not consent to the election. See section 1362(b)(2).

If a husband and wife have a community interest in the stock or in the income from it, both must consent. Each tenant in common, joint tenant, and tenant by the entirety also must consent.

A minor's consent is made by the minor or the legal representative of the minor, or by a natural or adoptive parent of the minor if no legal representative has been appointed. The consent of an estate is made by an executor or administrator.

Continuation sheet or separate consent statement.—If you need a continuation sheet or use a separate consent statement, attach it to Form 2553. The separate consent statement must contain the name, address, and employer identification number of the corporation and the shareholder information requested in columns J through N of Part I.

If you want, you may combine all the shareholders' consents in one statement.

Column L.—Enter the number of shares of stock each shareholder owns and the dates the stock was acquired. If the election is made during the corporation's first tax year for which it is effective, do not list the shares of stock for those shareholders who sold or transferred all of their stock before the election was made. However, these shareholders must still consent to the election for it to be effective for the tax year.

Column M.—Enter the social security number of each shareholder who is an individual. Enter the employer identification number of each shareholder that is an estate or a qualified trust.

Column N.—Enter the month and day that each shareholder's tax year ends. If a shareholder is changing his or her tax year, enter the tax year the shareholder is changing to, and attach an explanation indicating the present tax year and the basis for the change (e.g., automatic revenue procedure or letter ruling request).

If the election is made during the corporation's first tax year for which it is effective, you do not have to enter the tax year of any shareholder who sold or transferred all of his or her stock before the election was made.

Signature.—Form 2553 must be signed by the president, treasurer, assistant treasurer, chief accounting officer, or other corporate officer (such as tax officer) authorized to sign.

Part II

Complete Part II if you selected a tax year ending on any date other than December 31 (other than a 52-53-week tax year ending with reference to the month of December).

Box P1.—Attach a statement showing separately for each month the amount of gross receipts for the most recent 47 months as required by section 4.03(3) of

Revenue Procedure 87-32, 1987-2 C.B. 396. A corporation that does not have a 47-month period of gross receipts cannot establish a natural business year under section 4.01(1).

Box Q1.—For examples of an acceptable business purpose for requesting a fiscal tax year, see Revenue Ruling 87-57, 1987-2 C.B. 117.

In addition to a statement showing the business purpose for the requested fiscal year, you must attach the other information necessary to meet the ruling request requirements of Revenue Procedure 90-1, 1990-1 C.B. 356 (updated annually). Also attach a statement that shows separately the amount of gross receipts from sales or services (and inventory costs, if applicable) for each of the 36 months preceding the effective date of the election to be an S corporation. If the corporation has been in existence for fewer than 36 months, submit figures for the period of existence.

If you check box Q1, you must also pay a user fee of $200 (subject to change). Do not pay the fee when filing Form 2553. The Service Center will send Form 2553 to the IRS in Washington, DC, who, in turn, will notify the corporation that the fee is due. See Revenue Procedure 90-17, 1990-1 C.B. 479.

Box Q2.—If the corporation makes a back-up section 444 election for which it is qualified, then the election must be exercised in the event the business purpose request is not approved. Under certain circumstances, the tax year requested under the back-up section 444 election may be different than the tax year requested under business purpose. See **Form 8716**, Election To Have a Tax Year Other Than a Required Tax Year, for details on making a back-up section 444 election.

Boxes Q2 and R2.—If the corporation is not qualified to make the section 444 election after making the item Q2 back-up section 444 election or indicating its intention to make the election in item R1, and therefore it later files a calendar year return, it should write "Section 444 Election Not Made" in the top left corner of the 1st calendar year Form 1120S it files.

Part III

Certain Qualified Subchapter S Trusts (QSSTs) may make the QSST election required by section 1361(d)(2) in Part III. Part III may be used to make the QSST election only if corporate stock has been transferred to the trust on or before the date on which the corporation makes its election to be an S corporation. However, a statement can be used in lieu of Part III to make the election.

Note: *Part III may be used only in conjunction with making the Part I election (i.e., Form 2553 cannot be filed with only Part III completed).*

The deemed owner of the QSST must also consent to the S corporation election in column K, page 1, of Form 2553. See section 1361(c)(2).

*U.S. GPO:1991-518-941/20363

Page 2

Form 2553 – Election by a Small Business Corporation: Sample

Form **2553** (Rev. December 1990) Department of the Treasury Internal Revenue Service	**Election by a Small Business Corporation** (Under section 1362 of the Internal Revenue Code) ▶ For Paperwork Reduction Act Notice, see page 1 of instructions. ▶ See separate instructions.	OMB No. 1545-0146 Expires 11-30-93

Notes: 1. This election, to be treated as an "S corporation," can be accepted only if all the tests in General Instruction B are met; all signatures in Parts I and III are originals (no photocopies); and the exact name and address of the corporation and other required form information are provided.

2. Do not file Form 1120S until you are notified that your election is accepted. See General Instruction E.

SAMPLE

Part I Election Information

Name of corporation (see instructions)	**A** Employer identification number (see instructions)
Number, street, and room or suite no. (If a P.O. box, see instructions.)	**B** Name and telephone number (including area code) of corporate officer or legal representative who may be called for information
City or town, state, and ZIP code	**C** Election is to be effective for tax year beginning (month, day, year)

(left margin: Please Type or Print)

D Is the corporation the outgrowth or continuation of any form of predecessor? . . ☐ Yes ☐ No   **E ·** Date of incorporation

If "Yes," state name of predecessor, type of organization, and period of its existence ▶ ....

F Check here ▶ ☐ if the corporation has changed its name or address since applying for the employer identification number shown in item A above.   **G** State of incorporation

H If this election takes effect for the first tax year the corporation exists, enter month, day, and year of the **earliest** of the following: (1) date the corporation first had shareholders, (2) date the corporation first had assets, or (3) date the corporation began doing business. ▶

I Selected tax year: Annual return will be filed for tax year ending (month and day) ▶ ....
If the tax year ends on any date other than December 31, except for an automatic 52-53-week tax year ending with reference to the month of December, you **must** complete Part II on the back. If the date you enter is the ending date of an automatic 52-53-week tax year, write "52-53-week year" to the right of the date. See Temporary Regulations section 1.441-2T(e)(3).

J Name of each shareholder, person having a community property interest in the corporation's stock, and each tenant in common, joint tenant, and tenant by the entirety. (A husband and wife (and their estates) are counted as one shareholder in determining the number of shareholders without regard to the manner in which the stock is owned.)	K Shareholders' Consent Statement. We, the undersigned shareholders, consent to the corporation's election to be treated as an "S corporation" under section 1362(a). (Shareholders sign and date below.)*		L Stock owned		M Social security number or employer identification number (see instructions)	N Share-holder's tax year ends (month and day)
	Signature	Date	Number of shares	Dates acquired		

*For this election to be valid, the consent of each shareholder, person having a community property interest in the corporation's stock, and each tenant in common, joint tenant, and tenant by the entirety must either appear above or be attached to this form. (See instructions for Column K if continuation sheet or a separate consent statement is needed.)

Under penalties of perjury, I declare that I have examined this election, including accompanying schedules and statements, and to the best of my knowledge and belief, it is true, correct, and complete.

Signature of officer ▶ _____   Title ▶ _____   Date ▶ _____

See Parts II and III on back.   Form **2553** (Rev. 12-90)

Form 2553 – Election by a Small Business Corporation: Sample (continued)

Form 2553 (Rev. 12-90)   Page **2**

Part II Selection of Fiscal Tax Year (All corporations using this Part must complete Item O and one of Items P, Q, or R.)

O Check the applicable box below to indicate whether the corporation is:

  1. ☐ A new corporation adopting the tax year entered in item I, Part I.

  2. ☐ An existing corporation retaining the tax year entered in item I, Part I.

  3. ☐ An existing corporation changing to the tax year entered in item I, Part I.

P Complete item P if the corporation is using the expeditious approval provisions of Revenue Procedure 87-32, 1987-2 C.B. 396, to request: **(1)** a natural business year (as defined in section 4.01(1) of Rev. Proc. 87-32), or (2) a year that satisfies the ownership tax year test in section 4.01(2) of Rev. Proc. 87-32. Check the applicable box below to indicate the representation statement the corporation is making as required under section 4 of Rev. Proc. 87-32.

  1. Natural Business Year ▶ ☐ I represent that the corporation is retaining or changing to a tax year that coincides with its natural business year as defined in section 4.01(1) of Rev. Proc. 87-32 and as verified by its satisfaction of the requirements of section 4.02(1) of Rev. Proc. 87-32. In addition, if the corporation is changing to a natural business year as defined in section 4.01(1), I further represent that such tax year results in less deferral of income to the owners than the corporation's present tax year. I also represent that the corporation is not described in section 3.01(2) of Rev. Proc. 87-32. (See instructions for additional information that must be attached.)

  2. Ownership Tax Year ▶ ☐ I represent that shareholders holding more than half of the shares of the stock (as of the first day of the tax year to which the request relates) of the corporation have the same tax year or are concurrently changing to the tax year that the corporation adopts, retains, or changes to per item I, Part I. I also represent that the corporation is not described in section 3.01(2) of Rev. Proc. 87-32.

Note: *If you do not use item P and the corporation wants a fiscal tax year, complete either item Q or R below. Item Q is used to request a fiscal tax year based on a business purpose and to make a back-up section 444 election. Item R is used to make a regular section 444 election.*

Q Business Purpose—To request a fiscal tax year based on a business purpose, you must check box Q1 and pay a user fee. See instructions for details. You may also check box Q2 and/or box Q3.

  1. Check here ▶ ☐ if the fiscal year entered in item I, Part I, is requested under the provisions of section 6.03 of Rev. Proc. 87-32. Attach to Form 2553 a statement showing the business purpose for the requested fiscal year. See instructions for additional information that must be attached.

  2. Check here ▶ ☐ to show that the corporation intends to make a back-up section 444 election in the event the corporation's business purpose request is not approved by the IRS. (See instructions for more information.)

  3. Check here ▶ ☐ to show that the corporation agrees to adopt or change to a tax year ending December 31 if necessary for the IRS to accept this election for S corporation status in the event: (1) the corporation's business purpose request is not approved and the corporation makes a back-up section 444 election, but is ultimately not qualified to make a section 444 election, or (2) the corporation's business purpose request is not approved and the corporation did not make a back-up section 444 election.

R Section 444 Election—To make a section 444 election, you must check box R1 and you may also check box R2.

  1. Check here ▶ ☐ to show the corporation will make, if qualified, a section 444 election to have the fiscal tax year shown in item I, Part I. To make the election, you must complete **Form 8716**, Election To Have a Tax Year Other Than a Required Tax Year, and either attach it to Form 2553 or file it separately.

  2. Check here ▶ ☐ to show that the corporation agrees to adopt or change to a tax year ending December 31 if necessary for the IRS to accept this election for S corporation status in the event the corporation is ultimately not qualified to make a section 444 election.

Part III Qualified Subchapter S Trust (QSST) Election Under Section 1361(d)(2)**

Income beneficiary's name and address	Social security number
Trust's name and address	Employer identification number

Date on which stock of the corporation was transferred to the trust (month, day, year) ▶

In order for the trust named above to be a QSST and thus a qualifying shareholder of the S corporation for which this Form 2553 is filed, I hereby make the election under section 1361(d)(2). Under penalties of perjury, I certify that the trust meets the definition requirements of section 1361(d)(3) and that all other information provided in Part III is true, correct, and complete.

_____   _____
Signature of income beneficiary or signature and title of legal representative or other qualified person making the election   Date

**Use of Part III to make the QSST election may be made only if stock of the corporation has been transferred to the trust on or before the date on which the corporation makes its election to be an S corporation. The QSST election must be made and filed separately if stock of the corporation is transferred to the trust after the date on which the corporation makes the S election.

*U.S. GPO:1991-518-943/20365

Notes

Chapter 3

Buying an Existing Business

Trust in Allah. But always tie your camel.

— Arab proverb

3.1 General Considerations

Obviously, it may not be necessary for you to build your business from the ground up. If you wish to go into a particular type of business, you may find an appropriate existing business that is for sale. Buying an existing business can have considerable advantages over starting one from scratch, and one of the most important of these is the chance to start out with an established customer base. It is also sometimes possible to have the seller stay on as an employee or consultant for a transitional period to help you become familiar with the operation of the business.

Other advantages of purchasing a going business include:

- You may be able to take a regular draw or salary right from the start, if it is a profitable operation. This is usually not the case in a start-up operation, which typically starts off losing money.

- Your risk is frequently less when you buy an established, profitable business. You know that it has a viable market if it is already profitable. Your main risk would be that something would change after you acquire the business, such as new competition or product obsolescence, and this would adversely affect your business. Another risk is that you will mismanage the business.

- Getting started is simpler. By buying an established business, you can focus your attention on giving good service and operating profitably. Since most facilities, operating systems, and employees will already be in place, your efforts will not be diluted by remodeling the premises, trying to hire employees, setting up accounting systems, acquiring initial inventory, and the like. With an existing business, in most cases, you should be able to step right into an operation that has already been established by someone else.

While there are some definite advantages to buying an established business, as compared to starting a new business, it can also be a lot more complicated and involves many potential pitfalls that you must avoid. The watchword in buying any kind of business should be *caveat emptor* — let the buyer beware.

Because the process of buying and selling businesses is very complicated even for experts, do not attempt it without retaining the services of a reliable attorney and, usually, a good accountant. Even skilled professionals, however, can generally only protect you from certain legal, financial, or tax pitfalls that arise in connection with the purchase of a business. Many of the potential problems that would not become obvious until it is too late can only be spotted in advance, if at all, by the exercise of your good judgment and as a result of your doing the necessary homework. Important pitfalls you should look out for in connection with buying an existing business are discussed in Section 3.3.

3.2 Finding a Business for Sale

How do you go about finding a business that is for sale? You have a number of ways to approach the problem, none of which are ideal, so you will probably want to use two or more of the approaches discussed below to find and buy an existing business.

Advertisements

The business opportunities section of your local newspaper, regional magazine, or trade association journal can be a major source of leads to businesses that are for sale. Such ads often do not tell you very much about the nature of the business, but at least they can be a starting point in your search. In many cases, the ads will have been placed by a business broker rather than the owner. The business broker will often be representing people who are seeking to sell their businesses.

Business Brokers and Realtors

Business brokers and realtors can be excellent sources in your search for a business that is for sale. The main drawback of going through a business broker or realtor is that his or her fee (paid by the seller) is usually a percentage, often 10%, of the sales price of the business; so the broker or realtor, like the seller, is trying to get the highest possible price for the business. At the same time, the seller will usually want more than he or she would if the sale were made without a broker, since he or she knows that the broker will take a healthy commission out of the negotiated sales price.

Your local chamber of commerce can usually tell you a great deal about the local business community and also provide you with leads to firms that are for sale.

Local Chambers of Commerce

Professionals, such as accountants, attorneys, and bankers, can often provide leads regarding good businesses even before they are on the market. Frequently, a business client will tell his or her accountant, attorney, or banker that he or she is planning to sell out or retire, long before making any formal attempt to put the business up for sale. So, if you have friends who are accountants, attorneys, or bankers, take them to lunch and tell them what you have in mind. Typically, they will have a vested interest in finding a friendly buyer for a retiring client's business, since they may loose that account if the firm is sold to buyers who have their own professional advisers.

Accountants, Attorneys, and Bankers

Certified public accountants (CPAs) can be excellent sources of leads. Not only will they usually not charge you any kind of finder's fee, but they usually know which of their clients' businesses are little gold mines. In some cases, a CPA who has a very profitable client who wishes to sell out may even want to go into the business with you as a financial partner, leaving the day-to-day operations to you. In these cases, you can generally be sure that if the CPA is putting up his or her money, he or she has studied the client's business carefully and feels that it is a real money-maker. In short, the CPA will have already done much of the prescreening for you.

Often, if you see a small business you think you might like to buy, the simplest approach will be to talk to the owner and see if he or she is interested in selling. While an owner may have had no serious thoughts about selling the business before, the appearance of an interested potential buyer is not only somewhat flattering, but it may even cause him or her to decide to sell out to you. Many businesses are bought and sold this way.

The Direct Approach

3.3 What to Look for Before You Leap

One of the first questions you may want to ask is: "Why are you selling your business?" Often, the response will be the owner wants to retire or is in poor health. While such an explanation may be true in many cases, it is also quite likely to be a well-rehearsed cover story. The real reason may be the business is in a declining neighborhood and the owner has been robbed several times recently and wants out. Or, the owners of a profitable little corner grocery store may be anxious to sell out while they can because they have learned that a major chain-store supermarket will

Why Is the Business for Sale?

be opening in the neighborhood in a few months. Another common reason behind a planned sale is that the business is either losing money or is not sufficiently profitable to make continuing worthwhile.

Whatever the real reason behind the owner's attempt to sell the business, you are unlikely to discover it without rolling up your sleeves and doing some independent and in-depth investigation. Perhaps the best way to find that needle in the haystack is to talk to a number of other businesspeople in the vicinity of the business you are investigating, particularly competitors in the same business. The firm's suppliers can also be a source of important information.

Even if you are very diligent and thorough, you may not be able to discover the hidden reason — if there is one — underlying an owner's desire to sell out. You may simply have to rely on your intuition in deciding whether the seller's reason for getting out of the business is the real reason. Just remember that in most cases a good and profitable small business is not something that most people walk away from, unless there is a very good reason to do so or the price offered is too good to turn down.

What Kind of Reputation Does the Firm Have?

One of the great advantages of taking over an existing business can be the opportunity to enjoy the reputation and goodwill that the existing owner has built up with customers and suppliers over the years. On the other hand, you may be much better off starting your own business from scratch than acquiring a business that has a poor reputation because of inferior work or merchandise or inferior service. It could take you years of hard work and reduced profits to overcome a former owner's poor reputation.

Even if the present owner has an excellent business reputation, you will want to know whether or not that goodwill is based on personal relationships built up between the owner and customers. These types of relationships aren't easily transferable. If the business relies heavily on a few key customers with whom the owner has very favorable business arrangements based on personal relationships, you may find those business arrangements could be lost when you attempt to take the owner's place. In short, satisfy yourself the goodwill you are buying is not based solely on personal relationships.

How Profitable Is the Business Now?

Unless you have some very good reasons to believe that you can operate the business more profitably than the current owner, you should not purchase a going business that does not produce a satisfactory profit under its current ownership. Thus, it is extremely important to find out how the business has fared financially for the last few years. This is where the services of a good accountant, who has knowledge of the particular type of business, will be invaluable.

Insist on having the seller make available the business' financial and business records to your accountant. Be particularly wary of a business that keeps poor records. Often, the most reliable sources of financial information can be the owner's income tax and sales tax returns, since it is not very likely that a business owner will report more income than was actually earned for tax purposes.

If the owner is not willing to make financial records available, make it clear that you are not willing to negotiate any further. Buying a business is a lot like buying a used car; you want to make sure it runs before you pay for it.

Assets and Liabilities

You will need to review both the tangible and intangible assets of the business to see if they are worth the price you will be paying and also to determine just what assets you will be acquiring under the sales agreement.

Personally inspect the business premises, and look for things like obsolete or unsalable inventory, out-of-date or rundown equipment, or furniture or fixtures that you may have to repair or replace. Also, determine whether the business is able to expand at its present location or if it is already too cramped. What you determine might require you to buy or lease additional facilities, if you wish to expand.

Review the terms of any leases. Some businesses close because of the imminent expiration of a favorable long-term lease or because the landlord plans to either raise the rent drastically or not renew the lease at all when the current lease expires.

If you will be acquiring the accounts receivable of the business, review them in detail. An aging of the accounts should be performed to determine how long various receivables have been outstanding. As a general rule, the longer a given receivable has been outstanding, the more likely it will prove to be uncollectible.

If a few large accounts of credit customers make up a significant portion of the receivables, you will want to particularly focus on those accounts and perhaps even have credit checks run on those customers. The bankruptcy of a major credit customer can ruin an otherwise successful business.

Part of your job in investigating a business that you want to buy is to find out what makes it tick — and make sure you will be getting whatever it is. For example, a business that has well-developed customer or mailing lists should ordinarily include those lists in the sales agreement. If there is a favorable lease, make sure it can and will be assigned to you. If patents, trademarks, trade names, or certain skilled employees are vital to the business, be sure that you will get them as part of the package.

You also need to be aware of potential problems with the government that the seller is experiencing or expects to experience in the near future, such as zoning problems or new environmental restrictions that may hamper the business' profitability.

Hidden Liabilities

Liabilities of the business may not always show up on its accounting records. There may be any number of hidden claims against the business, such as security agreements encumbering the accounts receivable, inventory, or equipment, unpaid back taxes of various kinds, undisclosed lawsuits or potential lawsuits, or simply unpaid bills.

If you are going to assume the liabilities of the business, the written agreement of sale should specify exactly which liabilities are being assumed and the dollar amount of each.

Other examples of hidden liabilities to look out for are:

- Pension liabilities — You may be taking on significant termination liability as a successor employer if the seller maintains or contributes to a pension fund and has unfunded pension fund liabilities.
- Vacation liabilities — If you are a successor employer, you may be liable for accrued but unpaid vacation leave of employees, which can be a significant hidden liability in some cases.
- Environmental liabilities — In many instances, environmental law imposes liability for past environmental abuses on current land owners or lessors. Many banks and savings and loans have recently learned about this the hard way, after foreclosing on land which had been contaminated over the years by toxic substances, and being held liable for clean-up costs as the contamination problems came to light.

  Many companies, when buying land or other companies that own land, now require the sellers to make detailed representations and warranties concerning environmental matters and to undertake extensive and costly environmental audits as a condition to buying a business. See Section 9.9 for a more detailed discussion of these issues.

If you intend to buy a corporation, you will be well advised to buy the business assets from the corporation rather than purchase its stock. The latter approach will subject the business to all hidden or contingent liabilities of the old corporation, whether or not you have agreed to pay for any liabilities of the corporation that predated the sale.

One exception to this general rule would be for a corporation that had substantial tax loss or tax credit carryovers that you might be able to utilize if you bought the stock of the corporation rather than the assets. Be aware, however, the tax law is a minefield when it comes to taking over someone else's tax loss or credit carryovers.

So before you do so, seek good advice from a tax attorney or tax accountant. If you don't, you may find that the carryovers you thought you were acquiring have evaporated like a mirage.

A change in ownership of more than 50% of the stock of a corporation in a three-year period will generally result in a severe restriction on the amount of its prior net operating losses that can be deducted in any subsequent taxable year.

3.4 Should You Consider a Franchise Operation?

Many small businesses, particularly fast food restaurants and print shops, are operated under franchises from a large national company (a franchisor). There can be substantial advantages to operating a franchised business, such as the benefits of national advertising, training programs, and assistance in setting up and running the business. If you are investigating a franchise, determine whether the franchise can be transferred to you, and if so, provide for the transfer as part of the sale in the sales agreement.

Carefully review the franchise agreement with the help of your attorney to determine whether the franchisor must approve the transfer, what the costs of operating are under the franchise, and the other terms of the agreement.

If the franchisor is not a well-known and respected company, contact your local Better Business Bureau or an appropriate state agency to see if they have any information regarding the history, ethics, and reputation of the franchisor. You do not want to sign on with one of the less-than-reputable franchising operations that charge substantial franchising fees for very little in the way of useful services.

The Federal Trade Commission (FTC) and a number of states provide franchising laws and regulations that offer you protection. These laws and regulations mandate the timing and content of the various disclosures which the franchisor must make to you, as the potential franchisee. You or your attorney should make sure that you ask for all of these disclosures on a timely basis, and be wary of any franchisor who does not provide these disclosures to you unless you ask for them.

A number of excellent publications, including *Franchise Bible* by Erwin J. Keup, can be obtained to help you evaluate various franchise opportunities. *Franchise Bible* explains what the franchise system entails and presents how both the franchisor and the franchisee should approach a franchising venture or opportunity.

For more information on *Franchise Bible* and additional franchise publications, refer to Section 10.9.

If you acquire a franchise, either from the franchisor or as a transfer from another franchisee, you may be able to amortize (write off) the cost of acquiring the franchise, under certain circumstances, for federal income tax purposes. Consult your tax adviser as to whether or not this will be possible in your case. If it is amortizable, you may want to allocate a significant part of the purchase price for the business to the cost of the franchise, which could save you major tax dollars in the long run.

Once you have focused on a particular franchise opportunity, you will find the checklist located at the end of this chapter very useful for evaluating the franchise operation.

3.5 Negotiating the Purchase

The Purchase Price

No book can tell you how much you should pay for the business you are planning to buy. You are on your own on that one. If, however, you have done your homework thoroughly in investigating the business in question and have talked to bankers and other businesspeople about what the normal purchase price for a business of that type and size should be, you should have a fairly good basis for determining whether the purchase price is a reasonable one.

For example, you may find that small businesses of the type you are considering generally sell for about one and one-half times their annual gross sales. That could be very important to know if the seller is asking three times last year's gross sales.

Even if you conclude the purchase price is a fair one, or even a bargain, you still must decide whether the price is one you can afford. Assuming that you can get the purchase price together, will it so deplete your liquid resources that you will not have enough working capital to make the business go or put you in a bind if income from the business drops off while you are at the learning stage? Or, if you are financing a substantial part of the purchase price, will your operating budget be able to stand the cost of making the payments on the debt and still leave enough for you to live on?

Remember, just because you can get the purchase price or down payment together does not necessarily mean that you can afford to buy a particular business even when the price is right.

Disclosure of Financial Information

At an early stage in the negotiations, specify that you want access to tax returns, books of account, and other financial records of the business, and make it clear that you have no interest in continuing the negotiations unless the seller cooperates fully in this respect.

Also, be sure this condition is expressed in any informal "memorandum of understanding" or letter of agreement between you and the seller that is written up before the final contract of sale.

Allocation of Purchase Price

One very important item that is often omitted in business sales agreements, perhaps because it is not absolutely necessary, is a provision in the agreement that shows how the parties agree to allocate the purchase price between the various assets that are being acquired.

For tax purposes, however, it is often very important to both you, as the purchaser, and the seller to have a written allocation agreement.

Since you and the seller usually have opposing interests in making an agreed allocation, the courts and IRS have generally been willing to abide by any allocation agreement between the parties.

The passage of the Clinton Deficit Reduction tax legislation on August 10, 1993 has greatly simplified the allocation process and made it easier, on an after-tax basis, to acquire a business when a significant portion of its assets are intangibles.[1]

Under the 1993 tax law, a broad new category of amortizable assets, called "Section 197 Intangibles," has been created. Section 197 Intangibles may be amortized over a 15-year period for assets purchased after August 10, 1993. Taxpayers may elect to have the new law apply retroactively to acquisitions of intangible assets that occurred after July 25, 1991. Consider amending your tax returns if you have recently purchased a business, after the latter date, and acquired any intangible assets that were not amortizable under prior law.

Before passage of this new law, a business buyer would seek to allocate as much of the purchase price as possible to depreciable tangible assets and amortizable intangible assets, such as technical know-how, customer lists, or covenants not to compete. In addition, buyers usually sought to minimize the portion of the purchase price allocated to other intangible items, such as goodwill or going concern value, which could never be amortized.

However, there was often little choice but to allocate most of the purchase price to intangibles because the value of tangible assets, such as office equipment and furniture and a few supplies, made up only a small portion of the purchase price. Since the IRS clearly would not accept a purchase price allocation that put a $50,000 value on $5 worth of paper clips, buyers were forced to become creative and try to define some asset, such as a customer base or insurance renewals list, and allocate some part of the purchase price to that asset.

In the past, when a buyer attempted to write off the cost of such intangible assets, the result was the IRS disallowed the amortization deduction. To sustain the deduction, the buyer often had to litigate the issue with the IRS and prove to a court that the intangible assets had a short, reasonably ascertainable economic life, and could thus be amortized for tax purposes. The courts frequently allowed taxpayers to write off various types of intangible assets over various periods of time, but only when the taxpayers convincingly demonstrated that such assets lost their economic value over a given period. The costs of such litigation, however, were and remain usually prohibitive for small businesses.

Thankfully, the new law should put an end to most such disputes with the IRS over intangible assets. For the first time ever, the tax law allows goodwill and going concern value to be amortized as Section 197 Intangibles over 15 years. Also included in the definition of Section 197 Intangibles are:

- Workforce in place;
- Information base;
- Any license, permit, or other right granted by a governmental unit or agency;

- Know-how, such as patents, copyrights, formulas, designs, patterns, or similar items (special rules apply to computer software and interests in films, tapes, books, and videos);
- Any customer-based intangible, such as customer lists, depositor lists, subscribers, and insurance expirations;
- Any supplier-based intangible, such as favorable supplier contracts;
- Covenants not to compete; and
- Any franchise, trademark, or trade name.

Computer software is considered an intangible asset, but it is generally not subject to the 15-year amortization requirement of Section 197. Software that is readily available for purchase by the general public is not considered a Section 197 Intangible asset and can now be amortized over three years rather than the five-year period that previously applied.[2] Other computer software is a Section 197 Intangible asset only if acquired in a transaction that involves the purchase of a whole business or a substantial portion of a business.

Section 197 will benefit most business buyers by preventing many disputes with the IRS regarding the purchase price of a business and by allowing amortization of the cost of intangible assets that were not deductible in the past. The new law, however, is not entirely favorable. Previously, business buyers who were allowed to amortize certain intangibles were often able to do so over a period of only a few years, which was far better than the new 15-year amortization requirement.

Allocation Agreements Are Still Important

Do not assume that the new law makes a purchase price allocation agreement unnecessary or unimportant. Certain assets that might be acquired in a business purchase, such as land, are still not depreciable or amortizable, so it will be advisable to try to allocate as little as possible to the cost of land in a purchase price allocation agreement. Also, it will still be advantageous to allocate as much as possible of the purchase price to inventories or depreciable assets whose costs can be written off in a time frame shorter than the 15-year amortization period for Section 197 Intangibles.

A tax deduction you can take today or in the near future is usually worth a great deal more than a tax deduction 15 years from now.

Required Filing

Tax regulations require both you and the seller to file *Form 8594* with the IRS any time a business is bought or sold. *Form 8594* reports certain information about the purchase price allocation.[3] Penalties for failure to file this form can be extremely large. Needless to say, the information on your *Form 8594* and that of the seller's should be identical, or you both will be inviting IRS audits.

In most cases, whatever value of an asset you and the seller agree on is binding for tax purposes. So, it is very important from a tax standpoint to negotiate the best possible allocation of the purchase price among the assets you acquire and have that allocation reflected in the contract of sale.[4]

3.6 Closing the Deal

The legal procedures involved in buying an existing business are rather complex. To ensure you are protected as fully as possible from liabilities you have not agreed to assume, have your attorney take the steps described below.

Legal Steps in Buying a Business

In most states, the purchaser of a retail or wholesale establishment or certain other types of businesses must prepare a notice to creditors of bulk transfer and file it in counties where the business operates and publish it in a general circulation newspaper before the purchase of the business. If this is not properly done, the seller's unsecured creditors may be able to attach the property that you thought you were buying free and clear. See Section 11.3 for specific state requirements regarding bulk sales law.

File Bulk Transfer Notice

Before closing the purchase, your attorney should check with the secretary of state's office to determine whether anyone has recorded a security interest — a lien or chattel mortgage — against the personal property of the seller's business. Naturally, if the transaction involves a purchase of real property, you should also have a title search performed to see if the seller has good title and if there are any recorded mortgages or other claims against the property that the seller has not disclosed to you.

Check Security Interests

For a fee, the secretary of state's office (or its equivalent) will provide a listing of any security interests that have been recorded as a lien against the assets of the business you are buying.

As a condition of the sale, have the seller obtain the necessary form that certifies all state employment taxes have been paid by the seller from the appropriate state agency. If you fail to withhold enough of the purchase price to cover any of the seller's unpaid employment taxes, you may be liable to the state for those taxes. See Section 11.3 for specifics on state requirements.

Get Tax Releases

Similarly, require the seller to obtain and provide you with a sales and use tax certification showing that all outstanding sales and use tax payments due have been made by the seller. You do not want to end up paying for the seller's unpaid sales or use taxes.

File *Form 8594* with the IRS regarding the purchase price allocation and other information in connection with the transaction. The penalty for intentional disregard of this filing requirement is 10% of the amount that was not correctly reported, which could mean up to 10% of the entire purchase price. Don't forget to file *Form 8594*.

File with IRS

Do not attempt to buy or sell a business without the assistance of an attorney to review and structure the deal. Preferably, the attorney should

Retain a Lawyer

be one who specializes in business law practice rather than a litigation specialist or general practitioner. Obtain competent tax advice, either from your attorney or from an accountant, when negotiating and structuring aspects of the deal, such as the allocation of the purchase price and the disposition of any employee benefit plans carried on by the seller for the employees of the business.

Use an Escrow

In general, both you and the seller will be protected — from the time the sales agreement is signed until the deal closes — if an escrow is used to handle the sale of the business. The escrow holder, which is usually an escrow company or escrow department of a financial institution, will hold the agreement, escrow instructions, funds, and important documents until all conditions for closing the deal or releasing the funds or documents are fulfilled.

When the deal closes, the escrow holder will disburse the funds to the seller and deliver the documents of title to you. If the deal is not completed, the escrow instructions will specify how the items held in escrow are to be distributed to the parties.

Your attorney or the seller's attorney may also act as escrow holder, but you probably will not want the seller's attorney to act in that role in most cases, for obvious reasons.

Build in Holdbacks

If the seller has made misrepresentations to you in the contract of sale regarding assets that do not exist, or the like, you may always seek satisfaction by suing for damages. In view of the cost, delay, and uncertainty in bringing a lawsuit, however, you would generally be far better off if there were some simple way you could merely offset any such overstated asset or understated liability against the purchase price, retroactively.

To make this possible, seek to structure the deal so part of the purchase price is held back for some period, say a year, just in case such a contingency arises. Then, if you discover false representations as to assets or liabilities, it will be relatively simple — compared to bringing a lawsuit against a seller who may have skipped town — to have your claim deducted from the amount held back. Discuss with your attorney the possibilities of structuring the transaction so you either:

- Give the seller a note as part of the purchase price, with a right to reduce the principal amount of the note if certain contingencies occur; or
- Have part of the cash payment price held in escrow for six months or more after the sale occurs.

3.7 Summary Checklist for Buying an Existing Business

☐ Why does the present owner want to sell the business?   **Investigation**

☐ Will the reputation of the business be helpful or harmful if you take it over?

☐ Obtain tax returns, bank deposit records, and other financial records.

☐ If the business is not currently very profitable, why do you think you can run it more profitably than the present owner?

☐ Thoroughly investigate the business' financial records and history, its reputation, and any factors that might unfavorably impact on its future. You may need the help of an accountant or other experts.

☐ Review or have reviewed the provisions of key contracts, leases, franchise agreements, or any other legal arrangements which have a significant effect on the business. Be sure you are not assuming an unfavorable lease or contract or losing the benefits of a favorable one.

☐ Make sure that the purchase price is fair. Even if it is, can you afford   **Negotiations**
it? Will you have enough working capital to run the business properly after you pay the purchase price?

☐ Insist on getting accurate financial information and access to the supporting data, early in the negotiations.

☐ Push for an allocation of the purchase price to specific assets in the sales agreement. Seek to maximize the amounts allocable to depreciable assets and any noncompetition covenant. Seek to minimize allocations to goodwill or land purchased.

☐ Look for hidden liabilities, such as pending lawsuits, accrued vacation liabilities, unfunded pension plan liabilities, or potential exposure to environmental clean-up costs.

☐ Retain an attorney to participate in drawing up the sales agreement.   **Closing the Transaction**

☐ Comply with the requirements of the Bulk Transfer Act, if it applies to the particular type of business being acquired.

☐ Be sure that the acquired property is not subject to any recorded security interests or other liens beyond those disclosed by the seller.

☐ Have the seller obtain and furnish a certification that all employment taxes due have been paid.

☐ Have the seller obtain and furnish a certification that all sales and use taxes due have been paid.

☐ Seek to hold back part of the purchase price as security to reimburse yourself for any misrepresentations as to assets or liabilities by the seller.

☐ Prepare *Form 8594*, and file it with the IRS.

☐ See Section 11.3 for state law considerations.

Other Tax Considerations

☐ Determine whether the sale of the business will result in a sales tax liability with respect to part or all of the purchase price. If so, is there a way to reshape the transaction to reduce or avoid sales tax? For example, allocate more of the purchase price to assets not subject to sales tax and less to assets that are.

☐ If you are buying a corporation that has not been paying income taxes because it has carryovers of net operating losses or investment tax credits, be aware you may be able to use only a small portion of those carryovers to shelter the income of the business once you become the owner.

☐ If the seller has a favorable experience rating for unemployment tax purposes, make sure you act promptly so that you can succeed to that rating as a successor employer.

☐ If you are acquiring intangible assets, including previously non-deductible intangibles, such as goodwill or going concern value, you may now amortize the cost of most such intangible assets over 15 years, under 1993 tax legislation.

Endnotes

1. I.R.C. §197.

2. I.R.C. §167(f)(1).

3. Temp. Treas. Regs. 1.1060-1T.

4. I.R.C. §1060(a).

Checklist for Evaluating a Franchise

The Franchise

YES NO

☐ ☐ After studying it paragraph by paragraph, did your lawyer approve the franchise contract you are considering?

☐ ☐ Does the franchise call upon you to take any steps which are, according to your lawyer, unwise or illegal in your state, county, or city? If yes, what are the steps? _____

_____

_____

☐ ☐ Does the franchise give you an exclusive territory for the length of the franchise? or

☐ ☐ Can the franchisor sell a second or third franchise in your territory?

☐ ☐ Is the franchisor connected in any way with another franchise company handling similar merchandise or services? If yes, what is your protection against this second franchisor organization?

_____

_____

☐ ☐ Can you terminate the franchise contract? Under what circumstances can you do it and at what cost to you, if you decide for any reason at all that you wish to cancel it?

_____

_____

☐ ☐ If you sell your franchise, will you be compensated for the goodwill you have built into the business?

The Franchisor

How many years has the firm offering you a franchise been in operation? _____

☐ ☐ Does the firm have a reputation for honesty and fair dealing among the local firms holding its franchise?

☐ ☐ Has the franchisor shown you any certified figures indicating exact net profits of one or more going firms?

☐ ☐ Have you personally checked these certified figures with the franchisor?

☐ ☐ Will the firm assist you in the following areas?

YES NO

☐ ☐ A management training program?

☐ ☐ An employee training program?

☐ ☐ A public relations program?

YES NO

☐ ☐ Capital?

☐ ☐ Credit?

☐ ☐ Merchandising ideas?

☐ ☐ Will the firm help you find a good location for your new business?

☐ ☐ Is the franchising firm adequately financed so it can carry out its stated plan of financial assistance and expansion?

Checklist for Evaluating a Franchise (continued)

YES NO

☐ ☐ Is the franchisor a one-person company? or

☐ ☐ Is the franchisor a corporation with an experienced management trained in-depth (so that there would always be an experienced person at its head)?

Exactly what can the franchisor do for you which you cannot do for yourself? _____

_____

_____

☐ ☐ Has the franchisor investigated you carefully enough to assure itself that you can successfully operate one of the franchises at a profit both to the franchisor and to you?

☐ ☐ Does your state have a law regulating the sale of franchises? and

☐ ☐ Has the franchisor complied with that law?

You – The Franchisee

How much equity capital will you have to have to purchase the franchise and operate it until your income equals your expenses? _____

Where are you going to get the capital? _____

_____

☐ ☐ Are you prepared to give up some independence of action to secure the advantages offered by the franchise?

☐ ☐ Do you really believe you have the innate ability, training, and experience to work smoothly and profitably with the franchisor, your employees, and your customers?

☐ ☐ Are you ready to spend much or all of the remainder of your business life with this franchisor, offering its product or service to your public?

Your Market

☐ ☐ Have you made any study to determine whether the product or service which you propose to sell under franchise has a market in your territory at the prices you will have to charge?

Will the population in the territory given you increase ☐, remain static ☐, or decrease ☐ over the next five years?

Will the product or service you are considering be in greater demand ☐, about the same ☐, or in less demand ☐ five years from today?

What competition already exists in your territory for the product or service you contemplate selling:

From nonfranchise firms? _____

From franchise firms? _____

Source: *Franchise Opportunities Handbook*, U.S. Department of Commerce, Washington, D.C., 1982.

Starting the Business

Part II

Chapter 4
A Trip through the Red Tape Jungle:
Requirements that Apply to Nearly All New Businesses

Chapter 5
The Thicket Thickens:
Additional Requirements for Businesses with Employees

Chapter 6
Businesses that Require Licenses to Operate

Chapter 4

A Trip through the Red Tape Jungle: Requirements that Apply to Nearly All New Businesses

*The difference between a taxidermist and a tax collector is that
the taxidermist leaves the skin.*

— Old American proverb

4.1 General Considerations

This chapter outlines the most common governmental requirements and
other red tape that virtually everyone starting a new business must attend
to. The requirements discussed will also generally apply if you have
bought an existing business, unless you have acquired the stock of an
incorporated business. This chapter assumes your business has no
employees. If you expect to have one or more employees, a large number
of additional legal requirements will affect your business immediately.
Chapter 5 covers the additional requirements that apply to new businesses that have employees. This chapter does not discuss the special
licenses that many types of businesses are required to have. If you do not
know whether the type of business you are considering going into
requires a special license or licenses from federal, state, or local government agencies, refer to Chapter 6 and Section 11.6.

4.2 Choosing a Name for the Business

The name you choose for your business can be important from a business
image standpoint and also in communicating to the public what you have

to offer. Most small businesses should select a name that, at least in part, clearly describes the product or service provided. If you ignore this basic common-sense rule, you run the risk of losing many potential customers for the simple reason they will pass right by without realizing what you do. A fanciful or whimsical name is fine from an image standpoint, but it should also give the public a clear idea of what it is your business provides in the way of goods or services. For example, if you call your restaurant "The Comestible Emporium," a lot of hungry people will probably drive right by without realizing that you serve food.

It is advisable, however, from the standpoint of protecting your business' name as a trademark or service mark under federal or state law, to adopt a name that is also partially arbitrary or nondescriptive, in conjunction with a name that is descriptive of the services or goods provided. An example would be the "21 Club Restaurant." The reason for selecting a name that is partially whimsical or arbitrary is that trademarks or service marks that are merely descriptive of the goods or services cannot be legally protected from use by others unless it can be proven that the name has acquired a secondary meaning, which is very difficult to establish for a new small business.[1]

You also need to think of the possible consequences of putting your name out before the public. You may want to consider using some sort of fictitious name (see Section 4.10) for your business, rather than your name. There is nothing illegal or shady about using a fictitious business name. If you put your name on the business and the venture goes belly up, as so many new businesses do, many people in the community will automatically associate your name with the defunct or bankrupt business. This may make it very difficult if you try to start another business or to obtain credit in the same community in the future.

Once you have settled on a name for your business, you or preferably your attorney, should find out whether the same name, or a confusingly similar name, has already been preempted by someone else. This involves making an inquiry with the state's secretary of state's office to find out whether the name is already being used in the state. Inquiry should also be made of the county clerk, in each county where you will do business, to see if another business is already using the same or a confusingly similar name in the county and has filed a fictitious business name statement. If so, you may have to choose a different name. See Section 9.5 for more information on trademark protection.

4.3 Local Business Licenses

Almost every business will need city or county business licenses, or both. These licenses can be obtained at the local city hall or county offices. Failure to obtain a license when you start business will usually result in a penalty when the local government eventually catches up with you; therefore, obtaining the necessary licenses should be among the first steps taken when you start a business.

Some cities and counties impose a gross receipts, income, or payroll tax on most businesses. Certain types of businesses, such as restaurants, may also be required to obtain special permits from local health authorities and fire or police departments.

If your business will construct its own building, it will be necessary to consult your local city or county zoning ordinances. A building permit must be obtained for both new construction and remodeling in most areas.

In addition, whether or not you plan to carry on any construction activity or do any remodeling, you will need to make certain that the business activity you intend to carry on does not violate any zoning regulations or any ordinances regarding hazardous activities. You may also be required to obtain a use permit from the city or county planning commission.

4.4 State Licenses

Most states impose license fees or taxes on a wide range of businesses, occupations, and professions. The fees often vary widely among the different types of businesses and occupations, ranging from relatively nominal to substantial amounts or rates, depending upon the activity. The many different types of licenses and permits are usually granted based on some combination of requirements such as registration, bonding, education, experience, and passage of licensing examinations.

Since you may not legally operate any of these regulated businesses or professions without being licensed, you should find out whether there is a state licensing requirement for the business you plan to start. If so, determine whether and how you will be able to comply with the licensing requirements.

See Section 11.6 for a partial listing of businesses, occupations, and professions that must be licensed under the laws of this state.

4.5 Federal Licenses

Most new small businesses are unlikely to require any type of federal permit or license to operate, unless they are engaged in rendering investment advice, making alcohol or tobacco products, preparing meat products, or making or dealing in firearms. Federal permits or licenses would also be necessary to commence certain large-scale operations, such as a radio or television station or a common carrier and the production of drugs or biological products. If you wish to engage in any of the foregoing activities, all of which are heavily regulated, consult an attorney regarding regulatory requirements well in advance.

4.6 Estimated Taxes

Individual

As a sole proprietor or partner in a partnership, you will have to make advance payments of estimated federal — and possibly state — income taxes and federal self-employment tax once your business begins to turn a taxable profit. Individual estimated tax payments are due in four annual installments on April 15, June 15, September 15, and January 15 of the following year for an individual whose tax year is the calendar year. Any remaining unpaid federal tax is due with your tax return on April 15 of the following year — which is also the date when the first estimated tax installment is due for that year. An individual files *Form 1040-ES* with his or her federal estimated tax payments. During a year, you must make estimated tax payments equal to 90% of the current year's tax or 100% of the prior year's tax, whichever is less.

Certain high-income taxpayers, however, are not allowed to base their payments on the prior year's tax. Starting in 1994, taxpayers with more than $150,000 of adjusted gross income in the prior year may base their payments on 110% of the prior year's tax.[2]

Corporate

If your business is incorporated, the corporation will generally have to make corporate estimated tax payments, if it has taxable income, as early as the fourth month of its first tax year. For tax years beginning after June 30, 1992, the percentage your corporation must pay as estimated tax to avoid underpayment penalties has increased from 93% to 97%. For tax years beginning after December 31, 1993, your corporation must pay estimated tax equal to 100% of its current year tax or 100% of its tax for the prior year, whichever is less.

Federal estimated tax payments should be computed on *Form 1120-W* — which can be obtained, along with other federal tax forms, from any IRS office — and must be deposited in a bank that is authorized to accept federal tax deposits. The corporate estimated tax deposits must be accompanied by federal tax deposit coupons. Your corporation will be issued one coupon book which contains coupons that are preprinted with your corporate tax identification number. These coupons can be used for deposits of all types of federal taxes. On each coupon, you must indicate, by checking the applicable box, the kind of tax being deposited and the calendar quarter to which payroll tax deposits are to be applied. The boxes on the coupon indicate the form name for the type of tax being paid.

Type of Tax	Box to Check on Coupon	
Payroll tax deposits	941	
Federal unemployment tax	940 (or 940-EZ)	
Corporate income tax estimates (and year-end payments)	1120	

Federal Tax Deposits

For deposits of corporate estimated income tax, you must indicate the calendar quarter which most closely corresponds to your fiscal year end, not the calendar quarter to which the payment relates. Example: If your corporate year end is May 31, you would check the "1120" box and darken the box which indicates 2nd quarter. For each of the four quarterly estimates, 2nd quarter would be indicated on each deposit coupon.

Fiscal Year Ends	Applicable Quarter	
January, February, March	1st quarter	
April, May, June	2nd quarter	
July, August, September	3rd quarter	
October, November, December	4th quarter	

Tax Periods

The coupon books will be sent to you automatically when you file *Form SS-4*, which requests a tax identification number for the corporation. When you receive your coupon book, a reorder form, *Form 8109A*, will be provided so you can request additional coupon books for the current year, if needed.

A penalty may be imposed for failure to make deposits directly to an authorized government depository bank. In the past, when tax deposit cards were unavailable, it was common practice to mail payments to the Internal Revenue Service accompanied by a letter indicating the nature of the tax payment and requesting additional tax deposit cards. This method of paying business taxes is no longer acceptable. Thus, it is important to mail the reorder form in time to receive additional coupon books before you run out; however, the IRS will sometimes send you blank coupons for temporary use. Refer to Section 11.4 regarding state filing requirements for individual and corporate estimated income taxes.

4.7 Miscellaneous Tax Information Returns

As a general rule, every person engaged in a trade or business must report to the IRS any payments of $600 or more made to any person during the calendar year, for items such as rent, compensation for services, commissions, interest, and annuities, plus other items of fixed or determinable income.[3] To make these filings, you will use a series of 1099 forms. A number of additional tax reporting requirements are listed below. Be aware there are stiff new penalties for failure to comply with them.

Reporting Payments to Individuals

Obtaining Social Security Numbers

It is necessary to obtain the name and Social Security number or other tax identification number of any person to whom you make payments of $600 or more. There is a $50 penalty for failure to obtain their tax identification number — unless you have a reasonable excuse, such as their refusal to give you the number.[4] If they do refuse to give you the number, you must withhold 31% of whatever amount you owe them and deposit it with the IRS, or you will be subject to a penalty for failure to withhold.[5]

Reporting Sales to Direct Sellers

In addition, you must report sales of $5,000 or more of consumer products to any individual who is engaged in direct selling — that is, selling in any way other than through a permanent retail establishment.[6] This will mainly apply to sales made to people in direct sales organizations, such as Tupperware, Amway, or Shaklee. It would also apply in many other situations, such as where the person you sell to sells the goods by mail order. Use *Form 1099-MISC* to report these sales.

1099 Forms

Reportable payments you make that are in excess of $600 per year are usually filed for each payee on *Form 1099-MISC* (information return) or *Form 1099-INT* (for interest); a duplicate must be sent to the payee. In addition, you must prepare and file a *Form 1096* return summarizing all the information on the 1099-MISC forms and on the other forms in the 1099 series. Each of these forms is due by February 28 each year, for the prior calendar year, and a copy must also be sent to the recipient of the payment by January 31.

Be aware that instructions for *Form 1099* say you should use your personal Social Security number rather than your business' employer identification number on the form. Putting down the wrong taxpayer identification number in such a case will subject you to a penalty.

Payments of compensation in excess of $600 made to nonemployees — independent contractors — are also reportable on *Form 1099-MISC*. Businesses must also report royalty payments of $10 or more made to any person.

Penalties

There are stiff IRS penalties for not filing the above 1099 forms. The penalty for not filing or not giving a 1099 to a payee is $50 per failure. Since there is a separate penalty for not giving a copy of the 1099 to the payee as well as for not filing a copy with the IRS, it can cost you $100 for each person for whom you fail to prepare 1099s.[7] The $50 penalty for late-filed 1099s, and certain other information returns, can be reduced to $30, if you file more than 30 days late but before August 1 of the year the filing is due. Or, if you file within 30 days after the due date, the penalty can be reduced to only $15.

In addition, if you erroneously, but in good faith, treat a person as an independent contractor, and it is later shown that the person was actually an employee, you will only be liable as an employer for 20% of the employee's Social Security tax that should have been withheld and for income tax withholding equal to 1.5% of what you paid the individual provided that you properly filed *Form 1099-MISC* with the IRS.[8] If you failed to file *Form 1099-MISC* for that person, the amount of withholding tax you are liable for is doubled.[9]

Fortunately, a number of important exemptions from the 1099 filing requirements will eliminate most of the people or companies to whom you are likely to make payments of $600 or more. You do not have to report:

Exemptions for 1099 Filings

- Payments to corporations — except certain corporations in the medical field;[10]
- Payments of compensation to employees that are already reported on their W-2s;[11]
- Payments of bills for merchandise, telegrams, telephone, freight, storage, and similar charges;[12]
- Payments of rent made to real estate agents;[13]
- Expense advances or reimbursements to employees that the employees must account to you (the employer) for;[14] and
- Payments to a governmental unit.[15]

If your business is incorporated, your corporation will have to file a *Form 1099-DIV* for each person to whom it pays dividends of $10 or more each year.[16] You must also file *Form 1099-INT* for each person to whom you pay $10 or more in interest on bonds, debentures, or notes issued by the corporation in registered form.[17] *Form 1099-DIV* or *Form 1099-INT* is also required for any other payment of dividends or interest on which you are required to withhold tax. Payments reported on *Form 1099-DIV* and *Form 1099-INT* must also be reported on the *Form 1096* summary. *Form 1099-S* must be given to recipients of the proceeds from the sales of real estate, in general.

Reporting Dividends and Interest

Any business that receives a payment of more than $10,000 in cash, in cash equivalents — such as cashier's checks or traveler's checks — or in foreign currency in one transaction, or in two or more related transactions, is required to report the details of the transactions within 15 days to the IRS[18] and to furnish a similar statement to the payor by January 31 of the following year.[19] The form for reporting such "suitcase" transactions is *Form 8300*.

Reporting Large Cash Transactions

The penalties for noncompliance are generally the same as for not filing 1099s, except that in cases of intentional failure to file, there is an additional penalty equal to the higher of $25,000 or the amount of the cash or cash equivalent received in the transaction, up to $100,000.[20] In addition to the requirement that you file 1099s with the IRS, you may have to file similar forms with the state.

Reporting Mortgage Interest Received

Federal law requires that you give *Form 1098* to any individual from whom you receive $600 or more in mortgage interest during the year, in the course of your trade or business. *Form 1098* has the same filing requirements as *Form 1099*.[21]

Reporting on Magnetic Media

Note that the IRS permits you to file *Form 1098* and *Form 1099*, as well as certain other information returns, on magnetic media (computer tapes or disks) rather than the actual paper forms, if very specific formats for the computer tape or disk are met. The IRS requires that certain information returns be filed on magnetic media, if your business files 250 or more such returns for a calendar year.[22] These include *Form 1098*, all of the 1099 series and W-2 series of information returns, and various others, such as *Form 5498* and *Form 8027*.

A "hardship waiver" to excuse you from having to file in magnetic media format may be granted under certain circumstances, if you file a request on *Form 8508* at least 90 days in advance of the due date.

Failure of a taxpayer to file an information return on magnetic media — or on a machine-readable form where magnetic media filing is not required — when required to do so is treated as a failure-to-file and can result in the imposition of applicable penalties for failure to file, as noted earlier.

If your business finds it will be required to file information returns on magnetic media, there are many data processing firms and computer programs you can buy that will encode the data for you, at a relatively small cost, in a way that meets the IRS' highly technical specifications.

4.8 Sales and Use Tax Permits

With a limited number of exceptions, every business that sells tangible personal property, such as merchandise, to customers must obtain a seller's permit from the state sales tax agency. Usually, a separate permit must be obtained for each place of business where property subject to tax is sold. See Section 11.4 for a discussion of the state's sales and use tax laws and permit requirements. Some states have a gross income or a gross receipts tax rather than a sales tax.

In general, as a wholesaler or manufacturer, you will not have to collect sales tax on goods you sell to a retailer for resale, if the retailer holds a valid seller's permit and provides you with a resale certificate in connection with the transaction. Likewise, if your business, as a retailer, buys goods for resale, you need not pay sales tax to the wholesalers if you provide them with resale certificates. You may buy blank resale certificate forms at most stationery stores in states where such certificates are required.

The sales and use tax laws typically require a business that sells or leases tangible personal property to keep complete records of the gross receipts from sales or rentals whether or not the receipts are believed to be taxable. You must also keep adequate and complete records to substantiate all deductions claimed on sales and use tax returns and of the total purchase price of all tangible personal property bought for sale, lease, or consumption in the state.

4.9 Real Estate Taxes

As a rule, you do not need to worry about contacting the county tax assessor's office regarding payment of any real property taxes on real property acquired for your business. They will usually contact you by mailing a property tax bill to the owner of record. See Section 11.4 for a general description of how state or local real property and personal property taxes are assessed and collected.

Property Taxes

In addition to local property taxes, U.S. citizens and residents who acquire U.S. real estate from foreign persons — including partnership interests or stock in certain firms owning U.S. real property — must withhold up to 10% of the purchase price and remit it to the IRS under the Foreign Investment in Real Property Tax Act (FIRPTA). If you fail to withhold the tax, you are liable for it. This is a potentially dangerous tax trap for unsuspecting American buyers of real estate, since it is often difficult to determine whether a seller is a foreign person.

FIRPTA Withholding Tax on Purchase of Real Property

While there is an exception for residences costing $300,000 or less — if you will live in it for at least 50% of the time for two years — it is far safer to obtain a certificate of nonforeign status from the seller if there is any possibility that the seller is a nonresident alien or a foreign company.

To protect yourself when purchasing real estate — or your client, if you are in the real estate business — you should require, as a condition of closing the transaction, that the seller provide you with an affidavit certifying whether or not the seller is a nonresident alien or a foreign company.

If the seller refuses to sign the affidavit and provide the required information, you should withhold 10% of the gross purchase price and transmit it to the IRS within ten days of the sale along with IRS *Form 8288* and *Form 8288-A*. This can be a real problem in a highly leveraged deal where less than 10% of the purchase price is paid in cash at the closing.

Some states have adopted similar withholding provisions with regard to purchases of real estate within such states where the seller is a nonresident of the state.

In short, if the seller is a foreign person, you will owe the IRS 10% of the purchase price if you fail to withhold the tax, unless you received a certificate of nonforeign status from the seller.

4.10 Fictitious Business Name Statement

Almost every state has laws requiring any person who regularly transacts business in the state for profit under a fictitious business name to file and publish a fictitious business name statement. For a sole proprietorship or partnership, a business name is generally considered fictitious unless it contains the surname of the owner or all of the general partners and does not suggest the existence of additional owners. Use of a name that includes words like "company," "associates," "group," "brothers," or "sons" will suggest additional owners and will make it necessary for a business to file and publish a fictitious business name statement.

Putting a name that would be considered fictitious on your company letterhead, on your business cards, in advertising, or on your products will be considered a use of the name.

Many newspapers will provide the form for filing, publish the notice, and file the required affidavit. See Section 11.4 regarding specific requirements for filing a fictitious business name statement in this state.

4.11 Insurance — A Practical Necessity for Businesses

Insurance, like death and taxes, is an inevitable necessity for the owner of any small business. For almost any business, even one that has no employees, insurance coverage for general liability, product liability, fire and similar disasters, robbery, theft, and interruption of business should be considered.

If your business will have employees, workers' compensation insurance is usually mandatory under state law. Employee life, health, and disability insurance have also become virtual necessities in many businesses and professions, if you wish to be competitive with other firms in hiring and retaining capable employees.

Fidelity bonding should be considered for employees who will have access to the cash receipts or other funds of the business. If you have an employees' pension or profit-sharing plan subject to the Employee Retirement Income Security Act of 1974 (ERISA), employees involved in administering the plan or handling its funds are required to be covered by a fidelity bond.[23] See Section 5.5 for further information.

Insurance Agents

Since it isn't realistic to expect you to become a sophisticated comparison shopper for insurance while you are trying to get a business off the ground, seek out a good insurance agent whom you can trust and rely upon to give you good advice.

There is no easy way to find such an agent, just as there is no sure way of finding a good lawyer or accountant. In general, the best approach will be to ask friends, lawyers, accountants, or other businesspeople you know to refer you to a topflight insurance agent.

Agents who have earned the Chartered Life Underwriter (CLU) designation will, as a rule, be more experienced and capable than those without the CLU credential. This can be an additional factor to consider when selecting your insurance agent.

Agents who deal primarily in property and casualty insurance will not usually have CLU on their business cards. Instead, they may have the initials CPCU — Chartered Property/Casualty Underwriter — after their name, which is a similar mark of distinction in the field of property/casualty insurance.

Another good tip in finding an insurance agent is to analyze your own insurance needs. There are several how-to books that can help you analyze your risks and compare insurance prices.

Insurance Consultants

If you cannot find an agent with whom you feel comfortable, call an insurance consultant. Be sure the consultant is a member of the Society of Risk Management Consultants. To belong to the group, the individual or firm cannot be an insurance broker. These consultants are insurance experts and can give you an objective analysis on risk management and insurance.

Society of Risk Management Consultants
300 Park Avenue
New York, NY 10022
(800) 765-SRMC

The usual hourly fees may seem high, but most new businesses probably will not need more than an hour of their time. Most will bill in quarter-hour increments.

You will probably recoup the consultant's fee several times over in premium savings in just the first year alone. Be wary, however, of a consultant who wants to increase the number of hours by offering to create specifications and provide additional services.

Once you have met with an independent consultant and know what is needed, shop for the insurance you need from insurance brokers. Don't let them bid up the amount of coverage or add on additional types of insurance.

Use the insurance consultant as you would an attorney or physician — follow his or her advice.

4.12 Requirements Specific to the Legal Form of the Business

Sole Proprietorships

There are no significant government regulatory requirements that apply specifically to sole proprietorships; although, as a sole proprietor of a business, you will need to attach a form *Schedule C* to your individual federal tax return, on which you will report the income or loss from the business.

Also, if your sole proprietorship shows a profit, you will usually have to pay a self-employment tax equal to 15.3% of your net self-employment income from the business or at least on the first $57,600 of such income, plus an additional 2.9% on self-employment income of more than $57,600 and up to $135,000, in 1993. The 2.9% tax will apply to all of your self-employment income after 1993. The self-employment tax is computed on *Schedule SE*, which must also be attached to your federal income tax return. See Section 11.4 for how to report business profits on your state income tax returns.

Partnerships

Like a sole proprietor, as a partner, you will have to pay a self-employment tax on your share of your partnership's net self-employment income. Net self-employment income usually includes all partnership income less all partnership deductions allowed for income tax purposes. Some types of income, such as interest, may or may not be considered self-employment income. The source of your income and your involvement in the activity from which your income is received will determine whether it is self-employment income.

If your earnings from self-employment is $400 or more for the year, you will have to figure self-employment tax on *Schedule SE* of your federal *Form 1040*. The self-employment tax is a Social Security and Medicare tax for those who work for themselves.

Schedule E of your federal *Form 1040* deals with your personal income tax and includes all other taxable income, such as royalties, rentals, and interest. You report your share of partnership ordinary income or loss on *Schedule E*.

In addition, your partnership must file a partnership information return, federal *Form 1065*, reporting the partnership's income and each partner's share of income and other items. The partnership must also file *Form SS-4* with the IRS to obtain a federal employer identification number, even if it has no employees. See Section 11.4 for state partnership return filing requirements, and the end of this chapter for a sample *Form SS-4*.

When a partner buys, sells, or exchanges a partnership interest, the partnership must file a special information return if the partnership's assets include unrealized receivables or substantially appreciated inventory that might cause the seller to have ordinary gain, rather than all capital gain, on the sale or exchange.[24] Statements also have to be sent to the partners involved in the transaction.[25]

A limited partnership, to qualify as such, is usually required to file a *Certificate of Limited Partnership* with the secretary of state or other state agency. In most states, a limited partnership should also file certified copies in each county where it does business or owns real estate.

Corporations are subject to the following requirements. These requirements are not applicable to other legal forms of business organization.

Corporations

- Filing articles of incorporation;
- Adopting a set of bylaws;
- Observing other corporate formalities on a regular basis, such as the election of directors by shareholders and appointment of officers by action of the board of directors;
- Filing federal income tax returns on *Form 1120* — or *Form 1120-S* for an S corporation — and state income or franchise tax returns in most states where they do business. See Section 11.4 for various filings, taxes, and fees required of corporations that are incorporated or doing business in this state;
- Reporting certain information relating to the transfer of tax-free property under Internal Revenue Code Section 351 on the corporation's income tax return for that year;[26]
- Filing *Form SS-4* with the IRS to obtain an employer identification number, even if there are no employees; and
- Qualifying with the secretary of state to do business, if the corporation was organized under the laws of another state.

4.13 Checklist of Requirements for Nearly All New Businesses

☐ Obtain local business licenses.

☐ Check on local zoning ordinances, regulations, and other land use restrictions.

☐ Determine if your particular business requires a state license to operate.

☐ Determine whether any type of federal permit or license is required.

☐ Be prepared to make estimated income tax payments almost immediately after starting business or incorporating.

☐ Apply for a sales and use tax seller's permit if you will sell tangible personal property.

☐ File sales and use tax returns, if you must collect sales or use tax.

☐ File with the county clerk and publish a fictitious business name statement if the business operates under a fictitious name, and then file an affidavit of publication with the county clerk (in most states).

☐ Locate a good insurance agent or retain and meet with an insurance consultant regarding fire, accident, liability, theft, and other types of commercial insurance. Then obtain the necessary insurance coverage.

☐ If you purchase real estate, you must withhold up to 10% of the purchase price and remit it to the IRS if the seller is a foreign individual or foreign-owned company, under the Foreign Investment in Real Property Tax Act.[27] Otherwise, you should insist upon receiving an affidavit that the seller is not a nonresident alien, with his or her taxpayer identification number, unless you are certain that he or she is a U.S. citizen or resident.

☐ For a sole proprietorship, report any self-employment income on *Schedule SE* of federal *Form 1040*, and report income or loss on *Schedule C* of *Form 1040*.

☐ A partnership files *Form 1065* reporting partnership income. Each partner reports his or her share of self-employment income on *Schedule SE* of *Form 1040* and income or loss from partnership operations on *Schedule E* of *Form 1040*.

☐ For a limited partnership, file a *Certificate of Limited Partnership* with the secretary of state and copies in counties where the partnership has places of business or real estate (in most states).

☐ For a corporation, file articles of incorporation, adopt bylaws, and observe necessary corporate formalities. File federal income tax return *Form 1120*; *Form 1120-S* for an S corporation. If property is transferred to the corporation tax-free under Internal Revenue Code Section 351, report required information relating to the transfer on the corporation's income tax return for that year.

☐ For a corporation or a partnership, apply for a federal employer identification number on *Form SS-4*, even if the business has no employees. See sample at the end of this chapter.

☐ File annual tax information returns, *Form 1096* and the *Form 1099* series, for payments of $600 or more for items such as rent, interest, and compensation for services, and send 1099s to the payees.

☐ File *Form 1098* for mortgage interest of $600 or more your business receives in a year from an individual.

☐ Also, report any cash payments or cash equivalents of more than $10,000 that you receive to the IRS within 15 days. Such filing may have to be done on computer-readable magnetic media.

☐ If your business is a corporation, be sure to obtain an adequate supply of federal tax deposit coupons in time to make your estimated tax payments.

The above requirements apply to any business, whether it has employees or not. There are many additional requirements for businesses that do have employees, and these are covered in the next chapter. See Section 11.4

for a checklist of additional state law requirements that apply to nearly all new businesses.

4.14 Securities Laws

Inherent in the choice of the legal form of the business is the potential application of federal and state securities laws, if the new business is to have more than one owner or should it become necessary to raise capital for an existing business. Because of the potentially dire consequences of violating federal or state securities laws, it is important to consult with your attorney as early as possible when considering issuing or transferring a security. Corporate stock and limited partnership interests generally are considered securities, and even a general partnership interest can be a security in appropriate circumstances, as can certain types of debt instruments.

Registration of Securities

Since the Securities Act of 1933, federal law has required registration as a prior condition to the issuance or transfer of securities. The law exempts various types of securities and certain types of transactions. The most important of these exemptions for small businesses have been the exemption for securities sold to persons residing within a single state and transactions by an issuer not deemed to involve any public offering. The Securities and Exchange Commission (SEC) from time to time has issued regulations exempting small securities issues, attempting to balance the needs of small businesses to raise capital against the public policy of protecting investors. In 1982, the commission adopted Regulation D as its primary method of regulation of securities offerings by small businesses, although not to the exclusion of other exemptions which might apply.

Rule 504 Exemption

Rule 504 under Regulation D exempts the issuance of securities by an entity if the aggregate offering price of all exempt securities sold by the entity during a twelve-month period does not exceed one million dollars — not more than $500,000 of securities can be offered and sold without registration under some states' securities laws.[28] The securities cannot be offered or sold by any form of general solicitation or general advertising, and the securities so acquired cannot be resold without registration or an exemption from registration.

This rule does not require any specific information to be given to the purchasers of the securities; however, since the anti-fraud provisions of the securities laws apply even though the transaction is exempt from registration, it is helpful to memorialize in writing the material information regarding the offering.

Rule 505 Exemption

Rule 505 exempts offers and sales of securities if the offering price for all exempt securities sold over a twelve-month period does not exceed five million dollars.[29] To obtain this exemption, the issuer must reasonably believe that there are not more than 35 purchasers exclusive of accredited investors.

Examples of accredited investors include banks, insurance companies, a natural person whose net worth at the time of purchase exceeds one million dollars, or a person who has individual income in excess of $200,000 — or $300,000 jointly with a spouse — in each of the two most recent years and expects the same in the current year. Exceptions are also made for certain large investors, including corporations, partnerships, or business trusts with total assets in excess of five million dollars, unless formed for the specific purpose of acquiring the securities.

For purposes of Rule 505, the issuer must furnish extensive information and certified financial statements to the investors, unless securities were sold only to accredited investors. The prohibition against advertising and solicitation applies to this rule, as do the anti-fraud provisions of the securities laws.

Rule 506 Exemption

Rule 506 provides exemptions similar to those under Rule 505, including the 35-purchaser limitation, with the same exception for accredited investors described above.[30] However, Rule 506 requires that an issuer of securities must reasonably believe, immediately before making a sale to a nonaccredited investor, that the investor is sufficiently knowledgeable to adequately evaluate the merits and risks of the investment. Alternatively, the issuer can rely on the knowledge and experience of a person who represents the investor. The other main difference between Rule 505 and Rule 506 is that there is no five million dollar or other maximum size limitation on the amount of securities that can be issued in a Rule 506 offering.

Regulation D Filing Requirements

Issuers utilizing any of the above exemptions must file *Form D* with the SEC generally no later than 15 days after the first sale of securities and at other specified times thereafter. Rule 507 disqualifies any issuer found to have violated the *Form D* filing requirement from future use of the Regulation D exemptions, if the issuer has been enjoined by a court for violating the notice filing requirement — but apparently will not disqualify prior issuances of securities merely due to failure to file *Form D*.[31]

The exemptions available under the federal securities laws are more liberal than those available under the securities laws of many states. In connection with any issuance or transfer of securities, it is necessary to consider the possible application of securities laws in the state where the business entity is established or operates, and, if different, the states where purchasers of the securities live. See Section 11.2 for further information concerning state securities laws.

Through its 1993 Regulation S-B, the SEC provides a new set of rules designed to make it easier and simpler for small businesses to raise capital in the public market. Regulation S-B is an integrated system of rules, forms, and reporting requirements designed especially for small firms, which have traditionally found the costs and complexity of "going public" to be prohibitive. To make a public offering of securities that qualifies under the streamlined procedures of Regulation S-B, an issuing company must meet all the following requirements:

Going Public Easier for Small Companies

- A company must be a U.S. or Canadian company and cannot be an investment company.

- A company's revenues must be less than $25 million per year.

- The aggregate value of a company's outstanding securities (not counting those held by affiliated companies or persons) must not exceed $25 million.

- If the issuer is a majority-owned subsidiary of another corporation, the parent company must also meet the above criteria.

Endnotes

1. *Armstrong Paint and Varnish Works v. New and U-Enamel Corp.* 305 U.S. 315 (1938); *Carter-Wallace, Inc. v. Proctor and Gamble Co.* 434 F.2d 794 (9th Cir. 1970). The author wishes to acknowledge Henry C. Bunsow, esq. of the San Francisco patent and trademark law firm of Townsend and Townsend for alerting him to this important point.

2. I.R.C. § 6654.

3. I.R.C. § 6041(a).

4. I.R.C. § 6724(d)(3).

5. I.R.C. § 3406(a).

6. I.R.C. § 6041A(b).

7. I.R.C. §§ 6721–6722.

8. I.R.C. § 3509(a).

9. I.R.C. § 3509(b).

10. Treas. Regs. § 1.6041-3(c).

11. Treas. Regs. § 1.6041-3(a).

12. Treas. Regs. § 1.6041-3(d).

13. Treas. Regs. § 1.6041-3(e).

14. Treas. Regs. § 1.6041-3(i).

15. I.R.C. § 6041(a) requires filing of information returns for payments made to another "person." As defined in IRC § 7701(a)(1), "person" does not include governmental bodies.

16. I.R.C. § 6042(a).

17. I.R.C. § 6049(a).

18. I.R.C. § 6050I.

19. I.R.C. § 6722.

20. I.R.C. § 6721.

21. I.R.C. § 6050H.

22. Rev. Proc. 93-24, 1993-20 I.R.B. 7.

23. 29 U.S.C. § 1112 (§ 412 of ERISA).

24. I.R.C. § 6050K(a).

25. I.R.C. § 6050K(b).

26. Treas. Regs. § 1.351-3.

27. I.R.C. § 1445(a).

28. 17 C.F.R. § 230.504.

29. 17 C.F.R. § 230.505.

30. 17 C.F.R. § 230.506.

31. Rule 507, as interpreted in Securities Act Release No. 6825, March 14, 1989 (17 C.F.R. § 230.507).

Form SS-4 – Application for Employer Identification Number: Sample

Form **SS-4** (Rev. April 1991) Department of the Treasury Internal Revenue Service	**Application for Employer Identification Number** (For use by employers and others. Please read the attached instructions before completing this form.)	EIN OMB No. 1545-0003 Expires 4-30-94

Please type or print clearly.

1 Name of applicant (True legal name) (See instructions.)

2 Trade name of business, if different from name in line 1   **3** Executor, trustee, "care of" name

4a Mailing address (street address) (room, apt., or suite no.)   **5a** Address of business (See instructions.)

4b City, state, and ZIP code   **5b** City, state, and ZIP code

6 County and state where principal business is located

7 Name of principal officer, grantor, or general partner (See instructions.) ▶

8a Type of entity (Check only one box.) (See instructions.)
☐ Individual SSN ____   ☐ Estate   ☐ Trust
☐ REMIC   ☐ Personal service corp.   ☐ Plan administrator SSN ____   ☐ Partnership
☐ State/local government   ☐ National guard   ☐ Other corporation (specify) ____   ☐ Farmers' cooperative
☐ Other nonprofit organization (specify) ____   ☐ Federal government/military   ☐ Church or church controlled organization
☐ Other (specify) ▶   If nonprofit organization enter GEN (if applicable) ____

8b If a corporation, give name of foreign country (if applicable) or state in the U.S. where incorporated ▶   Foreign country   State

9 Reason for applying (Check only one box.)
☐ Started new business   ☐ Changed type of organization (specify) ▶
☐ Hired employees   ☐ Purchased going business
☐ Created a pension plan (specify type) ▶   ☐ Created a trust (specify) ▶
☐ Banking purpose (specify) ▶   ☐ Other (specify) ▶

10 Date business started or acquired (Mo., day, year) (See instructions.)   **11** Enter closing month of accounting year. (See instructions.)

12 First date wages or annuities were paid or will be paid (Mo., day, year). **Note:** *If applicant is a withholding agent, enter date income will first be paid to nonresident alien. (Mo., day, year)* ▶

13 Enter highest number of employees expected in the next 12 months. **Note:** *If the applicant does not expect to have any employees during the period, enter "0."* ▶   Nonagricultural | Agricultural | Household

14 Principal activity (See instructions.) ▶

15 Is the principal business activity manufacturing? ☐ Yes ☐ No
If "Yes," principal product and raw material used ▶

16 To whom are most of the products or services sold? Please check the appropriate box. ☐ Business (wholesale)
☐ Public (retail)   ☐ Other (specify) ▶   ☐ N/A

17a Has the applicant ever applied for an identification number for this or any other business? ☐ Yes ☐ No
Note: *If "Yes," please complete lines 17b and 17c.*

17b If you checked the "Yes" box in line 17a, give applicant's true name and trade name, if different than name shown on prior application.
True name ▶   Trade name ▶

17c Enter approximate date, city, and state where the application was filed and the previous employer identification number if known.
Approximate date when filed (Mo., day, year) | City and state where filed | Previous EIN

Under penalties of perjury, I declare that I have examined this application, and to the best of my knowledge and belief, it is true, correct, and complete | Telephone number (include area code)

Name and title (Please type or print clearly.) ▶

Signature ▶   Date ▶

Note: *Do not write below this line.   For official use only.*

Please leave blank ▶ | Geo. | Ind. | Class | Size | Reason for applying

For Paperwork Reduction Act Notice, see attached instructions.   Cat. No. 16055N   Form **SS-4** (Rev. 4-91)

Instructions for Form SS-4: Sample

Form SS-4 (Rev. 4-91)   Page **2**

General Instructions

(Section references are to the Internal Revenue Code unless otherwise noted.)

Paperwork Reduction Act Notice.—We ask for the information on this form to carry out the Internal Revenue laws of the United States. You are required to give us this information. We need it to ensure that you are complying with these laws and to allow us to figure and collect the right amount of tax.

The time needed to complete and file this form will vary depending on individual circumstances. The estimated average time is:

Recordkeeping. . . . . . . 7 min.
Learning about the
law or the form . . . . . . 21 min.
Preparing the form . . . . . 42 min.
Copying, assembling, and
sending the form to IRS . . . . 20 min.

If you have comments concerning the accuracy of these time estimates or suggestions for making this form more simple, we would be happy to hear from you. You can write to both the **Internal Revenue Service**, Washington, DC 20224, Attention: IRS Reports Clearance Officer, T:FP; and the **Office of Management and Budget**, Paperwork Reduction Project (1545-0003), Washington, DC 20503. **DO NOT** send the tax form to either of these offices. Instead, see **Where To Apply.**

Purpose.—Use Form SS-4 to apply for an employer identification number (EIN). The information you provide on this form will establish your filing requirements.

Who Must File.—You must file this form if you have not obtained an EIN before and

● You pay wages to one or more employees.

● You are required to have an EIN to use on any return, statement, or other document, even if you are not an employer.

● You are required to withhold taxes on income, other than wages, paid to a nonresident alien (individual, corporation, partnership, etc.). For example, individuals who file **Form 1042**, Annual Withholding Tax Return for U.S. Source Income of Foreign Persons, to report alimony paid to nonresident aliens must have EINs.

Individuals who file **Schedule C**, Profit or Loss From Business, or **Schedule F**, Profit or Loss From Farming, of **Form 1040**, U.S. Individual Income Tax Return, must use EINs if they have a Keogh plan or are required to file excise, employment, or alcohol, tobacco, or firearms returns.

The following must use EINs even if they do not have any employees:

● Trusts, except an IRA trust, unless the IRA trust is required to file **Form 990-T**, Exempt Organization Business Income Tax Return, to report unrelated business taxable income or is filing Form 990-T to obtain a refund of the credit from a regulated investment company.

● Estates

● Partnerships

● REMICS (real estate mortgage investment conduits)

● Corporations

● Nonprofit organizations (churches, clubs, etc.)

● Farmers' cooperatives

● Plan administrators

New Business.—If you become the new owner of an existing business, **DO NOT** use the EIN of the former owner. If you already have an EIN, use that number. If you do not have an EIN, apply for one on this form. If

you become the "owner" of a corporation by acquiring its stock, use the corporation's EIN.

If you already have an EIN, you may need to get a new one if either the organization or ownership of your business changes. If you incorporate a sole proprietorship or form a partnership, you must get a new EIN. However, **DO NOT** apply for a new EIN if you change only the name of your business.

File Only One Form SS-4.—File only one Form SS-4, regardless of the number of businesses operated or trade names under which a business operates. However, each corporation in an affiliated group must file a separate application.

If you do not have an EIN by the time a return is due, write "Applied for" and the date you applied in the space shown for the number. **DO NOT** show your social security number as an EIN on returns.

If you do not have an EIN by the time a tax deposit is due, send your payment to the Internal Revenue service center for your filing area. (See **Where To Apply** below.) Make your check or money order payable to Internal Revenue Service and show your name (as shown on Form SS-4), address, kind of tax, period covered, and date you applied for an EIN.

For more information about EINs, see Pub. 583, Taxpayers Starting a Business.

How To Apply.—You can apply for an EIN either by mail or by telephone. You can get an EIN immediately by calling the Tele-TIN phone number for the service center for your state, or you can send the completed Form SS-4 directly to the service center to receive your EIN in the mail.

Application by Tele-TIN.—The Tele-TIN program is designed to assign EINs by telephone. Under this program, you can receive your EIN over the telephone and use it immediately to file a return or make a payment.

To receive an EIN by phone, complete Form SS-4, then call the Tele-TIN phone number listed for your state under **Where To Apply.** The person making the call must be authorized to sign the form (see **Signature block** on page 3).

An IRS representative will use the information from the Form SS-4 to establish your account and assign you an EIN. Write the number you are given on the upper right-hand corner of the form, sign and date it, and promptly mail it to the Tele-TIN Unit at the service center address for your state.

Application by mail.—Complete Form SS-4 at least 4 to 5 weeks before you will need an EIN. Sign and date the application and mail it to the service center address for your state. You will receive your EIN in the mail in approximately 4 weeks.

Note: *The Tele-TIN phone numbers listed below will involve a long-distance charge to callers outside of the local calling area, and should only be used to apply for an EIN. Use 1-800-829-1040 to ask about an application by mail.*

Where To Apply.—

If your principal business, office or agency, or legal residence in the case of an individual, is located in:	Call the Tele-TIN phone number shown or file with the Internal Revenue service center at:
Florida, Georgia, South Carolina	Atlanta, GA 39901 (404) 455-2360
New Jersey, New York City and counties of Nassau, Rockland, Suffolk, and Westchester	Holtsville, NY 00501 (516) 447-4955
New York (all other counties), Connecticut, Maine, Massachusetts, New Hampshire, Rhode Island, Vermont	Andover, MA 05501 (508) 474-9717
Illinois, Iowa, Minnesota, Missouri, Wisconsin	Kansas City, MO 64999 (816) 926-5999
Delaware, District of Columbia, Maryland, Pennsylvania, Virginia	Philadelphia, PA 19255 (215) 961-3980
Indiana, Kentucky, Michigan, Ohio, West Virginia	Cincinnati, OH 45999 (606) 292-5467
Kansas, New Mexico, Oklahoma, Texas	Austin, TX 73301 (512) 462-7845
Alaska, Arizona, California (counties of Alpine, Amador, Butte, Calaveras, Colusa, Contra Costa, Del Norte, El Dorado, Glenn, Humboldt, Lake, Lassen, Marin, Mendocino, Modoc, Napa, Nevada, Placer, Plumas, Sacramento, San Joaquin, Shasta, Sierra, Siskiyou, Solano, Sonoma, Sutter, Tehama, Trinity, Yolo, and Yuba), Colorado, Idaho, Montana, Nebraska, Nevada, North Dakota, Oregon, South Dakota, Utah, Washington, Wyoming	Ogden, UT 84201 (801) 625-7645
California (all other counties), Hawaii	Fresno, CA 93888 (209) 456-5900
Alabama, Arkansas, Louisiana, Mississippi, North Carolina, Tennessee	Memphis, TN 37501 (901) 365-5970

If you have no legal residence, principal place of business, or principal office or agency in any Internal Revenue District, file your form with the Internal Revenue Service Center, Philadelphia, PA 19255 or call (215) 961-3980.

Specific Instructions

The instructions that follow are for those items that are not self-explanatory. Enter N/A (nonapplicable) on the lines that do not apply.

Line 1.—Enter the legal name of the entity applying for the EIN.

Individuals.—Enter the first name, middle initial, and last name.

Trusts.—Enter the name of the trust.

Estate of a decedent.—Enter the name of the estate.

Partnerships.—Enter the legal name of the partnership as it appears in the partnership agreement.

Corporations.—Enter the corporate name as set forth in the corporation charter or other legal document creating it.

Plan administrators.—Enter the name of the plan administrator. A plan administrator who already has an EIN should use that number.

Line 2.—Enter the trade name of the business if different from the legal name.

Note: *Use the full legal name entered on line 1 on all tax returns to be filed for the entity. However, if a trade name is entered on line 2, use only the name on line 1 or the name on line 2 consistently when filing tax returns.*

Line 3.—Trusts enter the name of the trustee. Estates enter the name of the executor, administrator, or other fiduciary. If the entity applying has a designated person to receive tax information, enter that person's name as the "care of" person. Print or type the first name, middle initial, and last name.

Lines 5a and 5b.—If the physical location of the business is different from the mailing address (lines 4a and 4b), enter the address of the physical location on lines 5a and 5b.

Instructions for Form SS-4: Sample (continued)

Form SS-4 (Rev. 4-91)   Page **3**

Line 7.—Enter the first name, middle initial, and last name of a principal officer if the business is a corporation; of a general partner if a partnership; and of a grantor if a trust.

Line 8a.—Check the box that best describes the type of entity that is applying for the EIN. If not specifically mentioned, check the "other" box and enter the type of entity. Do not enter N/A.

Individual.—Check this box if the individual files Schedule C or F (Form 1040) and has a Keogh plan or is required to file excise, employment, or alcohol, tobacco, or firearms returns. If this box is checked, enter the individual's SSN (social security number) in the space provided.

Plan administrator.—The term plan administrator means the person or group of persons specified as the administrator by the instrument under which the plan is operated. If the plan administrator is an individual, enter the plan administrator's SSN in the space provided.

New withholding agent.—If you are a new withholding agent required to file Form 1042, check the "other" box and enter in the space provided "new withholding agent."

REMICs.—Check this box if the entity is a real estate mortgage investment conduit (REMIC). A REMIC is any entity

1. To which an election to be treated as a REMIC applies for the tax year and all prior tax years,

2. In which all of the interests are regular interests or residual interests,

3. Which has one class of residual interests (and all distributions, if any, with respect to such interests are pro rata),

4. In which as of the close of the 3rd month beginning after the startup date and at all times thereafter, substantially all of its assets consist of qualified mortgages and permitted investments,

5. Which has a tax year that is a calendar year, and

6. With respect to which there are reasonable arrangements designed to ensure that: (a) residual interests are not held by disqualified organizations (as defined in section 860E(e)(5)), and (b) information necessary for the application of section 860E(e) will be made available.

For more information about REMICs see the Instructions for **Form 1066,** U. S. Real Estate Mortgage Investment Conduit Income Tax Return.

Personal service corporations.—Check this box if the entity is a personal service corporation. An entity is a personal service corporation for a tax year only if

1. The entity is a C corporation for the tax year.

2. The principal activity of the entity during the testing period (as defined in Temporary Regulations section 1.441-4T(f)) for the tax year is the performance of personal service.

3. During the testing period for the tax year, such services are substantially performed by employee-owners.

4. The employee-owners own 10 percent of the fair market value of the outstanding stock in the entity on the last day of the testing period for the tax year.

For more information about personal service corporations, see the instructions to **Form 1120,** U.S. Corporation Income Tax Return, and Temporary Regulations section 1.441-4T.

Other corporations.—This box is for any corporation other than a personal service corporation. If you check this box, enter the type of corporation (such as insurance company) in the space provided.

Other nonprofit organizations.—Check this box if the nonprofit organization is other than a church or church-controlled organization and specify the type of nonprofit organization (for example, an educational organization.)

Group exemption number (GEN).—If the applicant is a nonprofit organization that is a subordinate organization to be included in a group exemption letter under Revenue Procedure 80-27, 1980-1 C.B. 677, enter the GEN in the space provided. If you do not know the GEN, contact the parent organization for it. GEN is a four-digit number. Do not confuse it with the nine-digit EIN.

Line 9.—Check only one box. Do not enter N/A.

Started new business.—Check this box if you are starting a new business that requires an EIN. If you check this box, enter the type of business being started. **DO NOT** apply if you already have an EIN and are only adding another place of business.

Changed type of organization.—Check this box if the business is changing its type of organization, for example, if the business was a sole proprietorship and has been incorporated or has become a partnership. If you check this box, specify in the space provided the type of change made, for example, "from sole proprietorship to partnership."

Purchased going business.—Check this box if you acquired a business through purchase. Do not use the former owner's EIN. If you already have an EIN, use that number.

Hired employees.—Check this box if the existing business is requesting an EIN because it has hired or is hiring employees and is therefore required to file employment tax return for which an EIN is required. **DO NOT** apply if you already have an EIN and are only hiring employees.

Created a trust.—Check this box if you created a trust, and enter the type of trust created.

Created a pension plan.—Check this box if you have created a pension plan and need this number for reporting purposes. Also, enter the type of plan created.

Banking purpose.—Check this box if you are requesting an EIN for banking purpose only and enter the banking purpose (for example, checking, loan, etc.).

Other (specify).—Check this box if you are requesting an EIN for any reason other than those for which there are checkboxes and enter the reason.

Line 10.—If you are starting a new business, enter the starting date of the business. If the business you acquired is already operating, enter the date you acquired the business. Trusts should enter the date the trust was legally created. Estates should enter the date of death of the decedent whose name appears on line 1.

Line 11.—Enter the last month of your accounting year or tax year. An accounting year or tax year is usually 12 consecutive months. It may be a calendar year or a fiscal year (including a period of 52 or 53 weeks). A calendar year is 12 consecutive months ending on December 31. A fiscal year is either 12 consecutive months ending on the last day of any month other than December or a 52-53 week year. For more information

on accounting periods, see **Pub. 538,** Accounting Periods and Methods.

Individuals.—Your tax year generally will be a calendar year.

Partnerships.—Partnerships generally should conform to the tax year of either (1) its majority partners; (2) its principal partners; (3) the tax year that results in the least aggregate deferral of income (see Temporary Regulations section 1.706-1T); or (4) some other tax year, if (a) a business purpose is established for the fiscal year, or (b) the fiscal year is a "grandfather" year, or (c) an election is made under section 444 to have a fiscal year. (See the Instructions for **Form 1065,** U.S. Partnership Return of Income, for more information.)

REMICs.—Remics must have a calendar year as their tax year.

Personal service corporations.—A personal service corporation generally must adopt a calendar year unless:

1. It can establish to the satisfaction of the Commissioner that there is a business purpose for having a different tax year, or

2. It elects under section 444 to have a tax year other than a calendar year.

Line 12.—If the business has or will have employees, enter on this line the date on which the business began or will begin to pay wages to the employees. If the business does not have any plans to have employees, enter N/A on this line.

New withholding agent.—Enter the date you began or will begin to pay income to a nonresident alien. This also applies to individuals who are required to file Form 1042 to report alimony paid to a nonresident alien.

Line 14.—Generally, enter the exact type of business being operated (for example, advertising agency, farm, labor union, real estate agency, steam laundry, rental of coin-operated vending machine, investment club, etc.).

Governmental.—Enter the type of organization (state, county, school district, or municipality, etc.)

Nonprofit organization (other than governmental).—Enter whether organized for religious, educational, or humane purposes, and the principal activity (for example, religious organization—hospital, charitable).

Mining and quarrying.—Specify the process and the principal product (for example, mining bituminous coal, contract drilling for oil, quarrying dimension stone, etc.).

Contract construction.—Specify whether general contracting or special trade contracting. Also, show the type of work normally performed (for example, general contractor for residential buildings, electrical subcontractor, etc.).

Trade.—Specify the type of sales and the principal line of goods sold (for example, wholesale dairy products, manufacturer's representative for mining machinery, retail hardware, etc.).

Manufacturing.—Specify the type of establishment operated (for example, sawmill, vegetable cannery, etc.).

Signature block.—The application must be signed by: (1) the individual, if the person is an individual, (2) the president, vice president, or other principal officer, if the person is a corporation, (3) a responsible and duly authorized member or officer having knowledge of its affairs, if the person is a partnership or other unincorporated organization, or (4) the fiduciary, if the person is a trust or estate.

★ U.S.GPO:1992-0-312-699/60110

Chapter 5

The Thicket Thickens: Additional Requirements for Businesses with Employees

Man is a thinking animal, a talking animal, a tool-making animal, a building animal, a political animal, a fantasizing animal. But in the twilight of a civilization, he is chiefly a taxpaying animal.

— Hugh MacLennan

5.1 General Considerations

As the previous chapter indicated, there is a considerable amount of governmental red tape involved in starting almost any new business. If your business will have any employees — even if it is incorporated and you are the only employee — the level of government regulation and red tape will multiply several times over in a typical case. This chapter outlines the bases you must cover, in addition to those described in Chapter 4, if you start a business that will have employees.

5.2 Social Security and Income Tax Withholding

Once you go into business and begin paying salary or wages to employees, you will find that you have been appointed, as an agent of the government, to collect taxes from your employees. In addition to various payroll taxes, you will also be required to collect income taxes and Social Security (FICA) tax from employees' wages.

The first order of business is to apply for a federal employer identification number (EIN) with the IRS. This number will be used to identify your

Employer Identification Number

business on payroll and income tax returns and for most other federal tax purposes. To apply for an EIN number, you need to file a completed *Form SS-4* at the earliest possible time, especially if you have employees. This will ensure that you will get tax deposit coupons in time for depositing federal payroll taxes or corporate income tax. Corporations and partnerships must file *Form SS-4* even if they have no employees. A sample of this form is located at the end of Chapter 4.

The IRS can provide you with a business tax kit that is specifically put together for new employers. You can also obtain *Circular E, Employer's Tax Guide*, an IRS publication that explains federal income tax withholding and Social Security tax requirements for employers. *Circular E* contains up-to-date withholding tables that you must use to determine how much federal income tax and Social Security tax is to be withheld from each employee's paycheck.

Employer Social Security Tax

In addition to withholding Social Security tax from an employee's paycheck — at the rate of 7.65% on gross wages up to $60,600, 1.45% on wages in excess of $60,600 in 1994. The employer must also pay an equal amount of employer's Social Security tax. The withheld federal income tax, withheld employee Social Security tax, and employer's Social Security tax are lumped together and paid to the IRS at the same time. In some cases, these taxes can simply be mailed in with your payroll tax return (*Form 941* series) at the end of the calendar quarter or year; however, if you have significant amounts of these taxes to pay, you will generally be required to deposit the taxes with a federal tax deposit form, a precoded coupon, at an authorized commercial bank or a federal reserve bank. As a rule, the greater the amount of taxes due, the sooner they must be paid.

The complex tax deposit deadlines of previous years have been totally revised and considerably simplified and revised under recent IRS regulations. Rules for how and when federal income and Social Security taxes are to be mailed in or deposited are summarized briefly as follows:

Type of Depositor	Deadline
Small depositor — An employer with less than $500 of combined income and Social Security taxes for the calendar quarter.[1]	Deposit by last day of month following the end of the quarter, or mail with *Form 941* return by then.
Monthly depositor — An employer, who for the 12-month period ending June 30th of the preceding calendar year, reported $50,000 or less of employment taxes.[2]	Deposit by 15th day of the following month.
Semi-weekly depositor — All other employers:[3]	
For Wednesday–Friday semi-weekly period:	Deposit on or before next Wednesday.
For Saturday–Tuesday semi-weekly period:	Deposit on or before next Friday.

Some exceptions to the above tax deposit schedules do exist. For example, any employer with $100,000 of employment taxes accumulated at the end of any day — for the current month or semi-weekly period only, whichever applies — must deposit those taxes in an authorized bank by the end of the next banking day, subsequently becoming a semi-weekly depositor.[4] Shortfalls in required deposits will result in underpayment penalties. No penalty, however, will be imposed if the shortfall does not exceed 2% of the required deposit (or $100, if greater) provided the shortfall is made up within specified periods. For a more detailed explanation of federal tax deposits, see IRS *Notice 109*. Deposits of payroll and withholding taxes may be mailed to a depository bank, if postmarked at least two days prior to the tax deposit due date. But tax deposits of $20,000 or more by employers making more than one deposit a month must reach the bank by the due date, regardless of the postmark date.[5]

New Employees

When a new employee is hired, give the employee a federal *Form W-4*. He or she must then complete and return the form to you. When completed, *Form W-4* provides the employee's Social Security number and the number of withholding exemptions the employee is claiming. The number of exemptions is used to determine how much income tax you must withhold from his or her wages. You keep *Form W-4*. Neither it nor the information on it is filed with the IRS, except in the case of an employee who claims more than ten withholding exemptions, or who claims exemption from income tax withholding.

By January 31 of each year, you must furnish each employee with copies of *Form W-2, Annual Wage and Tax Statement*, showing the taxable wages paid to an employee during the preceding calendar year and the taxes withheld, including state income tax. By February 28, the original of *Form W-2* and a summary form, *Form W-3*, should be filed with the IRS.

Independent Contractors

A person who performs services for your business does not necessarily have to be your employee. In many cases, you can structure your legal relationships with persons who provide services to you so they are considered independent contractors for tax and other legal purposes. From an employer standpoint, it is preferable to treat someone as an independent contractor rather than as an employee of your business because you do not have to pay Social Security tax or federal or state unemployment taxes on his or her compensation. An independent contractor is considered to be self-employed for tax purposes and pays self-employment tax.

In addition, you don't have to withhold income and payroll taxes from compensation paid to independent contractors or file payroll tax returns with respect to their compensation. You must, however, file a *Form 1099-MISC* for each independent contractor to whom you make payments of $600 or more during a calendar year (with certain exceptions), or in the case of a direct seller of consumer goods, for each such direct seller to whom you sell $5,000 of goods during a year.

Because of the obvious advantages employers obtain by treating their employees as independent contractors, the IRS has been very aggressive in attempting to reclassify so-called independent contractors as employees where they perform functions in a manner that is more typical of an employer/employee relationship. Requiring businesses to file *Form 1099-MISC* is an attempt by the IRS to identify those businesses that may be improperly treating employees as independent contractors.

Before you decide to treat anyone who works for you as an independent contractor, consult your tax adviser because there can be serious consequences if those individuals are reclassified as employees by the IRS. See Section 9.11 for a discussion of the risks involved.

Each state has its own withholding taxes. For information on the withholding tax requirements for this state, see Section 11.5.

5.3 Unemployment Taxes

With relatively few exceptions, all businesses with employees must pay both federal and state unemployment taxes. These taxes are imposed entirely on you, the employer. Theoretically, the federal unemployment tax is 6.2% of the first $7,000 of annual wages per employee.[6] In actuality, however, the rate is usually only 0.8% because a credit for up to 5.4% is given for state unemployment taxes paid and for a favorable experience rating for state unemployment tax purposes.[7]

The state unemployment tax rate for an employer can be either more or less than the basic rate, depending upon the amount of unemployment claims by former employees. The more unemployment benefits claimed by your former employees, the higher your unemployment tax rate will be, within certain limits.

Federal Unemployment Tax

Your business will be required to pay federal unemployment tax (FUTA) for any calendar year in which it pays wages of $1,500 or more[8] or if it has one or more employees for at least a portion of the day during any 20 different calendar weeks during the year.[9] Needless to say, this will cover almost any business that has one employee, even if that employee is part-time.

If the FUTA liability during any of the first three calendar quarters is more than $100, you must deposit the tax with a federal tax deposit coupon, *Form 8109*, at an authorized bank during the month following the end of the quarter. If the tax is $100 or less, you are not required to make a deposit, but you must add it to the taxes for the next quarter. For the fourth quarter, if the undeposited FUTA tax for the year is more than $100, deposit the tax with a tax deposit coupon at an authorized bank by January 31. If the balance due is $100 or less, either deposit it with the coupon or mail it to the IRS with your federal unemployment tax return, *Form 940*, by January 31. *Form 940* is not due until February 10 if all of the FUTA tax for the prior year has already been deposited when due.

The IRS also provides *Form 940-EZ*, a greatly simplified FUTA return for certain small employers. In general, the small employers who can use *Form 940-EZ* are those:

- Who pay unemployment tax to only one state;
- Who pay state unemployment taxes by the *Form 940-EZ* due date; and
- Whose wages subject to FUTA are also taxable for state unemployment tax purposes.

The state also imposes an unemployment tax which meshes closely with the federal unemployment tax. Refer to Section 11.5 for details on state unemployment taxes, rates, returns, and registration as an employer.

5.4 Workers' Compensation Insurance

A business is generally required by state law to obtain workers' compensation insurance for its employees. This means that you, as an employer, may have to immediately seek out and obtain a workers' compensation insurance policy covering all your employees, or you will be subject to possible legal sanctions. Workers' compensation insurance coverage provides various benefits to an employee who suffers a job-related injury or illness.

Many insurance companies offer workers' compensation coverage, though many may be reluctant to write a policy that covers only one or a few employees, unless it is tied to other types of insurance policies. See Section 11.5 for a description of other formal requirements applicable to employers under the workers' compensation laws.

5.5 Compliance with ERISA — Employee Benefit Plans

If you have employees and provide them with fringe benefits, such as group insurance — other than workers' compensation — or other types of employee welfare plan benefits, or if you adopt a pension or profit-sharing retirement plan, you will almost certainly have to comply with at least some aspects of the Employee Retirement Income Security Act of 1974 (ERISA).

There are criminal penalties for willful failure to comply with two types of ERISA requirements: 1) reporting to government agencies, and 2) disclosure to employees.[10] In addition, there are a number of different types of civil penalties, which are incredibly numerous and complex, for unintentional failures to comply with ERISA requirements.[11] In short, compliance with ERISA is not a simple matter.

This section lays down some relatively simple and straightforward guidelines you, as a layperson, can follow in trying to recognize when you might have an ERISA compliance obligation. If you recognize your need to be in compliance, call your attorney, accountant, or benefit consultant for help. ERISA deals with two kinds of employee benefit plans: pension plans and welfare plans.

Pension Plans

Pension plans under ERISA are pretty much what you might expect — tax qualified retirement plans including both pension and profit-sharing plans (including Keogh plans), plus other types of benefit programs that defer payments until after employment has terminated.[12]

Because these compliance requirements are so very complex and are constantly in a state of flux, no attempt to spell them out in detail is made here. Instead, the basic ERISA compliance requirements for most pension and profit-sharing plans are summarized in the table on page 22.

If your business maintains a pension or profit-sharing plan, it should be obvious from this summary of basic ERISA compliance requirements that you need some expert help from an attorney, accountant, or pension consulting firm — or all of them — if you are going to be able to properly comply with the requirements of ERISA and avoid potential fines and other civil and criminal penalties.

The cost of maintaining these plans has unfortunately multiplied several times over since the passage of ERISA in 1974, followed by a labyrinth of ERISA regulations issued by several different federal agencies. In short, unless you make substantial contributions to and obtain significant tax savings from an employee retirement plan, it may not be worth having because of the heavy costs of compliance with ERISA.

Welfare Plans

Welfare plans under ERISA include most other types of employee benefit plans that are not considered pension plans.[13] These include typical fringe benefit plans adopted by small firms, such as health insurance, long-term disability, group-term life insurance, and accidental death insurance plans. ERISA compliance for welfare plans is usually less of a burden than for pension plans, but is required for almost every business that provides any kind of benefits for employees of the type mentioned above.

A number of so-called fringe benefits that are in the nature of payroll practices, such as paid holidays, vacation pay, bonuses, overtime premium pay, and most kinds of severance pay arrangements, are usually not considered to be either pension or welfare plans under ERISA.[14] Thus, these kinds of payroll practices are not subject to ERISA at all. Compliance requirements for reporting and disclosure under ERISA are briefly discussed below.

Summary Plan Descriptions

The one ERISA compliance requirement that applies to almost all small businesses is the requirement for you to prepare a summary plan description (SPD) for distribution to all employees covered by any type of welfare plan you sponsor, such as typical health, accident, life, or disability insurance plans.[15] An SPD must contain more than 20 specific items of information listed in the U.S. Department of Labor Regulations,[16] including an ERISA rights statement which must be copied more or less verbatim from the regulations.

An SPD must be prepared for each plan and distributed to covered employees within 120 days after the plan is first adopted.[17] Each new employee must be given a copy of the SPD within 90 days after becoming a participant in the plan.[18] Since an SPD must be prepared for each employee plan subject to ERISA, even a very small business may find that it has to produce three or four of these documents, each of which must meet detailed technical requirements.

One important consideration in taking out insurance coverage for employees should be a firm commitment from the insurance company or brokers that they will prepare the necessary SPDs for the insurance plans they are selling you. Otherwise, you may need to have your attorney or benefit consultant prepare the SPDs, which can result in substantial professional fees.

Other than the need for you to prepare SPDs and distribute them to employees, there are no significant ERISA requirements that apply to most kinds of insured-type welfare plans that cover fewer than 100 employees.[19] You must, however, make available the insurance policies and other plan documents for inspection by your employees and you must furnish copies to them upon request.[20]

Additional ERSIA Requirements

If your business should grow to have 100 or more employees who are covered by a plan, or if you adopt any type of uninsured funded welfare plan, you will suddenly become subject to a whole array of additional ERISA requirements, including:

- Filing a copy of the SPD with the U.S. Department of Labor;[21]
- Filing an annual return/report or registration (*Form 5500* series) with the IRS each year;[22]
- Preparing and distributing a summary annual report to covered employees each year;[23]
- Preparing a summary of material modifications of the plan, if necessary, and filing it with the U.S. Department of Labor and distributing it to covered employees;[24] and
- Filing a terminal report if the plan is terminated.[25]

Bonding and Withholding Requirements

Besides the ERISA reporting and disclosure requirements listed in the summary on page 22, you should be aware of two other points regarding ERISA: the bonding requirement and withholding requirements on pension or profit-sharing plan distributions. If any of your employees are deemed to handle assets of an employee benefit plan that is subject to

ERISA, they must be covered by a fidelity bond.[26] Consult your attorney or benefit consultant to see if any required bonding needs to be paid regarding any benefit plans you maintain for your employees. This is particularly important if you have a pension or profit-sharing plan.

Secondly, withholding is mandatory on distributions of pension, profit-sharing, and IRA benefits.[27] There is an exception for certain periodic distributions on which the recipient elects, in advance, not to have any tax withheld.

In addition to reporting and disclosure requirements under ERISA, there are other federal reporting and recordkeeping requirements for certain types of fringe benefit plans.[28] For example, employers maintaining educational assistance programs, group legal services plans, and so-called cafeteria plans are currently required to file annual reports with the IRS on *Form 5500*, *Form 5500-C*, or *Form 5500-R* and, if needed, to maintain records to show that those plans qualified for tax purposes for each year after 1984.[29]

5.6 Employee Safety and Health Regulations

As has been discussed in Section 5.4, employers are required by state law in many states to carry workers' compensation insurance for the protection of employees who develop job-related illnesses or who are injured on the job. In addition, there are comprehensive and far-reaching federal laws that set safety standards designed to prevent injuries arising from unsafe or unhealthy working conditions. The primary federal law regulating job safety, the Occupational Safety and Health Act of 1970 (OSHA), imposes several reporting and recordkeeping obligations for employers.

Federal OSHA

Over the years, the Occupational Safety and Health Administration has issued reams of regulations and standards for workplace safety. If you have employees, you will need to consult an attorney, preferably one with OSHA expertise, to determine what, if any, steps you must take to comply with federal and state safety standards at your place of business. Otherwise, you may be subject to fines and other legal sanctions if any employee is injured on the job or OSHA inspectors find that you are not in compliance with applicable safety standards at your place of business.

You may also want to contact the nearest regional U.S. Department of Labor – OSHA office and request information on any free consultative services or publications the office may have available. Many state occupational safety and health agencies provide confidential, on-site consultations for no charge. These consultations point out state compliance issues at your place of business. These state agencies would also know if any federal OSHA consultants are available.

OSHA requires that you post a permanent notice to employees regarding job safety.[30]

Under OSHA, it is necessary to keep a log of industrial injuries and illnesses.[31] Records maintained under an approved state OSHA plan can be used to satisfy this federal requirement.[32] The information in the log must also be summarized and posted prominently in your workplace from February 1 to March 1.[33] This requirement has been eliminated for most retail, financial, insurance, and service firms,[34] but not for:

- Building material and garden supply stores;
- General merchandise stores;
- Food stores;
- Hotels and other lodging places;
- Repair, amusement, and recreation services; and
- Health services.[35]

Under OSHA, a supplementary record must be prepared after a recordable injury or illness occurs, using federal *Form 101* or any of the substitutes state law permits to be used for this purpose.[36]

Neither of the above recordkeeping forms are ordinarily filed with the government. Instead, these records must be retained and kept available for inspection for five years.[37] In addition, special recordkeeping requirements will generally apply if your employees are exposed to toxic substances, asbestos, radiation, or carcinogens on the job.

You can obtain more detailed information on OSHA recordkeeping requirements by calling the nearest OSHA office (usually listed in the phone book under U. S. Government – Department of Labor) and asking for the booklet entitled, *Recordkeeping Requirements for Occupational Injuries and Illnesses.*

OSHA exempts any employer with ten or fewer employees from most of its reporting and recordkeeping requirements;[38] however, these small employers are not exempt from keeping a log of all injuries and accidents or reporting job-related fatalities and multiple injuries.

Federal OSHA reporting requirements include:

- The Bureau of Labor Statistics may require certain selected employers, including small employers, to report certain summary information on job-related injuries and illnesses annually on an occupational injuries and illness survey form.[39]
- In the event of a fatality or an accident resulting in the hospitalization of five or more employees, you must notify the area OSHA director within 48 hours, describing the circumstances of the accident, the extent of any injuries, and the number of fatalities.[40] There are penalties in the event you fail to give notice as required.[41]

See Section 11.5 for a discussion of laws this state may have that govern employee safety and health.

5.7 Employee Wage-Hour and Child Labor Laws

Not all businesses nor all employees of a given business are covered by federal and state wage-hour and child labor laws. The coverage of these laws is a crazy quilt patchwork of exceptions. Thus, there is no simple way to tell you whether your business will be subject to one or more of the federal and state laws relating to minimum wage, overtime pay, and child labor, or, if it is, which employees are covered and which are not. To find out which laws apply to your business, contact your attorney or the local wage-hour office.

Federal Wage-Hour Laws

The Federal Fair Labor Standards Act (FLSA) includes a number of requirements regarding compensation of employees covered under the act. There are two major requirements you need to know about — the minimum wage and overtime requirements.

Minimum Wage Requirement

The minimum wage provisions of the FLSA set an hourly minimum wage that you must pay to an employee. The current federal minimum wage is $4.25 per hour.[42] Certain states provide for a minimum wage in excess of the federal requirement or that applies to some employees who are not covered under the federal minimum wage law. Refer to Section 11.5 for the requirements in this state.

Overtime Pay Requirement

The overtime pay requirement rule states you must pay a covered employee at one and one-half times the employee's regular hourly rate for any hours worked in excess of 40 in a week.[43] The regular hourly rate cannot be less than the minimum wage. For the overtime pay requirement, the FLSA takes a single workweek as its measuring period and does not permit averaging of hours over two or more weeks. For example, if an employee works 30 hours one week and 50 hours during the next, he or she must receive overtime compensation (time and one-half) for the 10 overtime hours worked in the second week, even though the average number of hours worked in the two weeks is 40.

Note that the FLSA only requires overtime pay based on the number of hours worked during a week and not for working long hours on a particular day.

The above rules generally apply to salaried workers as well as to those paid on an hourly basis. To determine the regular hourly rate for a salaried employee, it is necessary to divide the employee's weekly salary by the number of hours in his or her regular workweek (40 or less).

Executives, administrators, professionals, and outside salespeople are not covered by federal wage-hour laws and thus are not entitled by law to a minimum wage or to any pay for overtime hours worked.[44] The theory behind this exemption is apparently the view that these types of employees are independent and sophisticated enough to take care of themselves and do not need to be protected by the government from possible exploitation by their employers.

Under the Code of Federal Regulations (Title 29, Section 541.5), an employee qualifying for the exemption as an outside salesperson must meet the two requirements listed below.

- The employee customarily and regularly works away from the employer's place of business while making sales or obtaining orders or contracts for services or for the use of facilities for which a consideration will be paid by the client or customer.
- The employee cannot do any other kind of work for the company (besides that of selling) for more than 20% of the usual workweek put in by the company's nonexempt employees; for example, the outside salesperson or exempted employee could do receptionist work for only 8 hours of each 40-hour workweek.

Various indicators of an employee's bona fide status as an outside salesperson include:

- A contractual designation or job title that reflects involvement in sales;
- Significant compensation on a commission basis;
- Special sales training; and
- Little or no direct or constant supervision in carrying out daily tasks.

Employee Exemptions

Employees of certain small companies, other than those enterprises engaged in commerce, are exempt from coverage under the wage-hour laws. Translated from the legalese, this means certain smaller businesses that do not significantly affect the flow of goods and services in interstate commerce are exempted from FLSA overtime and minimum wage requirements.

An "enterprise engaged in commerce" is one that "has employees engaged in commerce or in the production of goods for commerce, or that has employees handling, selling, or otherwise working on goods or materials that have been moved in commerce or produced for commerce by any person," and "is an enterprise whose annual gross volume of sales made or business done is not less than $500,000."[45]

All of which means that, if your firm does less than a half million dollars in sales a year, it will generally be exempt from FLSA overtime and minimum wage requirements.[46]

Even if you are exempt from the FLSA wage-hour rules, state wage-hour laws may apply and may be more stringent than federal laws in many states.

Small Enterprise Exemption

Numerous other exemptions from the wage-hour laws are based on the type of business, the nature of the work performed by the employee, where the work is done, and other factors.[47] Before you assume your employees are covered by the FLSA, consult your attorney, or at least call the local wage-hour office on an anonymous basis and ask for an informal and nonbinding opinion over the phone.

Detailed Records Required

Probably the most important thing you should be aware of, if you have employees subject to FLSA standards, is the need to keep detailed records of hours worked, the type of work, and wages or salary paid.

Under the law, if an employee files a claim against you for alleged failure to pay required wages in the past, you will need to be able to produce proof that you met the statutory requirements. Keeping detailed pay and work records for each employee is the only way to protect yourself against such claims for back pay. In addition, the FLSA requires employers to preserve such records for up to three years.

Poster Requirement

If you have employees whose wages, hours, and working conditions are subject to FLSA regulations, you will need to post the official wage-hour poster that is provided by the U.S. Department of Labor. In addition, you will most likely be required to post an official wage-hour poster for this state. For a discussion of the basic wage-hour and other significant labor law requirements under the law, refer to Section 11.5.

Child Labor Laws

Both the FLSA and various state laws regulate or prohibit the employment of children in businesses, with very few exceptions. If you intend to hire children to work in your business — other than hiring your own children, which is usually permitted, except in hazardous situations — you need to be aware of the following basic child labor law provisions.

As a general rule, the FLSA prohibits the employment of children under 16 years of age;[48] however, there are a number of exceptions to this rule.[49] In addition, all children under age 18 are excluded from certain occupations that are designated as hazardous by the secretary of labor.[50] Children under 16 years of age cannot be hired under any of the following circumstances:

- To work in any workplace where mining, manufacturing, or processing operations take place;
- To operate power machinery, other than office equipment;
- To operate or serve as a helper on motor vehicles — with certain exceptions for vehicles not exceeding 6,000 pounds gross weight, during daylight hours.
- To work in public messenger services; and
- To work in the following occupations: transportation, warehousing or storage, communications or public utilities, or construction — except in sales or office work.[51]

Children 14 or 15 years of age can be hired in other occupations not considered to be hazardous, but there are numerous limitations on the hours and times when they may work, particularly when schools are in session.

A few occupations, such as delivering newspapers and doing theatrical work, are exempt from the federal child labor laws, even for children under 14 years of age.[52]

Most states also strictly regulate the employment of children. See Section 11.5 regarding state child labor laws in this state. Thus, if you intend to employ children under 18 years of age in a business, you will probably need legal guidance as to the conditions under which they may work, if at all, under federal and state child labor laws.

5.8 Fair Employment Practices

As an employer, you will also need to be alert to your obligations under a number of federal and state laws that prohibit discrimination in employment on the basis of sex, age, race, color, national origin, religion, or on account of mental or physical handicaps. These anti-discrimination laws are not just limited to hiring practices, but relate to almost every aspect of the relationship between an employer and employee, including compensation, promotions, type of work assigned, and working conditions.

In addition to outlawing discrimination in employment, companies contracting for business with the federal government are generally required to adopt affirmative action programs in the employment of minorities, women, the handicapped, and Vietnam veterans.

Affirmative action programs are employment programs that go beyond elimination of discrimination. Under such programs, employers consciously make an effort to hire more women and minority group members and to upgrade the pay and responsibility levels of women and other groups that have historically been subject to patterns of discrimination.

Affirmative action programs are generally required for businesses that are government contractors. Most businesses are only required to refrain from discriminating in employment.

Federal Anti-discrimination Laws

If your small business employs fewer than 15 employees and is not working on government contracts or subcontracts, the federal anti-discrimination laws listed on the following page will generally not apply to you. The one exception to this would be the Equal Pay Act of 1963, which requires equal pay for equal work for women. This act is applicable to employers with two or more employees.

Employers Subject to Federal Anti-discrimination Laws

Name of Law	Employers Who Are Covered	What the Law Requires
Title VII of the Civil Rights Act of 1964 and Americans with Disabilities Act (ADA)	Employers with 15 or more employees during 20 weeks of a calendar year (25 employees under ADA until 1994)	No discrimination in employment practices based on race, religion, disability or national origin
Pregnancy Discrimination Act	Same as for Title VII above	Equal treatment for pregnant women and new mothers for all employment-related purposes, including fringe benefits
Executive Order 11246 as amended	Employers with federal contracts or subcontracts of $10,000 or more	No discrimination in employment practices based on race, sex, color, religion, or national origin
Equal Pay Act of 1963	Nearly all employers with two or more employees	Equal pay for women
Age Discrimination in Employment Act of 1967	Employers with 20 or more employees during 20 or more weeks in a calendar year	No discrimination in hiring or firing on account of age, for persons age 40 or older
Rehabilitation Act of 1973	Employers with federal contracts or subcontracts of $2,500 or more	No discrimination in employment practices on account of mental health or physical handicaps
Vietnam-Era Veteran Readjustment Assistance Act of 1974	Employers with federal contracts or subcontracts of $10,000 or more	Affirmative action programs for certain disabled veterans

Employers who violate any of the above laws may be sued by either the complaining individuals or by the various government enforcement agencies, or both.

Formal Compliance Requirements

Small businesses are not required to do a lot of paperwork or filling out of forms when it comes to federal anti-discrimination laws. An employer with more than 100 employees, however, must file *Form EEO-1* with the Equal Employment Opportunity Commission (EEOC) each year.[53]

As an employer you are required to keep detailed records — and should, for your own protection — as to the reasons for hiring or not hiring, promoting or not promoting, any employee or job applicant. In the event it is ever necessary to demonstrate that your firm has not discriminated against any group or individual member of a group in violation of federal laws, these records will provide the needed documentation.

Besides these requirements, there are a number of official posters you may be required to post in your place of business. These may include:

Display Posters

Type of Poster	Who Must Post	Source of Poster
Civil rights poster regarding sexual, racial, religious, and ethnic discrimination or because of physical or mental disability (*WH Publication 1088*)	Employers with 15 or more employees during 20 weeks of the year or with federal contracts or subcontracts of $10,000 or more[54]	EEOC offices, the nearest Office of Compliance
Age discrimination poster	Employers with 20 or more employees who work 20 or more weeks a year[55]	EEOC offices
Notice to employees working on government contracts (*WH Publication 1313*)	Any employer performing government contract work subject to the Service Contract Act or the Public Contracts Act	U.S. Department of Labor, Employment Standards Division
Poster required under the Vietnam Era Veterans Readjustment Assistance Act	Employers with federal contracts or subcontracts of $10,000 or more	From the federal contracting officer administering the contract

To obtain these posters, contact each of the appropriate federal agencies and request a copy of their required poster.

Sexual Harassment

You need to be keenly aware of your potential liability for sexual harassment in the workplace, another increasingly significant area of the anti-discrimination laws under Title VII of the Civil Rights Act. While the federal Civil Rights Act does not specifically refer to sexual harassment as a form of discrimination, the courts and the EEOC have long accepted it as such. There are two types of sexual harassment under Title VII, as it has been interpreted over the years.

One type of sexual harassment is where tangible job benefits are granted or withheld based on an employee's receptiveness to unwelcome requests or conduct. For example, a male supervisor tells a female employee to meet him in the hot tub of his mountain chalet on a Saturday afternoon to discuss a business contract. She refuses to meet him at his place and later receives a bad rating from him for a "poor attitude and unwillingness to work overtime," which costs her a raise or promotion. The female employee in such a case has been denied a tangible job benefit due to sexual harassment.

The second type of sexual harassment involves a hostile work environment; that is, a situation in which the work environment is oppressive and hostile to members of one sex. This occurs when such conditions either unreasonably interfere with the individual's work performance or create an intimidating, hostile, or offensive environment. This type of harassment may not have any economic effects on the individual, and management or supervisory personnel may not be involved. Nevertheless, an employer who allows such a condition to persist may still be liable if management was aware of the harassment by co-workers (or even by customers) and fails to take appropriate actions to remedy the situation.

Merely having a company policy that prohibits sexual harassment at your company won't automatically stop such activity or protect the firm from liability if harassment occurs, but the absence of such a policy makes such conduct somewhat more likely to occur and will also tend to strengthen an employee's claim against you if your firm is sued for allowing such acts to occur. Adopt a sexual harassment policy that not only prohibits such conduct, but which sets up a grievance mechanism for employees who are victims of any such harassment, and communicate this company policy strongly and clearly to your employees.

In addition to federal civil rights case law, the statutes of many states, or the regulations of many state civil rights commissions, now specifically prohibit sexual harassment in the workplace. Some of these laws go well beyond the protections afforded under federal law. For a more detailed discussion of anti-discrimination laws in this state, refer to Section 11.5.

5.9 Immigration Law Restrictions on Hiring

The Immigration Reform and Control Act of 1986 represents a major governmental requirement regarding the relationship between an employer and employee. Under this law, you are prohibited from hiring illegal aliens, and depending on the number of any prior violations, you are subject to fines of $250 to $20,000 for each illegal alien hired after November 6, 1986. At the same time, the act also prohibits employment discrimination on the basis of citizenship status and national origin; you may not fire or fail to hire anyone on the basis of foreign appearance, language, or name.

For all employees hired after November 6, 1986, you are required to verify their eligibility for employment within three business days of each new hire. As an employer, you will need to fill out and retain *Form I-9*. The employee fills out the top portion of the form, indicating whether he or she is a citizen or national of the United States; an alien lawfully admitted for permanent residence; or an alien authorized by the U.S. Immigration and Naturalization Service (INS) to work in the United States.

On the bottom portion of *Form I-9*, there are three separate lists of various forms of identification and employment eligibility documents the employee must provide for you. You must check off the documents you have examined, such as a passport or certificate of naturalization. These papers must include either one document in List A or one each in lists B and C. Both you and the employee must sign the form under penalty of perjury, and you must retain the completed form and make it available if the INS or U.S. Department of Labor requests it during an inspection.

You may obtain copies of *Form I-9* and a related *Employer's Handbook* from the nearest office of the U.S. Immigration and Naturalization Service. A sample *Form I-9* is also included at the end of this chapter. For more information on employer responsibilities, call:

U.S. Immigration and Naturalization Service
(800) 755-0777

5.10 Restrictions on Layoffs of Employees

If your business grows to where you have 100 or more full-time employees — or the equivalent, based on 40-hour workweeks — at a single location, you may be subject to the potentially onerous provisions of the plant closing law called the Worker Adjustment and Retraining Notification Act, or WARN Act.[56] This act would affect you if you laid off 50 or more employees, or one-third of the work force, in a 30-day period. It applies to virtually any plant closing or major layoff for any reason, with a few obvious exceptions, such as due to an earthquake or flood, or due to a labor dispute, such as a strike or lockout for which no notice need be given.

The WARN Act

A "layoff" under this act includes any of the following:

- A permanent termination of employment;
- A layoff of an employee for more than six months; or
- A loss of half the employees' working hours for six consecutive months.

In case of any major layoff or shutdown, the law requires you to give at least 60 days advance notice. If you give less than that, you are required to pay the laid-off workers for 60 days minus the actual number of days' notice you gave. The law requires you to notify the labor union that represents the employees, or, if none, the individual employees by mailing the notice to their last known address or including it in their pay envelope. You must also notify the local city or county government and state labor agency of the planned shutdown or cutback.

The WARN Act doesn't generally prohibit a company from making layoffs or shutting down a money-losing plant, but it makes it more costly for the employer to do so, and also gives local unions and politicians time to find some way to attempt to coerce or persuade a company into maintaining its operations, even if it is no longer economically viable.

The WARN law does impose stiff restrictions on a firm's ability to sell off, reorganize, merge, or consolidate operations, if such a decision would adversely affect the jobs of 50 or more employees. In other words, if your foreign competition renders your plant obsolete, you will not be allowed to sell it off to a competitor, if doing so would cost 50 or more employees their jobs. The act has made it much more costly to take a risk on building a plant in the United States — if it fails, you may have to close shop rather than restructure or sell.

As a result, there is expected to be a great deal of litigation over what does and does not constitute a mass layoff or shutdown under the WARN Act.

5.11 The Americans with Disabilities Act

In July of 1990, Congress enacted a revolutionary and wide-reaching piece of legislation, the Americans with Disabilities Act (ADA), which is designed to make both the workplace and most public facilities much more accessible to disabled persons.

The ADA and related regulations, which are being phased in over several years, will have a significant impact on a great many businesses, both in terms of employment practices and in terms of removing architectural barriers and other physical features that have limiting effects on the lives of disabled persons.[57]

Anti-discrimination Rules Regarding the Disabled

Title I of the ADA prohibits discrimination against any "qualified individual with a disability" in all aspects of employment, including hiring and discharging of workers, compensation, and benefits. Title I applies to employers who employ 25 or more employees — 15 or more as of July 26, 1994 — during 20 weeks of any calendar year. In addition, you must reasonably accommodate employees' or applicants' disabilities, which may mean modifying facilities, restructuring work schedules, or transferring disabled workers to vacant positions for which they are qualified, in appropriate circumstances. You are not required to accommodate a disabled worker, however, if doing so would impose an "undue hardship" on your business.

Medical Screening Tests

One area that will be significantly affected in the hiring process is the limitation on medical screening of applicants. Under the ADA, companies can no longer screen out prospective employees with disabilities because the applicant has an elevated risk of an on-the-job injury or a medical condition that might be aggravated because of job demands. The law specifically bans questions about a job applicant's physical or mental condition either on an employment application form or during a job interview. This would include general questions such as, "Do you have any mental or physical conditions that would prevent you from performing your job functions?"

Medical exams are still allowed, but they are greatly restricted. Pre-offer exams are prohibited, but an offer may be conditioned upon the satisfactory results of a medical examination. Results, however, cannot be used to withdraw an offer, unless they show that the individual in question is not able to perform the tasks required by the position.

The definition of "disabled" under the ADA includes people with AIDS, those who test positive for the HIV virus, and rehabilitated drug abusers and alcoholics; however, the ADA does not:

- Prohibit voluntary tests, such as employer-sponsored cholesterol or blood pressure tests; or
- Require employers to hire persons who are drug users or who have contagious diseases.

The ADA is neutral on the issue of drug testing of employees, in effect leaving that up to regulation by the states.

Title III of the ADA requires practically all businesses to make their facilities accessible to disabled employees and customers. Examples of various accessibility requirements with regard to public accommodations include:

Public Accommodations for the Disabled

- One designated parking space for the disabled must be provided for every 25 or fewer spaces. A lesser ratio applies if there are more than 100 total spaces.
- Hotels and motels must have 5% of their rooms accessible to wheelchairs and another 5% must be equipped with devices such as visual alarms for the hearing-impaired.
- Access ramps must be in place where the floor level changes more than one-half of an inch.
- Elevators must be provided in three-story or taller buildings and in those with more than 3,000 square feet per story.
- In retail or grocery stores, checkout aisles must be at least 36 inches wide. This is wide enough for wheelchairs.
- Theaters and similar places of assembly for 50 or more persons must have at least three wheelchair spaces dispersed throughout the seating area.

Companies spending money to remove architectural and transportation barriers to the disabled can deduct up to $15,000 a year of such expenses.[58] In addition, small firms — those with gross receipts under $1 million or fewer than 30 full-time employees — who spend between $250 and $10,250 a year on access for the disabled, can claim a tax credit for up to 50% of the cost of such expenditures, a maximum annual credit of $5,000.[59]

Tax Incentives

For more information on the ADA, contact:

Equal Employment Opportunity Commission   or   **U.S. Department of Justice**
2401 E Street   (202) 514-0301
Washington, DC 20506
(202) 663-4264 or
(800) 669-3362

5.12 Mandatory Family and Medical Leave Requirements

The Family and Medical Leave Act of 1993 became effective on August 5, 1993. This new law applies to all companies — as well as nonprofit entities — that have 50 or more employees within a 75-mile radius. As a result, many companies, who employ roughly half of all employees in the United States, are now subject to the family leave law's requirements.

The new act requires covered employers to:

- Offer their employees 12 weeks of unpaid leave after the birth or adoption of a child; to care for a seriously ill child, spouse, or parent; or for an employee's own serious illness.
- Maintain health care coverage for an employee who is on a leave of absence as described above; and
- Guarantee that employees will be able to return to either the same job or to a comparable position after the leave.

A serious illness must be verified by a physician's certification, and as the employer, you may require a second medical opinion if desired. An employee is required to provide you with 30 days notice for foreseeable leaves of absence for a birth, adoption, or planned medical treatment.

One major exception to the law's coverage is a provision that exempts certain "key employees" from coverage. Key employees are defined as the highest-paid 10% of the employer's workforce and those whose leave of absence would cause significant economic harm to the employer. Also exempted from the law's provisions are employees who haven't worked at least one year for the employer and who haven't worked at least 1,250 hours, or 25 hours a week, in the preceding 12 months. In addition, you are given the option of substituting an employee's accrued paid leave, if any, for any part of the 12-week period of family leave.

A number of states, such as California and Hawaii, have also enacted similar family leave laws. Refer to Chapter 11 for information on any such laws that have been adopted in this state.

Endnotes

1. Treas. Regs. §31.6302-1(f)(4).
2. Treas. Regs. §31.6302-1(b)(2).
3. Treas. Regs. §31.6302-1(b)(3).
4. Treas. Regs. §31.6302-1(c)(3).
5. I.R.C. §7502(e)(3).
6. I.R.C. §§3301(1) and 3306(b)(1).
7. I.R.C. §§3301(1) and 3302(b).
8. I.R.C. §3306(a)(1)(A).
9. I.R.C. §3306(a)(1)(B).
10. 29 U.S.C. §1131.
11. 29 U.S.C. §1132; I.R.C. §§4971, 4975, 6057–6059, and 6652.
12. 29 U.S.C. §1002(2); 29 C.F.R. §2510.3-2.
13. 29 U.S.C. §1002(1); 29 C.F.R. §2510.3-1.
14. 29 C.F.R. §2510.3-1(b); 29 C.F.R. §2510.3-2(b).
15. 29 C.F.R. §2520.104b-2.
16. 29 C.F.R. §2520.102-3.
17. 29 C.F.R. §2520.104b-2(a)(2).
18. 29 C.F.R. §2520.104b-2(a)(1).
19. 29 C.F.R. §2520.104-20.
20. 29 U.S.C. §1024(b)(4); 29 C.F.R. §2520.104b-1.
21. 29 C.F.R. §2520.104a-3.
22. 29 C.F.R. §2520.104a-5.
23. 29 C.F.R. §2520.104b-10.
24. 29 C.F.R. §§2520.104a-4 and 2520.104b-3.
25. 29 U.S.C. §1021(c).
26. 29 U.S.C. §1112.
27. I.R.C. §3405(a).
28. I.R.C. §6039 D.
29. Announcement 86-20, I.R.B. 1986–87, 34.
30. 29 C.F.R. §1903.2.
31. 29 C.F.R. §1904.2.
32. 29 C.F.R. §1904.10.
33. 29 C.F.R. §1904.5.
34. 29 C.F.R. §1904.16.
35. 29 C.F.R. §1904.12.
36. 29 C.F.R. §1904.4.
37. 29 C.F.R. §1904.6.
38. 29 C.F.R. §1904.15.
39. 29 C.F.R. §§1904.15 and 1904.21.
40. 29 C.F.R. §1904.8.
41. 29 C.F.R. §1904.9.
42. 29 U.S.C. §206(a)(1).
43. 29 U.S.C. §207(a)(1).
44. 29 U.S.C. §213(a)(1).
45. 29 U.S.C. §203(s).
46. 29 U.S.C. §207(a)(1).
47. 29 U.S.C. §213.
48. 29 U.S.C. §§203(1) and 212.
49. 29 U.S.C. §213.
50. 29 C.F.R. §570.50–570.71.
51. 29 C.F.R. §570.33.
52. 29 U.S.C. §213(c) and (d).
53. 29 C.F.R. §1602.7.
54. 29 C.F.R. §1601.30.
55. 29 U.S.C. §627 and 29 C.F.R. §1627.10.
56. 29 U.S.C. §§2101–2109.
57. 42 U.S.C. §§12101 *et seq.* and 29 C.F.R. §1630.
58. I.R.C. §190.
59. I.R.C. §44.

Summary of Basic ERISA Compliance Requirements for Pension Plans

Item	Provided to
Summary plan description.	U.S. Department of Labor; participants; beneficiaries
Annual return/report (*Form 5500, 5500-EZ, 5500-C*, or *5500-R*).	IRS (now required even for a simple one-person Keogh plan)
Schedule A, Form 5500 series (insurance information).	IRS
Schedule B, Form 5500 series (actuarial information prepared and signed by an enrolled actuary for "defined benefit" plans only).	IRS
Schedule SSA, Form 5500 series (registration statement).	IRS
Form W-2P (report of periodic plan benefit payments made during the year).	IRS; recipient of distribution
Form 1099-R (report of total distribution of benefits during the year).	IRS; recipient of distribution
Form W-3 or *W-3G* (transmittal of *Form W-2P* and *Form 1099-R*).	IRS
Form PBGC-1 (premium payment of required plan termination insurance — for "defined benefit" plans only).	Pension Benefit Guaranty Corporation (a government agency that insures pension plans of corporate employers)
Summary annual report.	Participants; beneficiaries
Individual deferred vested benefit statement to separated employee.	Former participant in plan
Summary of material modifications to a plan.	U.S. Department of Labor; participants; beneficiaries
Terminal report (when plan is terminated).	U.S. Department of Labor; participants; beneficiaries
Written explanation of joint and survivor annuity and financial effect of not electing to receive it (if plan provides benefits in the form of an annuity).	Participants
Written explanation of reasons for denying benefit claim and description of appeal procedures.	Person claiming entitlement to plan benefits
Various documents and information to be provided on request.	U.S. Department of Labor; participants
Various formal notices upon occurrence of certain events.	IRS; U.S. Department of Labor; Pension Benefit Guaranty Corporation; participants

Form I-9 – Employment Eligibility Verification: Sample

U.S. Department of Justice
Immigration and Naturalization Service

OMB No. 1115-0136
Employment Eligibility Verification

Please read instructions carefully before completing this form. The instructions must be available during completion of this form. **ANTI-DISCRIMINATION NOTICE.** It is illegal to discriminate against work eligible individuals. Employers CANNOT specify which document(s) they will accept from an employee. The refusal to hire an individual because of a future expiration date may also constitute illegal discrimination.

Section 1. Employee Information and Verification. To be completed and signed by employee at the time employment begins

Print Name: Last	First	Middle Initial	Maiden Name

Address (Street Name and Number) | Apt. # | Date of Birth (month/day/year)

City | State | Zip Code | Social Security #

I am aware that federal law provides for imprisonment and/or fines for false statements or use of false documents in connection with the completion of this form.

I attest, under penalty of perjury, that I am (check one of the following):
☐ A citizen or national of the United States
☐ A Lawful Permanent Resident (Alien # A_____)
☐ An alien authorized to work until ___/___/___
(Alien # or Admission # _____)

Employee's Signature | Date (month/day/year)

Preparer and/or Translator Certification. *(To be completed and signed if Section 1 is prepared by a person other than the employee.) I attest, under penalty of perjury, that I have assisted in the completion of this form and that to the best of my knowledge the information is true and correct.*

Preparer's/Translator's Signature | Print Name

Address (Street Name and Number, City, State, Zip Code) | Date (month/day/year)

Section 2. Employer Review and Verification. To be completed and signed by employer. Examine one document from List A OR examine one document from List B **and** one from List C as listed on the reverse of this form and record the title, number and expiration date, if any, of the document(s)

List A	OR	List B	AND	List C
Document title: _____		_____		_____
Issuing authority: _____		_____		_____
Document #: _____		_____		_____
Expiration Date (if any): ___/___/___		___/___/___		___/___/___
Document #: _____				
Expiration Date (if any): ___/___/___				

CERTIFICATION - I attest, under penalty of perjury, that I have examined the document(s) presented by the above-named employee, that the above-listed document(s) appear to be genuine and to relate to the employee named, that the employee began employment on (month/day/year) ___/___/___ and that to the best of my knowledge the employee is eligible to work in the United States. (State employment agencies may omit the date the employee began employment).

Signature of Employer or Authorized Representative | Print Name | Title

Business or Organization Name | Address (Street Name and Number, City, State, Zip Code) | Date (month/day/year)

Section 3. Updating and Reverification. To be completed and signed by employer

A. New Name (if applicable) | B. Date of rehire (month/day/year) (if applicable)

C. If employee's previous grant of work authorization has expired, provide the information below for the document that establishes current employment eligibility.
Document Title:_____ Document #:_____ Expiration Date (if any): ___/___/___

I attest, under penalty of perjury, that to the best of my knowledge, this employee is eligible to work in the United States, and if the employee presented document(s), the document(s) I have examined appear to be genuine and to relate to the individual.

Signature of Employer or Authorized Representative | Date (month/day/year)

Form I-9 (Rev. 11-21-91) N

Form I-9 – Employment Eligibility Verification: Sample (continued)

LISTS OF ACCEPTABLE DOCUMENTS

LIST A		LIST B		LIST C
Documents that Establish Both Identity and Employment Eligibility	**OR**	**Documents that Establish Identity**	**AND**	**Documents that Establish Employment Eligibility**

LIST A — Documents that Establish Both Identity and Employment Eligibility

1. U.S. Passport (unexpired or expired)

2. Certificate of U.S. Citizenship (INS Form N-560 or N-561)

3. Certificate of Naturalization (INS Form N-550 or N-570)

4. Unexpired foreign passport, with I-551 stamp or attached INS Form I-94 indicating unexpired employment authorization

5. Alien Registration Receipt Card with photograph (INS Form I-151 or I-551)

6. Unexpired Temporary Resident Card (INS Form I-688)

7. Unexpired Employment Authorization Card (INS Form I-688A)

8. Unexpired Reentry Permit (INS Form I-327)

9. Unexpired Refugee Travel Document (INS Form I-571)

10. Unexpired Employment Authorization Document issued by the INS which contains a photograph (INS Form I-688B)

OR

LIST B — Documents that Establish Identity

1. Driver's license or ID card issued by a state or outlying possession of the United States provided it contains a photograph or information such as name, date of birth, sex, height, eye color, and address

2. ID card issued by federal, state, or local government agencies or entities provided it contains a photograph or information such as name, date of birth, sex, height, eye color, and address

3. School ID card with a photograph

4. Voter's registration card

5. U.S. Military card or draft record

6. Military dependent's ID card

7. U.S. Coast Guard Merchant Mariner Card

8. Native American tribal document

9. Driver's license issued by a Canadian government authority

For persons under age 18 who are unable to present a document listed above:

10. School record or report card

11. Clinic, doctor, or hospital record

12. Day-care or nursery school record

AND

LIST C — Documents that Establish Employment Eligibility

1. U.S. social security card issued by the Social Security Administration (other than a card stating it is not valid for employment)

2. Certification of Birth Abroad issued by the Department of State (Form FS-545 or Form DS-1350)

3. Original or certified copy of a birth certificate issued by a state, county, municipal authority or outlying possession of the United States bearing an official seal

4. Native American tribal document

5. U.S. Citizen ID Card (INS Form I-197)

6. ID Card for use of Resident Citizen in the United States (INS Form I-179)

7. Unexpired employment authorization document issued by the INS (other than those listed under List A)

Illustrations of many of these documents appear in Part 8 of the Handbook for Employers (M-274)

Form I-9 (Rev. 11-21-91) N

FPI-LOM

Chapter 6

Businesses that Require Licenses to Operate

The bureaucrat who smiles when something serious has gone wrong
has already found someone to blame it on.

— Anonymous

6.1 General Licensing

Almost any kind of business activity you engage in will require a city or
county business license, which is usually fairly simple to obtain. In addition, some types of businesses will have to obtain licenses from the federal government to operate, while other businesses, occupations, and professions are also licensed and regulated by the state.

Even though there are tremendous variations regarding the requirements
for obtaining necessary federal and state licenses, these requirements
generally relate to educational attainments, experience in the particular
field, passage of examinations, submission of detailed applications,
meeting financial or bonding requirements, or some combination of the
foregoing, plus payment of a licensing fee or tax.

In addition to the federal and state licensing requirements, certain local
city or county permits may have to be obtained. For example, if you will
be in the food business, you may have to get a license from the county
health department; or, if your business would like to do any construction
or remodeling, you might have to get approval from your local planning
commission.

Before you begin to operate any kind of business, find out whether you
will be required to obtain any special government licenses or permits,
since in most cases you must obtain the particular license before commencing operation.

This chapter and Section 11.6, respectively, provide a partial listing of the federal and state licensing requirements you are most likely to encounter as a small business owner. Because the number of activities that may require federal or state licenses is so large, no attempt has been made to try to list all of them in this book.

Thus, the lists of licensing agencies and businesses that require licenses found in this chapter and in Chapter 11 should be helpful in alerting you, as a small business owner, to possible licensing needs, but you should remember that these lists are not complete and are not a substitute for individualized legal advice.

6.2 Federal Licenses

If you are starting a small business, it is relatively unlikely that you will need any type of license or permit from the federal government; however, the following is a list of the federal licensing requirements you might possibly encounter:

Federal Licensing Requirements

Activity	Federal Agency
Rendering investment advice	Securities and Exchange Commission
Providing ground transportation as a common carrier	Interstate Commerce Commission
Preparation of meat products	Food and Drug Administration
Production of drugs or biological products	Food and Drug Administration
Making tobacco products or alcohol	Treasury Department, Bureau of Alcohol, Tobacco, and Firearms
Making or dealing in firearms	Treasury Department, Bureau of Alcohol, Tobacco, and Firearms
Radio or television broadcasting	Federal Communications Commission

For a partial listing of businesses and professions required to be licensed in this state, see Section 11.6.

Operating the Business

Part III

Chapter 7

Excise Taxes

Taxation without representation is tyranny.

— Patrick Henry

Taxation with representation is worse.

— Will Rogers

7.1 General Considerations

Both federal and state tax laws impose excise or similar taxes on a number of different types of businesses, products, services, and occupations. These taxes are usually imposed without any assessment or notice to the taxpayer. Thus, it is up to you to find out if you are subject to any of these taxes and, if so, to obtain the proper tax return forms and pay the tax on time.

It is not uncommon for a small business to operate for several years without the owner ever being aware of the need to pay excise taxes. Then comes the day of reckoning, when a formal notice is received from the government demanding immediate payment of several years' worth of back taxes on some particular item subject to excise tax, plus interest and penalties for not filing the returns and not paying the tax. This can be a disastrous surprise, especially since the business owner has not factored the cost of paying the excise into the price of his or her goods or services.

This chapter is designed to alert you in advance to the types of federal and state excise — and similar — taxes that you may need to know about. Some excise taxes, such as those on telephone service and insurance companies, are not discussed below since they are passed along or absorbed by the telephone company, insurance company, or other large institution with which your business may deal, and you have no obligation to file any returns or make any direct payment to the government of such taxes.

See Section 11.7 for a summary of various state excise taxes that may affect your business.

7.2 Federal Excise Taxes

Federal excise taxes on many products and transactions have been repealed over the last 20 years, so these taxes are much less pervasive now than in the past. The excise tax that the largest number of small businesses are likely to be subject to is the motor vehicle highway use tax on vehicles of more than 55,000 pounds gross weight.[1] *Form 2290* must be filed by owners of trucks and buses subject to the highway use tax. If you want information about the highway use tax, request a copy of IRS *Publication 349* from any IRS office.

The federal government imposes a number of excise taxes on various types of business activities. Some excise taxes are on the production or sale of certain goods. Some are on services or the use of certain products or facilities. Still others are imposed on businesses of a certain type.

Most federal excise taxes are reported on *Form 720, Quarterly Federal Excise Tax Return*, the most common excise tax form. Environmental taxes on petroleum and 42 designated chemical substances are reported on *Form 6627* and attached to *Form 720*. Federal excise taxes can be broken down into several major categories:

- The motor vehicle highway use tax — This tax is imposed on vehicles of more than 55,000 pounds gross weight.[2]

- Retailer taxes on certain fuels[3] — The federal gasoline tax is $0.183 (18.3 cents) per gallon on gasoline, and the tax on diesel is $0.243 (24.3 cents) per gallon.

  In addition, both of the taxes are increased by $0.01 (one-tenth of one cent) per gallon by the Leaking Underground Storage Tank Trust Fund tax. A reduced tax rate applies to qualified methane and ethanol fuel.

Other retail excise taxes are imposed on sales of:
- Heavy trucks and trailers;[4]
- Tires and tubes;[5]
- Recreation equipment, such as bows, arrows, fishing rods, reels, lures, and creels;[6] and
- Firearms and ammunition.[7]

Other excise taxes exist on the following as well:

- Air transportation — If you are in the business of transporting people by air, you may have to collect an excise tax;[8]
- Telephone and teletype services;[9]
- Wagering;[10]
- Coal mined in the United States;[11]
- Alcohol and tobacco products;[12] and
- Manufacturers of certain vaccines — Certain vaccines manufactured or imported into the United States are subject to an excise tax in order to create a Vaccine Injury Compensation Trust Fund, a no-fault program for compensating persons who are injured by, or die from, certain vaccines.[13] This tax temporarily expired as of January 1, 1993, but was permanently restored on August 10, 1993.

There are also several environmental excise taxes, such as:

- An excise tax on ozone-depleting chemicals;
- An oil spill liability excise tax of $0.05 (5 cents) a barrel;[14] and
- Environmental taxes on petroleum products, various chemicals, and hazardous wastes.[15]

Luxury Taxes

A luxury tax applies to retail purchases of passenger automobiles costing more than $30,000.[16] The tax is equal to 10% of the amount by which the purchase price exceeds $30,000. For example, the luxury tax on a new $35,000 automobile would be 10% of $5,000 — the excess of $35,000 over $30,000, or $500. Beginning in 1994, the $30,000 threshold amount will be indexed for inflation that has occurred since December 31, 1990.

The luxury tax does not apply to:

- Vehicles of more than 6,000 pounds unloaded gross weight; or
- Any vehicle, such as a taxicab, that is used exclusively in the active conduct of a trade or business of transporting people or property for compensation or hire.

The luxury tax on automobiles is collected by the retailer who sells the item. This luxury tax only applies to the first retail sale of an item. For example, if you buy a used $50,000 automobile, there is no luxury tax on the purchase.

Other luxury taxes on boats, aircraft, furs, and jewelry were repealed on August 10, 1993, retroactive to January 1, 1993. If you paid luxury taxes on any of those items in 1993, you are entitled to a refund of the tax from the retailer who collected it from you.

For further information on excise taxes and other federal taxes, you may wish to obtain IRS *Publication 334, Tax Guide for Small Business,* or for more detailed information on excise taxes, IRS *Publication 510, Excise Taxes.*

Endnotes

1. I.R.C. § 4481(a).
2. Id.
3. I.R.C. §§ 4041, 4081, and 4091.
4. I.R.C. § 4051.
5. I.R.C. § 4071(a).
6. I.R.C. § 4161(a) and (b).
7. I.R.C. § 4181.
8. I.R.C. §§ 4261(a) and 4271(a).
9. I.R.C. § 4251.
10. I.R.C. §§ 4401 and 4411.
11. I.R.C. § 4121(a).
12. I.R.C. §§ 5001, 5041(b), 5701, and 5801–5822.
13. I.R.C. §§ 4131–4132.
14. I.R.C. §§ 4611(c)(2) and 4681.
15. I.R.C. §§ 4611 and 4661.
16. I.R.C. §§ 4001–4012.

Chapter 8

Planning for Tax Savings in a Business

The words of such an act as the income tax merely dance before
my eyes in a meaningless procession: cross-reference to cross-
reference, exception upon exception — couched in abstract terms
that offer no handle to seize hold of — leave in my mind only
a confused sense of some vitally important, but successfully
concealed, purport, which it is my duty to extract, but which
is within my power, if at all, only after the most inordinate
expenditure of time. I know that these monsters are the result of
fabulous industry and ingenuity, plugging up this hole and
casting out that net against all possible evasion; yet at times
I cannot help recalling a saying of William James' about certain
passages of Hegel: that they were no doubt written with a
passion of rationality; but that one cannot help wondering
whether to the reader they have any significance save that the
words are strung together with syntactical correctness.

— Judge Learned Hand

referring to the 1939 Internal Revenue Code, a statute which was almost
childlike in its simplicity compared to our current tax law.

8.1 General Considerations

One of the most shocking and unpleasant realizations of many successful small business owners comes when they realize they have acquired
an unwanted silent partner — a partner who contributes nothing to the
business but who often lays claim to half or more of the owner's hard-
earned profits. That silent partner, of course, is the government income

tax collector, and this chapter is a summary of many of the best and most effective legal ways to reduce that silent partner's share of the profits from your business.

This chapter is not intended to be a substitute for professional tax advice regarding your individual situation. Because the tax laws are so enormously complex, a technique that may work brilliantly in most cases might be useless or even disastrous in your particular tax situation. This chapter will provide you with a working understanding of some of the key ways to plan for tax savings and to avoid tax pitfalls in your business.

After you have read this chapter, you may want to talk to your tax adviser about one or more of the ideas discussed, if you feel they might be useful for applying to your business. Your tax adviser should be able to tell you whether a particular idea will work in your situation. If it will, he or she can help you implement it.

Tax attorneys and accountants often have a very heavy workload and a large number of clients to serve. An unfortunate result of this situation is your tax adviser may tend to spend most of the time responding to inquiries by clients and meeting tax deadlines rather than taking the initiative in seeking out ways to minimize your taxes. Thus, by having some understanding of what you would like to do in the way of reducing taxes on your business income, you can propose ideas to your tax advisers and maximize the effectiveness of their expert knowledge and advice. In tax planning, as in so many areas of life, it pays to be assertive. "The wheel that squeaks is the one that gets the grease."

8.2 Using a Corporation as a Tax Shelter

One of the most effective ways to reduce your taxes, in many cases, is to incorporate your business. Incorporation is most likely to be advantageous if the business is generating about $75,000 or less in annual profits and salary for the owner — or per owner, if there is more than one. There are three basic ways, other than the adoption of employee fringe benefit plans, that incorporation can reduce your taxes on business income:

- Leaving profits in the corporation
- Income-splitting
- Investing in stock

Leaving Profits in the Corporation

If you are able to leave your first $75,000 of annual profits in your corporation, the profits will generally be taxed at corporate rates that are lower than your individual income tax rates. This provides a strong incentive for you to leave at least that much taxable income in the corporation rather than pay it all out to yourself as salary. At taxable income levels above $75,000, corporate income is taxed at roughly the same rates as individual income, except at very high income levels of $335,000 or more. Refer to the table of corporate income tax rates in Section 2.4 and compare those rates with the personal income tax rates for your filing status. Be careful about leaving too much profit in your corporation. Sections 8.5 and 8.9 discuss the potential benefits and risks of having your profits accumulate in your corporation.

By using a corporation, it is also possible to split your overall profit between two or more taxpayers, so that none of the income gets taxed in the highest tax brackets. For example, with an overall economic profit of $100,000, an incorporated business may be able to reduce its taxable income to $50,000 by paying (and deducting) a $50,000 salary to its owner, as an officer/employee of the corporation. The corporation would pay tax only on the remaining $50,000 profit, at a maximum federal tax rate of only 15%, while the owner would pay tax on the $50,000 salary received.

Income-splitting

Because of the progressive tax rate structure under the federal income tax laws, the tax on the $100,000 income divided between the owner and his or her corporation would typically be much less than if the whole $100,000 were taxable to the owner. In 1993, for example, a single individual would pay $26,522 in federal income taxes on $100,000 of taxable income, while if the income were split evenly between the owner and his or her corporation, the corporation's tax would be $7,500 and the owner's $11,127, a saving of $7,895 — assuming the corporation is not a personal services corporation subject to a 35% flat rate of tax.

Another way to split the income of a business between multiple taxpayers is for you to make your children part owners of the business. Ideally, the children should be given an interest in the business when it is started, since the value of the gifts to them will often be minimal for gift tax purposes at that time.

It is frequently more feasible to split corporate income with your children by giving them some of the corporation's stock. This approach, however, will work only if your corporation has filed for an S corporation election on *Form 2553* with the IRS. The taxable income of a corporation that qualifies as an S corporation is taxable to its shareholders — in proportion to the stock they own in the corporation — and is generally not taxed to the corporation.

By giving a number of shares of stock in such an S corporation to one or more of your children, part of the taxable income of the business can often be shifted to the children[1] and taxed at their low tax brackets — assuming, as is usually the case, that the children do not have a lot of taxable income from other sources.

If, however, the parents attempt to shift too much income to the children by drawing no salary or too little salary from the corporation, the IRS has the power to reallocate the corporation's income to the parents to reflect the value of services rendered to the corporation. Shifting significant income to your children will not work if the children are under 14 years of age.[2]

Investing in Stocks

By investing accumulated corporate funds in dividend-paying stocks of other corporations, you can take advantage of the 70% deduction that corporations are entitled to on the dividends they receive.[3] Because this special deduction makes most dividends received by a corporation — other than those received by an S corporation — practically tax-free to the recipient corporation, your incorporated business can be an excellent place to hold stocks you wish to invest in, if you do not need the dividend income to live on.

Before you get too excited about putting your whole stock portfolio into your incorporated business, take these potential drawbacks into account:

- If you decide to later withdraw your corporate dividends or the stocks themselves, the withdrawal will usually be taxable to you as ordinary income[4] or perhaps, if you liquidate the corporation, as capital gains.[5] Capital gains are taxed at a maximum rate of 28% for individuals.[6]

- If you should accumulate more than $250,000 — $150,000 for professional and certain personal service firms — in after-tax earnings in your corporation, including the 70% of dividends that the corporation doesn't pay income tax on, and invest part of those earnings in liquid, nonbusiness investment assets like stocks, you may be inviting an IRS audit and a potential penalty tax for unreasonably accumulating earnings and profits in the corporation.[7] See the discussion of the accumulated earnings tax in Section 8.9.

- If too much of your corporation's income is in the form of dividends and other passive types of investment income, the corporation may be classified as a personal holding company for tax purposes, and this can have drastic tax consequences, as outlined in Section 8.9.[8] As long as more than 40% of your corporation's gross income is from sales of goods and services, however, as a general rule, you should not have to be concerned about personal holding company taxes.[9]

- Putting your personal assets that are not needed in the business into your corporation will subject those assets to the risk of the business. That is, anything you put into the corporation will be subject to the claims of the corporation's creditors if it goes bankrupt. If you put all of your assets into the corporation, you will in effect have given up the benefits of limited liability.

- If your corporation borrows money to invest in or carry stock investments, the 70% dividend exclusion will be reduced in part by the interest paid on the borrowed funds.[10]

Your accountant will probably be the best person to consult for determining how and whether you can use a corporation to reduce taxes on your business profits.

8.3 Retirement Plans and Other Fringe Benefits

One advantage of being your own boss, either as a sole proprietor, a partner, or a shareholder of a closely held corporation, is the opportunity to be able to set up a Keogh plan or corporate retirement plan. In a C corporation, you can also obtain insurance and other important fringe benefits as an officer and employee of the corporation on a tax-favored basis. Some of the ways you can benefit from using retirement plans and other tax-favored fringe benefits are outlined in this section.

There are three types of tax-favored retirement plans:

Tax Advantages of Retirement Plans

- Corporate pension and profit-sharing plans;
- Keogh pension and profit-sharing plans for unincorporated business; and
- Individual Retirement Accounts (IRAs), which may be set up by any individual who has earned income, including an employee.

IRAs are of limited interest to most business owners, since the maximum annual contribution to an IRA is $2,000 a year — $2,250 if you have a nonworking spouse. Even these small deductions may not be available if you are a participant in a Keogh or corporate retirement plan and your adjusted gross income is over $50,000 ($35,000 if you are a single person). Accordingly, the discussion below focuses on corporate and Keogh retirement plans.

The primary tax advantages of the three types of tax-qualified retirement plans — corporate, self-employed (Keogh), and IRA — are these:

- Amounts contributed, up to certain limits, are deductible from the income of the corporation or individual taxpayer.[11] This deduction can be as much as 25% of the individual's compensation for the year (not counting the plan contribution) or $30,000, whichever is less. Even larger contributions can be made by so-called defined benefit plans.
- Contributed funds can be invested by pension or profit-sharing plans on a tax-free basis.[12] The qualified retirement trust that is usually set up to hold the retirement funds is exempt from state and federal income taxes on its income or capital gains from investments in stocks, bonds, savings accounts, gold, silver, real estate, and other passive investments. Note, however, that gold, silver, and other collectibles can no longer be purchased as investments by individually directed retirement plans or by an IRA. The only exception is for certain gold and silver coins minted by the United States.[13]
- When trust funds are paid out to you at retirement, you may be in a lower tax bracket than when you made the contributions to the plan. Thus, not only do you get to defer payment of any tax on amounts contributed to the plan until you retire, but the tax you finally pay at retirement is apt to be at a lower rate than you would have paid when you were working.

■ Receipt of all your retirement plan funds in a lump sum at retirement, or in certain other circumstances, may often qualify for special low tax rates if the distribution is from a corporate or Keogh plan but not from an IRA.

Corporate and noncorporate Keogh retirement plans are almost identical under the tax law in all major respects, except for the ability to borrow one's retirement funds from the plan, which will be subject to an excise or penalty tax in the case of a Keogh. It does not pay to incorporate your business just for pension and profit-sharing plan purposes. If you decide to establish a retirement plan, there are several practical points you should consider before reaching a decision.

Model SEP Plans from Financial Institutions

If you are setting up a Simplified Employee Pension (SEP) plan for yourself, or a Keogh plan, consider obtaining a "canned" plan from a bank, savings and loan, insurance company, or mutual fund. Usually, these preapproved plans will be suitable for you unless you have a significant number of employees to cover under your Keogh, in which case, you probably should be incorporated anyway. The great advantages of getting a canned SEP or Keogh plan from a financial institution are cost and simplicity. Most such institutions will charge you only $10–$25 to adopt their plan. Their profit comes from investing your funds for a management fee, in the case of a mutual fund; or maintaining your deposits in interest-bearing accounts, in the case of a bank or savings and loan.

By contrast, hiring a lawyer or benefit consultant to draw up a customized SEP or Keogh plan for you could cost anywhere from a few hundred to a few thousand dollars in fees. In addition, since the pension laws seem to be rewritten every time Congress meets, you may find yourself paying hundreds or even thousands of dollars each year to your attorney or benefit consultant to revise or amend a custom-designed plan, just to keep it in compliance with the never-ending changes in the tax and other laws affecting pension plans.

Model SEP and Keogh Plans from Stockbrokerages

If you are not content to invest your SEP or Keogh funds in or with a financial institution, you can still participate in a canned plan offered by some stockbrokerage firms. These plans usually permit you to direct your own stock and bond investments.

Model Corporate Plans

If you are setting up a corporate retirement plan, it is also possible to obtain canned prototype plans from banks, if you allow them to act as trustee — or from insurance companies, if you buy their insurance or managed fund accounts through the plan. These plans usually have variable terms that can be tailored somewhat to suit your needs, unless you want to do something out of the ordinary, such as allow each participant to direct the investment of his or her portion of the plan's funds. Other institutions, such as stockbrokerages and mutual funds, also offer corporate plans.

Even if you do need something unusual that requires a customized retirement plan for your corporation, you will probably find it more cost-effective to have a benefit consulting firm draw up the plan for you. This way, your attorney would only be involved in reviewing the plan and obtaining approval of the plan from the IRS. Typically, benefit consultants or pension consultants will charge only a fraction of what a law firm would charge to draw up the plan, and the larger benefit consulting firms are generally quite competent. Most of their fees come from helping you administer the plan under ERISA after it is set up — a service you will need anyway.

Customized Plans

Simplified Employee Pension (SEP) plans have gotten very little use since they were created by Congress several years ago; however, they now offer most of the attractive features of typical Keogh and corporate plans with virtually no administrative costs. This is in contrast to a Keogh or corporate plan that may cost up to $2,000 or $3,000 a year to maintain for only five or ten employees.

Saving with SEPs

A SEP is basically a glorified individual retirement account (IRA), but it is one where you contribute to each employee's IRA account an amount of up to 15% of an employee's compensation with a maximum of $30,000.

The amount contributed is not taxed to the employee and can be invested in any type of IRA account the employee chooses. SEPs can be set up by corporations, partnerships, or sole proprietorships. Participants can still contribute up to $2,000 a year to their SEP/IRA or to another IRA plan.

SEP participants with taxable income in excess of $25,000 (single) or $40,000 (married filing jointly), however, will have their IRA deductions reduced or eliminated.

The main existing drawback of an SEP is that any distributions from the plan at retirement are taxed as ordinary income. The special five-year averaging — which can result in a lower tax rate — for lump sum distributions from a Keogh or corporate qualified plan is not available for IRAs or SEPs. Even so, they strongly merit consideration as an alternative to Keogh or corporate retirement plans, due to their relative simplicity.

An increasingly popular form of qualified retirement plan is the Section 401(k) plan. This type of plan generally permits employees to elect to have a percentage of their salary — with various limitations — deducted from their paychecks, free of income tax, and deposited on their behalf in a profit-sharing-type plan. In many cases, as an additional incentive to employees to make such tax-favored savings, you, as an employer, may provide some degree of matching contribution to the plan on behalf of the employee.

Section 401(k) Plans

For example, a typical situation would be where you contribute $0.50 (50 cents) for every dollar the employee elects to have withheld from his or her pay. Your contribution is placed in the 401(k) plan and is tax-free to the employee.

Various Nonretirement Fringe Benefit Plans

The federal tax laws are replete with a whole host of tax-favored employee fringe benefits, which are characterized as being deductible to you and nontaxable to the employee. Some of the most common and important nontaxable fringes are discussed below.

Medical Insurance Plans

The corporation that maintains a medical insurance plan, such as Blue Cross or a prepaid health care plan, is permitted to deduct the premiums it pays to the insurer. In addition, the employee is not required to include either the cost of the premiums or the benefits provided by the insurer in his or her taxable income, as a general rule.[14]

Self-Insured Medical Reimbursement Plans

A corporation can set up a plan under which the corporation directly reimburses employees for medical expenses or even for such expenses as dental care, orthodontic work, and prescription eyeglasses or contact lenses.[15] If the plan satisfies tax law requirements prohibiting discrimination in favor of highly paid employees, the reimbursements paid can be deducted by the corporation and are not taxable to the recipients.[16]

Such plans are often set up in addition to medical insurance plans, either to cover deductibles that the insurance does not pay or to cover particular types of medical or dental costs that the insurance plan does not provide for. The costs of cosmetic surgery are no longer deductible as medical expenses.

Disability Insurance

Payment by a corporation of disability insurance premiums is deductible by the corporation and is not taxed to the employees covered by the insurance — except in the case of an S corporation.[17]

If an employee becomes disabled and receives disability benefits under a policy that the employer has paid the premiums for, the benefits will be included in the employee's income for tax purposes. On the other hand, if an individual, such as a sole proprietor or partner, has paid his or her own premiums for disability insurance, any disability benefits received are tax-free.[18]

Group-term Life Insurance

Your corporation may set up a group-term life insurance plan and deduct the insurance premiums it pays on behalf of employees. To the extent the life insurance coverage on an employee does not exceed $50,000 under the plan during the taxable year, the premiums paid by you are not taxable income to the employee.[19]

Even to the extent an employee's coverage exceeds $50,000, the amount the employee must include in taxable income from the additional insurance premiums paid by you for the excess coverage is sometimes considerably less than the premium actually paid and deducted.

Unless your business is a C corporation, it cannot deduct the premiums for your own coverage under a group life insurance plan because you are not considered an employee of the business for tax purposes.

The following fringe benefits are excludable both from income and employment taxes (FUTA and FICA) for you and the employee:

Section 132 Excludable Fringe Benefits

- No-additional-cost services provided to an employee — These services consist of benefits such as free airline, rail, or bus transportation provided by companies in those industries; rooms for hotel employees; or free phone service for telephone company employees.
- Employee discounts — Service companies can provide their services to employees at up to a 20% discount. For companies selling goods, the discount may not exceed the employer's gross profit percentage multiplied by the usual selling price of the item to customers.
- Working condition fringes — These fringe benefits are tax-free, up to the amounts that would have been deductible if paid by the employee. Benefits include such items as a company car or plane used for business purposes; subscriptions to trade or professional publications; on-the-job training; business travel; and others.
- Qualified transportation fringes — These benefits include employer-provided transit passes and commuter transportation worth up to $60 a month and parking provided to employees worth up to $155 a month. Parking fringes are not available to self-employed individuals.
- Minor fringes — These benefits are items that are considered to be minimal to justify the administrative costs for them, such as using the company's copier machine or having a secretary type a personal letter.
- On-premises athletic facilities — Providing and operating facilities such as gyms, pools, tennis or golf courses on the business premises, for employees, their spouses, and dependents is a nontaxable fringe benefit.[20]

If meals are provided on-premises to employees, for your convenience as the employer, the value of such meals is usually not taxable to the employee for income tax purposes;[21] however, you can deduct 50% of the cost of furnishing such meals.

Meals on Premises

You may pay educational expenses on behalf of an employee — free of employment taxes or income tax to the employee — if the purpose of such education meets one of the two following tests: 1) the education maintains or improves skills required by the job, and 2) the education meets requirements set by you or applicable laws, where such requirements are imposed as a condition of the retention of employment or rate of compensation.

Educational Assistance Plans

You may also set up tax-qualified educational assistance plans to provide other — not necessarily job-related — educational benefits for employees, in amounts up to $5,250 a year per employee.[22] To qualify, such a plan must be in writing, disclosed to employees, and no more than 5% of benefits paid under the plan can go to 5% owners of the firm or their spouses or dependents. This tax benefit expired on June 30, 1992, but has been retroactively extended again for the period from June 30, 1992 through December 31, 1994.

Dependent Care Plans

Dependent care plans are one of the most popular and rapidly growing types of employee fringe benefit plans in recent years, providing up to $5,000 a year of dependent care benefits for children or elderly dependents per employee. Not more than 25% of benefits provided, however, can be on behalf of 5% owners of the employer company, and other technical nondiscrimination rules also apply.[23]

Stock Option Plans

Companies have devised, or Congress has provided, a number of different stock option plans with various tax advantages, all of which are designed to encourage employees to acquire a proprietary stake in the companies they work for. Major types of such plans include:

- Nonqualified stock options — In this plan, you usually grant favored employees options to acquire stock of the company at a bargain price during a period of several years. Such an option is usually not a taxable event; although, the excess of the value over the option price of the stock received, when the option is eventually exercised, is then taxed as ordinary compensation income in most cases — unless the stock is restricted or forfeitable.
- Incentive stock options (ISOs) — ISOs are options granted under a plan that meets IRS requirements, where the term of the option is limited and the option price is not less than the value of the stock at the day the option is granted. That is, with an ISO, there is no bargain element built into the option. If the stock is worth $20 a share the day the option is granted to the employee, the option must be at an exercise price of no less than $20. Thus, the employee will not stand to profit from exercising the option unless the value of the stock subsequently rises to above $20 a share — which is good incentive for the employee to help make the company as profitable as possible. If certain requirements are met, the employee does not recognize taxable income when he or she exercises an ISO and may qualify for subsequent capital gains treatment if the stock received from exercise of the option is sold at a gain.[24]
- Employee stock purchase plans — Under a tax-qualified employee stock purchase plan, a company may allow employees to purchase its stock, directly from the company, for up to a 15% discount from the fair market value of the stock. The employee is not taxed when exercising the right to purchase stock under such a plan and may receive capital gain treatment when the stock is eventually sold at a gain.[25]

Flexible Spending Plans

In the last few years, the flexible spending plan, or flex plan, has become another increasingly popular type of tax-favored employee benefit plan.

Each of the three flex plans below are designed to permit employees to choose how much to spend on a tax-free basis for various employee benefits, such as health care or dependent care. Flex plans are for employees only and cannot cover sole proprietors, partners in a partnership, or 2% shareholders in an S corporation.

Premium-conversion Accounts

Premium-conversion accounts are the simplest kind of flex account. They primarily are set up to allow employees to pay for their share of health, disability, or group-term life insurance premiums with untaxed dollars by deducting specified amounts out of their regular paychecks to pay for such coverage. The amounts the employees agree to have withheld from their salaries or wages to pay such insurance premiums are excluded from their taxable income, but deductible by the corporation or unincorporated employer. Such plans, in effect, convert part of wages directly into insurance payments, without having the government first remove a slice for taxes. Premium-conversion accounts are practical for even the smallest companies with only one or two employees.

Flexible Reimbursement Accounts

Flexible reimbursement accounts are accounts where an employee may agree to contribute a specified amount to each year and draw on the account to pay for health care expenses not covered by the company. Health care expenses could include medical insurance deductibles, vision care, dental coverage, or for up to $5,000 a year for dependent care expenses.

Here is how these accounts work: Before the start of each year, the employees must estimate their medical and dependent care costs for the coming year that they want paid out of their accounts. The amount designated by an employee is withheld from his or her paycheck during the year (tax-free). As expenses are incurred during the year for health and dependent care, the employee submits requests for reimbursement out of the account to the plan administrator, up to the specified maximum. Employers may choose to supplement or match amounts employees choose to have withheld from their pay, as an additional tax-free benefit to the employee.

Flexible reimbursement accounts may stand alone, or may be combined with premium-conversion accounts. They are feasible for fairly small employers as well; although, administrative costs may tend to be greater than for premium-conversion accounts.

Cafeteria Plans

Cafeteria plans are more complex and are rarely adopted by companies with fewer than 50 employees. Under a cafeteria plan, a company gives employees a menu of benefit choices, provides a fixed number of tax-free dollars per employee each year, and allows the employees to each select or buy the particular benefits desired, such as:

- 401(k) contributions
- Health insurance

- Life insurance
- Disability insurance
- Vision or dental care, or both
- Vacation time

If the costs of the benefits selected exceeds the dollar amount provided by you, the employee may fund the balance with salary reduction amounts through premium-conversion or reimbursement accounts, or both, also on an untaxed basis.

Under flex plans, the golden rule is "use it or lose it." Any amount in an employee's account that is not utilized by the employee during the year is forfeited, and reverts back to you at the end of the year. Flex plans are required to meet nondiscrimination tests to ensure that highly compensated employees do not receive a disproportionate share of the benefits provided.[26] For more information on flex plans, contact:

Employers Council on Flexible Compensation
927 15th Street NW, Suite 1000
Washington, DC 20005
(202) 659-4300

8.4 Sheltering Profits on Export Sales

Many small and large American businesses have an unfortunate tendency to look at the United States as their only market and to ignore the vast potential markets for their products or services that lie outside the borders of this country. One way in which Congress has taken constructive steps to encourage more exports and to make American goods and services more competitive in foreign markets is to provide a form of indirect tax subsidy to American firms that export.

While this export subsidy has not succeeded in stemming the unfavorable trend in the balance of trade the United States has experienced in recent years, it does provide a very attractive tax benefit for U.S. companies that export. If your business is one of the many small firms that does sell its goods or services overseas, you may be able to qualify for this tax incentive by setting up either a Domestic International Sales Corporation (DISC) or a Foreign Sales Corporation (FSC).

In general, a DISC will allow you to accumulate profits earned from export sales in a specially treated corporation, free of U.S. taxes until you eventually choose to distribute the deferred income. An FSC will allow you to accumulate such income, whether or not distributed, free (in part) of U.S. corporate taxes. For an FSC, the exempt foreign trade income will not even be taxed when paid out as a dividend, if the shareholder is a corporation.[27] For small companies, DISCs may often be much simpler to operate and preferable to the FSCs, at least for the first few years of operation.

A DISC is usually just a separate dummy corporation that has no employees and does not carry on any sort of business, except on paper.

The tax law allows a U.S. firm that has qualified export receipts to set aside part of its profits on the export transactions by paying a so-called sales commission to a DISC.[28] As a corporation without any employees, the DISC does not actually do anything to earn the commissions; your firm pays the DISC the largest commission permitted by the tax law on each qualifying export sale. It is usually advisable to have a written commission agreement between your firm and the DISC for legal purposes, although this is not required for tax purposes.

The commission that can be paid to the DISC on an export sale is the larger of 4% of the gross sales price or 50% of the profit on the sale[29] — so long as the commission does not create a loss on the sale for your firm.[30] In addition, the DISC's commission income can be increased by 10% of certain export promotion expenses, if any, incurred by the DISC.[31] As you might suspect, some fairly elaborate tax accounting rules determine how much profit you have on an export sale, for purposes of computing the DISC's maximum commission.[32]

The tax benefits for your business arise because you or your business owns the DISC stock, and the commissions your business pays to the DISC are deducted from the business taxable income, while the DISC pays no tax on income it receives.

However, about 6% (or $1/17$) of the DISC's income each year is taxed to its corporate (but not individual) shareholders,[33] so the DISC will usually pay about 6% of its income back as a dividend to the business that owns the stock of the DISC — which is usually, but not necessarily — your corporation that paid the DISC the commissions. Thus, 94% (or $16/17$) of the income that is shifted to the DISC as export sales commissions escapes federal income tax indefinitely, until the DISC either pays out the accumulated income as dividends or is disqualified and loses its status as a DISC.[34]

For deferred DISC income that accumulates after 1984, however, each DISC shareholder must compute the amount of additional tax it would pay each year if all the deferred DISC income were taxed and pay the IRS interest on the deferred tax.[35] This interest will apparently be tax-deductible if paid by a corporation. The interest rate is based on the going rate for one-year T-bills.

Conceptually, having a DISC can be thought of as taking $100 of pre-tax income out of your left-hand pocket and putting it in your right-hand pocket, then putting $6 back into the left-hand pocket. You do not have to pay tax on the $94 that remains in the right-hand pocket as long as you leave it there. In fact, there are even legal ways in which you can borrow the $94 and put it back in the left-hand pocket (your business) without paying tax on it — another example of having your cake and eating it too.[36] But as long as you keep the $94 in the right-hand pocket, you pay interest on the tax saved.

DISCs — In a Nutshell

Another advantage of having a DISC is that the DISC can continue to accumulate its undistributed profits year after year without fear of incurring an accumulated earnings tax, since a DISC is exempt from the accumulated earnings tax as well as the regular federal income tax.[37]

FSCs — In a Nutshell

A Foreign Sales Corporation (FSC) is somewhat similar to a DISC, but it will probably be too great of an administrative burden for it to be worthwhile for your small business to consider. Unlike a DISC, an FSC cannot be a dummy or paper corporation set up in the United States. Instead, it must meet all of the following requirements:

- It must be a foreign corporation, incorporated in a U.S. possession or in a foreign country that, in general, has arrangements to swap tax information with the IRS.
- There can be no more than 25 shareholders in an FSC.
- An FSC cannot issue preferred stock.
- An FSC must maintain a foreign office, at which there is a permanent set of tax records, including invoices.
- The FSC's board of directors must include at least one person who is not a resident of the United States — although the nonresident member can apparently be a U.S. citizen.
- An FSC cannot be part of a controlled group of corporations that also includes a DISC. That is, you can set up either an FSC or a DISC, but not both.[38]

Summary

Here is a brief summary of this section on DISC and FSC tax benefits.

- If your business will be engaged or is engaged in selling goods or services abroad, consult your tax adviser as to the advisability of establishing a DISC or FSC to shelter a large portion of your export profits.
- Both DISCs and FSCs are extremely complex entities to establish and administer, although a DISC will probably be much less of a headache for a small business to operate than an FSC. In either case, you will need to hire some very sophisticated accounting talent, so unless you earn some fairly substantial export profits, the administrative costs of having a DISC or FSC may well exceed any tax savings you will generate.
- State tax treatment of DISCs and FSCs is discussed in Section 11.8.

8.5 Planning for Withdrawal of Corporate Funds with Minimum Tax Cost

Because of the many tax and other advantages of operating a corporation, there is a good chance you will choose, either initially or later on, to incorporate your business. If you do, and your business becomes profitable to the extent that it has significant profits even after paying you the largest salary that can be justified as "reasonable compensation" under the circumstances, you will eventually be faced with the problem of how to remove the accumulated profits from the corporation without excessive tax costs. That is, unless you decide to liquidate the corporation at some point and operate as an unincorporated business or decide to sell your stock to someone else. The proceeds you receive from liquidation or selling your stock would probably result in capital gains tax in most cases, in addition to a tax at the corporate level upon liquidation. For a definition of unreasonable compensation, see Section 8.9.

If the corporation simply pays dividends to you, this activity will normally be a tax disaster because the dividends you receive will probably be taxable to you as ordinary income at federal income tax rates up to 39.6% or somewhat more. Since the corporation will have already paid tax on the money it distributes to you as dividends, double taxation will result. If both you and the corporation are in the maximum tax brackets, the result can be an effective tax rate of approximately 60% (federal corporate and individual taxes) on the income that is paid out as dividends and an even higher rate if there are also state income taxes. There are better ways to get the money out of the corporation.

Personal Loans from the Corporation

Your corporation can often serve as a bank for your short-term financial needs; however, if you continually borrow from your corporation, the IRS can in some cases treat the loans as dividends to you, which is just what you want to avoid. Or, if your corporation has an accumulated earnings problem, as described in Section 8.9, the existence of loans to shareholders can make it very difficult to argue that the corporation is accumulating earnings for the reasonable needs of the business. So, while a loan from your corporation can be a very good way to tap its funds on a temporary basis, it is not a long-term solution.

If you do borrow, you should normally pay interest if the loan is greater than $10,000. The interest rate should not be less than the applicable federal rate established by the IRS.[39] This rate is announced by the IRS each month of the year for transactions that occur during the following month.

Preliminary Structuring

A number of different ways of structuring your corporation at its inception can give you a great deal of potential flexibility in getting money out of the corporation for yourself or family members later at no tax cost or, at worst, as only partially taxable. Some of these approaches can also make it possible to keep a great deal of the value of the corporation's stock out of your taxable estate for estate tax and inheritance tax purposes. Discuss the structuring of your corporation with your tax adviser before you form the corporation. Here are some of the strategies you might explore.

Putting Stock in Names of Spouse and Children

When the corporation is formed, consider putting a substantial part of the stock in the name of your spouse or children, or both. Later, when or if the business has prospered and the stock has become valuable, it may be possible to bail out a large chunk of the corporation's accumulated profits at a child's lower tax rates by having the corporation redeem (purchase) all of the stock of your spouse or child.

The redemption will usually be treated as a sale for a capital gain if your spouse or child agrees to notify the IRS if he or she reacquires any interest in the corporation within ten years after the redemption.[40] Working as an employee of the corporation would be an "interest" that would prevent the spouse or child from receiving favorable capital gains treatment. So if you want your son or daughter to work for you in the business, do not count on being able to redeem his or her stock as a capital gain.

Note that while capital gains are taxed at only slightly lower rates than ordinary income, it is still very desirable to have a stock redemption qualify for capital gains treatment, because part of the money received will be a nontaxable recovery of the shareholder's tax basis in the stock that is being redeemed. This is usually not the case if the redemption payment is treated as an ordinary income dividend.

Such redemption of stock as a capital gain could even be made on an installment basis.[41] For example, if your daughter had all her stock redeemed by the corporation for $150,000, the corporation could pay the $150,000 price, plus interest, in 15 annual installments of $10,000 each, so that your daughter would not have a "bunching" of all the capital gain on the sale in one tax year. Instead, the capital gains tax would be spread over a 15-year period, and the corporation should be able to deduct interest paid on the note held by the daughter.

Constraints in Community Property States

Unfortunately, this tactic does not work as well in community property states if you attempt to redeem your spouse's stock. Under the community property laws, half of your stock will generally be treated as owned by your spouse. This makes it difficult to completely terminate his or her interest, unless all of the stock that is community property is first split in half between you by agreement, so that you each own your shares as separate property.

Even in that case, your spouse may be considered to have reacquired a community property interest in your separately owned stock if you continue to work for the corporation and the value of the stock increases on account of your efforts. Thus, if you live in a community property state, you probably should not count on trying to redeem your spouse's interest in the corporation as a capital gain. The states that have community property laws are Arizona, California, Idaho, Louisiana, Nevada, New Mexico, Texas, Washington, and Wisconsin.

Gifts of Stock to Children

Even if the corporation never redeems your children's stock, it is useful to put some of the stock in their names when you form the corporation — especially at a time when a gift to them of the stock will be subject to little or no gift tax because of its low value. When you die many years later, the stock owned by your children may then be very valuable and will not be included in your estate in most instances, which could save your children a great deal in estate and inheritance taxes. The federal gift tax laws now permit you to make gifts worth up to $10,000 per child per year free of federal gift tax. If you are married, you and your spouse can jointly make gifts of up to $20,000 per year per child; however, you may be subject to state gift taxes in some states.

Debt Capitalization Pitfall

Until the Revenue Reconciliation Act of 1989 was passed, it was considered astute tax planning — when setting up a new corporation — to capitalize the company with both equity capital (stock) and debt capital (an interest-bearing note from the corporation to you); however, such a tactic can now be a tax trap.

This type of structuring can still be done without adverse tax consequences, but only if the assets you are transferring to the corporation are cash or other assets on which you would not have a taxable gain if sold at current fair market value. Otherwise, under the 1989 law, any notes or other debt capital you take back from the corporation will cause you to pay tax on appreciated assets (land, equipment, etc.) that you transfer to the corporation in return for the stock and debt instruments.

Debt Capitalization Still Can Be Advantageous

If, however, the only asset you are putting in the corporation to start it up is, for example, cash, you will not be affected by the 1989 tax law change mentioned in the preceding paragraph. As an illustration, if you plan to put $10,000 in the corporation to get the business started, you might take back stock for $5,000 and a $5,000 note when the corporation is set up, rather than having the corporation issue you stock for the whole $10,000. While the note is outstanding, you will be able to siphon off some funds from the corporation as interest on the note, which the corporation can deduct. By contrast, if the corporation distributed profits to you as dividends on its stock, it would result in double taxation of those profits, since, unlike interest, the corporation cannot deduct dividends it pays.

More importantly, when the note becomes due, the corporation will repay you the $5,000 principal of the note; if things have been handled properly, you should pay no tax on that $5,000. In contrast, if the corporation attempted to return part of your investment in the stock, whatever you received would probably be fully taxable to you as a dividend, even if you surrendered some of your stock in a redemption. Lending the corporation part of its start-up capital allows you to withdraw part of your investment without paying tax.

Thus, there are considerable advantages in partially capitalizing your corporation with debt in the form of a note or notes that you will hold from the corporation. You will need competent tax advice before you do so, however, since there are hundreds of court cases that have tried to define when debt instruments will be considered debt and when they will be considered stock. For example, if you capitalize your corporation with more than $3 of debt for each $1 of stock — say a $6,000 note and $2,000 of stock — the note (debt) may be treated as though it were stock for tax purposes. Thus, if the corporation paid you interest or principal on the note, whatever payments you received would be treated as dividends to you, and the corporation's deduction for the interest payments would be disallowed. So tread very lightly in lending money to your corporation. See Section 8.9 for more on the distinction between debt and equity for tax purposes.

Post-Incorporation Planning

Whether or not you take advantage of the above planning suggestions at the time you incorporate, there are a number of other ways you can get cash out of your corporation at a low tax cost later on.

Leasing to the Corporation

Instead of putting your own money into the corporation so it can buy property it needs, keep the money outside the corporation, and buy the property yourself and lease it all at a reasonable rental to the corporation. This way, you will be able to directly obtain the tax depreciation and other benefits of owning the property. At the same time, by keeping the property out of the corporation, you will be putting less of your assets at risk in the business, especially if the corporation goes broke. Also, if the leased property is real estate, it will probably appreciate in value.

You can personally and directly benefit from that appreciation, including the increased rent you will be able to charge the corporation as inflation continues. Furthermore, if you have used straight-line depreciation and sell the property at a gain, all of the gain will be capital gain. By contrast, if the corporation sells real property at a gain, 20% of the straight-line depreciation is recaptured as ordinary income.[42] Although a corporation's capital gains are currently taxed at the same rate as ordinary income, Congress restored preferential tax rates for individuals' capital gains in 1990, and it may do the same for corporations in the future.

Trusts for Your Children

You could make a gift of business property — or the funds to buy it — to a trust and have a bank or other independent trustee negotiate a reasonable lease of the property to the business, with the rental income going to the trust for distribution to your children. Upon the trust's termination, or earlier, such as when your children reach specified ages, the property and accumulated income can be distributed to the children, or if a child does not live until age 21, revert to you at his or her death.

This can be a useful way of taking cash out of the corporation for the benefit of your children, who have lower tax brackets; however, since the IRS regularly attempts to attack these types of arrangements, you should go into this only with the help of an astute tax adviser. Be aware that the Tax Reform Act of 1986 eliminated nearly all the tax advantages of trusts for children under 14 years of age.

DISC Deferrals

Consider setting up a DISC corporation if your corporation has foreign sales. You can then hold the DISC stock yourself or give it to your children.

This will not only enable you to indefinitely defer federal income taxes on part of the profits from export sales, it will also, in effect, allow you or your children to siphon off part of the profits on export sales — dividends paid by the DISC — in a manner that allows your corporation to deduct those dividends, thereby avoiding double taxation.

Consider adopting corporate pension or profit-sharing plans and various corporate fringe benefit plans. These types of benefit plans, in appropriate circumstances, can provide deferred retirement benefits or current insurance benefits to you tax-free — or on a tax-deferred basis, in the case of retirement plans — while reducing the corporation's current taxable income. See the discussion of these kinds of employee benefit plans in Section 8.3.

Benefit Plans

8.6 Deducting Expenses Related to Your Business

One major advantage of operating your own business is the opportunity it may give you to deduct the costs of certain activities or luxuries as business expenses. Some of these deductions are discussed below.

Some of the tax benefits that were available in the past, however, such as costs of attending foreign conventions[43] and treating part of your home as a business office[44] have been severely curtailed, and there are strict recordkeeping requirements for others.[45] For instance, deductions for attending foreign conventions are now completely disallowed, unless you can show that:

- It is just as reasonable for the convention to be held abroad as it would be to hold it in North America; and
- The meeting is directly related to your trade or business.

If these two requirements are met, you must then meet the general requirements for traveling outside the United States. Deductions for conventions or seminars on cruise ships are limited to $2,000, and other travel by "luxury water transportation" is deductible only up to certain per diem amounts.[46] For more on office-in-the-home expenses, refer to Section 8.14.

It is still possible to deduct business travel expenses, entertainment of your clients or customers, and business-related meals; however, you can only deduct 50% of qualifying business meals and entertainment. Consequently, this 50% rule considerably complicates recordkeeping for these types of expenses.

Travel, Entertainment, and Meal Expenses

For instance, if you stay in a hotel on a business trip and charge your meals to your room, you are required to separately break out your meal expenses for tax purposes because your meal expenses are only 50% deductible.

If you are an employee of your business, the 50% disallowance of meal and entertainment expenses does not apply to you individually, if your company reimburses you for the expenses; it applies only at the company level.

Detailed Records Required

To claim any of these kinds of deductions, you must keep daily, detailed records of such expenditures, including bills, receipts, and the following information for each expense:

- The relationship of the expenditure to the business;
- The time when the expense was incurred;
- Where the money was spent, and to whom it was paid;
- The amount of the expenditure; and
- The identities of the persons involved, including persons entertained.[47]

The law requires that taxpayers keep "adequate records or ... sufficient evidence corroborating the taxpayer's own statement."[48] It is strongly recommended that you pick up a daily expense record book or diary and enter all expenses for travel, meals, and entertainment you think should be deductible. Include the above information for each item.

Not All Expenses Deductible

Not all expenses for entertaining clients or customers will be deductible, even if you keep meticulous records. As a general rule, your records must show that you were engaged in a substantial and bona fide business discussion during or immediately before or after the entertainment.[49] Expenses of entertaining people just to create a good impression on them, in the hope they might send some business your way in the future, are classified as goodwill entertainment, and you cannot deduct them for tax purposes.

The rule allowing quiet business meals with clients or potential customers to be deductible, even if no business is discussed, has been repealed.[50] For more information on business-related expenses you can deduct, contact your local IRS office and request *Publication 463, Travel, Entertainment, and Gift Expenses.*

Automobile Expenses

If you use an automobile more than 50% of the time for business purposes, you will generally be able to deduct a percentage of the costs of owning and operating the car, if you can substantiate the business mileage. The expenses of using the car for commuting to and from work and for personal travel are not deductible.[51]

For example, if your business purchases a new car for your use as a business car, and 80% of the mileage on the car can be shown to be for business trips, and only 20% for commuting to work and other personal use, you should be able to deduct 80% of the gas, oil, insurance, and maintenance costs relating to the car. You can also depreciate the cost of the car, less 20% for personal use.

Rules are even more drastic for any automobile, airplane, boat or computer not kept in your place of business if you can't establish a business-use percentage in excess of 50%. Automobile depreciation is stretched out over at least six years, straight-line: 10% the first year; 20% a year thereafter, for four years; and 10% the final year. For boats, planes, or computers, it can be stretched out for longer periods.[52] There are also strict dollar limits on maximum annual depreciation deductions for so-called luxury automobiles costing more than about $15,000. For luxury automobiles, the maximum annual depreciation deduction allowed is limited to the amounts below.

Luxury Automobile Depreciation

1992 Acquisitions	1993 Acquisitions
$2,760 for the first year	$2,860 for the first year
$4,400 for the second year	$4,600 for the second year
$2,650 for the third year	$2,750 for the third year
$1,575 for each succeeding year	$1,675 for each succeeding year

Exemptions

These restrictions don't apply to business vehicles such as ambulances, hearses, taxis, delivery vans, or heavy trucks.[53]

Mileage Deduction

If you drive an inexpensive economy car on business, it may be simpler and more advantageous to elect to deduct a flat $0.28 (28 cents) per mile for 1993[54] for your business mileage rather than keep records of your various kinds of automobile expenses. If you use this method, you can still deduct tolls and parking incurred on business trips. If you drive an expensive car, you will probably get much larger tax deductions by reporting your actual operating expenses, plus depreciation, than by electing the mileage allowance. Be sure to keep an accurate record of your business mileage so you can substantiate the car was used for business purposes.

Form 4562 of your annual tax return requires you to answer a number of detailed questions if you claim an automobile deduction.

8.7 Choosing the Best Taxable Year for a Corporation

If your business is an S corporation or is considered a personal service corporation, you will generally have no choice but to operate on a calendar-year basis, and you can skip over the following discussion of how to select a taxable year. If, however, your business is incorporated and is neither an S corporation or a personal service corporation in which the services performed are "substantially performed" by owner/employees,[55] you will have an opportunity to choose any tax fiscal-year period you desire during your initial year of operation as a corporation. There are significant tax deferral and savings opportunities in selecting the right year end.

Unfortunately, in some cases, it will be necessary to be able to project with some accuracy how much your corporation will earn or lose each month for several months to a year ahead. If you expect to have start-up losses and show an overall net profit for your first year as an incorporated business, one good rule is to cut off your first taxable year at the end of the month in which you first get back to break even for the year-to-date.

For example, assume your first tax year starts on January 1, 1994, and you show a cumulative tax loss of $20,000 at the end of June. You then have taxable income of $10,000 a month in July, August, and September, and expect profits to continue. If you chose June 30 as your tax year end, you would have a $20,000 loss for your first tax period ending June 30, 1994. For federal income tax purposes, it is no problem, since you can carry over the loss and use it to offset $20,000 of taxable income during the next tax year. Some states, however, do not allow a carryover of losses.

Another approach would be to choose an August 31 year end, so that you would show no taxable income for your first year, assuming the corporation continued to net $10,000 a month.

If you do not mind paying some tax earlier, it might pay, in the above example, to wait until the end of October, November, or even December to cut off the first tax year. This would enable the corporation to isolate $20,000 to $40,000 or so of profit in a tax period subject to low federal corporate income tax rates, which are only 15% on the first $50,000 of corporate income.

If you do so, however, you are making an assumption that the corporation will be in a higher tax bracket in the following year, which cannot be known with any certainty. Also, the existence of tax credits would somewhat complicate the simple picture portrayed above. Obviously, your accountant can help you decide which tax year will produce the best result.

Start-up Losses Must Be Capitalized, Not Deducted

Remember, when projecting your start-up losses, you can't immediately deduct preopening expenses; instead, you must capitalize those costs and write them off (straight-line) over 60 months.[56] For example, if you are starting a restaurant and are paying salaries to a manager and to employees being trained before the day the restaurant opens for business, you might well think those expenses are immediately deductible. Not so! All such preopening expenses must be capitalized, and you can't begin to amortize them until opening day.

Another planning approach in adopting a year end, which may some-times conflict with the above strategy, is to adopt a January 31 year end. If you structure your employment contract with your corporation so that you receive a substantial part of your compensation in January each year, you can, in effect, defer the bonus to your following tax year, while the corporation can deduct it — if paid in January — for its fiscal year end-ing just after the bonus is paid. Naturally, the corporation will be required to withhold income tax from your bonus, but at reduced rates, compared to regular monthly salary payments. Federal income tax withholding on bonuses is at a flat rate of only 28%.

Benefits of Adopting January 31 Year End

If you have a seasonal business, you may want to defer taxes by selecting a tax year that ends just before your most profitable season begins. For example, if you are in the business of selling Christmas tree ornaments and do most of your business from October through December each year, you might choose a September 30 tax year end.

Seasonal Businesses

Remember, though, that tax considerations are not the only factors to take into account in choosing a fiscal year. If taking an annual inventory is a major task, consider adopting a year end that occurs when inventory is at a low ebb and when business is slow, if possible. You may also find that you will get somewhat quicker and better service from your CPA firm for annual tax returns, audits, etc. if you pick a fiscal year that ends several months before or after December. Most CPAs are at their busiest during their annual tax season from about February to May, preparing 1040s and doing audits for their many clients who have December year ends.

8.8 Selecting Tax Accounting Methods

Rely on your tax accountant's advice when choosing which tax account-ing methods you should adopt in your business. This section is provided for your information in case you are not sure whether your accountant has recommended the method that will produce the best results for you.

The two overall tax accounting methods most commonly used are the cash method and the accrual method. There are, however, other special overall methods, plus a number of special kinds of accounting elections a business can make with regard to particular items, such as installment sales, inventory valuations, and deduction of accrued vacation pay.

The cash receipts and disbursements method of accounting, called the cash method, is the simplest accounting method in use. Under this method, you include income only as it is actually or constructively received.

Cash Method

Likewise, you only become entitled to deductions when you actually pay expenses — except for certain special items like depreciation or amortization of certain kinds of expenditures — rather than when you receive bills for the expenses. Thus, you usually do not have to report your year-end accounts receivable in income for the year and cannot deduct your year-end accounts payable. This will normally allow you to defer some taxable income each year if your year-end receivables are larger than accounts payable and other accrued but unpaid expenses. Obviously, this gives you some flexibility, too, if you want to pay off a number of payables at year end to reduce your taxable income for the current year.

The cash method is the method used by most individual taxpayers and by businesses in the real estate, financial, and service fields, where inventories of goods are not material factors in producing income.

Businesses with significant inventories, such as manufacturers and wholesale or retail firms, are usually required to use an accrual method of tax accounting.[57] In some cases, however, it is possible even for those businesses to use a hybrid accounting method — accounting for income and the cost of goods sold on an accrual method — while using the cash method to report selling expenses and administrative expenses.

The Tax Reform Act of 1986 disallowed use of the cash method for C corporations — regular corporations — and for partnerships that have C corporations as partners. One exception is for small firms with an average gross receipts of five million dollars or less during the three preceding years.[58] Another exception is made for larger firms in the farming business and for certain employee-owned qualified personal service corporations in fields such as law, medicine, accounting, architecture, or consulting.

Sole proprietorships, S corporations, and partnerships with no C corporation partners are not affected by these restrictions, unless they are considered tax shelters, and may remain on the cash method if that is a permissible accounting method for their particular type of business. Firms that are forbidden from using the cash method must adopt the more complex accrual method of accounting.

Accrual Method

As noted above, most large corporations and businesses with significant inventories are required to report income on the accrual method of accounting for tax purposes. This method requires you to report income when income is earned rather than when you receive it. Similarly, expenses can be deducted when all events have occurred that fix the amount and the fact of your business' liability for a particular expense, even if it is paid in a subsequent tax year. However, if economic performance required of the other party does not occur until a subsequent tax year, you may not be able to deduct an accrued expense until economic performance occurs.

For example, if you sign a contract with your accountant in 1993 to prepare your tax return in 1994, "economic performance" does not occur until 1994, and you may be unable to accrue the deduction in 1993, unless you meet several requirements, such as recurring expenses or performance occurs within a reasonable time after the end of the tax year.[59]

Even though the accrual method may not be required for your business, you may find it preferable to use, if most or all of your income is from cash sales and you pay a large part of your expenses on a delayed credit basis. In this case, you would have few, if any, receivables at year end but might have substantial accrued payables you could deduct in the current year without having to actually make payment before year end.

Accrual of bonuses to employees, in an incorporated business, is a good example of a deduction that can be accelerated by a business using the accrual method. But expenses owed to you or a related owner of the business can't be deducted until actually paid.[60]

Special Accounting Methods Long-term Contracts

If your business is engaged in heavy construction work on a long-term contract basis, it may be difficult to tell in advance whether a particular contract will result in a profit or loss, since many unforeseen difficulties may arise. The tax regulations recognize this problem and allow such contractors to utilize special methods of accounting which may delay the time at which profit or loss is recognized on a long-term contract. They are:

- The percentage of completion method; and
- The completed contract method.[61]

The Tax Reform Act of 1986, however, and subsequent legislation has eliminated the use of the completed contract method of accounting for most large companies, except for certain ship contracts and for some home construction and other residential building contractors.

Fortunately, small businesses, whose average annual gross receipts for the three preceding years do not exceed ten million dollars, are still allowed to use completed contract accounting for tax purposes, at least for contracts that are estimated to take no more than two years to complete.[62]

Even those completed contract method deferrals that survive the new restrictions are now mostly considered tax preference items under the alternative minimum tax rules.[63] In other words, heads you lose, tails the tax collector wins.

Installment Sales

If your business makes casual or occasional sales of personal property — other than merchandise held for sale — or makes sales of real estate it owns, the profit on any such sale can, in general, be reported on the installment basis as and when payments are received, rather than in the year of sale.[64] The installment method of reporting, however, is not available for "dealers," such as retailers, in personal or real property, except for certain dealers in real property. This is an election that sellers of residential lots or time-shares may make to use the installment method. The catch is that the dealer making such an election must agree to pay interest on any tax that is deferred by using installment reporting.[65]

In the case of nondealer sales of property for more than $150,000, if the total face amount of all installment notes exceeds five million dollars for the year, at the end of the year, the seller must pay interest on the deferred tax liability.[66] Sales of personal-use property or of farm property, for any amount, are exempt from the interest-on-deferred-tax provisions.[67]

Inventory Valuation Methods

If you maintain substantial inventories, discuss with your accountant the pros and cons of using the last-in-first-out (LIFO) method of valuing year-end inventories[68] versus the more common and simpler first-in-first-out (FIFO) method.

FIFO Method

Under the FIFO method, the cost of ending inventory is calculated under the assumption that the first items of inventory bought were the first ones to be sold, so that only the most recently purchased items are assumed to be left in inventory at the end of each year. This usually means the highest-cost items, in times of inflation. That is, if a company turns all its inventory over every three months each year, FIFO assumes, in effect, that the inventory remaining on hand at December 31 was all bought in the last three months of the year, rather than at some earlier date when prices may have been lower.

Most companies use the FIFO method because:

- FIFO is much simpler to use in terms of maintaining accounting records;
- When prices of goods are generally rising, FIFO has the effect of making a company's net income appear to be greater than if the more conservative LIFO method were used — but it also tends to inflate the amount of a company's taxable income; and
- Their accountants never mention to them that there is an alternative method (LIFO) of inventory accounting that can be used.

LIFO Method

In contrast to FIFO, the LIFO method assumes that the items in your ending inventory are the first or oldest ones that were acquired. Thus, under LIFO, ending inventory values for many of the items of inventory will be based on what that item cost in the very first year in which the business began using the LIFO method. The difference in inventory valuation can be dramatic if, for example, a business using LIFO for ten years was paying $10 each ten years earlier for the widgets it keeps in inventory versus a current price of $75 per widget. Under LIFO, the widgets would still be carried on the accounting records at a cost of $10 apiece versus $75 under FIFO.

Accordingly, the difference in inventory cost, or $65 per widget in the above example — called the LIFO reserve — would be the amount of taxable income per widget that the company has deferred over the ten years. Thus, for a company with large amounts of capital invested in inventories, it is easy to see how LIFO can result in a huge tax saving.

At present, using the LIFO method is extremely complex, and the tax savings may in some cases be offset by increased accounting fees incurred and additional management time spent in attempting to comply with the LIFO tax regulations. The tax requirements for using LIFO, however, are somewhat relaxed for those small businesses with less than five million dollars a year in sales.[69]

Any firm with inventories may elect to use either FIFO or LIFO. If a firm is already using FIFO, it may be able to change over to LIFO, if a number of technical requirements set by the IRS are met. Or, a company using LIFO may also change over to FIFO. Note, however, that if a firm uses LIFO and changes to FIFO for some reason, it will usually have to pay a large amount of tax, when it recaptures the LIFO reserve described above, at the time of the changeover. Any such changes in inventory accounting methods should not be attempted without the assistance of a competent tax adviser. If your C corporation already uses LIFO inventory accounting and elects S corporation status, your corporation will be required to pay tax, in four annual installments, on the LIFO reserve at the time of the changeover to an S corporation.[70]

Regardless of whether a company uses LIFO or FIFO for inventory accounting, it generally must allocate a wide range of its indirect costs to inventory, rather than simply deducting them as expenses, under the IRS's uniform capitalization rules. The practical effect of this is that any such costs that have been absorbed into the cost of inventory on hand at the end of the tax year do not get deducted currently for tax purposes. Manufacturing and processing operations of any size are subject to these complex capitalization rules. Fortunately, the uniform capitalization rules do not apply to a wholesale or retail business in any year when the company's annual gross receipts for the preceding three years have averaged ten million dollars or less.[71]

Vacation Pay Accrual Method

If you accrue employees' vacation pay for internal business purposes, you normally can only deduct your liability for such accruals when an employee actually uses his or her vacation pay. The only exception is for accrual-basis taxpayers, where vacation pay is vested at the end of a tax year and paid within two and a half months afterwards.

8.9 Tax Problems Unique to Corporations

While this book has outlined some of the many tax and other advantages inherent in operating a corporation, you need to be aware of a number of traps in the tax law if you go overboard in trying to take advantage of the tax benefits bestowed on corporations.

As is emphasized in this chapter, the most basic goal in corporate tax planning for many high-income individuals is to leave as much profit in the corporation as possible so it can be taxed at the relatively low corporate tax rates and later withdrawn tax-free or at capital gains rates, such as by selling or having the corporation redeem the stock or by liquidating the corporation.

The government's role is to prevent the taxpayer from reaching these goals except where the corporation has good business reasons — as opposed to the individual's tax and investment reasons — for virtually everything it does. In attempting to plug up all the possible loopholes taxpayers might use to take advantage of low corporate rates, the tax law contains a whole array of penalties for corporations:

- That unreasonably accumulate earnings;[72]
- That are used as "incorporated pocket books" for holding personal investments;[73] or
- That are capitalized too heavily with debt.[74]

These and other operating problems of corporations under the tax law are briefly outlined below to give you a sense of what the limits are and how far you can go in utilizing corporate tax advantages. None of these problems are significant concerns for S corporations.

Penalty Tax on Accumulated Earnings

The accumulated earnings tax might well be called the scourge of the overly successful small corporation.[75] This tax potentially applies to almost every corporation that accumulates more than $250,000[76] in after-tax profits (with certain adjustments),[77] unless the corporation can demonstrate that it needs to retain the profits for use in its business operations.[78]

Your corporation can accumulate up to $250,000 — $150,000 for professional and certain personal service firms — in earnings without having to be concerned about this penalty tax.[79] If additional accumulations cannot be justified as being made for the "reasonable needs of the business," however, the corporation will be faced with the choice of paying out the excess earnings as dividends or paying the accumulated earnings tax. The tax is imposed at the rate of 39.6% on the improperly accumulated earnings.[80] Since this is a tax that is imposed in addition to the corporate income tax, it is one you probably do not ever want to be forced to pay.

As long as you are able to keep plowing profits back into your business; buying more facilities, equipment, and inventory; and maintaining needed working capital, you will not have much cause for worry about the accumulated earnings tax. If, however, you reach a point where the corporation has more liquid funds than it needs, and you are beginning to look for places to invest the surplus cash, like real estate or the stock market, that should serve as a signal to you that there may be a potential accumulated earnings problem. In that case, you will need some good tax advice as to what you can do to protect the corporation from imposition of the penalty tax.

Fortunately, there are a number of acceptable reasons that can justify accumulating funds that are not currently being used in the corporation's business. Some of the more important ones include:

- Setting up a reserve to redeem enough of the stock of a shareholder (yourself, for example) who dies, in order to enable the individual's estate to pay certain expenses related to his or her death — estate and inheritance taxes, funeral expenses, and expenses of administering the estate.[81] This reserve can only be created by the corporation after the death of a shareholder, prior to the repurchase of the shareholder's stock;

- Creating a fund to allow for a bona fide plan to replace facilities or expand the business, including the acquisition of another business;[82]

- Creating a reasonable reserve fund to pay potential uninsured product liability claims;[83]

- Accumulating funds to retire indebtedness created in connection with the business of the corporation;[84] and

- Setting up a defined benefit pension plan with an initial "past service liability" to be funded over a number of years.

A number of ways also exist to reduce the accumulated earnings without paying them out as dividends. Some typical examples would be to redeem part of the stock of the corporation, such as the stock of one of your children. This will not only reduce accumulated earnings but will reduce the amount of excess cash not needed in the business.

Another useful approach is to have the corporation purchase real estate that it might currently be leasing. This can sometimes be particularly advantageous where you are the landlord who is leasing the property to the corporation, as suggested in Section 8.5. This tactic technically will not reduce the corporation's accumulated earnings, but will use up excess cash that would otherwise raise questions by IRS auditors.

Another effective solution if you have an accumulated earnings problem is to convert your C corporation to an S corporation, if that is possible. S corporations are not subject to the accumulated earnings tax because all their earnings are deemed to be distributed to shareholders.

Justifiable Accumulations

Penalty Tax on Personal Holding Company Income

If a closely held corporation gets a large proportion of its gross income, usually 60% or more, in the form of personal holding company income,[85] such as dividends, interest, rents, and royalties, it will generally be considered a personal holding company for tax purposes.[86]

Other kinds of income considered personal holding company income include income received by a service business from anyone (other than the corporation) who has the right under a contract to designate a particular individual to perform the contracted services. The person designated, however, must own at least 25% of the corporate stock.[87] Also, payments a corporation receives from a 25% shareholder for use of its property is personal holding company income.[88] This puts a damper on schemes such as having your corporation buy a yacht and charter it to you.

As a rule, if a corporation comes within the definition of a personal holding company, the tax law imposes a 39.6% penalty tax on any personal holding company income not distributed as a dividend.[89]

Most actively conducted small businesses will not need to be very concerned about being treated as personal holding companies since they will seldom get 60% or more of their gross income from passive sources like dividends and interest.

The kind of small business most likely to have a personal holding company problem is the incorporated personal service business — when the corporation enters into contracts and agrees to provide the services of an employee who is a major shareholder.

The best way to avoid this problem is to specify in the contract that the corporation reserves the right to designate the person who will provide the services. You will need to consult your tax adviser, however, before entering into any such personal service contract since the tax rules in this area are quite subtle and the tax penalty is very heavy if the income under the personal service contract is considered to be personal holding company income.

Another type of operating company that frequently encounters personal holding company tax problems is the developer of computer software that generates much of its income from software licensing agreements.

While the Tax Reform Act of 1986 included a special exemption from the personal holding company provisions for corporations actively engaged in the computer software business, the terms of this exception are quite technical and many software firms will only be able to qualify for this relief with very careful planning.[90]

Possible Treatment of Corporate Debt as Stock

As discussed in Section 8.5, there are two significant advantages to putting part of your investment in an incorporated business into the corporation in the form of debt, rather than all of it in exchange for stock. These advantages are:

- The interest paid to you is normally deductible by the corporation, unlike dividends paid on its stock.
- Repayment of the money you loaned to the corporation allows you to take part of your investment out of the corporation free of tax.

Because the use of debt in structuring a closely held corporation is so advantageous, Congress has taken steps to limit the extent to which you can use debt to capitalize a corporation and still enjoy these advantages.[91]

Over the last few years, the IRS has proposed several sets of new and complex regulations as to when loans to a corporation by its shareholders will be treated as equivalent to an investment in its stock — in which case interest payments will not be deductible by the corporation and principal payments would be taxable to the recipient.

These regulations raised such a storm of protest each time they were proposed that the IRS has finally withdrawn them. So, to determine what constitutes debt and stock, guidelines are used from hundreds of different court decisions. Nevertheless, there are a few generally accepted ground rules that you should follow to avoid having corporate debt reclassified by the IRS as equity or stock:

Debt-Equity Distinction

- The loan should not have any equity-type features, such as interest or payments, pegged to the corporation's income.
- The loan should be made at a reasonable interest rate, such as the rate at which the IRS imputes interest between related parties.
- The corporation's total debts — other than trade accounts payable — should not be more than about three times its net worth.
- The loan should be documented by a written note and should have a specified maturity date. All interest and principal payments on the note should be made on time.

If you follow each of the above rules, you will generally avoid the problem of having debt reclassified as stock. If you fail to comply with one or more of those rules when lending money to your corporation, the loan may be treated as a stock investment. This can be a serious tax trap if, when the loan is to be repaid, you are unaware that the repayment to you may constitute taxable income.

The most basic tax problem resulting from incorporating a business is the possibility of double taxation of the business income if it is paid out as dividends. That is, if the corporation has any profit after payment of salaries and other expenses, it must pay tax on those profits, unless it is an S corporation. Then, if those profits left after taxes are distributed to stockholders as dividends, the stockholders must also pay tax on the dividends they receive.

Double Taxation of Corporate Income

Fortunately, the problem of double taxation is generally quite manageable and most small incorporated businesses never pay dividends. The owners normally are also the officers of the corporation and can take enough income out in the form of salary and fringe benefits to live on, usually leaving some profit in the corporation to be plowed back into the business.

Also, as outlined briefly in Section 8.5, there are a number of better ways to get the accumulated profits out of the corporation than by paying dividends.

If you own an incorporated business or own a portion of its stock and are actively involved in operating the business, you will be an employee of the corporation and will draw a salary. Drawing a large salary from the corporation may enable you to withdraw much of the profits of the business without any problem of double taxation, since the corporation can deduct reasonable compensation it pays to you as your salary.[92]

Unreasonable Compensation

Thus, taking salary out of the corporation is preferable to taking money out in the form of dividends, since the corporation cannot deduct dividends it pays. The salary you receive, if reasonable, is deductible by the corporation; however, the key word here is reasonable. If you try to take too much income out of the corporation as salary, including bonuses and fringe benefits like pension and profit-sharing contributions, the IRS may try to treat part of your salary as unreasonable compensation. If you are fortunate enough to be worried about the one-million-dollar limitation on executive compensation that goes into effect in 1994, you can relax. That limitation will only apply to executives of publicly held corporations. So unless your company has gone public, you don't need to be concerned about this limitation.[93]

There are no hard and fast rules as to how much compensation is reasonable, but if you are taking no more than the officers in similar businesses of the same size are paid, you should not have any problem establishing that your compensation from the corporation is reasonable under the circumstances.

If, however, the IRS does succeed in treating part of your compensation as excessive, there will be two serious tax consequences:

- The deduction by the corporation for the unreasonable portion of your salary will be disallowed.
- Part of your salary will be reclassified as dividend income, and thus pension and profit-sharing plan contributions based on that salary may not be fully deductible, which could even result in disqualification of your pension or profit-sharing plan.

8.10 Estate Planning in Connection with Your Business

As the owner of part or all of even a moderately successful business, you may find that after a few years the value of your business accounts for a very large portion of your personal net worth. As such, your business will probably be the most important single asset you have to be concerned with for estate planning purposes, both during your lifetime and at the time of your death. No attempt will be made here to go into the intricacies of the estate-planning possibilities that may be available; instead, the fundamental approaches you need to be aware of are outlined below. Discuss how to relate these concepts to your own situation with your tax adviser and attorney.

Income-Splitting

A useful method of reducing lifetime income taxes is to split the taxable income from your business between two or more persons or entities. Usually a corporation, particularly an S corporation, is a useful vehicle for doing this; you can split income between you and your children by giving them stock in the corporation. A corporation that has not elected S corporation treatment can also be used to split income between you and the corporation. See Section 8.2.

Often, the best time to remove potential wealth from your taxable estate at death is by giving your children part of the stock in your incorporated business when the business is formed — when the value of the stock is likely to be negligible. If you wait until the business has become a valuable and profitable enterprise, gifts of stock at that time may result in substantial taxable gifts for gift tax purposes, even though the tax cost of those gifts may not be felt until you die, in some cases. You can now make gifts of up to $10,000 ($20,000 if married) per year to each of your children completely free of federal gift taxes.

Reducing Estate and Gift Taxes

Assuming that you want part of your stock in your incorporated business to pass to your children at your death, it obviously makes sense to give them a portion of the stock — but not enough to affect your control of the corporation — during your lifetime. By doing this, there will be little or no gift tax cost if it is done when the business is started. Thus, they will already own the stock when you die, and that valuable asset will have passed to them free of death taxes in most instances. In addition, as noted above, lifetime gifts of stock to your children may also save on income taxes.

If you have one or more partners or business associates who also own a part of the business, it is very important that you enter into a buy-sell agreement with them that spells out what happens if one of you dies, becomes disabled, or wants to sell his or her interest in the business.

Buy-Sell Agreements

Often these agreements are funded by life insurance on the owners, so that if you die, the business or the other owners will collect the life insurance proceeds and use those funds to buy out your interest in the business. Otherwise, your surviving family members might find it very difficult to sell the interest in the business they inherit from you, except at a give-away price.

Many small business owners ignore the need for buy-sell agreements or, like having a will drawn up, they keep putting it off. When one of the partners or shareholders dies, the survivors may have a problem in raising enough cash to pay the death taxes. This is only one of the problems that may arise when there is no buy-sell agreement.

The few hundred dollars you may spend in legal fees to have a buy-sell agreement with your business partners or associates drawn up is probably one of the best investments you and your associates will ever make.

Since 1982, it has been possible to leave your entire estate to your surviving spouse free of federal estate taxes.[94] In some cases, however, it is

Unlimited Estate Tax Marital Deduction

not the best strategy to fully use the unlimited estate tax marital deduction, so see a lawyer to get a current will that takes the best approach for your situation. This exemption from the estate tax also applies to pension benefits you leave to your spouse when you die, unless the accrued value of your pension benefits exceeds $750,000 (less in some instances). If so, your estate will have to pay a special 15% excise tax on the amount over $750,000.[95]

Since not all state inheritance tax laws permit an unlimited marital deduction, it can create inheritance tax problems in those states if you leave too much property to your spouse. Refer to Section 11.8 for details regarding this state's marital deduction rules under its inheritance tax laws.

Wills or trusts executed before September 13, 1981 may not qualify for the unlimited estate tax marital deduction.[96] If you have such a will or trust, you need to have it updated immediately, unless your state has enacted protective legislation to ensure that such older wills of its residents qualify for the federal unlimited marital deduction.

8.11 Targeted Jobs Tax Credit

Are you aware that if you hire members of certain economically disadvantaged groups, the federal government will pay you a subsidy of up to $2,400 in the form of tax credits per employee? Unfortunately, most employers, particularly small businesses, seem to be unaware of this substantial tax subsidy.

Part of the reason so many employers fail to take advantage of this tax incentive appears to be on account of a Catch-22 in the way the program works. To qualify for the targeted jobs tax credit for hiring a disadvantaged category person, he or she must be certified as such by a designated state employment security agency, and the certification must be received by the employer (or requested in writing) at least one day before the employee begins work.[97]

At the same time, state and federal anti-discrimination laws make it very difficult for you as an employer to ask prospective job applicants if they belong to any of the disadvantaged groups that are eligible for the targeted jobs tax credits, since to do so could be considered a discriminatory hiring practice.

Your best bet is to check first with your local state employment department or division to find out how to take advantage of state and federal job credit programs. The department will either refer you to the proper agency or organization that can assist you, or the department itself will help you find an individual who qualifies under this program and matches your specific job requirements.

The targeted group individuals for whom you can claim the jobs tax credit are:

Targeted Groups

- Vocational rehabilitation referrals — These referrals are for certain handicapped individuals who have completed rehabilitation programs. Tax credits aside, handicapped individuals often are extremely good and conscientious employees.
- Economically disadvantaged youths — These individuals are between 18 and 22 years of age and are certified as members of economically disadvantaged families.
- Economically disadvantaged Vietnam veterans.
- Supplemental Security Income (SSI) recipients — SSI recipients are people who are 65 or older, or blind, or have a disability and who don't own much or have a lot of income. SSI payments are not just for adults; they can also go to disabled and blind children.
- General assistance recipients — These persons receive state or local welfare payments.
- Economically disadvantaged ex-convicts.
- Youths participating in a cooperative education program — Youths in this category are 16–20 years of age and have not finished high school.
- Eligible work incentive program employees.
- Qualified summer youth employees — These economically disadvantaged youths are 16 or 17 years old and are hired to work between May 1 and September 15. They cannot have been previously employed by you.

On the first $6,000 you pay an eligible target group employee, you will earn tax credits of 40% of the wages. This is limited to $3,000 of wages for qualified summer youth employees during the first 90 days they work for you.

Here is how the federal targeted jobs tax credits apply for eligible and certified new employees:

Category of Employee	Federal Tax Credit	Minimum Work Period
All qualified employees as listed above	40% of wages on first $6,000 of wages or a maximum credit of $2,400 per employee	90 days or 120 hours
Qualified summer youth employees	40% of first 90 days' wages for up to $3,000 of wages or maximum credit of $1,200	14 days or 20 hours

One drawback with all of these tax credits is that you must reduce the wages you can deduct dollar-for-dollar for credits you claim.[98] That is, if you pay someone $1,000 and claim a $400 targeted jobs tax credit, you can only deduct $600 for wage expense, not the full $1,000. The credit is not allowed for wages paid to strikebreakers.

Drawbacks

The 1993 Deficit Reduction Act retroactively extended the targeted jobs credit to June 30, 1992. It will expire on December 31, 1994, unless Congress extends it again.

8.12 Hiring a Spouse as an Employee

If you run an unincorporated business and your spouse works with or for you, there are three ways your spouse can be treated for tax purposes:

- As an employee;
- As a partner in the firm; or
- As an uncompensated employee, which is probably the most common approach.

Social Security Tax

Congress, by enacting the Omnibus Budget Reconciliation Act of 1987, ended the exemption from Social Security (FICA) taxes for wages paid to a spouse, parent, or minor child — with the exception of a child under 18 years of age. There are, however, still some advantages to having your spouse be a paid employee of your proprietorship, as described below.

Individual Retirement Account for Spouse

If your spouse works for you without pay and has no other income from an outside job, the most the two of you can put into an individual retirement account (IRA) is $2,250. If you start compensating your spouse, even as little as $2,000 a year, you should each qualify for a $2,000 IRA deduction or a total of $4,000 a year, rather than only $2,250. Note that IRA deductions may be limited if either of you is an active participant in another retirement plan.

Medical Insurance

You can deduct any medical insurance premiums that you pay for employees, but you can only deduct 25% of your own medical insurance premiums. If your spouse works for you, however, you can put your spouse on the payroll and provide a medical expense reimbursement plan or medical insurance for your spouse and his or her family — which includes you — you can then deduct the payments or premiums in full since your spouse is an employee.[99] See Section 11.8 regarding state tax exemptions and other implications of hiring a spouse as an employee.

8.13 How to Save on Unemployment Taxes

The unemployment tax rate you pay as an employer is one of the few taxes where you have some control over the rate you pay. The state maintains a reserve account for each employer, in which it monitors the unemployment taxes you pay in and the unemployment benefits it pays out to your former employees. The more benefits the state pays to your former employees, the higher your individual company's tax rate will be and vice versa.

So it pays for you to have as few former employees as possible who are collecting unemployment benefits, since these are charged to your reserve account.

To succeed in keeping down the unemployment claims charged to your account, you need to challenge any former employees' claims that appear to be unjustified. Often, you will be surprised to learn that an employee you had fired for stealing or who had quit on you has filed for benefits and has lied about his or her reasons for leaving. In general, an ex-employee can't collect unemployment from you if he or she left your employment for one of these reasons:

- Refusal to work;
- Voluntarily quitting;
- Inability to continue work due to illness or injury; or
- Misconduct, such as theft, not showing up for work, or the like.

An employee who leaves your employ for virtually any other reason, such as being fired for incompetence, can generally collect benefits, which will cost you money by raising your unemployment tax rate. Here are some tips on how you can keep down the number of unemployment claims filed against your account.

Reducing Claims

- When you are hiring, be aware of the cost you may have if you lay off these people in the future. You may hire a number of new employees for an expansion or new project with the view that if things don't work out as planned, you will simply lay them off and cancel the project with no further cost. Count the cost. Remember that if you do have to lay them off, you may pay a much higher unemployment tax rate for several years.

- Document in writing your reasons for firing an employee, if for reasons such as theft, insubordination, absence, or intoxication on the job. This will buttress your argument that the fired employee is not entitled to benefits if he or she should file a claim.

- Be aware that if you change an employee's hours of work and he or she quits as a result, it will be considered involuntary dismissal and the employee will probably be eligible for benefits. So it pays to have a written agreement signed by the employee to work any shift or hours that are required, if needed. Then, if the employee quits, it will not be due to a change in job conditions in the eyes of the law.

- If you decide to fire someone for misconduct, do it on the spot. If you keep them on at your convenience until you find a replacement, it will not usually be considered a discharge for misconduct, and the fired employee will most likely be eligible for benefits.

- If new employees do not work out, consider firing them before they have worked three months. In most states, a person has to work for you at least three months before they can earn unemployment benefits that are chargeable to your reserve account.

In general, it pays to keep a close eye on your employer reserve account and be aware of who is filing benefit claims that will cost you money. Contest any claims that you feel are not legitimate.

8.14 Deductions for Office-in-the-Home Expenses

If you use part of your residence for business purposes, you may be able to deduct part of your office-in-the-home expenses; however, the rules are rather stringent, and the general rule is that office-in-the-home expenses are not deductible for tax purposes, unless you meet a number of quite technical requirements.

There are several types of situations under which you may be able to claim deductions for part of your rent or expenses related to ownership of your residence, as well as other occupancy expenses, despite the home-office deduction limitations.

Exclusive-use Tests

If you use part of your residence exclusively for business purposes and on a regular basis, you may be able to claim office-in-the-home deductions, if you also qualify under one of these tests: [100]

- You use a portion of your home as your principal place of business.
- You use your home as a place to meet clients, customers, or patients.
- Your home office is a separate structure that is not attached to your house or living quarters.

The ability to treat a home office as your "principal place of business" has been sharply limited by the U.S. Supreme Court's 1993 decision in the *Soliman* case. Under this holding, even if your home office is your *only* office, it won't qualify if it is not also your *most important* place of work. In *Soliman*, the Supreme Court disallowed home-office deductions of a physician who had no office other than a room in his home, where he kept his business records and made business-related phone calls. Most of his actual work was done at various hospitals where he performed services as an anesthesiologist.

As a result, the rule for determining whether your home office is your principal place of business now depends on two primary considerations:

- The relative importance of the activities performed at each work location; and
- The amount of time spent at each location.

Nonexclusive Uses that Qualify

Two special exceptions are made where part of a home is regularly, but not exclusively, used for business purposes.

- Storage of inventory — A wholesaler or retailer who uses part of a home to store inventory that is being held for sale; if the dwelling unit is the taxpayer's sole fixed location of the trade or business; or
- Day care facility — Part of the home is used for day care of children, physically and mentally handicapped persons, or individuals age 65 or older.

If you can show that a portion of your residence qualifies as a home office, you have cleared the first hurdle. But note that, even if you don't meet any of the above requirements, these rules will not disallow your deductions that are otherwise allowed for tax purposes, such as interest on your home mortgage, real estate taxes, or casualty losses from damage to your residence. Also, business expenses that are not home-related, such as business supplies, cost of goods sold, wages paid to business employees, and other such operating expenses, are not affected by the limitation on home office-related deductions.

If the business use of your home qualifies under one of the above tests, then you may be able to deduct part of the home office expenses that are allocable to the portion of your home that is used in your business, in addition to home mortgage interest, property taxes, and casualty losses.

For example, if 15% of your home is used exclusively and regularly as your principal place of business, you could possibly deduct up to 15% of your occupancy costs, such as gas, electricity, insurance, repairs, and similar expenses, as well as 15% of your rent or depreciation expense on 15% of the tax basis of your house. The IRS and the tax court don't agree on the deductibility of certain other types of expenses, such as lawn care.

Deductions Limited to Income

Note, however, that the amount of qualifying home office expense you can actually deduct for the year is limited to the gross income from your home business, reduced by regular operating expenses (wages, supplies, etc.) and an allocable portion (15% in the above example) of your mortgage interest, property taxes, and casualty loss deductions. If you still have net business income after taking those deductions, then you may deduct the allocable portion of your home office expenses, up to the amount of such net income.

Any portion of your home office expenses that aren't deducted due to the income limit in one year can be carried over to future years until usable, if ever. Thus, it pays to keep track of any such disallowed expenses, in case your home-based business becomes more profitable in the future, and you are then able to deduct the carried-over expenses from earlier years.

Your federal individual return, *Schedule C*, no longer asks you whether expenses for business use of a home are being deducted. Instead, you must determine a tentative profit or loss on *Schedule C*, without taking into account home use expenses. Home office expenses are now computed separately on *Form 8829*. On this form, you must compute the amount of deductible expenses for business use of the home, which (if any) can then be deducted from the net *Schedule C* income. This will make it impossible, or at least illegal, for taxpayers filing *Schedule C* to simply bury the home office expenses in with other business expenses.

Potential Tax Trap

The downside of taking home office deductions is a potential tax bite when you sell your home. For example, if 15% of your home has been used for business and you sell your home for a gain, you will have to pay tax on 15% of the gain, even if you reinvest in a new house, or even if you qualify for the once-in-a-lifetime $125,000 exclusion of gain — for persons over age 55 — when you sell the house. Thus, a few hundred dollars of home office deductions now, could later result in many thousands of dollars of tax on the "business" part of your house, if you sell it for a gain a few years down the road. For more information on the deductibility of home-office expenses, obtain IRS *Publication 587, Business Use of Your Home*.

Endnotes

1. I.R.C. § 1366(e).
2. I.R.C. § 1(g).
3. I.R.C. § 243(a).
4. I.R.C. §§ 301 and 302(d).
5. I.R.C. § 331.
6. I.R.C. § 1(h).
7. I.R.C. § 531.
8. I.R.C. § 542.
9. I.R.C. § 542(a)(1).
10. I.R.C. § 246A.
11. I.R.C. §§ 219 and 404(a).
12. I.R.C. § 501(a).
13. I.R.C. § 408(m).
14. I.R.C. §§ 105–106.
15. I.R.C. § 105(b).
16. I.R.C. § 105.
17. I.R.C. § 106.
18. I.R.C. § 104(a)(3).
19. I.R.C. § 79(a).
20. I.R.C. § 132.
21. I.R.C. § 119.
22. I.R.C. § 127.
23. I.R.C. § 129.
24. I.R.C. § 422.
25. I.R.C. § 423.
26. I.R.C. § 125.
27. I.R.C. § 245(c)(1).
28. I.R.C. §§ 991–997.
29. I.R.C. § 994(a).
30. Treas. Regs. § 1.994-1(e).
31. I.R.C. § 994(a).
32. Treas. Regs. § 1.994.
33. I.R.C. § 995(b)(1)(F)(i) (as amended by The Tax Reform Act of '86).
34. I.R.C. § 995.
35. I.R.C. § 995(f).
36. Rev. Rul. 75-430, 1975-2 C.B. 313; Rev. Rul. 76-284, 1976-2 C.B. 236.
37. Treas. Regs. § 1.991-1(a).
38. I.R.C. § 922(a)(1).
39. I.R.C. § 7872.
40. I.R.C. § 302(c)(2) permits the complete termination of the interest of a family member in a corporation by means of a stock redemption to qualify for capital gains treatment, if certain conditions are met.
41. I.R.C. § 453(g).
42. I.R.C. § 291(a).
43. I.R.C. § 274(h).
44. I.R.C. § 280A.
45. I.R.C. § 274(d).
46. I.R.C. § 274(m)(1).

47. I.R.C. §274(d).

48. I.R.C. §274(d), as amended by Pub. L. No. 99-44.

49. I.R.C. §274(a)(1)(A).

50. I.R.C. §274(e)(1). (Repealed as of 1-1-87.)

51. I.R.C. §262; Treas. Regs. §1.212-1(f).

52. I.R.C. §280F(b)(2).

53. I.R.C. §280F(d)(5)(B).

54. Rev. Proc. 92-104, 1992-2 C.B. 583.

55. I.R.C. §441(i).

56. I.R.C. §195.

57. Treas. Regs. §1.446-1(c)(2)(i).

58. I.R.C. §448.

59. I.R.C. §461(h).

60. I.R.C. §267(a)(2).

61. Treas. Regs. §1.451-3.

62. I.R.C. §460.

63. I.R.C. §56(a)(3).

64. I.R.C. §453(b).

65. I.R.C. §§453(1)(2)(B) and 453(1)(3).

66. I.R.C. §453A(b).

67. I.R.C. §453A(b)(3).

68. I.R.C. §472.

69. I.R.C. §474.

70. I.R.C. §1363(d).

71. I.R.C. §263A(b)(2)(B).

72. I.R.C. §531.

73. I.R.C. §541.

74. I.R.C. §385.

75. I.R.C. §531.

76. I.R.C. §535(c)(2).

77. I.R.C. §535(a) and (b).

78. I.R.C. §537(a).

79. I.R.C. §535(c)(2).

80. I.R.C. §531.

81. I.R.C. §537(a)(2).

82. Treas. Regs. §§1.537-1(b)(1) and 1.537-2(b)(2).

83. I.R.C. §537(b)(4).

84. Treas. Regs. §1.537-2(b)(3).

85. As defined in I.R.C. §543.

86. I.R.C. §542.

87. I.R.C. §543(a)(7).

88. I.R.C. §543(a)(6).

89. I.R.C. §541.

90. I.R.C. §543(d).

91. I.R.C. §385.

92. I.R.C. §162(a)(1).

93. I.R.C. §162(m).

94. I.R.C. §2056.

95. I.R.C. §4980A(d).

96. Economic Recovery Tax Act of 1981, Pub. L. No. 97-34, §403(e)(3).

97. I.R.C. §51.

98. I.R.C. §280C(a).

99. Rev. Rul. 71-588, 1971-2 C.B. 91.

100. I.R.C. §280A(c)(1).

Notes

Chapter 9

Miscellaneous Business Pointers

Money is not the root of all evil. The lack of money is the root of all evil.

— Reverend Ike

9.1 General Considerations

This chapter provides a number of general pointers and suggestions in connection with operating a small business, some of which may be of interest to you.

9.2 Accounting — Some Basics

Maintaining good accounting records is a must for any small business. Without accurate and up-to-date records, you will be operating your business without vitally important information. Meaningful financial statements can only be prepared if the underlying records of transactions are accurate and current.

Accounting Systems

It may help to think of your accounting system as being like an airplane's radar system. If you are not getting current and correct feedback from either system, you will not have enough time to react to prevent a potential crash.

While most schools and colleges teach only the double-entry method of bookkeeping, which provides a series of checks and balances in recording income and expenditures, some small business owners use a single-entry method of accounting.

Single-Entry Method

If you are not knowledgeable about double-entry bookkeeping and handle most of the funds directly yourself, you may find that a single-entry system is acceptable for your needs and much simpler to use. The single-entry method is only slightly more involved than keeping a checkbook record of cash income and disbursements and usually consists of three basic records:

- A daily cash receipts summary — This summary may come from a cash register tape or sales slips. It will not only give you a total of your daily cash receipts, but it will break down your sales by product, by salesperson, or by store, depending on how much detail you need.
- A monthly cash receipts summary — This is simply a monthly summary of the daily cash receipts.
- A monthly cash disbursements report — This is a report on expenses and other payments, such as debt repayments, purchases of capital assets, or distributions of profits.

A number of simplified write-it-once systems for all different kinds of businesses are available at office supply stores.

Double-Entry Method

While a single-entry system is easy to use, it is not a complete accounting system because it focuses mainly on profit and loss and does not provide a balance sheet. For all but the very smallest of businesses, a single-entry accounting system is likely to be inadequate. Even if your business is very small, but expects to grow, it is usually advisable to start out with a full set of books, using the double-entry method.

You can avoid many future problems if you get a CPA to help you set up the accounting system for your business. He or she will tailor a chart of accounts to your specific needs and build in internal controls to record all transactions and to reduce the possibilities of employee theft or embezzlement that might go undetected with a poorly designed system.

If you use a personal computer in your business, there are any number of general ledger accounting software packages you can buy if your accounting needs are fairly straightforward and if you have a reasonable understanding of how double-entry accounting works. For a very small business, there are adequate software packages available for under $100.

Accounting Firm Services

If you are going to use an outside accounting firm to prepare financial statements, they can provide three different levels of service — compilations, reviews, and audits.

Compilations

Most financial statements prepared for small businesses are compilations because they are far less expensive than an audit or review. In a compilation, the outside accountant has no obligation to do any investigation unless he or she becomes aware of something that looks suspicious or that could be misleading. Generally, all an accountant is required to do in preparing compilation statements is to take the financial data you give him or her and present it in a manner that conforms with generally accepted accounting principles (GAAP).

In a compilation, the accountant expresses no opinion on the accuracy of the information presented. The accountant is simply taking what you gave him or her and putting it in a proper financial statement format. It is important for you to remember that regardless of what type of assurance your accountant expresses, you are ultimately the one responsible for ensuring your financial statements are prepared accurately.

Reviews

A review involves some limited analysis or testing of the financial records, but the certified public accountant (CPA) expresses only a very limited opinion as to the accuracy of the information in the financial statements. A review is somewhat less expensive than an audit but more expensive than a compilation. Most small businesses hire a CPA firm to do a review only if their bankers or other lenders or financial backers insist on a review rather than a compilation.

Audits

An audit is invariably the most involved and most expensive level of service in connection with financial statements. An accounting firm that audits financial statements must not only verify that your financial statements are presented fairly and in accordance with GAAP, but it also checks and verifies some or all of the accounts to satisfy itself that they are real.

To verify accounts, an accounting firm can request confirmations of bank accounts or receivable and payable account balances from banks, customers, and vendors to uncover possible errors or fraud in recordkeeping. Because audits are relatively expensive, many small businesses elect to have review or compilation statements done; however, lenders or bonding companies often insist that you have a certified audit.

Depreciation

The Tax Reform Act of 1986 effectively repealed the highly favorable accelerated cost recovery system (ACRS) tax depreciation system that was in force from 1981 until the end of 1986. In January 1987, taxpayers learned to live with another whole new complex system of depreciation. Unfortunately, it is still necessary to know the former ACRS rules for assets acquired during the 1981–86 period, as well as the old depreciation rules for items acquired before 1981, to compute current depreciation on those assets.

The Modified ACRS System

The modified ACRS (MACRS) law from 1986 does not provide depreciation tables, unlike the previous ACRS system. Instead, all assets (with a few special exceptions) placed in service after 1986 are assigned to 3-, 5-, 7-, 10-, 15-, or 20-year recovery period categories, except for real estate, which must be depreciated over 39 years — 27.5 years for residential rental property.[1]

Under the MACRS system, most personal property is depreciated under the 200% declining balance method over a specified number of years (called a recovery period). The only exceptions are for 15- or 20-year property, for which the 150% declining balance method is used. Real estate may only be depreciated under the straight-line method.

Assets other than real estate are mostly assigned to the various recovery periods that vary from industry to industry and are far too voluminous and technical to reproduce in a book of this nature. MACRS, however, specifically assigns some types of assets to recovery classes. For example, autos and light trucks are five-year property. The MACRS provisions have also reduced the maximum annual depreciation deductions on luxury automobiles as discussed in Section 8.6.

One small ray of sunshine in the MACRS tax depreciation nightmare is a liberalization of the former $10,000 first-year expending election for tangible personal property. You may elect to expense up to $17,500 in cost of furniture and equipment in the year such assets are placed in service.[2] For example, if the only depreciable items you buy in 1994 are $15,000 of office equipment, you may be able to deduct the full $15,000 in 1994. Note, however, that this special deduction is not allowed to the extent that it would create a loss for your trade(s) or business(es) for the year. Also, the deduction is phased out if you acquire more than $200,000 of eligible property during the tax year.

Internal Accounting Controls

Poor internal accounting controls and recordkeeping procedures are a weakness for many small business owners. Lax procedures are frequently to blame when a secretary or bookkeeper departs for Brazil with thousands of dollars of stolen or embezzled funds belonging to his or her employer. Ideally, you would consult a good accountant to set up and review your internal financial controls; however, that will cost you a good deal of money, so before you do so, you may want to do your own review of your internal controls, utilizing the checklist located at the end of this chapter.

9.3 Cash-flow Management

Cash flow is the lifeblood of any business organization; yet, often small business operators are so concerned with other matters, they don't pay attention to managing their cash resources properly. Good cash management can make a significant contribution to the competitiveness and profitability of your business. Poor cash management is one of the main causes of business failures, particularly among smaller firms, since a cash shortage due to poor planning can set off a chain reaction of disastrous consequences, even in a profitable business.

Cash-flow management has two aspects: 1) projecting future cash flow, and 2) controlling and maximizing the cash available from operations at all times.

Projecting Cash Flow

Perhaps the most important part of cash-flow management is accurately projecting your business' near- and long-term cash needs and making your business decisions reflect those needs. Often, to project what your sales will be in coming months, it will be necessary to rely on what has happened in the past — what percentage will be credit sales and when your receivables are likely to be collected.

Similarly, you have to estimate and project what you will have to pay out in the way of payroll, rent, taxes, servicing debts, purchasing inventory, and paying off existing payables, plus extraordinary outlays you can anticipate.

The purpose of making these detailed projections of expected cash inflows and outflows is to point out any future cash shortages or deficits, so you can take steps in advance to prevent such occurrences. For example, if your projections indicated you were going to experience a severe cash crunch in about three months, you might take any of a number of steps to avert it, such as:

- Seeking to raise new capital;
- Borrowing money;
- Liquidating some of your inventory by cutting prices; or
- Cutting back on planned expenditures.

If you have a computer, microcomputer models are available to assist you in preparing projections of cash flows. If you don't own a computer, your accountant may have such models available to assist you.

Controlling and Maximizing Cash Flow

If you are able to increase available cash by speeding up collections, delaying payments, or by other means, you can use the extra cash to reduce your borrowings — thus saving interest expenses — or you can invest the surplus cash to earn interest. Either way, improving your cash flow should increase your net earnings and should also help you avert cash shortages.

Here are some basic ways to improve your business' cash flow.

- Bill your customers promptly. The later they receive the bill, the later you will usually collect for a particular sale.
- If you know that certain large customers must receive bills by certain days of the month so you can get paid in that month, try to bill them before those deadlines.
- Deposit your cash receipts daily, if possible.
- Keep close tabs on credit customers. Send them past due notices as soon as payments become overdue.

- If you can do so without hurting business, add late charges to overdue accounts.
- Never pay bills until just before they become due, unless there is a worthwhile discount for quick payment.
- Try to keep inventories as lean as possible. Even if you occasionally lose a small sale because you are temporarily out of an item, you should be far ahead of the game by substantially reducing the amount of cash you have tied up in inventory.
- Look for items in your inventory that are moving slowly or not at all. Consider slashing the price on those articles to convert them to cash and also to reduce the cost of storing them or having them take up valuable shelf space.
- Consider leasing equipment items instead of buying.
- Do not pay more on your estimated income taxes than you have to. You may qualify — without incurring interest charges or late payment penalties — under one or more exceptions that will allow you to delay paying much of your tax for the year until the tax return is due. If you realize that you have already overpaid your corporate estimated tax for the year, there is a procedure for obtaining a refund prior to the time when you can file a return.[3]
- If your business has a net operating loss for tax purposes that can be carried back to prior years, a procedure exists for filing a claim for a quick refund of the prior years' taxes. File it as early as you can because the IRS no longer pays interest on these refunds.
- Instead of keeping all your business cash in a local bank account, consider putting a significant portion of your cash in an out-of-town money market-type fund that pays interest and allows you to write checks against the account. Since you continue to earn interest on funds on deposit until the checks clear, consider using a fund in a distant part of the country, since it will take longer for your checks to clear when you make payments to local firms.

9.4 Protecting Your Assets

Starting a new business is almost always a risky proposition, and if the business fails, you may be forced into bankruptcy and could lose everything except what the bankruptcy laws allow you to keep. This is one reason why many small businesses incorporate at the outset, since a corporation will generally limit your liability to business creditors to the amount you invest in the corporation, plus any loans to the corporation you guarantee.

Accordingly, if you incorporate, be cautious about committing too much of your personal assets to the business. For example, instead of putting a building or piece of land you own into the corporation, it may be better —

and may save income and property taxes — for you to keep the property and lease it to the corporation. Even if you incorporate, the leases or bank loans you find it necessary to guarantee on behalf of the corporation could still wipe out your personal assets if the business folds. Thus, it often makes sense to have your corporation set up a tax-qualified pension or profit-sharing plan and to have it contribute as much as possible to the plan on your behalf. Not only does this provide substantial tax savings and deferral, but the law in most states will in many cases protect your account under such a plan from your creditors or the corporation's creditors.

So, if you can build up a significant retirement fund in your corporation's pension plan, you have at least some degree of assurance that the failure of the business or a disastrous lawsuit will not touch that nest egg. In a divorce, however, your spouse may be able to claim his or her share of the pension plan account.

9.5 Protecting Trade Names and Trademarks

If you intend to use some type of distinctive trade name for your business or trademark for your product or in advertising your services, consider taking steps to protect the use of the name or mark by registering it under state or federal law, or both. When considering your trade name or trademark, it may be necessary to perform a search, which can be expensive, to determine whether someone else has already registered the same or a very similar name or symbol. You do not want to open yourself up to a lawsuit for infringement. Since not every trade name can be registered, you will need to consult a trademark attorney if you are interested in protecting a particular name used by your business.

Federal registration of a name confers a number of significant benefits to registering your trade name or trademark, including:

Advantages to Trade Name or Trademark Registration

- Nationwide notice to others of your exclusive right to use the name or mark.
- Prima facie evidence of the validity of the registration and your exclusive right to use the mark throughout the country.
- With certain exceptions, registration gives you an unquestionable right to use the name or mark.
- If you prove in court that someone violated your rights under the Trademark Act of 1946,[4] you will be entitled to recover their profits and damages from its use.
- The right to sue in federal court for trademark infringement regardless of the amount at stake and whether or not there is diversity of citizenship — that is, regardless of whether you and the defendant operate in the same or different states.

■ The right to have customs officials halt importation of counterfeit goods using your trademark.

Federal registration is permitted only if you will use the trade name or trademark in more than one state.

9.6 Section 1244 Stock

If you invest directly in a small corporation by transferring money or property (other than securities) to the corporation in exchange for its common stock — or preferred stock, if issued after July 18, 1984 — the stock will usually qualify as Section 1244 stock.[5] If it does, and the stock later becomes worthless or you sell it at a loss, Section 1244 of the Internal Revenue Code permits you to deduct up to $50,000 of your loss — $100,000 for a couple filing a joint return — as an ordinary deduction instead of as a capital loss for that year. This can be very important, since you can fully deduct an ordinary loss from your taxable income, while capital losses can only be used to offset capital gains, if you have any, or $3,000 of ordinary income per year until your capital losses are used up.[6] The $50,000/$100,000 limit on the amount of loss that can qualify for ordinary loss treatment is an annual limitation.

Any stock issued by a small business corporation will generally qualify as Section 1244 stock unless the corporation obtained half or more of its gross receipts from passive kinds of income, such as interest, dividends, and the like, in the five years before your loss is incurred.[7] A corporation qualifies as a small business corporation if the total invested in its stock is one million dollars or less.[8]

If the stock issued by your corporation meets the requirements of Section 1244, it will automatically qualify for ordinary loss treatment, up to the first one million dollars of stock issued. You should be aware, however, that capital contributions you make, where no stock is received by you for such money, will not qualify for ordinary loss treatment.[9]

See Section 11.9 as to whether state law also provides favorable tax treatment for losses on stock in a small business corporation.

9.7 U.S. Small Business Administration and Other Government Loans

If you need to borrow money for your business and cannot obtain regular bank financing, don't overlook the possibility of obtaining a loan through the U.S. Small Business Administration (SBA). Many small business owners are under the impression that it is virtually impossible to obtain an SBA loan unless a member of a minority group; this is not the case. Although the SBA does make special efforts to provide financing for minority-owned businesses, only a relatively small percentage of SBA loans are made to minority firms. Furthermore, a very high percentage of applications for SBA loans are approved when applications are properly submitted.

SBA Loan Programs

The SBA, an agency of the U.S. government, guarantees intermediate and long-term loans to small firms, and to a limited extent, also makes direct loans to some small businesses. The SBA is not allowed to grant such financial assistance unless the borrower is unable to obtain private-sector financing on reasonable terms. The SBA does not compete with banks or other lenders; instead, it works with private lenders to assure availability of capital to potentially profitable small firms. Contrary to what you may have heard on late-night television infomercials, the SBA does *not* have a grant program for starting a small business.

For your firm to qualify for SBA financial assistance, it must come within the current definition of a "small business." In general, these are the types of small businesses eligible for SBA financing:

- Manufacturers with a maximum of 500 to 1,500 employees, depending upon the industry in which the applicant is engaged;
- Retailers with less than $3.5 million in annual sales — up to $13.5 million for some types of retailers;
- Wholesaling firms with 100 or fewer employees;
- General construction firms, whose annual sales have averaged less than $9.5 million for the last three fiscal years; lower limits apply to various special trade construction firms;
- Service firms with annual receipts not in excess of $3.5 to $14.5 million, depending on the industry; and
- Other definitions apply for businesses engaged in activities, such as agriculture and transportation.

Private lenders that are eligible to make SBA-guaranteed loans or participate in SBA financing packages include banks, savings and loans, and certain other lenders. The SBA has several types of loan programs for small businesses.

Guaranteed Loans

Most SBA financing actually consists of loans by banks or other lenders that are guaranteed by the SBA. This enables the small business to obtain such loans at reasonable interest rates because the bank's risk is largely eliminated.

As the borrower, you put up a reasonable amount of equity or collateral. These loans are usually secured by fixed assets, real estate, and inventory and are limited in term to 7 years for working capital loans or 10 years for purchasing fixed assets. Construction loans can be for as long as 25 years.

Under this program, the bank or other private lender deals with the SBA, and you deal with the bank, not the SBA. You will, however, need to do the following in applying for such a loan or any other SBA financing:

- Define the amount you need to borrow and the purposes for which the funds will be used.
- Describe the collateral you will offer as security.
- Determine from a bank that a conventional loan is not available.
- Prepare current financial statements, preferably with your accountant's assistance. These would include, at a minimum, a relatively current balance sheet and an income statement for the previous full year and for the current year up to the date of the balance sheet.
- Prepare personal financial statements of the owners, partners, or stock-holders owning more than 20% of the stock of the company.

Direct Loans

If you are unable to obtain sufficient conventional financing or SBA guaranteed loan funds, you may in some cases be able to obtain a direct loan from the SBA of up to $150,000.

These direct loans are hard to get and can only be made if the SBA has funds available. When made, these loans are usually offered on a participation basis with a bank or other lender, where the bank oversees the loan payments and loan servicing on behalf of itself and the SBA.

Other SBA Programs

New legislation frequently adds to and modifies the number and scope of SBA loan programs. Other such programs include:

- Seasonal lines of credit;
- Economic opportunity loans for entrepreneurs who are physically handicapped or members of a minority group;
- Short-term contract loan guarantees;
- Energy loans to small firms to install, sell, service, develop, or manufacture solar energy or energy-saving devices; and
- Disaster recovery loans to firms harmed by natural disasters.

Since the nature, scope, and availability of funds under these numerous programs are constantly changing, consult your bank or local SBA offices if you think your firm may qualify under one of these special financial assistance programs.

U.S. Department of Housing and Urban Development

The U.S. Department of Housing and Urban Development (HUD) makes Urban Development Action Grants (UDAG) to cities in economically distressed areas. The cities are then able to use these UDAG funds to make second-mortgage loans to private developers who are able to leverage these loans by borrowing at least five times such amounts — three times in small towns — from private sources. The purpose of such loans is to encourage new investment and development in depressed areas.

The Economic Development Administration (EDA) of the U.S. Department of Commerce makes direct loans and offers loan guarantees to businesses in areas with low family incomes or areas suffering from high unemployment. The purpose of these loans is to promote creation or retention of jobs for the residents living in these areas.

To qualify for this financing, your business must be located in an EDA redevelopment area and you need to demonstrate that the venture will directly benefit local residents and will not create local over-capacity for the industry in question. Application for EDA loan assistance is a long and complex process, taking much longer for processing than typical SBA loans.

U.S. Department of Commerce

The Farmers Home Administration (FmHA) can perhaps be thought of as an SBA for rural areas. It offers insured and guaranteed loans to develop business and industry in nonurban areas with populations of under 50,000. Like the SBA program, FmHA loan guarantees are for up to 90% of the total amount of the loan and are made for up to 30 years for financing real estate acquisition, 15 years for machinery and equipment, and 7 years for working capital. FmHA loan guarantees are not available for agricultural production.

Unlike SBA loan guarantees, there is no dollar limit on FmHA loan guarantees, nor does the FmHA make direct loans. Applicants for FmHA loan guarantees must not only have adequate collateral and good business histories, they must also demonstrate that the project will have a favorable economic impact and will create new jobs in the area — not merely shifting business activity and jobs from one area to another. Preference is given:

Farmers Home Administration

- To businesses who are expanding rather than transferring into an area;
- To projects in open country areas or towns with populations of under 25,000; and
- To business owners who are military veterans.

Other major federal loan programs are provided through the Federal Land Bank Association, Production Credit Association, and the Federal Intermediate Credit Bank. These organizations offer loans to businesses that provide services to farmers. These loans can be for purchasing land and equipment and for obtaining start-up working capital.

Other Federal Loan Programs

In addition to direct loans and guarantees from government agencies, don't overlook possible loans or equity financing from Small Business Investment Companies (SBICs) and Minority Enterprise Small Business Investment Companies (MESBICs). Both are licensed and regulated by the SBA to provide equity capital, long-term loans, and management assistance to small businesses.

SBICs and MESBICs

SBIC and MESBIC loans are usually subordinated to loans from other creditors and are typically made for five- to seven-year terms. Both types of investment companies are privately owned and thus tend to favor loans to established companies with significant net worth rather than new business start ups.

You may have to give up a large part of the equity in your business if you obtain SBIC financing. An SBIC is not permitted to control a company (50% or greater ownership) it lends to, but typically an SBIC lender will insist on debt that is convertible into common stock, warrants, and options, which may give it up to 49% ownership in your company. An SBIC will also want seats on your board of directors, will impose controls and restrictions on the way your business operates, and may insist upon salary limits for the principal owners. SBIC financing does not come without a price.

MESBICs serve only those small firms that are owned by members of economically or socially disadvantaged minority groups.

Business Development Corporations

Business Development Corporations are Local Development Companies (LDCs) and Certified Development Companies (CDCs) organized by local residents to promote economic development in their particular communities. These entities do not make working capital loans or loans to purchase free-standing equipment.

Instead, LDCs or CDCs will arrange for SBA-guaranteed bank loans and sale of SBA-guaranteed debentures for up to 90% financing for 25 years for land acquisition, building construction, or renovation and purchase of fixed assets, such as machinery and equipment.

For information on what state business loan programs may be available in this state, refer to Section 11.9.

9.8 Mail Order Sales

If your business involves selling goods by mail order, become familiar with Rule 435.1, a regulation issued by the Federal Trade Commission (FTC).[10] This federal regulation requires any business soliciting mail order sales to be prepared to ship the merchandise within 30 days after an order is received, unless it has clearly stated in its solicitation that orders will not be shipped for a longer period. Otherwise, the solicitation will be considered as an unfair and deceptive trade practice.

In addition, if you receive an order and for some reason you cannot ship it within 30 days, or the period stated in your solicitation, you must:

- Immediately notify the customer and offer to either cancel the order and receive a refund or consent to the delay in shipment.

- Indicate when you will be able to ship or that you do not know when you will be able to ship the order.
- Provide other required information to the customer, which will vary in content depending upon when you expect to be able to ship.

If you are going into the mail order business and want a single source of information on state and federal mail order laws, obtain the *Mail Order Legal Guide*, by Erwin J. Keup, from your book source or:

The Oasis Press
(800) 228-2275

Rule 435.1 is fairly complex and difficult to understand, but you need to understand and be familiar with it if you sell goods by mail order. For a free guide on this FTC rule, contact the FTC at the number listed below and request *A Business Guide to the Federal Trade Commission's Mail Order Rule*.

Federal Trade Commission
(202) 326-2222

State Sales and Use Taxes

If you sell across state lines to customers in states where you have no offices, employees, or other presence, the sale is usually not subject to sales tax in either state, since it is an interstate sale; however, technically, such sales are subject to use tax in the customer's state. A use tax is sort of a shadow of the sales tax and, in most states, applies where the sales tax doesn't.

The U.S. Supreme Court and other courts generally have not supported attempts of the various states to force out-of-state retailers to collect use tax on mail order or other sales made to residents of the taxing state, so that most mail order firms tend to treat such interstate sales as being tax-free, or tell the customers that it is up to them to report the purchase and pay the use tax, which they rarely do.

Unfortunately, in the last few years, many states have enacted new and broader sales and use tax laws. Many of these laws require out-of-state retailers, who advertise in the local media or send substantial amounts of direct mail/catalog solicitations into the state, to register as retailers subject to sales or use tax in the state and to treat such direct sales as taxable. The U.S. Supreme Court has finally ruled that these aggressive new sales tax laws are unconstitutional in the 1992 case of *Quill Corporation v. North Dakota*. Thus, it appears most of the broad new mail order sales and use tax laws — which have been adopted in some 34 states and are targeted to hit out-of-state mail order firms — may be invalid. While this is good news for mail order retailers, the bad news is the court also indicated in its decision that Congress could, if it chose to do so, constitutionally enact legislation that would permit the states to require use tax collection on mail order and similar sales by out-of-state retailers. Expect a real battle if such a bill is introduced in Congress, which seems likely.

9.9 Environmental Laws Affecting Your Business

As the world becomes more crowded and as the damaging effects of two centuries of unrestrained industrial development becomes more apparent on the environment, political attempts to remedy these problems, particularly the problems of pollution and toxic emissions, have resulted in a flood of legislation, regulations, and litigation involving environmental matters. While this is probably all to the good in the larger sense, some of the immediate effects of these new environmental restrictions have been to create another whole layer of complex and often conflicting government regulations on business, plus a virtual minefield of legal exposure for companies of all sizes.

For small businesses, most of which do not have in-house legal staffs and can hardly afford the large legal fees needed for professional guidance through this maze of regulations, the effect of the growing body of environmental laws is especially harsh. Small businesses are also disproportionately affected by the heavy costs of complying with various mandated emissions requirements, which often require large capital expenditures for sophisticated new pollution control equipment.

While this section cannot do much more than scratch the surface of the environmental law exposure and increased operational complexities most firms are going to face, the discussion below explains some of the main problem areas you need to be at least passingly familiar with. This section also provides a capsule description of the major areas of federal environmental law that may currently apply to your business or which may apply at some time in the future.

Environmental Clean-up Laws

Perhaps the most pervasive of the environmental laws, with the most devastating potential consequences for the unwary, are the environmental clean-up laws, and the legal liability these laws attach to real estate that has been contaminated by hazardous substances. The main laws that apply in this area are the Comprehensive Environmental Response, Compensation and Liability Act[11] (CERCLA or the Superfund law) and the Resource Conservation and Recovery Act (RCRA).[12]

CERCLA and RCRA apply to virtually every real estate transaction. While RCRA applies primarily to currently generated hazardous waste, including limits on creation of waste and requirements for disposing of it, CERCLA is more focused on cleaning up hazardous substances that have been spilled or dumped in the past.

CERCLA Liability

CERCLA deals with all kinds of pollution: air, surface water, groundwater, and soil. It covers virtually every type of hazardous substances as defined under CERCLA, the Clean Water Act, the Clean Air Act, or the Toxic Substances Control Act. There are, however, major exceptions for petroleum and certain petroleum derivatives. The main thrust of CERCLA is to impose liability on private owners of property to clean up hazardous wastes they have created. CERCLA would also apply to owners of the inherited property, if the property in question was already contaminated when it was acquired.

In short, even if you were not responsible for creating a contamination problem, if you acquire real estate that is already contaminated — and it later becomes apparent there has been a spill or dumping that requires an environmental cleanup, possibly at astronomical cost — you are liable for the costs of the cleanup, if you are the current owner. You can't simply walk away from the property and let the government take it in lieu of paying the clean-up costs.

Once the owner, you are the responsible party and may be held liable for costs that exceed the value of the property many times over. You may even become liable somewhere down the road if you sell a business — an existing corporation, for instance — that has formerly owned contaminated property. The government could eventually institute environmental proceedings against the current property owner, who then sues all the prior legal owners of the property, including you, for indemnity or reimbursement.

Of course, you may be able to sue the prior owner or anyone in the chain of prior owners for indemnification, if they are still in existence and can be found. However, since that is a pretty slim thread upon which to hang your financial survival, you need to take precautions up front, before acquiring any real property, to protect yourself from possible environmental liability for cleanup under CERCLA.

The following are some things you can and should do to reduce your risk in any real estate or existing business acquisition:

- Exercise considerable diligence concerning the current condition and past uses of any real estate involved in a transaction. Also, if buying an existing corporation, you need to find out what properties it owned in the past and be concerned whether any such properties may have been contaminated by hazardous substances.

- Be particularly wary of any sites that have been used as gas stations, landfill areas, locations of dry cleaners, chemical or other industrial production processes, battery production, recycling, or metal plating. Be extremely cautious if the site contains underground storage tanks.

- Consider retaining an environmental audit firm to do detailed site inspections and evaluations to determine if there may be a contamination problem.

- In a business or real estate purchase agreement, require written representations and warranties about the site from the seller and include provisions under which he or she will indemnify you if there is a problem. Be mindful of the seller's financial viability, in case you should be forced to seek indemnity from him or her. A promise isn't worth the paper it is written on, if the seller doesn't have the wherewithal to make good on it.

Even though under the Superfund law there is an innocent purchaser defense, you must be able to demonstrate that you made appropriate inquiry before acquiring the property to determine any pre-existing contamination problem. There is little guidance in the law at this point as to what constitutes an appropriate inquiry, so perhaps you should not expect to escape liability under that rule. The best defense is to avoid purchasing property that is contaminated by taking the steps outlined above. Even if such steps fail to discover a lurking environmental problem, at least you will have a much stronger argument to make under the innocent purchaser defense if you have done a due-diligence survey and had an environmental audit performed by a reputable firm.

RCRA Requirements

RCRA contains a comprehensive set of rules for managing hazardous wastes, including petroleum-based substances, and regulating those who generate hazardous wastes, transport them, and store, treat, or dispose of them. Penalties for violations include fines of up to $25,000 a day, plus imprisonment.

One important focus of RCRA is on underground storage tanks (USTs), many of which are known to be leaking gasoline or other contaminants into the surrounding soil and groundwater. Under RCRA, much of the regulation of USTs is left to state governments. Thus, under federal regulations, the owner of a UST must notify the state of the tank's existence, including tanks that were taken out of service after January 1, 1974.[13]

New USTs must satisfy federal performance standards, which generally require that they be constructed of fiberglass-reinforced plastic or steel that is cathodically protected from corrosion.[14] Furthermore, all existing USTs must be upgraded to federal standards by December 22, 1998,[15] which will result in some major expenditures for many small businesses, such as service stations.

Clean Water Act

Under the Clean Water Act, the federal Environmental Protection Agency (EPA) and individual states are the watchdogs of water pollution standards.[16] It also allows private citizens to sue to enforce the act. Penalties for violations can be as high as $50,000 a day, and even negligent, but unintentional, violations can result in imprisonment. For certain existing facilities, this law provides for a system of EPA permits for discharging certain amounts of water pollutants.

Wetlands Development

Portions of the Clean Water Act require that all proposed development activities, which involve the dredging or filling of wetlands, obtain permits from the U.S. Army Corps of Engineers.[17] Thus, before you acquire real property that you plan to develop in any way, you need to do a careful survey to determine if the property lies within an area that is considered to be a wetland. Otherwise, you may end up with a piece of property which is undevelopable and which can hardly be sold at all, even for a huge loss.

This has been a trap for more than one unwitting buyer of land in wet-lands districts, since wetlands include much more than swamps and marshes. Many dry-looking parcels may also fall within the regulatory definition. Furthermore, be aware that many states have adopted wet-lands restrictions, which may require you to also obtain state develop-ment permits.

Clean Air Act

The Clean Air Act of 1970, which was substantially amended and streng-thened by the Clean Air Act of 1991, among other things, restricts the ability of stationary sources of air pollutants to emit various pollutants into the atmosphere at new or modified facilities.[18] States are allowed to implement their own rules for controlling air pollution levels. The Clean Air Act of 1991 has greatly expanded the impact on small businesses. As this act's amendments go into effect, they will require a diverse number of air pollution controls. Some will include:

- Gasoline stations will need vapor-recovery devices on gasoline pumps.
- Furniture makers may need incinerators to burn off hydrocarbons released from spray-paint booths.
- Restaurants in smoggy areas will have to install containment units that collect hydrocarbon emissions from charcoal grills.
- Many bakeries will have to install oxidation devices or catalytic con-verters to neutralize the gases produced by fermenting yeast when dough is baked.
- Auto-body paint and repair shops will have to install extremely expen-sive equipment to catch hydrocarbon emissions from spray painting.
- Print shops will have to neutralize or eliminate use of chemicals that contribute to ozone formation.

As the above examples indicate, the requirements under the Clean Air Act of 1991 are very pervasive and will affect many nonindustrial types of businesses who would never have considered themselves to be pol-luters in the past. Companies that are sources of air pollutant emissions will have to obtain state-issued construction and operating permits under EPA rules. Small businesses will have to apply for permits at least every five years and file reports of their compliance with the law every six months, if they produce more than 100 tons per year of any ozone-forming pollutant. Ozone-forming pollutants are the main targets of the act.

According to some experts, once these rules go into effect, a small busi-ness' main cost of complying with the clean air regulations is likely to be all the required paperwork. Penalties for violations are also very severe, with civil penalties as high as $25,000 a day for each violation, plus felony imprisonment and huge fines for willful or negligent releases of hazardous air pollutants. In addition, the EPA has set emissions fees of $25 a ton for every ton of regulated pollutants that a firm emits, up to $4,000 per year.

Toxic Substances Control Act

If your business is one that engages in the manufacturing, processing, or distribution of chemical substances, you may be required under the federal Toxic Substances Control Act (TSCA) to report certain information to the EPA regarding the chemical substances and mixtures you use.[19] The TSCA requires manufacturers to give a 90-day notification before producing a new chemical substance and, in some cases, for older chemicals. The EPA may require safety testing before approval of such a chemical. The TSCA also has extensive recordkeeping rules regarding use and disposal of toxic chemicals.

There are severe penalties for failing to make the required reports to the EPA, including civil and criminal penalties of $25,000 and up, plus up to a year's imprisonment for each violation. Each day the violation continues is considered a separate violation for purposes of the fines levied under the TSCA.

Pesticide Regulations

The Federal Insecticide, Fungicide and Rodenticide Act (FIFRA),which amends the Federal Environmental Pesticides Control Act of 1972 (FEPCA), regulates both the manufacture and distribution of pesticides.[20]

Environmental Impact Statements

The National Environmental Policy Act of 1969 (NEPA) requires an environmental impact statement (EIS) to be prepared with respect to major federal actions that significantly affect the quality of the human environment.[21] While this would not, at first impression, seem to directly affect you, as a small business owner, the EIS requirement also applies in any situation where a federal agency approves some action by other persons, such as a private company.

In addition, many states have adopted similar EIS requirements; for instance, when a local planning board approves a real estate development, an EIS may be required under state law, if not federal.

Asbestos Regulation

As lung disease, cancer, and other health risks attributed to the exposure to asbestos have come to light, a number of state and federal laws have been enacted to deal with this problem. In addition, huge numbers of individual damage suits for alleged harm to individuals, who were exposed to asbestos in the workplace and elsewhere, have resulted in enormous judgments against many companies, even forcing a giant building materials firm, Johns-Manville Corporation, into Chapter 11 bankruptcy to protect itself from a host of asbestos-related lawsuits.

Federal amendments to the TSCA and the Asbestos Hazard Emergency Response Act of 1986 (AHERA) have given the EPA power to issue regulations regarding asbestos in school buildings. In addition, Occupational Safety and Health Administration (OSHA) regulations have been issued to limit asbestos exposure in the workplace and to set construction standards regarding use of asbestos.[22]

Both OSHA and the EPA have issued regulations on noise emission standards, ranging from aircraft noise to protections of workers from hearing impairment in the workplace.

Noise Control

9.10 Consumer Credit Laws and Regulations

Many of the largest and most successful companies in America have gotten where they are, in part, by providing consumer credit to persons who buy their products. Classic examples would include such giant companies as Sears and General Motors, although countless smaller companies have also found that financing their customers' purchases can be a major boon to sales and that the interest earned on such credit can also become an important profit center in its own right.

The definition of consumer credit does not refer to the practice of allowing a client or customer to charge it and pay you at the end of the month, which is largely unregulated by the government. Instead, the following discussion deals with the situation where your business extends credit and charges interest during the period over which the loan amount (or amount financed) is being paid off by the customer.

The three main areas of the law regulating the extension of consumer credit, which affects nearly all businesses that grant such credit, are the federal Equal Credit Opportunity Act, the federal Truth-in-Lending Act, and state laws that prohibit usury.

If your business is engaged in providing consumer credit, you will most likely be subject to the provisions of the federal Equal Credit Opportunity Act (ECOA).[23] In general, the ECOA prohibits discrimination in credit transactions on the basis of race, color, religion, national origin, sex, age, or marital status.

Equal Credit Opportunity Act

The basic principle of this law is that each person applying for credit must be considered as an individual. This means, primarily, that there are very strict limits regarding what you may ask about marital status and about the spouse of the applicant. You may ask about marital status, but only to determine what rights and remedies you might have as a creditor — such as in a community property state — to refuse an applicant's credit.

The ECOA also forbids discrimination in providing credit because some or all of the applicant's income derives from public assistance programs, or because a person exercised a right, in good faith, under the Consumer Credit Protection Act.

If your business activities involve lending money, or if you sell to consumers on credit terms, you may have to comply with the federal

Truth-In-Lending Act

Truth-in-Lending Act and state laws such as those that prohibit the charging of usurious interest rates on loans or other credit transactions.[24]

Regulations under the Truth-in-Lending Simplification and Reform Act provide that a business is not subject to the truth-in-lending rules unless it extended consumer credit at least 25 times in either the previous year or the current calendar year.[25] For loan transactions, required disclosures include:

- The annual percentage rate of interest;
- When the finance charge begins to accrue;
- The total amount of the finance charge;
- The number of payments to be made and the dollar amount of each payment;
- When payments are to be made;
- The total dollar amount of all payments;
- How any prepayment penalty and any late charges are to be computed;
- The amount of any prepaid finance charges and any deposit, plus the sum of the two;
- The amount financed;
- The existence of any balloon payment and its dollar amount;
- Annual statements of billing rights;
- Other information regarding security interests and rights to rescind; and
- Periodic billings to credit customers must include a number of disclosures regarding outstanding balances, how finance charges have been computed, and other items.

The rules regarding the Truth-in-Lending Act are far too complex to cover satisfactorily in a book of this nature; it can only alert you to the possibility that you may be required to comply with those rules and give you some sense of what will be required if the rules do apply to you. If you plan to extend credit to consumers — other than sending out bills requesting payment in full, without interest charge, after you have provided goods or services — you need to consult an attorney experienced in this area.

Fortunately, legislation has considerably simplified the truth-in-lending rules, and the Federal Reserve Board has published model disclosure statements and billing rights statements that can be used to satisfy the requirements of the truth-in-lending regulations.

Cash Discount Act

The Cash Discount Act permits sellers to offer a discount of any amount to customers who pay in cash or by check without running afoul of the truth-in-lending rules. The discount, in this case, has to be clearly disclosed and made available to all customers.[26] In the past, if you offered more than a 5% cash discount, you were considered to be imposing a finance charge on credit customers and had to give them all the required truth-in-lending disclosures.

See Section 11.9 for a brief description of how this state's usury laws may apply to your business. **Usury Laws**

9.11 Employee or Independent Contractor?

As was pointed out in Section 5.2, there are some major advantages in hiring independent contractors rather than employees to work in your business. Not only do you gain considerable payroll tax savings by retaining independent contractors, but there are far fewer administrative headaches.

Unfortunately, just because you hire someone and you agree that he or she will be an independent contractor, it does not necessarily make it so for tax and legal purposes. So before you hire anyone to work for you as an independent contractor, you need to take a hard look at whether the IRS or a court of law would consider that person to be your employee rather than an independent contractor. While the IRS uses a 20-factor test to evaluate whether a person is or is not an employee, a few major warning flags will indicate to you whether or not the person is your employee. These include:

- The person works mostly or only for your firm. That is, the person is not like a lawyer, for example, who has a number of clients besides you that he or she works for.
- The worker is subject to your control, and you have the right to direct how the work is done, not just to demand a particular result.
- The person works in your office or establishment and does not have his or her own place of business, business cards, business name, etc.
- The kind of work the person does for you is normally done by employees, such as secretarial work.
- The person is not a licensed professional of any type.

Unless you are quite clear that the work relationship will not be considered that of employer/employee, be very careful about hiring someone as a so-called independent contractor. The consequences of being wrong can be severe. Here are just a few of the things that can happen if your independent contractor is determined to be an employee:

- You are liable for not only the employer payroll taxes you failed to pay, but also for a portion of the employee taxes you failed to withhold, for example, income taxes and FICA tax.
- If you treat someone as an independent contractor, report payments of $600 or more a year to that person on IRS *Form 1099-MISC*. If you do, and the IRS later determines the person was really an employee, the back taxes you are liable for are limited to the employer payroll taxes, 20% of the employee's FICA tax you failed to withhold, and income tax withholding equal to only 1.5% of the wages you paid the person.

If you do not file *Form 1099-MISC* and the person is reclassified as an employee, you are liable for 40% of the employee's FICA tax and income tax withholding equal to 3% of the wages — twice as much as if you would have filed *Form 1099-MISC*. Furthermore, there is a $100 penalty for failure to file *Form 1099-MISC* and you will owe interest on the taxes due. It is no longer a bargain to "borrow" from the IRS.

You may also be assessed other penalties if you did not have a reasonable basis for treating the person as a nonemployee and may be liable for up to 100% of the employee's FICA and income tax which you failed to withhold.

- If the person is hurt on the job and you have not provided workers' compensation insurance coverage, you will be liable for extensive legal damages.

- If your firm has a qualified retirement plan and you have not contributed to the plan on behalf of the person because he or she was not thought to be an employee at the time, the retirement plan could be disqualified for tax purposes for failing to cover the employee in question.

Thus, do not get stampeded into the independent contractor game by your friends and business associates who tell you how simple it is to avoid all those payroll taxes.

The above discussion of independent contractors summarizes federal rules only. Many states take an even more restrictive view than the IRS on the employee versus independent contractor issue.

Independent Contractor Treatment Tips

There are a number of steps you may be able to take to make a stronger case for someone who works for you to be treated as an independent contractor. Obviously, not all of the following will necessarily be feasible in every case, and a number of these steps, if implemented, may require some significant changes in the way you do business.

But if you can follow most of the suggestions below with regard to a given worker, you will improve your odds against having that worker reclassified as an employee by the IRS.

- Have a written agreement, signed by both parties, that makes it clear the company doesn't have the right to control the methods or procedures for the worker to accomplish the work contracted for. Include language in the agreement that states it is the worker's obligation to pay income and self-employment taxes on amounts earned, and that he or she will receive a 1099 reflecting amounts earned, if the amount earned is $600 or more.

- Try to avoid setting working hours by hour or week. It would be all right to specify starting and completion dates for the work.

- Make it clear that if additional workers are needed to help, the contractor will hire and pay them.

- The arrangement should make it clear that the contractor is not limited to working exclusively for you, but is free to take on other work from other customers.
- Compensation should be based on what work is performed rather than the time spent to do it. This may require careful estimates so that the worker is fairly paid, not overpaid, for the work done.
- Avoid providing office space to the contractor on a regular basis.
- Let the workers be responsible for their own training, if that is possible.
- Each worker should be advised, in writing, to provide for their own liability, workers' compensation, health, and disability insurance coverage.
- Costs such as meals, transportation, and clothing should be built into the contract price of the job, rather than being billed directly to your account.
- It should be clear in your agreement with the worker that he or she can't be fired and can't quit. The worker's job is to fulfill a given work contract.
- Don't give the worker other work to fill in during downtime. This may mean, of course, that you will have to pay the worker somewhat more for the work done than you otherwise would, if you wish to keep him or her happy.
- Don't pay bonuses to a person you treat as an independent contractor.

Other Alternatives

Hiring individuals as your own employees or treating them as independent contractors may sometimes pose a difficult choice. Fortunately, you have other available options. You could:

- Hire temporary employees from a temporary help agency; or
- Lease employees from an employee leasing company.

An increasing number of companies are utilizing these two worthwhile alternatives.

Hiring "temps" is usually quite straightforward, at least for many kinds of positions, but it may cost you a bit more than straight hiring. A temporary help agency has to charge you enough to make a profit, as well as pay for any benefits it provides to the temps, who are the agency's employees — not yours. One benefit to you, other than the simplicity of having someone else handle payroll, benefits, workers' compensation, and other costs of retaining such workers, is that you can send such workers home the moment you no longer need them, with no adverse consequences.

Of even greater importance to many companies is the opportunity to try out temps and offer permanent jobs to those whose performance they like. In effect, you get to "test out" such individuals for as long as you wish, before deciding if you want to offer them employment as your own employee, not the agency's, which is exactly what many temps are seeking.

Employee leasing is a bit more complicated, because in many cases, you do the "hiring." In some cases, you may even transfer your existing staff over to the payroll of the leasing company, which then leases them back to you for a fee equal to the salaries, taxes, and benefits paid by the leasing company, plus its mark-up percentage.

Leasing tends to be more of a long-term solution than hiring temps. Do your homework in checking out the reputation and background of any leasing company you will be dealing with. A number of leasing companies have gone broke or absconded with the payroll taxes withheld from employees' salaries, frequently leaving the firms that leased from them holding the bag. While there are many reputable leasing firms, they tend not to be as large and well known as the major temp firms, such as Kelly Services, Manpower, and other well-established firms in the industry.

Similar to hiring temps, leasing can be a major time- and energy-saving convenience. For example, if you lease all of your employees, you may be freed up to do what you do best, such as selling, rather than spending most of your time bogged down with payroll, benefits, and other employee-related paperwork.

You may also actually save money on your costs for workers, particularly if the leasing company is large and has been able to negotiate much less expensive, pooled rates for health insurance or workers' compensation than you could as a small employer.

Thus, leasing can offer substantial advantages to small companies, and usually avoids the problems and risks involved in seeking to treat workers as independent contractors, where such status is somewhat questionable. Be sure you deal with a reputable, established, financially responsible employee leasing company.

9.12 Whether You Should Incorporate Outside Your State

For most small businesses, there is little reason to consider incorporating your business under the laws of some state other than where you live. In fact, there are a few good reasons why you should not incorporate in a different state.

- Your corporation may have to pay a qualification fee to transact business in your home state as a foreign corporation. See Section 11.2 on this point.

- If your attorney is a local lawyer, he or she is likely to be much less familiar with the corporate laws of some other state than those of your state. Thus, your attorney is likely to either charge you more for corporate law advice if he or she has to research the law of an unfamiliar jurisdiction or give you less accurate advice than he or she could about your state's corporate laws.

- In many states, your corporation will have to pay some sort of minimum annual franchise tax or capital tax to the state of incorporation, even if you do no business there.

Don't believe the newspaper ads that tell you to incorporate in wonderful, tax-free Nevada or some other state and avoid your state's corporation income or franchise taxes. It doesn't work. If your corporation does business in your state, it pays the same taxes on its taxable income regardless of whether it is incorporated in your state, Nevada, or in the Grand Duchy of Luxembourg.

Perhaps the only valid reason why you might want to incorporate elsewhere would be to take advantage of some particular provision or flexibility available under the corporate laws of a particular state. If you own all the stock of your company, it is unlikely you would ever need to take advantage of any such provisions, which are usually more important where different groups are struggling for control of a corporation's board of directors or the like.

9.13 Foreign Investment in U.S. Businesses

Under the Foreign Direct Investment and International Financial Data Improvements Act of 1990, foreign individuals owning or acquiring 10% or more voting interest in U.S. businesses, including interests in U.S. real estate, must report certain information, including annual financial and operating data, to the U.S. Department of Commerce. Failure to file can result in civil penalties of $2,500 to $25,000.[27] For more information on this law, write to:

Bureau of Economic Analysis
U.S. Department of Commerce
BE-50 (IN)
Washington, DC 20230
(202) 606-5577

9.14 Emerging Trends and Issues

Today, businesses of every size and type are being buffeted by the ever-accelerating rate of change in the business, economic, social, and political environment in which they must operate. Part of the reason is that Congress, along with 50 state legislatures and countless government agencies, spew out reams of new laws and regulations all year long, in ever greater volume. As Benjamin Franklin once put it, "No man is safe in his bed when the Congress is in session."

To blame all of the disorienting changes that are occurring on lawmakers, however, is unfair since it seems that life in general is becoming more complex and unpredictable by the day. Accordingly, this section attempts to provide you, as a business owner, with a brief overview of developing and current trends in the business environment.

Labor Rates

Low labor rates abroad are causing the permanent shutdown of many large and small U.S. manufacturers, who can no longer keep up with foreign competition or U.S. manufacturers who move their operations overseas where wages are lower. This trend seems likely to continue and will have a rippling effect throughout the U.S. economy, adversely affecting many of the small firms that are either suppliers to large U.S. manufacturers or whose service operations will be drastically affected as larger companies close plants and make massive and permanent layoffs of thousands of employees.

Automation

Increasing automation, both here and abroad, is also likely to have a dramatic effect on employment and competitiveness in this country and throughout the world. Automation has been a factor in replacing blue-collar labor for decades. With the continual explosion in computing power and sophistication, vast numbers of middle managers and other white-collar workers are beginning to be displaced. With the advent of expert systems and "artificial intelligence," which are still in their infancy, but rapidly coming into their own, it is difficult to say whose job, if anyone's, will be safe in a few years.

While the ability to replace workers with computers or computer-driven machinery may be very attractive from a cost-savings standpoint to an employer, its societal effects are hard to predict and may prove to be very adverse to the overall business environment. The field of information processing is moving rapidly, and it is difficult to visualize how the world and the U.S. economy may look in as little as five or six years.

Downsizing

According to an American Management Association (AMA) survey for the year ending in June 1991, 55.5% of the organizations polled engaged in downsizing and 60% of those firms had also made significant staff cutbacks in the previous year, suggesting that firms are now cutting even deeper and deeper. The survey revealed that the cuts were heaviest on the Pacific Coast, averaging 12.6% of the workforce among firms reporting downsizing. Middle management jobs, which are estimated to make up something like 5% to 8% of the total workforce, accounted for more than 16% of the jobs cut in the 1991 survey period.

This trend seems to be continuing into 1993, as many of the nation's largest, most successful corporations, including IBM, General Motors, and Boeing, have announced one round of massive layoffs after another. Challenger, Gray & Christmas, a placement firm, says the pace of layoffs among large companies so far in 1993 is running well ahead of 1991, which was supposedly the bottom of the recent recession. [28]

While much of this change seems frightening to businesspeople, as well as to their employees, it may also give rise to fantastic new opportunities. Many of these people are likely to start their own smaller businesses due to the permanent disappearance of so many middle management or automatable jobs. Many may even keep working for their former firms as independent contractors or consultants.

In addition to enriching the overall business environment by creating a major upsurge in the formation of new, small, and flexible business entities, firms that cater to the needs of other small businesses may find the coming decade to be one of explosive growth and unparalleled opportunity.

One of the most predictable trends, which is already well under way, is the growth of telecommuting, where more and more people work out of their homes, communicating with their clients or employers by use of personal computers, modems, faxes, or multiple phone lines. Already, some employers, like certain government agencies in Washington, D.C., are taking an intermediate step by setting up satellite telecommuting offices in suburban areas. By going to these nearby satellite offices, equipped with computer workstations, many workers can, on most days, avoid long and arduous commutes to downtown offices by piping their work product electronically to the main office instead.

Telecommuting

A 1992 survey by Link Resources Corporation, a research and consulting firm, showed telecommuting has become a major factor in the economy almost overnight. The survey estimated that company employees who work at home part- or full-time increased in 1992 by 39%, over 1991, to 39 million individuals, most of whom are believed to be telecommuting. The survey apparently did not even take into account home-based businesses, which are also believed to be proliferating at startling rates.

Not all the consequences of increased telecommuting are positive. Some unforeseen side effects are already beginning to surface, such as rising workers' compensation costs for employers who have substantial numbers of employees working at home.

Apparently, employees who injure themselves at home tend to claim in many cases that such injuries are work-related, and therefore compensable under the workers' compensation system. In addition, injuries sustained while commuting are also more likely to be compensable, where such workers are constantly taking work back and forth between the office and home.

As a result, workers' compensation insurers have already begun to raise their rates for telecommuting employees. Don't overlook this potential expense when analyzing the costs and benefits of having more of your workforce telecommute.

Pending Law Changes

Now that one political party controls both the White House and Congress, look for significant law changes in 1994 and during the remainder of the Clinton administration. Many of these future law changes are sure to affect your business, for better or worse. Major new legislation to look for in the near future may include:

- Mandatory health care coverage — This is currently the Clinton administration's number one priority. The exact shape of change in this area is anyone's guess at this time. However, it looks as though the initial proposal to pay for universal health care with a payroll tax will not be part of the final plan, due to the enormous opposition to such a tax. Instead, look for some sort of mandated insurance coverage, probably with insurance rates and medical coverage terms set by the government.

  Part of the final package may also include a limit on deductions for medical insurance. Under such a limit, excess premiums paid for health care plans providing more than a defined "standard" level of benefits would not be deductible by employers and the excess payments would also be taxable income to the covered employee. Some portion of the additional costs of universal health care will be borne by the government. It seems likely the government will seek to fund the costs by imposing increased "sin" taxes on alcohol and cigarettes, and a national sales tax or value-added tax (VAT) of some kind cannot be ruled out as a possibility.

- Full deductibility of health insurance for the self-employed — In a 1993 speech to the National Governors Association regarding health care reform, President Clinton endorsed an increase in the percentage of self-employed persons' health insurance deduction from the current 25% to 100% and said this will be part of the health care reform plan he will offer to Congress.

  The president also indicated this deduction — which has expired and been renewed after the fact several times in recent years — will be made permanent. Such provisions, if enacted, would finally put self-employed business owners on a par with those who are incorporated, with regard to deductibility of their medical insurance costs.

- Federal legislation regarding limited liability companies (LLCs) — Now that over two-thirds of the states have adopted LLC laws and the tax benefits of LLCs threaten to reduce federal income tax revenues, one congressional committee is already looking into the possibility of requiring LLCs to be taxed as corporations. LLCs are generally taxed as partnerships under current federal tax law.

- Striker replacement law — Congress now appears close to passing a striker replacement law, which would overturn a 1938 Supreme Court decision that held employers could fire workers who go on strike over economic issues, such as wages. The proposed law would prohibit employers from hiring permanent replacement workers during a strike and would require them to give the strikers their jobs back after the strike ends. The proposed legislation contains other provisions that would also shift power to labor unions and impose major burdens on small, nonunion employers. This bill seems likely to be passed by Congress very soon, unless opponents can muster the 41 votes needed in the Senate to sustain a filibuster and thereby prevent a vote on the bill itself. President Clinton has already announced he will sign the bill if it passes in Congress.

- Information returns (1099s) for payments to corporations — Under current law, businesses do not have to file 1099 information return forms for most payments they make to corporations; however, Congress may soon eliminate this important exemption. Doing so would greatly increase the paperwork burden on nearly all businesses.
- Increase estimated tax "safe harbor" to 115% — The ink is not yet dry on the 1993 Deficit Reduction Act, which will allow high-income individual taxpayers to base their estimated tax payments in 1994 on 110% of the prior year tax, and the House Ways and Means Committee is already considering raising the "safe harbor" percentage to 115% of the prior year tax liability.

Civil Rights Laws

The federal Civil Rights Act of 1991 (CRA91) makes life a lot more complicated for all covered employers in the area of employment practices. The law's most controversial aspect is in the "disparate impact" cases, where a company's employment practices, although not shown to be intentionally discriminatory, have a disparate (unequal) impact on employment of protected groups.

For example, if a company is located in an area where 80% of the population consists of Native Americans, but only 5% of its employees are Native Americans, there may be grounds for a disparate impact claim against the employer, under prior civil rights law as well as the new CRA91 provisions, regardless of employer intent.

Under prior law, the U.S. Supreme Court held that the burden of proof was on the employee who alleged discrimination. The employee had to identify the particular business practice of the employer that resulted in the disparity.

By contrast, under the new CRA91, the employee is relieved of this burden of proof if he or she can simply show that the employer failed to select an alternative employment practice, such as hiring quotas, that would not have had a disparate impact — meaning the employment practice would not have had a negative impact on the minority or other protected group.

Instead, the burden of proof in these cases is now shifted to the employer, who must show that the challenged employment practice regarding hiring, promotions, pay, or other aspects of employment is job-related for the position in question and consistent with business necessity.

This vagueness regarding job-relatedness business necessity is what former President Bush initially expressed concerns over, arguing that many firms would find it easier to simply adopt minority hiring quotas than to attempt to prove the "business necessity" defense in court. There are no easy answers as to what policy a company should adopt in this regard. It may seem that one safe way to avoid discrimination suits under the new law would be to adopt some sort of quota system; yet, using the quota system generates issues of unfairness and possible employee morale problems.

CRA91 also considerably expands the monetary damages that can be awarded in cases of intentional discrimination. Before, an employer who lost such a discrimination suit was usually liable only for back pay, front pay, lost benefits, attorney's fees, and court costs. Under CRA91 — which may even be retroactive in effect — compensatory damages may also be allowed in addition to other monetary damages. CRA91 also overrides a U.S. Supreme Court case that had limited fees — a flat $40 — recoverable by a claimant for expert witness fees.

In light of the foregoing changes in the Civil Rights Act of 1991, the odds, as well as the costs, of losing a discrimination action have increased significantly for employers. The act makes it much more attractive for plaintiffs to file such suits, both for claims of intentional discrimination and in disparate impact cases.

Employers can now expect a great many more such claims to be filed. Thus, however fair you may feel your firm's employment practices are, if you are a large enough firm — generally 15 or more employees — to be subject to the Civil Rights Act, this may be a good time to consult an attorney who is familiar with employment discrimination matters to see what, if any, steps you may need to take to protect your business from liability in this area.

Other Legal Trends and New or Pending Legislation

Listed and discussed below are some other legal trends and new or pending legislation you should know about for future reference. This information provides possible tips for issues or rules which may affect your business.

Minimum Wage

From all indications, the Clinton administration will support an early increase in the federal minimum wage, which is currently $4.25 an hour. Look for an increase in the $5.00-an-hour range before the end of 1994.

While changes in the minimum wage in the past have usually occurred only at intervals of several years, depending upon the mood and makeup of Congress, current proposals call for indexing the minimum wage so it would automatically increase each year with the cost-of-living or other index.

Video Display Terminals

Until recently, white-collar workplaces or offices generally created very little liability exposure for employers, with regard to hazardous working conditions. This, too, is beginning to change.

In recent years, there have been an increasing number of lawsuits filed by employees in connection with hazards of working long hours on computers; and in late 1990, the city of San Francisco adopted an ordinance that provides regulatory safeguards for workers using video display terminals (VDTs) for four or more hours per shift.

Apparently, Los Angeles and a number of other city and state governments around the nation are now considering similar laws or ordinances, since use of computers in the workplace is now a universal phenomenon and because a number of threats of employees' health have arisen in connection with the heavy use of computers.

These range from excessive exposure to radiation emitted by VDTs to carpal tunnel syndrome, a now common and debilitating nerve entrapment disorder that can cause severe pain and weakness in the wrist. Carpal tunnel syndrome can result from too many hours spent typing on a computer keyboard — as well as from many other tasks requiring repetitive flexing and extensions of the wrist.

Laws regulating VDTs are likely to begin appearing all over the country in the near future, and offices that don't pay attention to ergonomics — the study of equipment design to reduce workplace injury — may well become sitting ducks for lawsuits or fines. While most legal claims by employees regarding VDT usage have been imposed on workers' compensation insurers thus far, employers may become directly liable:

- If they participate actively in the design of computer systems or workstations that allegedly caused the injury to an employee; or
- If new state legislation removes such claims from the workers' compensation system and places financial responsibility directly upon employers.

Helpful Organizations

Communicate your thoughts on government policy and pending legislation to groups like the National Federation of Independent Business (NFIB), the U.S. Chamber of Commerce, your local chamber of commerce, or a trade association for your industry. It also can be helpful to call or write your senator, U.S. representative, or state legislator to voice your opinion in favor of or opposition to pending legislation or regulations that will affect your business.

Small business has been hit very hard by the government at all levels in recent years, and the more small business owners join and work together through helpful organizations, the better the chances of shaping the future.

Endnotes

1. I.R.C. §168.
2. I.R.C. §179(b)(1).
3. I.R.C. §6425.
4. 15 U.S.C. §§1051–1127.
5. I.R.C. §1244(c). The Tax Reform Act of 1984 §481(a).
6. I.R.C. §1211(b).
7. I.R.C. §1244(c)(1)(C).
8. I.R.C. §1244(c)(3).
9. I.R.C. §1244(d)(1)(B).
10. 16 C.F.R. §435.
11. 42 U.S.C.A. §§9601 *et seq.*
12. 42 U.S.C.A. §§6901 *et seq.*
13. 40 C.F.R. §280.22(a) and (b).
14. 40 C.F.R. §280.20.
15. 40 C.F.R. §280.21.
16. 33 U.S.C.A. §§1251–1376.
17. 33 U.S.C.A. §1344(a).
18. 42 U.S.C.A. §§7401–7626.
19. 15 U.S.C.A. §§2601–2629.
20. 7 U.S.C.A. §§135 *et seq.*
21. 42 U.S.C.A. §§4321–4347.
22. 29 C.F.R. §§1910 and 1926.58.
23. 15 U.S.C. §1691.
24. 15 U.S.C. §§1601 *et seq.*
25. 12 C.F.R. §226.2(a)(17).
26. 12 C.F.R. §226.4(c)(8).
27. 15 C.F.R. §806.
28. *Barron's National Financial Weekly.* August 30, 1993.

Internal Accounting Controls Checklist

☐ The same person who handles your cash receipts should not be the same person who makes the bank deposits. Cash is too easily misappropriated. Don't tempt an employee by letting him or her handle both of these duties.

☐ The person who writes checks should not also sign them or have the authority to sign checks. A different person should sign checks.

☐ Whoever signs checks should only sign them when the bill that is being paid is presented at the same time. The check number should be written on the bill to avoid double payments or payments to a nonexistent vendor. When you sign the check, be sure you know what the bill is for.

☐ Consider using some type of mechanical check imprinting equipment for all checks that are written, as a further means of preventing unauthorized payments. Such machines keep a record of the amount of any checks written.

☐ Use only prenumbered checks and keep all of the cancelled or voided checks in your records. This will help make it readily apparent if any additional checks are written without your knowledge.

☐ Complete a monthly bank reconciliation yourself or have your outside accountant do it. Never let the person who writes checks do the reconciliation.

☐ Deposit your daily cash receipts in the bank each day. Do not let cash collections for one day get mingled with the next day's collections.

☐ Use prenumbered sets of sales checks, invoices, and receipts to keep control of payments made and received. Duplicates will be kept track of by the individuals making sales, etc., and the master copy will enable you to make sure they account for all of their transactions.

☐ Use a petty cash fund and voucher system for stamps, small bills, and other small cash outlays. Do not use cash from the day's receipts to pay bills! Put a voucher or bill in the petty cash box each time money is taken out. When the fund is depleted, write a check to bring it back up to the maximum amount (say $50), and record all the vouchers at the time the check is cashed to replenish the fund.

☐ Maintain a master or control account for all of your accounts receivable, and reconcile it each month to the subsidiary accounts receivable. If someone is stealing money from customer payments, it will be easier to spot if the master and subsidiary accounts are reconciled regularly.

Notes

Chapter 10

Sources of Help and Information

If you're going to sin, sin against God, not the bureaucracy.
God will forgive you, but the bureaucracy won't.

— Admiral Hyman G. Rickover

10.1 General Considerations

Many government and private organizations provide free or low-cost services and publications to small business. Unfortunately, most small business owners only find out about a few of these sources and then only on a haphazard basis. This chapter summarizes many of the services and publications you may need to draw on as an owner or operator of a small business.

10.2 Professional Services

Select your accountant carefully. This is the one person outside your business who is most likely to be closely in touch with almost everything going on in your operation. Besides helping to set up your books and to establish systems for handling cash receipts and disbursements, a good accountant can provide a wealth of practical advice on a wide range of subjects that are important to your business, including planning for taxes, managing your money, obtaining financing, and evaluating business opportunities. Attorneys and bankers are often in a good position to recommend accountants.

Accountants

Attorneys

Unless you are starting out as a sole proprietor, you will usually need an attorney to prepare a partnership agreement or to set up a corporation. You will probably do well to consult an attorney anyway to make sure you are obtaining necessary licenses and permits or to help you obtain them in some cases. In most parts of the country, local bar associations have lawyer referral services that can put you in touch with attorneys in your area. In most cases, you will do better to ask an accountant or banker to recommend a good business lawyer. If you need highly specialized legal advice or representation, ask an attorney you know to recommend a specialist.

Bankers

Establish a good relationship with officers of the bank branch where you open an account for your business. While you may find it tough to borrow from your banker when you first go into business, he or she will be interested in keeping an eye on your business to see how it develops. It pays to cultivate the relationship to create a good impression before you want to apply for a business loan from the bank. Ask around before opening an account; find out if there is a bank in your area that is well known for lending to small businesses. Many of the large banks tend to be more interested in larger accounts, although different branch managers of the same bank may have very different ideas about working with small businesses. Your banker can be a useful source of free financial advice and a good connection when wanting to meet other business owners in your community.

Benefit Consultants

If you intend to establish a corporate pension or profit-sharing plan — or Keogh plan, if you have a number of employees — you may want to seek out a benefit consulting firm and obtain its proposals as to the type of benefit plan you need and how it should be structured. Since many such firms are primarily engaged in selling insurance products, such as life insurance, annuities, and investment contracts, designed for pension plans, the plan these firms design for you will almost invariably involve building in their products. Since an insured retirement plan may not necessarily make sense in your particular situation, ask your attorney or accountant to recommend a benefit consulting firm that does not have products to sell other than its consulting and plan administration services.

10.3 U.S. Small Business Administration and Other Helpful Agencies

The federal Small Business Administration (SBA) is one government agency that is genuinely helpful to small businesses. The SBA not only guarantees financing for many small businesses (see Section 9.7) but it also provides a number of valuable services.

One service you might find helpful is the Service Corps of Retired Executives (SCORE). SCORE is a program in which retired executives with many years of business experience volunteer their services as consultants to small businesses and charge only for their out-of-pocket expenses. Other SBA programs designed to provide assistance to small businesses include:

- Small Business Development Centers (SBDCs) — SBDCs are local centers operated by the state or community, with SBA assistance, to provide a wide range of business counseling and training. To see if your state has an SBDC network, refer to Section 11.10.
- Small Business Institutes (SBIs) — SBIs provide in-depth business counseling at hundreds of universities across the country.

In addition, SBA offices perform a variety of seminars and workshops on topics of interest to people who are starting or operating small businesses. Here are some of the seminars offered by the SBA.

- *Building a Business Plan*
- *Starting a New Business*
- *Preparing the Loan Proposal*

Contact your local SBA office for more information.

Business Information Centers

The SBA has also opened new Business Information Centers — each of which has a full set of all 51 of the books in this *Starting and Operating a Business* series — in Seattle, Houston, and Atlanta, with more coming soon in St. Louis, Los Angeles, and elsewhere. Each of these centers is designed to assist in disseminating helpful information to small business.

Telephone Hotlines

The SBA and several other government agencies maintain toll-free telephone hotline information services to assist businesses and taxpayers. Some of the more important ones to know about are listed below.

SBA Answer Desk

The SBA Answer Desk has a toll-free number of a small business information and referral service offered by the SBA, which you can call from anywhere in the continental United States, except Washington, D.C. For the number in D.C., check the local directory. The telephone Answer Desk offers a wide range of prerecorded, informational messages, any of which you may access if you have a touch-tone phone.

SBA Answer Desk
(800) U-ASK-SBA or 827-5722

SBA On-Line

The SBA has set up an electronic bulletin board system (BBS), called SBA On-Line, to help distribute information about its services and publications to anyone with a personal computer and modem. To log onto the BBS, dial:

SBA On-Line
(800) 859-INFO (for 2400 baud service)
(800) 697-INFO (for 9600 baud service)

There is no charge for access, and even the phone lines are toll-free. You can browse through various files remotely or download them for free to your computer.

Small Business Hotline

The Small Business Hotline is a specialized free service offered by the Export-Import Bank to small exporters needing general information or problem-solving assistance relating to doing business abroad. It provides information on export credit and on assistance available from other government agencies and the private sector.

Small Business Hotline
(800) 424-5201

Internal Revenue Service

The IRS has an assistance program called Tele-Tax. The program allows you to call a toll-free number in your state to listen to pre-recorded tax information that will answer many federal tax questions.

About 140 topics are available, including information on the Small Business Tax Education Program (STEP), business income, sole proprietorships, and the self-employment tax.

For more information on Tele-Tax, call the IRS's toll-free number to request *Publication 910, Guide to Free Tax Services*. This publication not only lists the many tax publications you can order, but it also lists the Tele-Tax phone numbers and topic numbers in your state.

Internal Revenue Service
(800) 829-3676

Trade Information Center

The Trade Information Center has a hotline where you can receive general information on exporting that is provided by various U.S. government agencies.

Trade Information Center
(800) USA-TRADE or 872-8723

For information on doing business in the unified European Market after 1992, call for written information and a quarterly newsletter from:

U.S. Department of Commerce's Single Internal Market – 1992 Information Service
(202) 377-5276

European Center – Washington, D.C. Office
(202) 862-9500

Ernst & Young

Ernst & Young, one of the Big Six accounting firms, publishes some helpful guides for anyone interested in expanding their business into the global markets. They are:

- *The Ernst & Young Guide to Expanding in the Global Market* — This guide is for those managers who want to succeed in complex international ventures. This hardcover book includes step-by-step programs and helpful examples.
- *The Ernst & Young Resource Guide to Global Markets 1991* — This guide is an up-to-date resource to global market trends and regional county data. This book is available in both paperback and hardcover.

For more information, contact:

John Wiley & Sons, Inc. – Sales Department
605 Third Avenue
New York, NY 10158-0012
(212) 850-6000

Environmental Protection Agency Ombudsman

Like certain Scandinavian countries, the Environmental Protection Agency (EPA) has a small business ombudsman who gives easier access to the EPA, helps you comply with EPA regulations, and makes sure you are treated fairly in any EPA disputes.

EPA Small Business Ombudsman
(703) 305-5938
(800) 368-5888

Social Security Administration

If you want to find out what records the Social Security Administration (SSA) has on your earnings and your projected benefits at retirement age, you can file a simple form requesting a detailed printout of this information. This is something everyone should do once every few years because if the SSA has made a serious mistake in your earnings record, you have only a limited number of years in which you can contact them and have your record corrected.

To obtain the request form, call the SSA's toll-free number or write the SSA for this form at the Consumer Information Center address below.

Social Security Administration
(800) 772-1213

Consumer Information Center
Department 72
Pueblo, CO 81009

Corporate Agents, Inc.

There are also companies who can assist in the incorporation process, providing a variety of incorporation kits and services. One such company, Corporate Agents, Inc., can help you form your corporation in any state for as little as $39 (plus state fees), depending on the state. Some examples of complete costs for other states are $115 for Delaware, $169 for Florida, $269 for New York, and $1,014 for California.

The fees cover all costs, including all state filing fees and recording costs, preparing and filing articles of incorporation, and a registered agent's service fee for the first six months. Also available for a nominal additional cost are the corporate kits, which include the corporate seal, minute book, stock certificates, and sample forms and bylaws. For more information on this company, you can send the preaddressed post card located at the back of this book or call Corporate Agents at the toll-free number below:

Corporate Agents, Inc.
1013 Centre Road
P.O. Box 1281
Wilmington, DE 19899
(800) 877-4224
FAX (302) 998-7078

10.4 Publications Regarding Small Business Operations

U.S. Small Business Administration

The U.S. Small Business Administration (SBA) has more than 50 helpful booklets and other publications on subjects of importance to new and existing small businesses. The publications, which sell for a nominal fee — usually about $0.50 (50 cents) to $1.00 each, and never more than $2.00 — can be obtained through your nearest SBA office or by calling the SBA Answer Desk and asking for a list of publications.

SBA Answer Desk
(800) U-ASK-SBA or 827-5722

You can also use the preaddressed post card in the back of this book to request lists of SBA publications.

Small Business Institutes

Small Business Institutes (SBIs) are located on university campuses throughout the United States. Part of a cooperative program with the SBA, SBIs offer you business assistance while furthering the education of college students. Students, supervised by faculty members, provide your business with:

- Free confidential consulting;
- In-depth analysis of your firm's business situation;
- Alternatives and recommendations to business problems; and
- Written and oral reports.

Headquartered at the University of Central Arkansas, the Small Business Institute Directors' Association (SBIDA) National Center and the Small Business Advancement Network perform research and gather information on small business. The SBIDA National Center is the link between all SBI universities and the government. The SBIDA also:

- Is the center of correspondence for SBI schools;
- Keeps records on all SBI schools;

- Publishes the *SBIDA News*;
- Processes SBIDA membership; and
- Is a center for advocacy.

The Small Business Advancement Network is an electronic bulletin board which provides information on grant opportunities, cooperative ventures between the SBA and SBI, and small business research. The network is available during regular business hours and is updated daily. For information on the SBI nearest you, contact:

SBIDA National Center
University of Central Arkansas
College of Business
UCA P.O. Box 4983
Conway, AR 72035-5002
(501) 450-5300

For more on the Small Business Advancement Network, contact:

Small Business Advancement National Center
University of Arkansas
College of Business
UCA P.O. Box 5018
Conway, AR 72035-5002
(501) 450-5377

The Oasis Press

The publisher of this book, The Oasis Press, has a number of how-to business guides and software programs targeted toward small businesses. Some of the most recent titles published by The Oasis Press include:

- *The Business Environmental Handbook* — A comprehensive book that shows you how any business can be environment-friendly and environment-profitable. Provides a listing of helpful resources, EPA regional offices, state environmental departments, and hazardous materials laws. $19.95 (paperback)
- *Export Now* — A recently updated book that will help anyone interested in exporting get the information and direction necessary for entering the international market. $19.95 (paperback)
- *People Investment* — This book provides timely information for hiring the right persons for your business. Learn about hiring practices, avoid legal problems, and start a personnel program the easy way. $19.95 (paperback)
- *Power Marketing for Small Business* — A hands-on, easy-to-read book that details all aspects of marketing. Full of helpful worksheets and examples that will help both the beginning and experienced marketer make a difference in sales and profits. $19.95 (paperback)
- *Start Your Business* — A complementary book to the *Starting and Operating a Business* series that is designed especially for the person wondering what steps to take before opening the doors of his or her new business. Handy checklists help simplify the plan of action needed to get started on the right foot. $8.95 (paperback)

Information on these and other related resources from The Oasis Press is provided at the back of this book or it can be obtained by calling:

The Oasis Press
(800) 228-2275

Magazines

Here are some magazines that provide continuing information for businesses in general and small businesses in particular. There are also a number of specialized publications you may find helpful. Most of these publications can be located through your local library or news stand.

The Wall Street Journal
200 Liberty Street
New York, NY 10281
(212) 416-2898

D&B Reports
299 Park Avenue
New York, NY 10171-0002
(212) 593-6723

In Business
419 State Avenue
Emmaus, PA 18049-3717
(215) 967-4135

Success Magazine
P.O. Box 3038
Harlin, IA 51537
(800) 234-7324

Entrepreneur Magazine
Business Start-ups
Subscriber Service
P.O. Box 19787
Irvine, CA 92713-9441
(800) 421-2300
(800) 352-7449 (in California)

Family Business Magazine
Subscriber Service
P.O. Box 420265
Palm Coast, FL 32142-0265
(800) 423-1780
(800) 858-0095 (in Florida)

Business Review
P.O. Box 777
Cypress, TX 77429-0777
(713) 373-3535

Business Week
Subscriber Service
P.O. Box 506
Hightstown, NJ 08520
(800) 635-1200

Nation's Business
U.S. Chamber of Commerce
1615 H. Street, NW
Washington, DC 20062
(202) 463-5650

INC.
Subscriber Service
P.O. Box 54129
Boulder, CO 80322-4129
(800) 525-0643

Small Business Opportunities
1115 Broadway, 8th Floor
New York, NY 10010
(212) 807-7100

Small Business Reports
Subscriber Services
P.O. Box 53140
Boulder, CO 80322-3140
(800) 234-1094

Independent Business
National Federation of Independent Business
Membership Development Office
600 Maryland Avenue, SW, Suite 700
Washington, DC 20024
(202) 554-9000

Home Business Opportunities
P.O. Box 1606
Ozark, AL 36360
(205) 774-0990

Some of the more important sources of statistical information that you will need if you do your own marketing research are:

Statistical Information

Title	Publisher
Survey of Buying Power Sales and Marketing Management Magazine Comprehensive data on population, retail sales, and consumer buying income for states, counties, and cities.	**Bill Communications, Inc.** 355 Park Avenue South New York, NY 10010 (212) 592-6000
Publication Price List Titles on corporate relations, human resources, management, economic and business environments, and consumer research.	**Conference Board** 845 Third Avenue New York, NY 10022 (800) 872-6273
Survey of Current Business U.S. Department of Commerce's monthly survey of business trends and conditions.	**Superintendent of Documents U.S. Government Printing Office** Washington, DC 20402 (212) 339-0345
The Complete Information Bank for Entrepreneurs & Small Business Managers, Second Edition An excellent sourcebook which lists and describes hundreds of leading business books and other sources of help and information for small businesses.	**Center for Entrepreneurship** Wichita State University 1845 Fairmont Wichita, KS 67260-0147 (316) 689-3000
Encyclopedia of Business Information Sources, Ninth Edition Arranged by industry, this guide lists trade associations and major sources of statistical information.	**Gale Research, Inc.** 835 Penobscott Building Detroit, MI 48226 (313) 961-2242

The U.S. Occupational Safety and Health Administration (OSHA) provides a number of useful, free publications on OSHA requirements for small businesses. Two of the more important ones are listed below. Each is available from one of OSHA's ten regional offices or from one or more local OSHA offices in every state.

U.S. Occupational Safety and Health Administration

OSHA Handbook for Small Business (OSHA 2209)	Helpful handbook designed to assist small business employers to meet their legal requirements under the OSHA laws and regulations.
Recordkeeping Guidelines for Occupational Injuries and Illness (O.M.B. No. 1220-0029)	Provides useful summary of what records must be kept, who must keep them, and for how long.

OSHA offices can also provide you with a package or folder entitled, *Information from the Occupational Safety and Health Administration,* which includes the above publications, plus required posters and about a dozen other OSHA informational booklets and pamphlets. See the pre-addressed postcard at the back of the book for ordering booklets and required posters.

Securities and Exchange Commission

The SEC's Office of Small Business Policy publishes *Q & A: Small Business and the SEC*, which is a guide to special services, rules, regulations, and suggestions regarding a company's first public offering of stock. It is available from:

Office of Small Business Policy
Securities and Exchange Commission
450 Fifth Street NW
Washington, DC 20549
(202) 272-2644

Equal Employment Opportunity Commission

The Equal Employment Opportunity Commission (EEOC) publishes a useful and comprehensive publication on all the discrimination laws that it enforces, such as civil rights, age discrimination, and equal pay. The publication is entitled, *Laws Enforced by EEOC*. Obtain it from:

Equal Employment Opportunity Commission
2401 E Street
Washington, DC 20507
(202) 663-4264
(800) 669-3362

10.5 Do-It-Yourself Incorporation

If you want to form your own corporation and save several hundred dollars in legal fees, there are books that tell you how to do it and provide the forms you need; however, think carefully before you attempt to do this on your own. In some cases, setting up a corporation is not that complicated, and if you follow the instructions in a self-incorporation book precisely — if one is available for your state — you should be able to do it properly. But you will have to spend many hours carefully figuring out and then doing all that is required. Your time might be worth much more than the money you would save in legal fees because you could concentrate more on getting the business off to a good start. Check Section 11.10 to see if there is an incorporation book for your state.

10.6 Information Regarding Payroll Taxes and Withholding

Major offices of the IRS frequently put on seminars for new employers regarding payroll tax requirements. Call your local IRS office for information as to when such seminars will be held in your area. In addition, you may want to obtain *Circular E, Employer's Tax Guide,* and *Notice 109, Information About Depositing Employment and Excise Taxes.* Both can be obtained from the IRS office nearest you. In addition, the Matthew Bender Company publishes an excellent book called the *Payroll Tax Guide*, which covers almost every aspect of federal payroll tax returns.

Matthew Bender Company
(800) 223-1940

10.7 Other Useful Tax Publications

The publications below can also be obtained from your local IRS office:

Publication	Subject
Publication 334	*Tax Guide For Small Business Income and other Federal Taxes*
Publication 349	*Federal Highway Use Taxes on Heavy Vehicles*
Publication 378	*Fuel Tax Credits and Refunds*
Publication 463	*Travel, Entertainment, and Gift Expenses*
Publication 510	*Federal Excise Taxes*
Publication 541	*Tax Information on Partnerships*
Publication 542	*Tax Information on Corporations*
Publication 544	*Sales and Other Dispositions of Assets*
Publication 552	*Recordkeeping Requirements*
Publication 583	*Taxpayers Starting a Business*
Publication 587	*Business Use of Your Home*
Publication 589	*Tax Information on S Corporations*
Publication 910	*Guide to Free Tax Services*
Publication 937	*Business Reporting*

To order these free tax publications or other tax forms, call:

Internal Revenue Service
(800) 829-3676

10.8 ERISA Compliance

If your business has a pension or profit-sharing plan and you wish to handle your own Employee Retirement Income Security Act (ERISA) filings for the plan, obtain a copy of Charles D. Spencer & Associates' publication, *5500 Annual Reports for Employee Benefit Plans*. This publication will help you prepare the necessary *Form 5500* series through its easy-to-understand, step-by-step instructions. For ordering information, contact:

Charles D. Spencer & Associates, Inc.
250 South Wacker Drive, Suite 600
Chicago, IL 60606
(312) 993-7900

10.9 Information on Franchising

Title and Author	**Publisher**
Franchise Bible Erwin J. Keup	**The Oasis Press** 300 North Valley Drive Grants Pass, OR 97526 (800) 228-2275
Miscellaneous titles on franchise topics. Write for a catalog.	**International Franchise Association** 1350 New York Avenue, NW, Suite 900 Washington, DC 20005
Business Franchise Guide	**Commerce Clearing House, Inc.** 4025 West Peterson Avenue Chicago, IL 60646
Miscellaneous titles on franchise topics. Write for a catalog.	**Pilot Books** 103 Cooper Street Babylon, NY 11702
Franchise Opportunities Handbook U.S. Department of Commerce	**Superintendent of Documents** **U.S. Government Printing Office** Washington, DC 20402
Franchising in the U.S. Michael M. Coltman	**Self-Counsel Press Inc.** 1704 North State Street Bellingham, WA 98225 (800) 663-3007
Franchisee Rights — A Self-Defense Manual *for The Franchisee* Alex Hammond	**Hammond & Morton** 1185 Avenue of the Americas New York, NY 10036
Franchising: Regulation of Buying and Selling *A Franchise* Philip F. Zeidman, Perry C. Ausbrook, and H. Bret Lowell	**Bureau of National Affairs, Inc.** 9435 Key West Avenue Rockville, MD 20850 (800) 372-1033
The Info Franchise Newsletter *The Franchise Annual*	**Info Press** 728 Center Street Lewiston, NY 14092-0550 (716) 754-4669
Survey of Foreign Laws and Regulations *Affecting International Franchising* Compiled by the Franchising Committee of the Section of Antitrust Law of the American Bar Association	**Publications Planning and Marketing** **American Bar Association** 705 North Lake Shore Drive Chicago, IL 60611

Notes

Notes

State Laws & Related Resources

Part IV

Notes to Georgia State Chapter

What's New

This update of the Georgia state chapter features new information and additions in several areas. The list below will help you locate the most significant changes by chapter–section number.

- New unemployment tax rate information – 11.5

- New addresses for Small Business Development Centers and Georgia business publications – 11.10

- Samples of Georgia tax registration forms are provided in the Appendix -- back of book

- A new post card for the centralized taxpayer registration unit – back of book

If changes have occurred since publication of this update, you are advised to contact the state office listed below for assistance or referral to the appropriate agency.

Administrative Office
Georgia Small Business Development Center
University of Georgia
1180 East Broad Street
Athens, GA 30602
(404) 542-5760

About the Authors

The state authors of *Starting and Operating a Business in Georgia* are Thomas J. Harrold, Jr. and Betsy Birns McCall, who have updated this chapter through May 1992.

Thomas J. Harrold, Jr. is a native Georgian and is currently the partner in charge of the Corporate and International Practice Group with the law firm of Glass, McCullough, Sherrill & Harrold of Atlanta, Georgia.

He received a Bachelor of Arts with honors from Columbia University and a Juris Doctor from the University of Georgia School of Law. Mr. Harrold served as Deputy Revenue Commissioner for the State of Georgia from 1976 to 1978 and is the author of numerous articles on state and local tax planning, particularly for foreign investors. He is a member of the International, American, Georgia, and Atlanta bar associations and the Society of International Business Fellows.

Betsy Birns McCall is an associate with the law firm of Glass, McCullough, Sherrill & Harrold of Atlanta, Georgia. She received an A.B. from Harvard University with honors, a master's degree from Harvard University in Middle East Studies, and a Juris Doctor from Harvard Law School with honors. She is a member of the State Bar of Georgia.

Chapter 11

State Laws and Taxes

11.1 Introduction

Georgia offers one of the most thriving and progressive business climates in the United States. In particular, this is evidenced by the rapid surge of both domestic and international activity by corporations that have chosen to locate within the state. Georgia's strong and healthy economy is characterized by a diverse mix of agricultural, manufacturing, service, and financial enterprises which have combined to make the state virtually "recession-proof."

A number of factors have contributed to the substantial economic growth in Georgia during the past 15 years, not the least of which is the superb quality of life and relatively low cost of living. Rand McNally recently selected the metropolitan Atlanta area as the most desirable place in the entire country to live and work. Atlanta also is recognized as the financial, transportation, and service center for the southeastern United States.

There is much more to Georgia, however, than the city of Atlanta. Savannah is one of the oldest cities in the South, with a unique charm and heritage. It also ranks as one of the busiest and most efficient ports on the Atlantic coast. The University of Georgia makes the city of Athens a particularly attractive place to live and work and has become the center of business and manufacturing in northeast Georgia. Augusta, the home of the Masters Golf Tournament, is the commercial center of the central eastern section of the state. Columbus, Macon, Valdosta, and Albany are developing into metropolitan business centers in their respective geographic areas.

Georgia is noted for its distinct geographic diversity. There are the flat coastal plains of southwest Georgia and the spectacular coastline of beaches and sea islands — including the Cumberland Island National Seashore — the rolling hills of dogwood trees characteristic of Atlanta and the Piedmont Plateau, and the nearly 3,000 square miles of mountain forests in the northern part of the state. The virtually unlimited supply of water, both subsurface and from a network of rivers, streams, and many recreational lakes, gives Georgia a natural resource advantage over the Sunbelt states of the West and Southwest. The utilities which provide natural gas, electricity, and telephone services are among the most efficient and economical in the United States.

The number of new businesses locating in Georgia during the past decade attests to the fact that Georgia is an attractive place to do business. Some of the factors contributing to Georgia's successful business development are discussed below.

Pro-Business Government

The state, county, and city governments of Georgia are noted for their pro-business attitude. They actively encourage business expansion and attempt to work in concert, rather than in conflict, with business and industry.

State Taxes

The corporate income tax rate of 6% and the statewide sales tax rate of 4% makes Georgia one of the lowest taxing states in the entire nation.

Skilled Labor Force Available

The work ethic is flourishing in Georgia, and Georgians provide a hard-working labor pool with relatively low union activity. The state government has established and vigorously pursues vocational training programs, which benefit new businesses and industries, as well as assists in manufacturing and high tech industries within the state.

Transportation

Atlanta's Hartsfield International Airport is one of the most modern airport facilities in the entire world and currently ranks as the busiest commercial airport in the United States. The abundance of regularly scheduled flights from Hartsfield enables a business executive to leave Atlanta almost any morning and arrive in any major city in the United States before 10:00 A.M. local time.

International flights now connect Atlanta and the Southeast with London, Dublin, Shannon, Paris, Frankfurt, Stuttgart, Munich, Hamburg, Zurich, Brussels, Amsterdam, Tokyo, Taipei, Bangkok, and Seoul, as well as with a number of cities in the Caribbean and Mexico. Savannah's port facilities have been expanded and modernized, making it one of the fastest growing ports on the Atlantic coast. Brunswick's port facilities are being expanded with an emphasis on agricultural exports.

In addition, Georgia is fortunate to have a sophisticated and well-developed rail service and highway system. These transportation resources contribute to making Georgia's transportation system the best in the Southeast.

Atlanta has become the undisputed financial center of the Southeast. Twenty-seven international banks, substantially all of the money center banks, and a strong network of regional and local banks have established permanent offices in the city. These financial institutions provide the business community with excellent services, enabling large and small companies to obtain the requisite financial support to operate successful businesses in Georgia. Furthermore, access to the international banks opens doors throughout the world for Georgia businesses seeking new opportunities.

Financial Center

Economic forecasters acknowledge that the foregoing dynamic factors will make Georgia one of the fastest growing states in the nation during the remainder of this century.

11.2 Choosing the Legal Form of the Business

One of the first decisions you must make when starting your new business is to choose which legal form of business organization you will adopt. There are three basic forms: the sole proprietorship, the partnership, and the corporation. General considerations for choosing a legal form of business are located in sections 2.1–2.4. More state-specific considerations are discussed below.

A sole proprietorship is a business that is owned by one person. Because there are no formal requirements by law for setting up a sole proprietorship, you will find it relatively simple to form and operate. A sole proprietorship offers you more control of your business, fewer tax requirements and filings than other forms of business, and all the profits (or losses). Be aware, however, that as a sole proprietor, you will be personally liable for your business' debts and obligations.

Sole Proprietorships

Since the owner of a sole proprietorship is not considered an employee of the business, you do not have to pay any unemployment tax on your own salary or obtain workers' compensation insurance for yourself.

Of course, once you hire additional employees, you will be responsible for paying unemployment tax — as well as other payroll taxes — and providing workers' compensation coverage for your employees. In addition, a variety of employee-related laws and regulations will also apply to your business. For more information on your responsibilities as an employer, refer to Section 11.5.

When first starting your business, you may need to register your business name if you intend to operate under any name other than your own true name. For specifics on how to register your fictitious or assumed business name, refer to Section 11.4. This section covers other basic requirements — such as tax collection and reporting, obtaining licenses and permits, and paying property taxes — you will need to consider when operating a business within the state.

From a tax perspective, the state of Georgia follows the federal system and uses the net income or loss figure from *Schedule C* of IRS *Form 1040*, which is added to other income using Georgia *Form 500*. Your proprietorship income is included on your individual income tax return and for married persons filing a joint return is taxed at a graduated rate from 1% to 5% on the first $10,000 of net taxable income, plus 6% on the excess net taxable income of more than $10,000.[1] The actual tax on the first $10,000 amounts to $340 on a joint return.

There are slight variations for single taxpayers or married taxpayers filing separately. Unless an extension is obtained, the tax return must be filed and the taxes paid no later than April 15,[2] subject to the estimated tax requirements discussed in Section 11.4. For more information on income tax requirements, contact the Georgia Department of Revenue.

Income Tax Division
Georgia Department of Revenue
507 Trinity-Washington Building
Atlanta, GA 30334
(404) 656-4291 (Individual returns)

Partnerships

Any two or more individuals or entities who agree to contribute money, labor, property, or skill to a business and who agree to share in its profits, losses, and management are considered to have a partnership. Georgia law recognizes both general and limited partnerships.

General Partnerships

As a partner in a general partnership, you have the right to share in management and have unlimited personal liability for the partnership's debts, taxes, and other obligations. Even though you are not required to submit or file any formal documents regarding your partnership, it is sound business practice for you and your partner(s) to draw up a partnership agreement that, at a minimum, outlines basic business issues. Consider consulting an attorney when writing your partnership agreement.

At least two different persons or entities are required to create a general partnership. No minimum amount of capital is required by Georgia law, and there are no filing requirements other than the annual filing of *Form 700*, which is discussed below.

A local business license is required, and although there is no requirement for the filing of articles of a general partnership, it is customary that a partnership agreement be filed in the county in which the partnership owns real property or conducts business.

Under the Uniform Partnership Act, title to any real property of the general partnership will vest in the partnership as a legal entity rather than in the individual partners.[3]

A general partnership cannot operate under a name containing the words "company," "corporation," "incorporated," or "limited" and should not use any name that would generally mislead the public or be confused with another business. Any general partnership which carries on any trade or business under a partnership name which does not disclose the individual ownership of the business or profession must, prior to commencing business, file a trade name registration statement. See Section 11.4 for a detailed explanation of trade name registration.

A general partnership in itself is usually not subject to an income tax; however, every Georgia partnership is required to file an informational return for each taxable year on *Form 700*. The return lists the partnership's gross income, the deductions allowed by statute, the names and addresses of individuals entitled to share in the net income of the partnership, if the net income were distributed, and the distributive share amount of each individual.[4]

The tax return must be filed with the Georgia Department of Revenue on or before April 15 of each year, unless the taxpayer uses a fiscal year other than the calendar year, in which case the return must be filed on or before the 15th day of the fourth month after the close of the partnership fiscal year.[5]

You and your partner(s) are required to report your share of the partnership's profit or loss on your personal individual income tax returns.

Limited Partnerships

A limited partnership can be formed between two or more individuals, partnerships, corporations, or other associations. In this type of partnership, limited partners have limited liability and are only liable for the amount of their investment in the partnership. In exchange for this limited liability, limited partners have no control of the partnership's management. That responsibility is left to the general partners who have unlimited liability. Under Georgia's Revised Limited Partnership Act, however, even a limited partner who takes an active role in the conduct of the partnership's business is not subject to unlimited liability.[6]

However, a third party who is misled by a limited partner's participation in the business may sue on partnership-by-estoppel or fraud grounds. A limited partnership must always have at least one general partner and at least one limited partner. To form a limited partnership, you must file a *Certificate of Limited Partnership* with the Georgia Secretary of State.

The *Certificate of Limited Partnership* must contain:

- The exact name of the limited partnership;
- The name and address of a registered agent and address of the registered office in Georgia to be used for service of legal process on the limited partnership;

- The name and business address of each general partner;
- The latest date on which the limited partnership may be dissolved; and
- The signature of each of the general partners.

The certificate may also include other matters as determined by you and your general partners.[7]

There is a $60 fee for filing the *Certificate of Limited Partnership* for a new domestic limited partnership. A certified copy can be obtained from the secretary of state at a cost of $10.

Proposed names for your new limited partnership may be reserved for a 90-day period.[8] When a request to reserve a name is made, the secretary of state's office will conduct a search of its records to determine whether the proposed name is available.

If the name is available, the secretary of state will issue a name reservation.[9] The name must contain the words "limited partnership" or the abbreviation "L.P." The name must also be distinguishable on the records of the secretary of state from the name of any other limited partnership organized in Georgia, any foreign limited partnership having authority to do business in Georgia, and any corporation, professional corporation, or association on file with the secretary of state.[10]

Each limited partnership is required to deliver and file an annual registration with the secretary of state between January 1 and April 1 of each year. This annual registration is filed on a form that is mailed to your limited partnership during December of each year. The annual registration must contain:

- The name of the limited partnership and the state under whose law it is organized;
- The name of the registered agent and the address of the registered office in Georgia;
- The correct mailing address of the limited partnership;
- Any additional information that is necessary to enable the secretary of state to carry out the provisions of the revised act; and
- The signature of an authorized representative of the limited partnership.[11]

Failure to file an annual registration on behalf of a limited partnership may result in the following sanctions:

- The limited partnership may not maintain an action or proceeding in any court in Georgia.
- A domestic or foreign limited partnership which fails for three consecutive years to meet filing requirements may be placed on inactive status.[12]

Careful attention must be given to compliance with applicable securities law requirements as discussed later in this section — particularly if a large group of people invest in the limited partnership.

Corporations

A corporation is a more complicated form of business because it is considered a distinct legal entity and has a legal status or existence separate from you, the incorporator or owner. One of the main advantages to incorporating your business is that you are not personally liable for the corporation's debts, as long as you comply with all the necessary corporate formalities and recordkeeping requirements.

To learn more about corporate formalities, obtain a copy of *The Essential Corporation Handbook* by Carl Sniffen from your local bookstore or through The Oasis Press.

If you are considering incorporating your business, consult an attorney to be sure you know what your responsibilities are and to better understand your options. Here is a brief overview of some of the issues you will need to address when incorporating your business. Keep in mind you will need to research more details if you do decide to incorporate.

Incorporation

To form a corporation, your articles of incorporation must be filed with the secretary of state's office.[13] They must be accompanied by a $60 filing fee.[14]

Your articles of incorporation must include:

- The name and address of each incorporator;
- The name and street address, not a post office box, of the registered agent and office for acceptance of service of legal process on behalf of the corporation;
- The amount of authorized stock;
- The corporate name; and
- The name and address of the corporation's initial principal office.

Your articles of incorporation may optionally include, among other things:

- The names and addresses of the initial board of directors;
- A specified duration of the corporation;
- A par value for the corporation's shares;
- Minimum capital requirements for the corporation;
- The purpose or purposes for which the corporation is organized; and
- Any provision for shareholder preemptive rights to acquire additional shares of the corporation.[15]

Prior to incorporation, you must mail a notice to the publisher of the legal newspaper of the county in which your corporation's initial registered office is located requesting that notice of the incorporation be advertised in that newspaper.

A $40 advertising fee, payable by check to the appropriate legal newspaper, must be filed with the notice. The notice of incorporation must be published once a week for two consecutive weeks.

Along with the articles of incorporation, you or an agent acting on behalf of your corporation, must also execute and file a certificate with the secretary of state, whose office verifies that the request for publication of the notice of incorporation was made, and the fee was paid.[16]

When selecting a name for your corporation, keep in mind that it must contain a word such as "corporation," "incorporated," "company," or "limited" — or abbreviations of such words.[17] Also, you may not use a name of any other corporation or entity doing business in Georgia. As with limited partnerships, it is a good idea to reserve a name with the secretary of state. Name reservations are limited to a 90-day period and are nonrenewable.[18]

Close Corporation Status

Under Georgia's corporate code, corporations with 50 or fewer shareholders may now elect statutory close corporation status by so stating in the articles of incorporation. This election subjects such corporations to certain statutory provisions designed for small closely held corporations.[19] All stock certificates in a statutory close corporation must carry a special legend in accordance with code provisions.[20]

Election of statutory close corporation status automatically restricts the transferability of shares, unless otherwise provided by the articles of incorporation, by subjecting them to a right of first refusal procedure. The share transfer restrictions are limited to written offers for cash.[21]

A corporation electing close corporation status has a right to buy shares from a third-party transferee who acquired the shares from a shareholder in violation of a transfer requirement. For example, a close corporation could reacquire shares even though the corporation failed to place a legend on the share certificates, or a restriction on transfer is held invalid by court.[22]

The close corporation election generally allows a corporation to provide in its articles that the executor or administrator of a decedent shareholder's estate may compel the corporation to purchase his or her shares.

The close corporation election also permits the articles, bylaws, or shareholder agreement to authorize one or more shareholders to dissolve the corporation at will. Shareholders in statutory close corporations have automatic preemptive rights, unless otherwise provided in the articles of incorporation.[23]

A statutory close corporation may also operate without a board of directors if its articles, bylaws, or shareholder agreement contains a statement to that effect. In such case, the shareholders will assume any liability the directors would have had.[24]

It should be noted that many of the characteristics of a statutory close corporation can be achieved under the regular corporate code by including the appropriate provisions in a corporation's articles or bylaws.

The S corporation election — previously known as the Subchapter S corporation — allows the flow-through of taxable income and losses to the individual stockholders who are subject to tax within the state of Georgia.

An S corporation which has one or more stockholders who are nonresidents of Georgia must file a consent, *Form 600-SCA*, and pay Georgia income tax on their allocated share of the net corporate income.[25] The S corporation election will not be recognized in Georgia unless all required nonresident forms are filed and the nonresident pays Georgia income tax.

S Corporations

If a corporation that is already incorporated in another state or another country wishes to transact business within the state of Georgia, it must first obtain a certificate of authority from the secretary of state.[26] The application for the certificate of authority must set forth:

Foreign Corporations

- The corporation's name;
- The names and business addresses of the officers and directors;
- The mailing address of its principal office;
- The date and place of original incorporation;
- Its period of duration; and
- The name and address of the registered agent and office within the state of Georgia.[27]

The application for a certificate of authority must be submitted with a certificate of existence, which is issued by the secretary of state or other official having custody of corporate records in the place of incorporation.[28] The certificate must be forwarded with a $170 filing fee.[29]

The foreign corporation must also obtain a city or county business license. Finally, each year the foreign corporation must file an annual registration,[30] together with a $15 filing fee.

A $500 penalty will apply if a company begins to do business in Georgia prior to obtaining a certificate of authority.[31]

Each year your corporation must file an annual registration with the secretary of state, setting forth the name of the corporation and its state or country of incorporation; the name and address of its registered office and the name of its registered agent at that office in Georgia; the mailing address of its principal office; and the names and addresses of its chief executive officer, chief financial officer, and secretary, or individuals holding similar positions.

Annual Registration

The annual registration must be filed between January 1 and April 1 each year,[32] together with the payment of an annual $15 registration fee. Any change in the information noted above is to be reflected on the annual registration.[33] If the annual registration is not filed within 60 days after it is due, together with all required fees and penalties, the secretary of state is authorized to involuntarily dissolve the corporation.[34]

Shortly after your corporation is formed, a state withholding tax identification number and a Georgia sales tax number must be obtained by completing Georgia Department of Revenue *Form G-5* and forms CRF-002, -004, and -005.[35] Samples of these forms have been provided at the back of this book. Local business licenses must be obtained by completing and filing the appropriate local forms.

On or before the fifteenth day of the third month following incorporation, the initial license and occupation tax return, Georgia Department of Revenue *Form 600*, must be filed and a tax paid based on the value of the stock actually issued by the new corporation — the corporation's "net worth" — according to the following schedule:[36]

Corporate Net Worth	Tax Due	Corporate Net Worth	Tax Due
$0 – $10,000	$10	$1,000,000 – $2,000,000	$ 750
10,000 – 25,000	20	2,000,000 – 4,000,000	1,000
25,000 – 40,000	40	4,000,000 – 6,000,000	1,250
40,000 – 60,000	60	6,000,000 – 8,000,000	1,500
60,000 – 80,000	75	8,000,000 – 10,000,000	1,750
80,000 – 100,000	100	10,000,000 – 12,000,000	2,000
100,000 – 150,000	125	12,000,000 – 14,000,000	2,500
150,000 – 200,000	150	14,000,000 – 16,000,000	3,000
200,000 – 300,000	200	16,000,000 – 18,000,000	3,500
300,000 – 500,000	250	18,000,000 – 20,000,000	4,000
500,000 – 750,000	300	20,000,000 – 22,000,000	4,500
750,000 – 1,000,000	500	22,000,000 – ∞	5,000

Franchise Tax

The Georgia corporation net worth tax, sometimes referred to as the franchise tax or the license and occupation tax, is based upon the amount of stock issued by the corporation, paid-in surplus, and retained earnings rather than upon the amount of stock authorized. Accordingly, the Georgia corporation net worth tax is less than the franchise tax imposed by other states which tax on the basis of amount of stock authorized by the corporation. The minimum tax is $10 for a corporation with a net worth under $10,000, and the maximum is $5,000 for a corporation with a net worth in excess of $22,000,000. If the corporation is formed after July 1, the amount of tax due will be one-half the amount shown above. The state of Georgia does not impose a documentary stamp tax with respect to the issuance or transfer of stock certificates.

State Income Tax

As a rule, every domestic corporation and foreign corporation authorized to do business within the state of Georgia must pay a nongraduated income tax equal to 6% of its Georgia taxable net income. Georgia taxable net income constitutes income from property owned or from business done within the state of Georgia, less all deductions authorized by state law. Thus, income includes profits realized from:

- Real or personal property situated in the state of Georgia; or
- Intangible property having an actual or business situs within Georgia.

For the most part, the Georgia return must be completed in the same manner as the federal return.[37] However, the following rules apply in determining net income:

- Interest and income derived from obligations of any state other than the state of Georgia are added to the taxable income to the extent that the interest income is not included in gross income for federal income tax purposes.
- The obligations of the United States, such as U.S. Bonds, are subtracted from taxable income to the extent such interest is included in gross income for federal income tax purposes.
- Any taxes on net profits accrued within the taxable year are added to the taxable income to the extent that such taxes are deducted to determine the federal taxable income.
- Profits, losses, and deductions previously used in computing Georgia taxable income shall not again be used in computing Georgia taxable income.
- Nonrecognition shall be allowed on the sale or exchange of real or personal property within the state of Georgia, if the taxpayer replaces such property with similar property within the state of Georgia.[38]

Net taxable income is subject to adjustments, allocation, and apportionment as provided by state law. If all of the corporation's business is conducted solely within the geographic boundaries of the state of Georgia, the Georgia taxable income is based upon the corporation's total taxable net income. The computation becomes more complex, however, when a corporation is actively engaged in business in several states. The Georgia corporate income tax applies only to that portion of the corporation's income generated within Georgia.[39]

Three-Factor Method

To determine the portion of a multistate corporation's income that is subject to tax in Georgia, the state uses the three-factor apportionment formula described below, which has been adopted by the majority of other states.

The corporation's net investment nonbusiness income — such as interest, rents, or gains from sales of property held for an investment that is deemed to have a situs in the state — is allocated to income taxable in Georgia. Interest received from bonds or other income received from intangible property held for investment is not subject to apportionment.[40]

The corporation's net business income attributable to the state of Georgia, is determined by multiplying the corporation's total net business income by a Georgia apportionment ratio using the following three-factor formula:

$$\frac{\dfrac{\text{Value of Georgia Property}}{\text{Total Property Owned (U.S.)}} + \dfrac{\text{Total Georgia Payroll}}{\text{Total U.S. Payroll}} + \dfrac{\text{Georgia Gross Receipts}}{\text{Total U.S. Gross Receipts}}}{\text{divided by 3}}$$

This ratio is applied to the corporation's total U.S. net income to determine the amount of income taxable in Georgia.

The Georgia income tax return is due on March 15, if your corporation is a calendar year taxpayer, or on the 15th day of the third month following the close of your corporation's tax year, if other than the calendar year.[41] Use *Form 600, Corporate Income Tax Return* to file your return. Affiliated corporations may file a consolidated return. Returns must be mailed to the Income Tax Division of the Georgia Department of Revenue.

Income Tax Division
Georgia Department of Revenue
507 Trinity-Washington Building
Atlanta, GA 30334
(404) 656-4165 (Corporate returns)

In certain cases, the Georgia Department of Revenue will grant extensions as long as it is no longer than six months from the due date of the return.[42]

Interest accrues at the rate of 12% per annum on any tax due after the normal filing date.[43] An additional late payment penalty of one-half of 1% per month accrues until the tax is paid.[44]

In the event the return is not filed on a timely basis, there is a delinquent filing penalty of 5% of the tax shown on the return for each month or fraction thereof — up to a maximum of 25% — as well as a 5% penalty for negligent underpayment of tax.[45] In the case of fraud, a penalty of an amount equal to 50% of the underpayment will be added to the tax.[46]

Tax Credit

Corporations which create a minimum of 10 new permanent jobs in a county designated by the commissioner of the Georgia Department of Community Affairs to be among the 25% of Georgia's less-developed counties shall be entitled to a $1,000 tax credit per new employee. This credit can be used each year from the second to the sixth year after the new job is created. The maximum tax credit is 50% of the tax liability. Unused credits may be carried forward for 10 years.[47]

For more information on incorporation or corporate filing requirements, contact the Corporations Division of the Georgia Secretary of State's office.

Corporations Division
Georgia Secretary of State
2 Martin Luther King, Jr. Drive
Atlanta, GA 30334
(404) 656-3900

State Securities Laws

When your newly formed corporation issues shares of its stock to you and to any other shareholders, you must be very careful to comply with both federal and state securities laws. Otherwise, you may be a target for lawsuits from disgruntled investors in your corporation and be subject to criminal prosecution.

In addition to regulation by the federal government, the offer or sale of securities in Georgia is subject to state regulation pursuant to the Georgia Securities Act.[48] Georgia securities laws apply not only to certificates of stock issued to corporations, but also to limited partnership interests, certificates of interest, or participation in any profit-sharing agreement. Security laws may also apply to general partnerships and business borrowings, including bonds, debentures, and evidence of indebtedness.

Under the Georgia Securities Act, it is unlawful for any person to offer or sell any security in Georgia unless the security is subject to an effective registration statement or the security or transaction is exempt. The Georgia Securities Act exempts certain securities transactions from its registration requirements as long as they comply with the following conditions:

- There are no more than 15 purchasers of securities of the issuer in Georgia during the 12-month period ending on the date of issuance — exclusive of persons acquiring securities that are not subject to the Georgia Securities Act — that are exempt under other provisions of the act or that have been registered.

- The securities are not offered for sale by means of publicly disseminated advertisements or sales literature.

- Any certificates representing securities issued or offered for sale under the exemption are marked for a period of one year from the date of issuance or sale to indicate clearly that they were issued or sold in reliance on the exemption.

  They cannot be sold or transferred except in a transaction that is exempt under the Georgia Securities Act, pursuant to an effective registration statement, or in a transaction that otherwise complies with the Georgia Securities Act.

- Each purchaser in Georgia executes a statement showing securities issued or offered for sale under the exemption have been purchased for investment for his or her own account.

  Any individual holding securities for one year past the date on which the securities were fully paid for by that individual is presumed to have purchased the securities for investment.[49]

State regulations issued pursuant to the Georgia Securities Act also create an exemption for certain transactions which are exempt from registration requirements imposed by federal securities laws under the federal law known as "Regulation D."[50]

Various conditions and limitations must be met if this exemption is to be available, including, but not limited to, the following:

- No commission, finder's fee, or similar remuneration can be paid to any unregistered securities dealer or salesperson in connection with the issue.

- All necessary reports, notices, and fees must be filed in a timely manner.
- The aggregate number of unaccredited purchasers cannot exceed 35 purchasers in Georgia during any 12-month period.

Exemptions from registration also exist for certain types of securities, including, for example, promissory notes which mature within nine months from the date of issuance and which are not offered for sale by advertisements publicly disseminated in the news media or through the mail.[51]

Transactional exemptions other than those previously discussed may also be available, depending upon the facts and circumstances of the particular contemplated transactions. If an exemption is not available for a particular issue, then the issue must be registered.

The filing of a registration statement can prove to be a very complicated and expensive undertaking. In offerings by an issuer, detailed information and documentation concerning the nature and extent of the offering and the parties involved must be filed and provided to potential investors to comply with the disclosure requirements.

Offerings that do not exceed $500,000 in the aggregate or involve 50 or fewer purchasers but which do not qualify for exemption may nevertheless qualify for registration as a small issue. Informational filings are required for a small issue registration under the Georgia Securities Act, but the filing requirements are not as burdensome as the general registration requirements.

Even though a security may be exempt from registration, there is no exemption from the anti-fraud provisions of the Georgia Securities Act. These provisions make it unlawful for any person to make an untrue statement of a material fact in conjunction with the offer or sale of a security. Statements may be oral or written.

It is also unlawful for anyone to omit a material fact when such an omission would render statements made in conjunction with the offer or sale misleading. Likewise, anyone who directly or indirectly engages in a scheme to defraud or deceive a purchaser or seller of a security — or who represents a registered or exempt security as recommended or approved, in any way, by the state of Georgia or the United States — is in violation of the Georgia Securities Act.

Any person who violates the provisions of the Georgia Securities Act is liable to the purchaser for the amount the purchaser paid for the security, plus interest from the date of purchase. If the purchaser has disposed of the security, he or she may recover the difference between the original purchase price of the security and his or her selling price, plus interest from the date of original payment to the date of repayment.

In addition, every director, officer, or partner, or the seller and any dealer or salesperson involved in the sale may be liable to the purchaser for damages.

A willful violation of any provision of the securities act is a felony, punishable upon conviction by a fine of not more than $500,000 or imprisonment for not less than one and not more than five years, or both.

Remember that sales of securities must comply with both state and federal laws. While there may be many similarities between certain state and federal laws, the requirements are by no means identical, and compliance under state law will not in and of itself constitute compliance under federal law.[52]

When forming a business entity in Georgia, consult an attorney to determine whether state or federal or both securities laws will apply to the formation or operation of your business and to ensure compliance with those laws.

Dividends Received Deduction

If your corporation owns stock in another corporation, your company may qualify for a dividends received deduction which could reduce the income tax it has to pay on dividends it receives. To find out if your corporation can take advantage of the dividends received deduction, consult with your accountant.

Georgia determines corporate taxable income by reference to taxable income as defined in the federal Internal Revenue Code.[53] This means that the applicable deduction for dividends received by a corporation under the federal Internal Revenue Code (70%, 80%, or 100%) is reflected in the taxable income of a corporation in Georgia. For additional information regarding the federal dividends received deduction, see sections 2.4 and 8.2.

11.3 Buying an Existing Business — State Legal Requirements

Buying a business is always a significant undertaking, and as a prospective purchaser, you must investigate the business being acquired as thoroughly as possible to avoid hidden liabilities and pitfalls. Be sure this investigation includes:

- A review of business books and records, including tax returns, payroll records, current receivables and payables, and minute books;
- A physical inventory of all furniture, fixtures, equipment, inventory and tangible personal or real property being acquired;
- A review of the status of any leases, contracts, or pending litigation;
- A search to determine if the seller has any overdue taxes, such as unemployment tax, owed to the state or federal governments;
- A review of all intangible property rights, such as patent, trade or service marks and copyrights; and
- Discussions with customers and suppliers of the business.

In many instances, you or the seller may want to keep the potential sale confidential, so your discussions with customers and suppliers may be limited. Any purchasing agreement should contain a detailed set of representations and warranties concerning the business being acquired. You may also wish to consider using an escrow or set-off provisions to provide recourse in the event a hidden liability is discovered after closing.

Purchasing an existing business is one endeavor you should not attempt without the assistance of an attorney. For more information on buying a business, refer to Chapter 3. Section 9.9 also discusses important new environmental laws you need to be aware of when purchasing an existing business.

At a minimum, as the purchaser of an existing business, you should become familiar with the state requirements outlined below.

Bulk Sales Law

The bulk transfer article of the Georgia Uniform Commercial Code[54] is designed to prevent commercial fraud. This article protects unsecured creditors from a merchant who would sell his or her company and abscond to the French Riviera without paying his or her bills. You may be surprised to discover that you may have to pay these debts.

The bulk sales article applies only to enterprises whose principal business is the sale of merchandise from stock, including those who manufacture what they sell.[55] A bulk transfer is defined as any transfer in bulk of a major part of the materials, supplies, merchandise, or other inventory of the transferor.[56] The grant of a security interest, the general assignment for the benefit of all creditors, and the settlement of a lien or other security interest is not subject to the bulk transfer article.[57]

The article sets forth specific requirements which must be satisfied by you and the seller. Generally, as the purchaser, you must:

- Require the seller to furnish a sworn list of existing creditors stating the names and business addresses of all creditors, amounts due, and any claims against the seller;[58]
- Prepare, along with the seller, a schedule of the property transferred;[59]
- Retain the list and schedule for six months following the transfer; or
  - If the seller is an individual, file the list with the clerk of the superior court in the county of residence of the seller;
  - If the seller is a partnership, corporation, or other business entity, file the list with the clerk of the superior court in the county of the principal place of business;[60] and
- Give notice personally or by registered or certified mail to all creditors on the list at least 10 days before taking possession or paying for the goods, setting forth certain information relating to the transfer.[61]

Unless you comply with the requirements imposed by the bulk transfer article, the property transferred remains subject to the claims of the seller's creditors.[62] These creditors may attempt to recover their losses by use of creditor's remedies such as levy, attachment, or garnishment. If you comply with the bulk sales law, the seller's former creditors cannot later claim the assets you have purchased. To meet the requirements of the bulk sales law when you buy or sell a business, consult with your attorney.

Before closing a deal, it is important for you to know if there are any security interests or liens against the business that would interfere with you receiving clear title to any part of it. A security interest is an interest in personal property or fixtures which secures payment or performance of an obligation.[63] Typically, the sale of goods on credit or the financing of business operations will include the grant of a security interest in inventory, equipment, or intangibles. The Georgia Uniform Commercial Code establishes the legal framework for the establishment and enforcement of security interests in personal property.[64]

Recorded Security Interests

To determine whether personal property being purchased is subject to a security interest and whether financing statements have been filed by the seller's creditors, your attorney should make a thorough search of the Uniform Commercial Code index kept by the clerk of the superior court of the appropriate county.[65] The table below details such a search.

Type of Seller	Place of Filing
Resident individual	County of residence
Partnership, corporation, or other business entity with an office in Georgia	County of principal place of business
Nonresident individual or business without an office in Georgia	County where the property is kept or used in Georgia

It is important to note that in addition to recording a financing statement in the appropriate county records, a security interest may also be perfected by possession.[66] Thus, you should take appropriate steps to ensure that the seller has actual possession of all of the assets which are part of the purchase.

In addition, if you are purchasing personal property, you should conduct a search of other public records maintained by the clerk of the superior court of the county in which the seller of such property resides and conducts business. At a minimum, the *General Execution Docket, Federal Tax Lien Digest*, and *Index of Pending Lawsuits* should be reviewed to determine their effect on the proposed purchase. A list of the Georgia counties and county seats is located in the Appendix.

Certain types of interests in personal property may be filed under other laws. For example, the motor vehicle certificate of title law provides that a lien on a motor vehicle may be perfected by filing an application for a certificate of title with the lien noted on the title.[67]

If you are purchasing real estate, you should search the records maintained by the clerk of the superior court of the county in which the real estate is located. You should also review the *Lis Pendens Index* as well as all county and city tax digests to insure that all ad valorem taxes have been paid on a timely basis. It is also recommended that an abstract of title be prepared on each tract of real property to discover all matters of record, including any liens, deeds to secure debt easements, and other matters affecting the title.

As a final note, if the seller is in bankruptcy, you should consider whether the sale must be approved by the trustee or bankruptcy judge.

Tax Experience Rating

As an employer, you are responsible for paying an unemployment tax to the state — see Section 11.5. Your company's unemployment experience rate determines how much you must pay or contribute to the state. These contributions are put aside as insurance for when employees lose their jobs and qualify to receive unemployment compensation while they are looking for work.

Your experience rate is based on your relationship between unemployment claims and your employee's taxable wages. For example, the more former employees who claim benefits, the higher your experience rating. Conversely, the fewer former employees claiming benefits, the lower your rate. If you are a new employer, you will be assigned a standard rate by the state. This rate may increase or decrease over the course of time, depending in large part on your unemployment experience history.

Unemployment Tax Release

If you purchase an entire business, the Georgia Department of Labor account held by the seller automatically passes to you.[68] This account consists of all amounts of unemployment taxes paid by the seller, as well as all liabilities for such taxes. Thus, you need to find out if the seller has properly paid all employment taxes up to the date of sale, because you will be responsible for any of his or her unpaid unemployment taxes.

Within ten days from the date of acquisition, you must complete and return a request for determination of status, and the seller must give notice to the Employment Security Agency of the acquisition by completing the Change of Status section on the back of the quarterly report.[69]

In the case of a purchase of a clearly identifiable part of an existing business, you still may succeed to a portion of the predecessor's account. This procedure begins with the steps outlined above. You must then, within two calendar quarters from the date of acquisition, complete and return an application for a partial transfer of the account on *Form ESA-641* and *Form 641A*. The application must also be accompanied by an agreement to the transfer by the seller.

Upon receipt of the application, a transfer percentage will be determined by relating the total taxable payroll of the acquired portion to the total taxable payroll of the predecessor for the 18-month period immediately preceding the date of acquisition. Then, that percentage of the predecessor's account will be transferred to you.

If you are already an employer subject to the regulation of the Georgia Department of Labor at the time of acquisition, your currently established tax rate will remain in effect until the next quarter, at which time the transferred record and your record will be combined and a rate computation made. If you are not an employer at the time of acquisition, you will be taxed based upon the tax rate that is already established for the seller.[70]

Because a new business must pay the standard rate of 2.64% on the first $8,500 of wages per employee, the ability to succeed to an existing rate of less than 2.64% can result in significant savings. For more information on unemployment experience ratings, taxes, and contributions, please contact:

Unemployment Insurance Division – Central Office
Georgia Department of Labor
148 International Boulevard, NE, Suite 900
Atlanta, GA 30303
(404) 656-3045

Sales Tax Release

A seller of a business liable for sales and use taxes must make a final return and payment of such taxes to the Georgia Department of Revenue within 15 days from the date of the sale of the business or its stock of goods.[71]

You are required to withhold a sufficient amount of the purchase price to cover the amount of taxes, interest, and penalties due and unpaid until the seller produces a receipt from the commissioner of the Georgia Department of Revenue showing that the taxes, interest, and penalties have been paid or that they are not due.[72] If you fail to withhold the required amount, you will be liable for the tax payment.[73]

Other Unpaid Taxes

If the seller has not paid real or personal property taxes, you may take the property subject to a tax lien. As indicated earlier in this section, it is your responsibility to search the tax digests and to check with the county and city tax collectors to determine whether all property taxes have been paid. Additionally, if you are purchasing a corporation, ensure that the corporate net worth tax[74] and the corporate income tax[75] have been paid.

Sales and Use Tax on Purchase

Generally, no sales or use tax liability will arise upon the purchase of an existing business. If the sale of the business is made in a "complete and bona fide liquidation" of the seller's business, the transaction is considered isolated and casual and does not fall within the reach of the Georgia Sales and Use Tax Provisions.[76]

11.4. State Requirements that Apply to Nearly All New Businesses

Regardless of the legal form of business organization you choose, your business will be required to comply with a number of state requirements, such as obtaining business licenses, paying various taxes, and registering your fictitious business name. This section introduces you to several basic state requirements and gives you a better understanding of what you need to do. For a quick overview of what your particular legal form must do, review the checklist of state requirements at the end of this section.

State Licenses

Many occupations and businesses are required to be licensed in Georgia. The secretary of state is responsible for managing most of the state licensing boards and for regulating the incorporation and domestication of businesses within the state of Georgia. Specific licensing requirements for various types of businesses are set forth by each licensing board and generally include a combination of a security bond for the protection of the general public, minimal educational and experience requirements, and successful passage of licensing examinations. For a listing of occupations and businesses that require state licenses, refer to Section 11.6, or contact:

Georgia Secretary of State
(404) 656-3900

Estimated Income Taxes

One of the most surprising concepts to new entrepreneurs is that, as a business owner, you will have to estimate how much money you will make before you make it, then pay taxes several times each year on the amount you have estimated, sometimes before you have even earned the money. No matter which business form you choose, filing and paying estimated taxes must now be part of your regular agenda.

If you don't have the money to pay estimated income taxes, get your accountant's advice on whether you should get a loan to cover the tax when due; or instead, pay interest in penalties to the government after the end of the year. Note that any state tax penalties you pay — unlike the state tax itself — will not be allowed as a deduction on your federal tax return.

Individual

If your business is a sole proprietorship or partnership, you must report the business income — whether it is actually distributed to you or not — on your personal tax return. Your estimated tax payments are due on the same dates as the federal estimated taxes — April 15, June 15, September 15, and January 15.[77] If you are just starting your business, contact your state income tax office to get estimated tax forms. To be sure you handle the estimating, filing, and paying correctly, get help from an accountant.

To make your estimated tax payments, complete *Form 500ES*, which is available from the Georgia Department of Revenue. After your first year of paying estimated taxes to the state, you will probably automatically receive forms to use in future years, but even if the forms don't come, you are still responsible for filing and paying on time. Failure to file an estimated return or to pay the proper amount of tax may result in a 9% per annum penalty assessed against the amount of the underpayments.[78]

Corporation

A corporation subject to the payment of corporate tax in the state of Georgia must file a declaration and pay estimated tax if taxable income can be expected to exceed $25,000 per year.[79] Generally, the estimated taxes are due on the same dates as federal corporate estimated taxes. The tax returns should be filed on Georgia Department of Revenue *Form 60T-ES*. Failure to file a declaration of estimated tax may result in a 5% penalty as well as a 9% annual interest penalty for underpayment.

Sales and Use Tax Permits

All businesses operating in the state of Georgia, regardless of form — proprietorship, partnership, or corporation — that engage in retail sales of tangible personal property must collect and remit the Georgia sales tax which has a statewide rate of 4%,[80] or $0.04 (four cents) of tax for each dollar of sales. For sales amounts with fractional parts of a dollar in excess of whole dollars, the tax on the fractional part is taken from the following table:

Amount of Sale	Tax Collected
$0.00–$0.10 (ten cents or less)	$0.00 (zero)
0.11– 0.25 (eleven to twenty-five cents)	0.01 (one cent)
0.26– 0.50 (twenty-six to fifty cents)	0.02 (two cents)
0.51– 0.75 (fifty-one to seventy-five cents)	0.03 (three cents)
0.76– 1.00 (seventy-six cents to one dollar)	0.04 (four cents)

For example, the sales tax on $3.35 is $0.14 (fourteen cents): $0.04 (four cents) for each whole dollar for a total of $0.12 (twelve cents), plus $0.02 (two cents) for the fractional part, as shown above.

Your new business must file an application for a *Certificate of Registration*, *Form ST-1*, with the Sales and Use Tax Division of the Georgia Department of Revenue.

Approximately two weeks after filing the application, a *Certificate of Registration, Form ST-2*, will be issued to your new business, assigning a sales tax number.

The *Sales and Use Tax Report, Form ST-3*, must be filed and sales taxes paid on or before the 20th of each month, reflecting all sales made during the previous month.[81] If your sales and use tax liability for each month will be less than $100, you may request permission to file the sales tax form on a quarterly basis.

Depending on which forms you are returning to the Sales and Use Tax Division, there are different mailing addresses. To obtain the correct mailing address or to ask sales and use tax questions, contact the director's office at:

Sales and Use Tax Division
Georgia Department of Revenue
310 Trinity-Washington Building
270 Washington Street
Atlanta, GA 30334
(404) 656-4060

Local Sales Tax

In addition to the statewide 4% sales tax rate, a number of cities and counties have adopted a local option sales tax which adds another 1% to the statewide total. In Fulton and DeKalb counties, where an additional 1% tax has been levied to fund the Metropolitan Atlanta Rapid Transit Authority (MARTA), the combined sales tax rate is 6%.

Georgia businesses are entitled to a vendor's compensation equal to 3% of the total amount of sales and use taxes submitted each month. In other words, the business may subtract 3% of the total tax due to compensate the business for the time and expense expended in collecting and remitting the sales tax. The vendor's compensation is allowed only if the sales tax returns are filed on a timely basis.[82]

Georgia will assess a 5% penalty for each 30-day period or fraction thereof in which the sales taxes are not paid. This penalty is not to exceed 25%.[83] Interest accrues on the unpaid sales and use tax at the rate of 1% per month.

Sales and use taxes are not assessed for the purchase of real property or raw materials, nor are they assessed for sales made from a wholesaler to a retailer who, in turn, sells his or her products to the general public. The sales tax applies only when the retailer sells to the general public.[84] The retailer must furnish a sales tax number to the wholesaler in order to avoid the payment of the tax at this transactional level.

Sales tax must be collected with respect to leases of tangible personal property, utility charges, and hotel and motel rentals, but will not be assessed against the accommodations for apartments or office space leased for more than 90 continuous days. Sales of tickets for sporting events and amusement and entertainment activities are also subject to sales tax.

Automobiles and other vehicles purchased within the state are subject to the payment of the sales tax and any out-of-state purchase is subject to the Georgia use tax which is collected at the time the motor vehicle is titled in the state of Georgia. As purchaser of a motor vehicle, you must furnish a copy of the bill of sale and manufacturer's statement of origin to the Motor Vehicle Licensing Division of the Georgia Department of Revenue.

Other tangible items of personal property purchased outside the state are also subject to the use tax if a sales tax was not paid previously. An out-of-state building contractor is required to file a bond with the state to ensure full and complete payment for all sales taxes due on the purchase of building materials.

The Georgia sales and use tax law requires that a licensed dealer retain the books and records for all retail sales transactions for examination and audit by revenue department auditors for a period of three years.[85] The burden of proof as to whether or not a sale of tangible personal property is subject to the sales tax rests upon the seller, unless he or she obtains a certificate from the purchaser stating that the property has been purchased for resale.

The Georgia Department of Revenue aggressively pursues owners of corporate businesses who have not paid the sales tax on a timely basis and may attach personal liability to the officers in control of these corporations who use the collected sales tax funds for other purposes.

Exemptions

The Georgia law provides a number of specific exemptions from the sales and use tax requirements including:

- Sales to federal, state, or local governments;
- Sales by counties and municipalities;
- Fares and charges collected by the urban transit system for the transportation of passengers;
- Sales of drugs dispersed by prescription and prescription eyeglasses or contact lenses;
- Sales to any state-created hospital authority and sales to the University System of Georgia and its educational units; and
- A host of agricultural exemptions.[86]

One of the most important exemptions available to new businesses is the exemption from the sales and use tax on new machinery and equipment used directly in the manufacture of tangible personal property and incorporated for the first time into a manufacturing facility located in the state of Georgia. Air and water pollution control equipment that is certified by the Georgia Department of Natural Resources will also qualify for a sales and use exemption[87] These exemptions should be confirmed prior to the final decision to locate a new manufacturing facility in the state of Georgia.

Property Taxes

Businesses operating in Georgia are subject to an ad valorem property tax on the real property, equipment, inventory of finished goods, work in process, and raw materials owned by the taxpayer on January 1 of each year.[88] The determination of the "fair market" value of the real property and equipment is made by a county or city tax appraiser and is assessed at a rate of 40% of its appraised value.[89] The tax rate or millage rate is multiplied against the 40% assessed value to determine the actual tax due. The millage rate is set by the city council, county commissioners, or the local boards of education.

As an example of this somewhat confusing procedure, assume a company's plant and equipment have a fair market value of $200,000 and its inventory is valued at $100,000. A 40% assessed value is applied against the total value of $300,000, giving a total taxable value of $120,000. The taxable value of $120,000 is multiplied by the millage rate of, for example, 27 mills or 27 x 120, since the millage rate is equal to 1 mill ($1/10$ of a cent) for each $1,000 of value. Thus, the total tax liability is $3,240.

The millage rates set by the local governments and boards of education vary greatly across the state of Georgia from a high in the city of Atlanta of 52.60 mills to a low of 12.30 in Burke County. This will be a significant planning consideration for a new business with a large volume of inventory or substantial investments in property and equipment.

Certain types of property and entities receive special treatment or exemptions from the ad valorem tax. Qualified rehabilitated historic property is eligible for a preferential ad valorem tax assessment equal to the acquisition cost on value at the time of certification. The subsequent improvements and "rehabilitation" expenses are not included in determining fair market value for ad valorem tax purposes.[90]

Certain agricultural property is eligible for a reduced assessment of its fair market value. The ad valorem property tax valuation applies to standing timber only during the year the timber is harvested.[91] Most public and government property is exempt from the ad valorem tax, as are nonprofit hospitals, churches, and publicly owned and supported nursing and convalescent centers.[92]

Most counties require that the ad valorem tax be paid on or before December 20 of each year, but there are counties and cities that have earlier installment payment dates. As the owner of a new business, you should contact the local county tax commissioner directly to verify these deadlines.

Real Property

Tax returns on real property purchased by a new business must be filed with the local tax office in the county in which the property is located. The returns must be filed between January 1 and April 1, unless an earlier filing is required by the county. After the initial return, the tax commissioner's office will generate annual statements setting forth the appraised value and the assessed value for the real property.

The resident property owner has 30 days — 10 days in Fulton County — and the nonresident owner has 15 days to file a protest if he or she feels the appraisal is too high. In determining the fair market value for the property, the tax assessor and the court will consider comparable sales of like kind of property in the general locale, the highest and best use of the property, and the original cost and the replacement cost for the property.[93]

Exemptions

A number of counties and cities in Georgia have adopted freeport amendments which allow a percentage exemption for raw materials, work in process, and inventories of finished goods destined for shipment to out of state customers. This tax incentive should be carefully investigated by new manufacturing businesses.

Furthermore, to encourage business development in low income areas, certain business property has been specifically exempted from the ad valorem property tax.

Individual homeowners in the state of Georgia are entitled to a homestead exemption of $2,000 on property owned and occupied as a permanent residence on January 1 of each year.[94] The $2,000 exemption is deducted from the 40% assessed value of the homestead property. A special homestead exemption of $4,000 is available for homeowners 65 years of age or older with a net income of $8,000 or less. Social Security is exempted from this computation.

A homestead exemption for school tax purposes is allowed on the first $10,000 of assessed value for persons 62 years of age or older with annual gross household incomes of $8,000 or less. Special homestead exemptions apply in a few jurisdictions. This should be confirmed directly with the county tax commissioner. Generally, an application for the homestead exemption must be filed before April 1 after a home is purchased.

Effective January 1, 1991, an additional homestead exemption of $32,500 or the maximum amount granted to a disabled veteran under Section 802 of Title 38 of the United States Code is available as long as the veteran qualifies under the statutory definition and files a letter from the U.S. Department of Veterans Affairs with the county tax commission.[95]

If industrial revenue bonds (IRBs) are used to finance a new manufacturing facility, consideration should be given to having the local development authority be the record title owner of the facility. This procedure may entitle the business to a graduated exemption from the ad valorem tax.

A few of the more developed counties in the state of Georgia have a policy against negotiating for a lower or reduced ad valorem tax, but other counties that are anxious to attract new industries are willing to make this concession.

Intangibles Tax

As previously noted, the ad valorem tax in the state of Georgia applies to real property, machinery and equipment, inventory of finished goods, work in process, and raw materials and other items of personal property owned by a business. In the case of an individual, this ad valorem assessment includes the home and personal automobile. Intangibles taxes, on the other hand, are assessed on the value of stocks, bonds, and cash owned by the individual taxpayer.

The Georgia intangibles tax is based upon the fair market value of stocks, bonds, cash, and accrued interest owned by the Georgia taxpayer on January 1 of each year.[96]

On January 1, if a taxpayer owns stocks or bonds worth more than $20,000 or has cash deposits of more than $200,000 or any combination of the two which creates an intangibles tax liability of $20 or more, he or she must file *Form PL-159, Intangible Personal Property Tax Return.*[97] *Form PL-159* is normally filed at the same time as the personal income tax return, *Form 500*, and should be mailed to:

Intangible Tax Section
Georgia Department of Revenue
P.O. Box 38068   or   270 Washington Street, Room 404
Atlanta, GA 30334   Atlanta, GA 30334
(404) 656-4247

After the first intangibles tax return is filed with the state, each subsequent year a separate return form will be mailed to the individual taxpayer who must reflect changes and additions to his or her investment portfolio occurring during the year.

The Property Tax Division of the Georgia Department of Revenue provides a booklet, *Instructions for Georgia Intangible Tax Form, PL-159,* at no charge to interested taxpayers. This booklet contains new information and a taxpayer's codebook, plus *Form PL-159*. To request this publication, contact the director's office:

Property Tax Division
Georgia Department of Revenue
405 Trinity-Washington Building
270 Washington Street
Atlanta, GA 30334
(404) 656-4240

The rate of taxation for each class of intangible tax property is shown below:[98]

Type of Property	Tax Rate
Money (including cash, certificates of deposit, savings accounts)	$0.10 (ten cents) for each $1,000
Accounts receivable notes not secured by real estate; short-term notes secured by real estate	$0.10 (ten cents) for each $1,000
Bonds and debentures of corporations	$1.00 for each $1,000
Stocks of out-of-state corporations not paying Georgia taxes	$1.00 for each $1,000
Credits extended in connection with the purchase of stocks or bonds	$0.25 (twenty-five cents) for each $1,000
All other intangible property	$0.10 (ten cents) for each $1,000

The Georgia Department of Revenue verifies the fair market value of the intangible property listed on the return, including the January 1st value of the stocks and bonds, and computes the amount of tax due. This information is forwarded to the tax commissioner of the county in which the taxpayer lives. The tax commissioner will forward a bill for the intangibles taxes directly to you.

Exemptions from the Georgia intangibles tax include:[99]

- U.S. Savings Bonds, treasury bills, and other evidence of debt of the federal government, as well as industrial revenue bonds issued under Georgia law and other debt obligations of governmental agencies and corporations established by an act of the U.S. Congress;
- Intangible personal property owned by a trust forming part of a pension, profit-sharing, or stock bonus plan exempt from income under Internal Revenue Code, Section 401;
- Intangible property held exclusively for the benefit of religious, educational, or charitable institutions;
- Intangible property which is taxed in another state and related to the conduct of the business in another state — excluding restricted foreign intangibles; and
- Stock of a Georgia corporation and its subsidiaries, which includes Georgia depository financial institutions.

Intangibles Recording Tax

Another type of intangibles tax is imposed to record a deed to secure debt on real estate, if the promissory note which the deed secures contains repayment obligations that exceed three years in duration. This type of intangibles tax is frequently referred to as a recording tax because it is paid to the clerk of the superior court of the county in which the land is located at the time the deed to secure debt is recorded. The tax is calculated at the rate of $1.50 for each $500.00 of the face value of the long-term indebtedness. This tax is a one-time levy and the maximum amount of any intangible recording tax payable on any single note is $25,000.[100]

The deed to secure debt may not be filed without proof that the tax has been paid. A lender who does not properly comply with the rules of the intangible recording tax may lose his or her secured priority position. The funds required to pay the tax are normally charged to the purchaser of the real property at the time of the closing of the transfer of the real estate. In past years, there has been confusion about this intangibles tax, as to whether it applied to value or was a recording tax similar to a documentary stamp tax in other states. A new law which took effect January 1, 1991, clarifies this tax as a recording tax.

Motor Vehicle Titles and Taxation

All automobiles, trucks, and trailers are required to be registered with the Motor Vehicle Division of the Georgia Department of Revenue.[101] Generally, both a title certificate and a license tag are required for each vehicle. The cost for most automobile license tags and small truck tags is $8. The application for a license tag must be made within seven days after the purchase of a new, unregistered vehicle. Ordinarily, the automobile or truck dealer will handle the application for both the title and the license tag. An individual who moves to Georgia must purchase Georgia license tags for his or her vehicles within 30 days after establishing residence in Georgia. Military personnel and out-of-state students are not required to obtain Georgia tags or titles.

Motor vehicle and ad valorem taxes are assessed against the owner of the motor vehicle on January 1 of each year. The Georgia Department of Revenue sets the value of each vehicle by make, model, and year, and distributes this information to the local tax commissioners who calculate the exact amount of the tax due based on the local millage rate. The owner of the vehicle must file the tag renewal application and pay the tax before May 1 of each year to receive a current year license tag or renewal decal.

Most counties have adopted the pre-bill system for the automobile ad valorem tax. After the initial purchase year, the system will generate a computer-prepared statement of the taxes due which is mailed directly to the owner of the motor vehicle. The owner may complete the pre-bill by entering the name of the owner's insurance company and the applicable motor vehicle liability policy number, signing the pre-bill, and returning it to his or her county tax commissioner with a check for the amount of taxes due. The tax commissioner will then send the renewal decal directly to the motor vehicle owner. The motor vehicle owner may also apply in person to the tag office of the county of his or her residence.

Fictitious Business Name

A trade or fictitious name is any name used in the course of business that does not include the full legal name of all the owners of the business. Georgia law requires that every person, firm, or partnership carrying on business in Georgia under a trade name that does not disclose the individual ownership of the business must file a trade name registration statement with the office of the clerk of the superior court of the county in which the business is located.[102] This statement must be verified by affidavit setting forth the nature of the business and the name or names of the person, persons, firm or partnership owing and carrying on the business. The fee for filing a trade name is $5.[103]

There are exceptions to this requirement for:

- Persons doing business under a limited partnership name already filed according to the Uniform Limited Partnership Act; or
- Persons practicing any profession under a partnership name.[104]

Notice of the filing of the trade name registration must be published once a week for two weeks in the legal publication of the county in which the trade name was registered.[105]

Failure to register a trade name, however, does not invalidate contracts signed by the unregistered entity. Rather, the court is authorized to assess court costs against the parties who have failed to register the trade or partnership name at the time an action is filed.[106] Thus, the registration of a trade name prevents a company from having to pay all court costs in an action by or against a company.

Trademarks and Service Marks

The term "trademark" refers to any word, name, symbol, or device used by a company to distinguish its goods from those of another company. A service mark is used to identify and distinguish services as opposed to goods.

Trademarks and service marks are registered with the secretary of state.[107] To register a trademark or service mark, you must submit three facsimiles of the trademark or service mark to the secretary of state.[108] These facsimiles may be obtained by advertising your business with the trademark or service mark in any newspaper or publication for three days or in three separate newspapers or publications for one day. The secretary of state may refuse registration of a trademark or service mark if it is likely to cause confusion regarding a previously issued trademark or service mark.[109]

Registration of a trademark or service mark with the secretary of state is permissive, not mandatory. Consequently, registration with the secretary of state does not deprive another trademark or service mark owner of his or her right to use the trademark or service mark which has been previously acquired, although not registered.[110] Furthermore, a business may not rely on registration with the secretary of state as evidence of superior rights in a trademark or service mark because a similar mark may have been registered federally before the state registration. The owner of a federally registered trademark has the right to prevent anyone from subsequently using a similar trademark and, in certain cases, to recover damages for an infringing use.[111]

Because of the interaction between federal and state trademark and service mark law and because Georgia law affords a trademark or service mark owner several alternative theories upon which to allege an infringement of a trademark or service mark, it is advisable to consult with an attorney to establish and fully protect any trademark or service mark used in your business.

Checklist of State Requirements

Shown below is a checklist of state and local requirements for each legal form of business. The asterisk (*) indicates requirements that apply to new corporations.

☐ Apply for a federal employer tax identification number by completing *Form SS-4*.

☐ Obtain any state, county, or city business licenses that apply to your business.

☐ Register with the Georgia Department of Revenue by using *Form ST-1*. Be sure to check out local sales taxes, too.

☐ File necessary income tax returns and make all required estimated income taxes.

☐ Apply for a state income tax withholding identification number using *Form G-5*.

☐ Apply for a Georgia unemployment number by completing *Form ESA-1*.

☐ File a trade name application if your business is not operating under a name which reflects its ownership.

☐ Check out your responsibilities regarding the various ad valorem taxes.

☐ Contact an insurance broker to obtain fire and accident liability, theft, and other types of commercial insurance needed to operate the business, as well as, workers' compensation insurance.

☐ If necessary, register your trademark or service mark with the secretary of state's office.

☐ Contact an accountant and provide him or her with all of the basic business information, so that the initial books may be opened in a timely and orderly manner.

☐ If you have acquired a new business, notify the local county tax commissioner to have the ad valorem records changed to reflect your name. Ascertain that the seller has withheld and remitted all employment taxes and sales and use taxes, paid state and federal corporate income taxes up to the date of the sale, and complied with the bulk transfer requirements of the Georgia Uniform Commercial Code.

☐ If operating as a limited partnership, prepare and file a *Certificate of Limited Partnership* with the secretary of state.

☐ File a partnership return each year on or before April 15 or on or before the fifteenth day of the fourth month following the close of the fiscal year.

☐ Contact the secretary of state and order a name reservation certificate.* This is not mandatory, but it is good practice.

☐ Prepare and file articles of incorporation with certificate indicating that a request for publication of the notice of incorporation has been made and the requisite advertising fees have been paid.*

☐ Prepare consent for appointment of registered agent.* This is not mandatory, but it is good practice.

☐ Arrange for the advertising of the incorporation for two successive weeks with the local newspaper designated to handle legal advertisements.*

☐ Prepare a consent action form or hold a meeting of the shareholders to elect directors of the corporation.*

☐ Prepare bylaws to be adopted at the organizational meeting of the board of directors which shall also include the election of officers.*

☐ Accept share subscription agreements and investment letters exempting the stock from state and federal securities laws.*

☐ Complete secretary of state's annual registration.*

☐ Complete the initial Georgia license and occupation tax return, *Form 600*, and pay the initial tax based on the corporate net worth.*

11.5 Additional Requirements for Businesses with Employees

Once you hire an employee to work in your business, you take on several additional requirements and responsibilities. You will need to withhold certain payroll taxes, obtain workers' compensation insurance, comply with safety and health regulations, and know your rights and those of your employees under various labor laws. This section discusses these requirements in further detail and recommends publications and assistance programs offered by various agencies.

Withholding Taxes

Georgia has a personal income tax and requires you to withhold tax payments from your employees' wages.[112] You must withhold an amount substantially equivalent to the income tax reasonably estimated to be due from the employee for the calendar year. The amount of wages subject to withholding is the amount of wages paid less any exemption allowance and less the standard deduction allowance applicable to the wage payment determination according to the payroll period and marital status of the employee.[113] The employee tax withheld must be remitted to the Income Tax Division of the Georgia Department of Revenue on a monthly basis unless the tax withheld is $200 or less per month, in which case it must be remitted to the Georgia Department of Revenue on a quarterly basis.[114] Georgia *Form G-1* must accompany your remittance.

Income Tax Division – Withholding
Georgia Department of Revenue
270 Washington Street, Room 504
Atlanta, GA 30334
(404) 656-4181

The *Employer's Tax Guide*, published by the Income Tax Division of the Georgia Department of Revenue, summarizes the tax withholding responsibilities of Georgia employers. Another publication by the department is the *Tax Guide for Georgia Citizens*, which summarizes the major taxes levied by the state of Georgia. These tax guides are available from:

Income Tax Division
Georgia Department of Revenue
504 Trinity-Washington Building
270 Washington Street
Atlanta, GA 30334
(404) 493-5603

State Unemployment Tax

Although all employers doing business in Georgia are subject to the provisions of the employment security laws, not all employers are subject to its taxing provisions. As an employer, you are automatically liable for payment of unemployment taxes if:

- You have acquired a business liable for unemployment insurance;
- You are liable to the United States for federal unemployment tax;

- You have one or more employees working for a portion of a day in 20 different weeks in a calendar year; and
- You have a gross payroll for any calendar quarter of greater than $1,500.[115]

If you are not otherwise subject to these taxing provisions, you may elect to become a covered employer.

If you have hired any employees in the state, you need to file *Form ESA-1, Employer Status Report* and, if those workers are covered under the statute, to submit the *Employer's Quarterly Tax and Wage Report, Form ESA-4. Form ESA-4* must be submitted quarterly and is used to report wage and tax information. It is due at the end of the month following the end of the calendar quarter. The form will be mailed to you, preprinted with your name, address, account number, and tax rate. The Georgia Department of Labor, however, stresses that failure to receive the form does not relieve the tax liability.

Georgia law requires that new businesses with no previous employment history in the state pay an initial unemployment tax rate of 2.64% on the first $8,500 of each employee's earnings through June 30, 1996, after which the rate increases to 2.7%.[116]

Your tax rate may be lowered if, as of June 30, you have four quarters of unemployment insurance chargeability, and there is a positive balance in the account — contributions exceeding charges.

If these conditions are met, until June 30, 1996, the tax rate will be dropped to between 0.04% and 2.125%. However, if the account shows a negative balance, the rate may be adjusted to between 2.16% and 5.4% until June 30, 1996.[117]

You must also post and maintain a notice in readily accessible places advising employees of their rights under the law as to unemployment insurance. This poster is provided by the commissioner of labor of the Georgia Department of Labor.

There are no other required withholding taxes in the state. The city of Atlanta has the authority to levy a payroll tax, but has not done so.

The Georgia Department of Labor publishes the *Employer's Handbook* which defines an employer's duties with regard to unemployment insurance. This publication is available through the central office of the Unemployment Insurance Division in Atlanta. You can contact this office or use the preaddressed post card which is provided for your convenience at the back of this book.

Unemployment Insurance Division – Central Office
Georgia Department of Labor
148 International Boulevard, NE, Suite 900
Atlanta, GA 30303
(404) 656-3045

The Georgia Workers' Compensation Law is designed to protect employees from the risks of injury, occupational disease, and death resulting from employment.[118] Generally, the workers' compensation system provides limited medical and income benefits for deaths, injuries, and occupational diseases which are job-related. The Georgia Workers' Compensation Law is administered by the State Board of Workers' Compensation. The principal office of the state board is located in Atlanta. The state board also maintains offices in Albany, Augusta, Columbus, Dalton, Gainesville, Macon, and Savannah.

With certain limited exceptions, every employer — whether a sole proprietorship, partnership, or corporation — that regularly employs three or more employees in the same business within Georgia is subject to the requirements imposed by the workers' compensation law.[119]

An employee is defined as any person in the full- or part-time service of the employer under any contract of hire or apprenticeship, written, or implied.[120] For purposes of counting employees, a partner is not considered an employee even though he or she may be receiving a salary or wages. Officers of a corporation, however, are considered employees. Neither employees nor employers can waive the provisions or any benefits of the workers' compensation law.[121] A corporate officer, however, may elect to be exempt from coverage under the workers' compensation law by filing written certification with the state board.[122]

Every employer subject to workers' compensation law must ensure payment of benefits by:

- Securing a policy of workers' compensation insurance;
- Qualifying as a self-insurer; or
- Participating in a group self-insurance plan.[123]

If you want insurance, contact an insurance agency representing a company licensed to write workers' compensation insurance in Georgia. If you wish to be self-insured, file an application with the state board and, if approved, post a bond of not less than $100,000. The group self-insurance plans provide an alternative mechanism through which members of trade or professional associations may provide coverage.

If you fail to provide the required coverage, you will be held responsible for the payment of benefits as if coverage had been obtained. Additionally, you are subject to civil and criminal penalties for failing to satisfy certain obligations imposed by the workers' compensation law.[124] Your agent, such as an officer or director of your corporation or your partner, may also be held personally liable for benefits if you fail to obtain coverage and are unable to satisfy your obligations.[125]

In addition to providing coverage, you need to:

- Post, in a conspicuous place, the notice of compliance, the insurer's name, and a list of at least three physicians who are reasonably accessible to employees for treatment;

Workers' Compensation Insurance

- Report any injury involving lost time of seven or more days to the state board; and
- Report other injuries and related information to the state board on a monthly basis.

Additional information and reporting forms may be obtained from the state board. Typically, insurers will assist you with these obligations.

As in most states, Georgia's workers' compensation law generally provides the exclusive recourse for an employee against his employer for on-the-job injuries.[126] The employee gives up his or her common law right to sue for injuries which arise out of and in the course of employment in return for the benefits provided by workers' compensation. Thus, you are protected from costly lawsuits and uncapped liability. For more information regarding worker's compensation, contact the nearest state board or insurance agency providing this type of coverage. The state board office in Atlanta can provide you with other state board addresses and phone numbers.

State Board of Worker's Compensation
South Tower #1, CNN Center, Suite 1000
Atlanta, GA 30303-7788
(404) 656-3875

For a $10 fee, you can obtain a copy of the worker's compensation law and rules and regulations of the state board. Send request and check to:

Atlanta Claims Association
P.O. Box 724627
Atlanta, GA 31139

Employee Safety and Health Regulations

Georgia defers to the federal government for the promulgation and enforcement of occupational safety and health regulations. These regulations are set forth in the Occupational Safety and Health Act of 1970 (OSHA). The federal agency that administers this act is the Occupational Safety and Health Administration. Some of the OSHA requirements include posting specific notices to employees; keeping accurate records of all job-related injuries or illnesses; and reporting these injuries or illnesses to the appropriate agencies in a timely manner. For a more detailed discussion of OSHA requirements and law, refer to Section 5.6.

The Occupational Safety and Health Administration has an office in Atlanta. If you are interested in learning more about OSHA requirements, this office will be able to answer your questions as well as send you some helpful OSHA-related publications at no charge. Some publications you may wish to request are listed below. For your convenience, a preaddressed post card requesting these publications is provided at the back of this book.

- *Your Workplace Rights in Action, OSHA 3035*
- *All About OSHA, OSHA 2056*

- *OSHA Handbook for Small Businesses, OSHA 2209*
- *OSHA Inspections, OSHA 2098*

U.S. Department of Labor – OSHA
1375 Peachtree Street, NE, Suite 587
Atlanta, GA 30367
(404) 347-3573

Before hiring your employees, you need to know about the various state labor laws that will affect such things as their rate of pay, overtime requirements, and working hours. You may have already addressed some of these issues in your company's policy manual. If you haven't yet written your policies on paydays, overtime, and work schedules, review the discussions below for guidelines and consider getting a copy of *A Company Policy and Personnel Workbook*, an easy guide to developing a company manual, from your local bookstore or through The Oasis Press. By having clear-cut policies, you can establish better communications with your employees right from the beginning.

Labor Laws

The state of Georgia has set a minimum wage law requiring covered employers to pay employees a minimum of $3.25 per hour. This rate, however, is preempted by the federal minimum wage of $4.25 per hour for most businesses. Georgia's minimum wage law is applicable to every employer and employee with the following exceptions:

Minimum Wage Requirement

- Farm owners;
- Sharecroppers;
- Land renters;
- Employers subject to federal minimum wage provisions;
- Employers of domestic employees;
- Employers having sales of $40,000 per year or less;
- Employers having five employees or less;
- Employees whose compensation consists wholly or partially of gratuities; and
- Employees who are high school or college students.[127]

The federal minimum wage provisions are found in the Fair Labor Standards Act (FLSA)[128] which is discussed in Section 5.7. Generally, any employee who produces, manufactures, mines, handles, transports, or works on goods that are shipped in interstate commerce or in farm commerce, or whose job is related to or essential to the production of goods shipped in foreign or interstate commerce, is covered under the federal minimum wage law.

Federal law requires you to pay at least one and one-half times the covered employee's base rate of pay for all hours worked in excess of 40 hours per week.[129]

Overtime Payments

In contrast, Georgia law does not provide for overtime compensation, and there is no general statutory limitation on the number of hours that an employee over age 16 may work per day, except that workers employed in cotton or woolen manufacturing establishments may not work more than 10 hours per day or an aggregate of 60 per week, unless they receive overtime compensation.[130]

Child Labor Laws

In addition to the federal regulations described in Section 5.7, Georgia law provides that minors under age 12 may not be employed other than in agriculture or in domestic service in a private home.[131] No children under age 16 may be employed in occupations designated as hazardous,[132] and children under age 16 may work only between the hours of 6:00 A.M. and 9:00 P.M.[133]

There are special provisions for delivering messages,[134] selling newspapers,[135] and the entertainment industry.[136] No child under age 16 may work during the hours when school is in session[137] or work more than four hours on any day in which school is in session.[138] Furthermore, a minor may work only eight hours a day and 40 hours a week if school is not in session.[139]

With limited exceptions, a child between the ages of 12 and 16 must provide you with a certificate showing his or her true age and that he or she is physically fit to perform the job at issue. The certificate may be obtained from a school superintendent (public schools) or principal (private school) upon presentation of a birth certificate and a statement of intent to hire from the employer.[140]

Rights of a Terminated Employee

In Georgia, the courts have followed the doctrine of employment at will with respect to claims for wrongful termination. The Georgia Supreme Court has held that in the absence of a controlling contract, "permanent employment," "employment for life," or "employment until retirement," is employment for an indefinite period, terminable at the will of either party, which does not give rise to a cause of action against the employer for wrongful termination.[141] Of course, a terminated employee may be entitled to unemployment insurance, as discussed in Section 11.5.

State Holidays

The Georgia statute on state holidays recently has been amended to provide that state holidays will correspond to federal holidays. The governor, however, may designate additional state holidays.[142]

Anti-Discrimination Laws

You cannot discharge or refuse to hire an individual between the ages of 40 and 70 solely because of that individual's age, unless age is a factor in suitable job performance.[143] It is permissible, however, for you to maintain a compulsory retirement program for individuals between 65 and 70 who have been in executive or high policy-making positions for at least two years prior to retirement, if each employee is entitled to immediate nonforfeitable retirement benefits aggregating at least $27,000 per year. Violation of this provision is punishable by a fine not to exceed $250.

It is also unlawful for you to discriminate by paying wages to employees of one sex at a lesser rate than that paid to employees of the opposite sex for comparable work in jobs that are substantially the same.[144]

You cannot discharge an employee who complains to you or to the commissioner of labor about sex discrimination.[145] Any violation will result in a fine not to exceed $100[146] and your liability to the employee for unpaid wages.[147] You are responsible for posting a copy of Chapter 5 of Title 34 of the Georgia Code Annotated (Michie), on sex discrimination, in a conspicuous place at the place of employment.[148]

As an employer, you also cannot refuse to hire, discharge, or discriminate against a handicapped individual, unless the handicap restricts the individual's ability to perform the job at issue.[149] Georgia law specifically provides that "[this] subsection shall not be construed to require any employer to modify his physical facilities or grounds in any way."[150] As is the case with sex discrimination, it is unlawful for you to discharge, refuse to hire, or discriminate against an employee who has opposed any labor practice that discriminates against the handicapped.

11.6 State Licenses

Numerous licensing requirements must be considered prior to establishing a business or practicing certain occupations or professions in the state of Georgia.[151] Listed on the following pages are the major Georgia licensing agencies and the activities or businesses under their control. Also listed are the examining boards operated under the control of the secretary of state, together with the professions and businesses required to be licensed.

Be sure you check the current status of specific licensing requirements with the Georgia Secretary of State, as well as with county and city authorities, when contemplating entering into a new business, occupation, or profession. For general information, contact:

Licensing Boards Division
Georgia Secretary of State
166 Pryor Street SW
Atlanta, GA 30303
(404) 656-3900

Licensing Agency	Nature of Activity or Occupation
Department of Agriculture	Licensing applies to dairy plants and manufacturers, food sales establishments, fish dealers, soft drink manufacturers, bottlers or distributors, bedding manufacturers, livestock dealers or establishments, packer buyers, poultry hatcheries or dealers, bird dealers, abattoirs and meat processing plants, nurserypersons and nursery dealers, apiaries, commercial and private pesticide applicators, pesticide products, persons engaged in structural timber processors and dealers, seed dealers, plant foods, lime materials, scale and L.P. gas repairpersons, gasoline service stations, moisture meter operators, agricultural products dealers, sales at state farmers' markets, grain, cotton and tobacco warehouses, grain dealers, tobacco dealers and tobacco storage facilities.
Department of Banking and Finance	Regulates state chartered financial institutions, state banks, state savings and loans, state credit unions, international bank agencies and facilities, loan production offices (representative offices) and sales of checks, money orders, and drafts.
State Office of Bar Admissions	Administers examination of attorneys.
Insurance Commissioner	Licensing of companies which transact insurance business; rating organizations; advisory organizations; joint underwriting or joint re-insurance organizations; funeral homes which operate under the Pre-Need Funeral Service Contract Act; premium finance companies; prepaid legal services plans; agents, counselors, brokers and adjusters; or insurers.
Georgia Industrial Loan Department	Licensing of industrial loan offices which handle loans to consumers of $3,000 or less.
Georgia State Fire Marshal	Licensing of storage, transportation and handling of hazardous materials, explosives; liquefied petroleum gases; control of anhydrous ammonia, self-service dispensing of motor fuels.
Board of Court Reporting of the Judicial Council	Licenses court reporters.
Department of Education	Licenses proprietary schools.
Department of Human Resources	Deals in licensing of day care centers, family and group day care homes, residential child care facilities, child placement agencies, maternity homes, therapeutic camps. Also licenses medical facilities such as hospitals, skilled nursing homes, interim care nursing homes, ambulatory surgical treatment centers, home health agencies, health maintenance agencies, eye banks, birthing centers, hospices, free standing emergency care clinics. Also licenses clinical labs, radioactive material users, X-ray machines, individual sewage disposal systems, ambulance services, emergency medical technicians, drug abuse treatment centers, alcohol treatment programs, food service establishments, food processing, tourist accommodations, among other activities.
Georgia Department of Labor	Licenses privately owned employment agencies; issues identification numbers to businesses for tax purposes and administers the state tax system.
Department of Natural Resources	Licenses issued in regard to air quality, water quality control discharge, ground water withdrawal, surface water withdrawal, public water system operations, solid waste management, erosion and sedimentation surface mining, dam safety, oil and gas deep drilling, radiation (storage/burial facilities), hazardous waste, marshlands, oil, gas and deep drilling surface mining, among other activities.

Licensing Agency	Nature of Activity or Occupation
Department of Public Safety	Issues permits for the sale of handguns; controls certification of vehicular safety and training.
Public Service Commission	Utilities Division – Issues certificates of public convenience and necessity to telephone companies, gas companies and radio common carriers, issues licenses for service observing equipment (i.e., to allow an airline's supervisors to monitor their reservation personnel while on the phone).
	Motor Carrier Division – Issues permits to any individual or business with respect to "hauling for hire" of either passengers or property.
Real Estate Commission	Licenses brokers and sales persons; approves real estate school programs.
Department of Revenue	Issues identification numbers to businesses for tax purposes, collects all state income taxes, sales and use taxes, motor fuel taxes, alcohol and tobacco taxes, issues automobile license tags and titles, administers the intangibles tax and supervises the preparation of county ad valorem property tax digests.
Secretary of State Examining Boards Division	Licenses the following professions and businesses through examining boards operating under its authority. These are:
State Board of Accountancy	Accountants
State Board of Architects	Architects
Georgia Board of Athletic Trainers	Athletic trainers
Georgia Auctioneers Commissioners	Auctioneers
State Board of Barbers	Barbers
Georgia Board of Chiropractic Examiners	Chiropractors
State Board of Cosmetology	Cosmetologists
Georgia Board of Dentistry	Dentists and dental hygienists
State Construction Industry Licensing Board	Electrical and air conditioning contractors
State Board of Registration for Professional Engineers and Land Surveyors	Professional engineers and land surveyors
Georgia State Board of Registration for Foresters	Foresters
State Board of Funeral Service	Funeral directors, embalmers, and funeral homes
State Board of Registration for Professional Geologists	Geologists
State Board of Hearing Aid Dealers and Dispensers	Hearing aid dealers and dispensers
Georgia Board of Landscape Architects	Landscape architects
State Board of Certification of Librarians	Librarians
Georgia Board of Examiners of Licensed Practical Nurses	Practical nurses
Georgia Board of Nursing	Nursing

(continued)

Licensing Agency	Nature of Activity or Occupation
Secretary of State Examining Boards Division	(continued)
State Board of Nursing Home Administrators	Nursing home administrators
State Board of Occupational Therapy	Occupational therapists
Georgia Board of Dispensing Opticians	Dispensing opticians
State Board of Optometrists	Optometrist
State Board of Pharmacy	Pharmacists
Georgia Board of Physical Therapy	Physical therapists
Composite State Board of Medical Examiners	Physicians, physician's assistants, osteopaths, and orthodontists
State Board of Podiatry Examiners	Podiatrists
State Board of Polygraph Examiners	Polygraph examiners
Georgia Board of Private Detective and Security Agencies	Private detective and security businesses
State Board of Examiners of Psychologists	Applied psychologists
State Board of Recreation Examiners	Recreation leaders, therapeutic recreation technicians, etc.
Georgia Board of Registered Professional Sanitarians	Registered professional sanitarians
State Board of Examiners of Speech Pathology and Audiology	Speech pathologists and audiologists
State Board of Registration: Used Car Dealers	Registration of used car dealers
State Board of Registration: Used Motor Vehicle Dismantlers, Rebuilders, and Salvage Dealers	Used motor vehicle parts dealers, dismantlers, and salvage dealers
State Board of Veterinary Medicine	Veterinarians and registered animal technicians
State Board of Examiners for Certification of Water and Wastewater Treatment Plant Operators and Laboratory Analysts	Water and wastewater treatment plant operators and laboratory analysts
Water Well Standards Advisory Counsel	Water well contractors
Department of Transportation	Issues a Permit of Enforcement to anyone hauling oversized loads of hazardous materials.

11.7 State Excise Taxes

The state of Georgia imposes a number of excise taxes on various types of activities, services, and products usage. A description of the major categories of such state taxes follows.

Alcoholic Beverages Taxes

The Georgia Department of Revenue collects an excise tax on distilled spirits by use of tax stamps placed on those items before they enter the market place. The state tax is $1.00 per litre of distilled spirits,[152] plus a local option tax of up to $0.22 (22 cents) per litre.[153] It is important to note that the Georgia tax is imposed in addition to the federal excise tax of $12.50 per gallon.

An excise tax on beer of $1.08 per standard case of 24 containers of 12 ounces of beer is levied by the state[154] in addition to a uniform local beer tax of $1.20 per standard case.[155] Wine made from fruits grown in Georgia or manufactured in Georgia that contains 14% or less alcohol is taxed at the rate of $0.11 (11 cents) per litre.

The tax is increased to $0.27 (27 cents) per litre if the wine contains more than 14% alcohol. If wine is manufactured or made from fruits grown outside the state and contains 14% or less alcohol, the tax is $0.40 (40 cents) per litre. Out of state wine containing more than 14% alcohol is taxed at $0.67 (67 cents) per litre. Wine that is fortified with distilled alcohol may be taxed as distilled spirits, if the alcohol content is greater than 21%.[156]

In the case of beer, wine, and distilled spirits, the wholesaler is responsible for collecting the appropriate excise tax. The retailer is responsible for collecting the appropriate sales tax. For more information, contact the Alcohol and Tobacco Tax Unit of the Georgia Department of Revenue.

Alcohol and Tobacco Tax Unit
Georgia Department of Revenue
305 Trinity-Washington Building
270 Washington Street
Atlanta, GA 30334
(404) 656-4252 (Director's office)

Severance Tax on Minerals

The state of Georgia does not impose a severance tax on minerals; although, it is necessary to have a license to mine phosphates.[157] See Section 11.6 for information on licensing.

Property Transfer Taxes

A seller of real property must pay a transfer tax if the consideration for the sale exceeds $100.[158] Also, a transfer tax must be paid by the transferor if property valued in excess of $100 is exchanged.[159]

The tax rate is $1.00 on the first $1,000.00 of the purchase price and $0.10 (10 cents) for every $100.00 in excess of $1,000.00. This tax must be paid upon recording the deed or any other instrument evidencing the sale or exchange. It is payable to the clerk of the superior court of the county in which the deed is recorded.[160]

Motor Fuel Tax

Georgia levies a tax on distributors who sell or use motor fuel within the state.[161] The tax is $.075 (7$\frac{1}{2}$ cents) per gallon of motor fuel and is charged in addition to a federal tax of $0.09 (9 cents) per gallon. The licensed distributor must submit a monthly report computing the tax to the Motor Fuel Tax Division of the Georgia Department of Revenue, together with the payment of tax due, by the 20th day of each month for the previous month.

In certain situations, a refund of a portion of the $0.075 (7^1/$_2$ cent) tax is available. For example, if the fuel is used in a farm vehicle for agricultural purposes, a refund of all but $0.01 (1 cent) per gallon is allowed,[162] and retail dealers of motor fuel are entitled to a refund of 2% of the first $.055 (5^1/$_2$ cents) per gallon of the tax to cover losses incurred by the retail dealer as a result of leakage, spilling, or evaporation.[163] In addition, some transactions are exempt from the motor fuel tax. They are statutorily listed[164] and you may request a list from the Motor Fuel Tax Unit of the Georgia Department of Revenue.

A second motor fuel tax, which is calculated at 3% of the fuel's retail sales price,[165] is collected by the Sales and Use Tax Division of the Georgia Department of Revenue.[166] However, for the purpose of this calculation, the motor fuel's retail sales price does not include the state tax of $0.075 (7^1/$_2$ cents) per gallon and does not include the federal excise tax on all other motor fuels.[167] The statutory exemptions mentioned above also apply to the second motor fuel tax.[168] If you would like more information on motor fuel taxes, contact:

Motor Fuel Tax Unit
Georgia Department of Revenue
421-C Trinity-Washington Building
270 Washington Street
Atlanta, GA 30334
(404) 656-4050

Cigarette Tax

The state tax on cigarettes is $0.12 (12 cents) per pack.[169] The federal government levies an additional $0.16 (16 cents) per pack of cigarettes. For additional details on this tax, contact the Alcohol and Tobacco Tax Unit of the Georgia Department of Revenue.

Other Special Taxes

Georgia imposes a road tax on motor carriers — defined as passenger vehicles having seats for more than 20 passengers in addition to the driver — road tractors, truck tractors, and trucks having more than two axles.[170] The tax is calculated on the amount of motor fuel used by the motor carrier in its operations within the state in the same manner as the first and second motor fuel taxes described above,[171] and the carrier is allowed a credit against the amount of road tax due for any motor fuel taxes actually paid within the state.[172]

Carriers subject to the road tax must pay the tax quarterly on or before the last day of January, April, July, and October on the *Carrier's Motor Fuel Tax Report, Form MFCO*.[173] Motor carriers operating solely within the state of Georgia may be exempt from the road tax.[174] See Section 11.4 for a discussion of ad valorem taxes and motor vehicle taxes.

11.8 Planning for Tax Savings in a Business — State Tax Laws

The tax burden imposed on businesses in Georgia is relatively low as a result of Georgia's pro-business environment. Additional opportunities for tax savings described below enhance the state's attractiveness to business.

If your company does significant export business, you may want to form a separate Domestic International Sales Corporation (DISC) or Foreign Sales Corporation (FSC) to take advantage of the federal export incentives described in Section 8.4. Georgia generally follows the federal tax rules for both DISCs and FSCs so that use of such special entities can reduce or defer both federal and Georgia's income taxes on export sales.

Sheltering Profits in Export Sales

The estate or inheritance tax levied in Georgia is equal to the amount of the maximum allowable credit for state taxes paid under Section 2011 of the federal Internal Revenue Code.[175] Therefore, the Georgia estate or inheritance tax never increases the total tax owed, but merely changes the recipient of a portion thereof (federal to Georgia). Georgia residents also enjoy the benefit of the unlimited marital deduction provided in Section 2056(a) of the federal Internal Revenue Code — provided the surviving spouse receiving property is a U.S. citizen.

Unlimited Estate Tax Marital Deduction

If a Georgia corporation, in computing its federal taxable income, has taken a federal jobs tax credit which requires the elimination of salary and wage deductions, the eliminated salary and wage deductions may be subtracted from the corporation's Georgia taxable income.[176] Georgia also allows individuals to make use of this deduction.[177]

State Job Tax Credits

If you operate your business as a sole proprietorship, keep in mind that there are some tax advantages in hiring certain family members as employees in your business. In Georgia, any wages your sole proprietorship pays to your spouse or children under 21 years of age are exempt from state unemployment tax. Keep in mind, however, that since you don't pay unemployment tax for them, they are not eligible to collect benefits if you fire or lay them off.

Saving on Unemployment Taxes

11.9 Miscellaneous Business Pointers

The following miscellaneous pointers should be considered by businesses seeking information regarding business loans, state aid, and other information not covered elsewhere in this chapter. Refer to Chapter 9 for information on federal assistance programs and other basic business pointers.

Section 1244 Stock

Small, closely held corporations may issue Section 1244 stock pursuant to Section 1244 of the Internal Revenue Code, as discussed in Section 9.6. The Georgia law follows the federal treatment of converting what would otherwise be a capital loss to an ordinary loss for such corporations.

The individual shareholder's investment in the stock of a liquidated Section 1244 company may be deducted as an ordinary loss in arriving at federal adjusted gross income. Since the federal adjusted gross income is the starting point for calculating Georgia taxable net income, the Section 1244 ordinary loss treatment is recognized to the extent the ordinary loss is recognized under the federal code.

Business Loan Programs

State funding to small businesses in Georgia is coordinated through the federal Small Business Administration (SBA).

The SBA has established a statewide network of Small Business Development Centers (SBDCs). These centers, which are under contract with various universities in Georgia, provide business counseling services, including advice for start-up operations. Complete information regarding SBA-Georgia business assistance can be obtained by contacting the SBA offices and SBDCs listed in Section 11.10.

Small Business Assistance Act

Another potential source of state aid to small businesses is the Small Business Assistance Act of 1975.[178] The Small Business Assistance Act requires the state to place a fair proportion of its total purchases with small businesses.[179] A small business is defined as a business independently owned and operated with less than 100 employees or less than $1 million dollars in annual gross receipts.[180]

Development Authorities

In addition to the above mentioned sources of state aid to small businesses, Georgia has approximately 300 economic or industrial development authorities. The Georgia Department of Community Affairs provides advice and assistance to local governments in Georgia regarding the establishment of development authorities.

The goal of these authorities is to further the redevelopment and revitalization of downtown areas, to promote and support commercial development, and to assist small businesses. In general, these authorities can own or lease property, make loans to finance projects, and issue industrial revenue and development bonds. For more information on development authorities, contact the Georgia Department of Community Affairs.

Georgia Department of Community Affairs
1200 Equitable Building
100 Peachtree Street, NE
Atlanta, GA 30303
(404) 656-3836

Industrial Revenue Bonds

Industrial Revenue Bond (IRB) financing is often an excellent method of financing the construction of manufacturing or processing facilities. An IRB is a bond or similar obligation issued by a government entity, the proceeds of which are used to construct a manufacturing plant or to purchase equipment for the benefit of a private commercial enterprise.

The advantage of IRB financing is that the interest paid on bonds is tax exempt if certain requirements under the Internal Revenue Code are met. An attorney should be consulted regarding the legal and tax consequences of this effective but complex means of financing.

Atlanta Economic Development Corporation

The Atlanta Economic Development Corporation (AEDC) assists small and medium-sized businesses in the city of Atlanta in acquiring loans through various governmental programs in conjunction with local lending institutions. These programs implement loans for:

- Land, buildings, and equipment for industrial purposes and in designated commercial districts;
- Pollution control and waste treatment facilities;
- Exterior facade and historic preservation of buildings in the city of Atlanta;
- Minority enterprises; and
- Other neighborhood projects which otherwise would not be economically feasible.

In addition, the AEDC, through the Venture Capital Network of Atlanta, Inc. (VCN), offers a computerized matching service program for potential investors and entrepreneurs. The registration fee for this computer matching service is reasonable. For prompt and confidential assistance for business projects in the city of Atlanta, contact the AEDC.

Atlanta Economic Development Corporation
230 Peachtree Street, NW
Suite 1650
Atlanta, GA 30303
(404) 658-7000

Usury Laws

The maximum legal rate of interest which may be charged in Georgia for loans in excess of $3,000 and evidenced in writing is 5% per month simple interest.[181]

If the principal amount of the loan is $3,000 or less, the general rule is that the rate of interest charged may not exceed 16% per annum simple interest. In the event that a rate of interest is not established in writing by the parties to a contract, the legal rate of 7% per annum is applied. Interest charged in excess of the allowed rate is usurious and can result in the forfeiture of the entire interest charged or contracted to be charged.[182]

Some state provisions may be displaced by federal laws concerning various aspects of loan transactions. Before engaging in any loan transactions, it would be advisable to consult an attorney to ascertain which federal or state laws, or both, are applicable to the contemplated transactions.

11.10 State Sources of Help and Information

Finding additional information and assistance is always beneficial when starting a new business. To help you in this process, Georgia has several agencies, programs, and organizations available.

Do-It-Yourself Incorporation

Before incorporating your business on your own, consult with your attorney or the Corporations Division of the Georgia Secretary of State's office. These two sources may be able to refer you to a do-it-yourself guide. Many general how-to books are available, but specific state guides are more difficult to find. Other helpful sources are your local library, the Small Business Development Center (SBDC), and your local bookstore. See Section 10.5 for general information on do-it-yourself incorporation.

For more information on incorporating your business, contact the Corporations Division of the Georgia Secretary of State's office.

Corporations Division
Georgia Secretary of State
2 Martin Luther King, Jr. Drive
Atlanta, GA 30334
(404) 656-3900

State Agency Assistance

Georgia is an active participant in facilitating and promoting business. All the state agencies mentioned throughout this chapter are more than happy to provide informational publications, forms, and general assistance.

Business Council of Georgia

In particular, you may wish to contact the Business Council of Georgia. The council is the successor to the state chamber of commerce and provides general business and research information to Georgia's businesspersons. They also publish the *Employer's Desk Manual*, which may be very helpful to you. For availability of this publication, contact:

Business Council of Georgia
233 Peachtree Street, Suite 200
Atlanta, GA 30303
(404) 223-2264

The Georgia Department of Revenue's Centralized Taxpayer Registration Unit is where you will need to go to register for:

Georgia Department of Revenue

- Alcohol and tobacco tax licenses;
- Motor fuel distributor tax licenses;
- Motor carrier truck tax permits;
- Sales and use tax registration; and
- Withholding tax identification numbers.

To help you complete the necessary forms for each of the above taxes, the unit offers a free publication called *Taxpayer Registration*. This booklet contains all the forms necessary to register for these taxes and provides general information with its question/answer format. To request this publication or learn more about tax registration, use the preaddressed post card provided at the back of this book or contact:

Centralized Taxpayer Registration Unit
Georgia Department of Revenue
270 Washington Street
P.O. Box 740001
Atlanta, GA 30374-0001
(404) 651-8651 (Information)
(404) 656-4092 (Forms)

The Georgia Department of Administrative Services, which administers the Small and Minority Business Program, offers two useful publications you may be interested in requesting. They are:

Georgia Department of Administrative Services

- *Yellow Pages for Small and Minority Businesses;* and
- *How to Do Business with the State of Georgia*

To request these publications, you can contact the Georgia Department of Administrative Services at the office listed below, or you can use the preaddressed post card which is provided for your convenience at the end of this book.

Small and Minority Business Coordinator
Georgia Department of Administrative Services
West Tower, Suite 1602
200 Piedmont Avenue
Atlanta, GA 30334
(404) 656-0928

In the Appendix, you will find a "Quick Reference" section which briefly lists the addresses and phone numbers of many of the state agencies you may need to contact when starting and operating your business. This reference also provides a brief description of an agency's responsibilities and often will provide regional and local office information.

Quick Reference

Local chambers of commerce will gladly provide helpful information and referrals to competent corporate attorneys, accountants, and tax advisers.

Chambers of Commerce

Federal Agency Assistance

Listed below are the federal agencies in Georgia which may be contacted for further assistance regarding business operations.

U.S. Small Business Administration

A federal agency, the U.S. Small Business Administration (SBA) is set up in practically every state to provide limited financing for qualified borrowers. It also publishes a variety of pamphlets and books on the many aspects of business. For more information, call or write to either of these two district offices.

Atlanta District Office
1720 Peachtree Road, NW, Suite 600
Atlanta, GA 30309-2482
(404) 347-2441

Statesboro District Office
Federal Building
52 North Main Street, Room 225
Statesboro, GA 30458
(912) 489-8719

Minority Business Development

The Minority Business Development organization offers management, marketing, and technical assistance to minority entrepreneurs. Services include:

- Assistance in starting a business;
- Referrals to business sources;
- Listings of minority vendors for government agency procurement opportunities;
- Accounting;
- Administration;
- Advocacy;
- Business planning; and
- Construction.

Minority Business Development Agency
Atlanta Regional Office
U.S. Department of Commerce
401 West Peachtree Street, Suite 1930
Atlanta, GA 30308-3516
(404) 730-3300 (Nationwide)

Federal Information Center

The Federal Information center is a one-stop source providing information and problem-solving assistance with the more than 100 federal government agencies, offices, and programs. For details, contact:

Federal Information Center
(800) 347-1997 (Nationwide)

Private Sector Sources

In addition to the state and federal sources of assistance discussed above, there are also private sectors in the state of Georgia which offer assistance to new businesses.

Advanced Technology Development Center

Committed to supporting the growth of Georgia's high-technology industry by stimulating new jobs and capital investment, the Advanced Technology Development Center offers a wide range of assistance programs and support services. Services include detailed information on state resources; office space on the Georgia Tech campus; and access to facilities and personnel in the state's University System, for the betterment of established high-technology companies and the development of early-staged firms. For further information, call or write to:

Advanced Technology Development Center
430 10th Street, NW, Suite N-116
Atlanta, GA 30318
(404) 894-3575

The Industrial Extension Division provides technical and management assistance to both small and medium-sized firms throughout Georgia. For more information on their services, contact the office listed below.

Industrial Extension Division

Economic Development Laboratory
Industrial Extension Division
Georgia Technology Research Institute
O'Keefe Building, Room 223
Atlanta, GA 30332
(404) 894-3830

Trade and business journals can assist you in keeping up-to-date on business-related activities and events in Georgia — several are listed below.

State Business Publications

Atlanta
Two Midtown Plaza
1360 Peachtree Street, #1800
Atlanta, GA 30309-3214
(404) 872-3100

Atlanta Business Chronicle
1801 Peachtree Street, #150
Atlanta, GA 30309
(404) 249-1000

The Atlanta Small Business Monthly
2342 Perimeter Park Drive, Suite 100
Atlanta, GA 30341
(404) 986-0447

Business Atlanta
6255 Barfield Road, Suite 100
Atlanta, GA 30328-4318
(404) 256-9800

Fulton County Daily Report
190 Pryor Street, SW
Atlanta, GA 30303-3607
(404) 521-1227

Georgia Trend
235 Peachtree Street, Suite 2400
P.O. Box 56447
Atlanta, GA 30343
(404) 522-7200

Georgia Farm Bureau News
1620 Bass Road
P.O. Box 7068
Macon, GA 31298
(912) 474-8411

Georgia Farmer
P.O. Box 150001
Raleigh, NC 27624
(919) 676-3276

Georgia Grocer
3200 Highland Parkway, SE, Suite 210
Smyrna, GA 30082
(404) 438-7744

Georgia Journal
624 South Milledge Avenue, Suite 212
P.O. Box 27
Athens, GA 30603

Georgia Sportsman
2250 Newmarket Parkway, #110
P.O. Box 741
Marietta, GA 30061
(404) 953-9222

Small Business Development Centers

The Georgia Small Business Development Center (SBDC) works hand in hand with the U.S. Small Business Administration in providing new and existing small businesses with various business information services.

The center's basic services include counseling, management training, continuing education, procurement networking, applied and basic research, and advocacy.

The Georgia SBDC has five areas of specialization:

- Center for Business and Economic Studies — This center develops and collects data for SBDC use. It also performs market analysis for individual projects, conducts feasibility studies and customer attitude surveys, forecasts business and economic conditions, and provides information for use in developing business plans most helpful to small business and economic development in Georgia.

- International Trade Development Center — This center assists Georgia small businesses in identifying potential overseas markets for their products. It provides consulting, continuing education, publications, and a variety of programs, including lumber and chemical initiatives.

- Center Operations — The Center Operations basically provides the small business community with information relevant to making wise business decisions. Its services include consulting and continuing education.

- Office of Minority Business Development (OMBD) — The OMBD is a business extension service throughout Georgia which was established to ensure that all Georgia minority businesses receive equal SBDC opportunities and services as Georgia nonminority businesses do.

  Its ongoing programs include the Entrepreneurship and Black Youth Program, Minority Outreach Program, and Computer-Assisted Minority Procurement Program (CAMP).

- Community Education — Community Education administers the REAL Enterprises Program which encourages and assists rural people, especially high school students, to identify service needs that are not being met in their communities.

While most SBDCs are affiliated with educational institutions, some of the offices are also operated with local chambers of commerce. For more information, contact the SBDC office nearest you.

SBDC: Northeast Georgia and Administrative Office
University of Georgia
Chicopee Complex
1180 East Broad Street
Athens, GA 30602
(404) 542-5760

SBDC: Southwest Georgia
Business Technology Center
230 South Jackson, Suite 333
Albany, GA 31701
(912) 430-4303

SBDC: Atlanta
Georgia State University
Box 874
University Plaza
Atlanta, GA 30303-3083
(404) 651-3550

SBDC: Augusta
1061 Katherine Street
Augusta, GA 30904
(404) 737-1790

**SBDC: Southeast Georgia Regional
Service Center**
1107 Fountain Lake Drive
Brunswick, GA 31525
(912) 264-7343

SBDC: West Central Georgia
928 45th Street
P.O. Box 2441-31902
Columbus, GA 31995
(404) 649-7433

SBDC: Savannah Area
6555 Abercorn Street, Suite 224
Savannah, GA 31405
(912) 356-2755

SBDC: Decatur Area Office
750 Commerce Drive
Decatur, GA 30030
(404) 378-8000

SBDC: Gainesville Area Office
Brenau College, Butler Hall
Box 4517
Gainesville, GA 30501
(404) 531-5681

SBDC: Gwinnet Area Office
1250 Atkinson Road
P.O. Box 1505
Lawrenceville, GA 30246
(404) 963-4902

SBDC: Central Georgia
P.O. Box 13212
Macon, GA 31208-3212
(912) 751-6592

SBDC: Kennesaw College
P.O. Box 444
Marietta, GA 30061
(404) 423-6450

SBDC: South Metro Atlanta
5900 Lee Street
P.O. Box 285
Morrow, GA 30260
(404) 961-3440

SBDC: Northwest Georgia
P.O. Box 1864
Rome, GA 30162-1864
(404) 295-6326

SBDC: Southeast Georgia
Georgia Southern College
Landrum Center, Box 8156
Statesboro, GA 30460
(912) 681-5194

Footnotes

1. GA. CODE ANN. § 48-7-20.
2. GA. CODE ANN. § 48-7-80.
3. GA. CODE ANN. § 14-8-8(f).
4. GA. CODE ANN. § 48-7-53.
5. GA. CODE ANN. § 48-7-56(a).
6. GA. CODE ANN. § 14-9-303.
7. GA. CODE ANN. §§ 14-9-201(a) and 14-9-204(a)(1).
8. GA. CODE ANN. § 14-9-103(a).
9. GA. CODE ANN. § 14-2-401.
10. GA. CODE ANN. § 14-9-102(a).
11. GA. CODE ANN. § 14-9-206.5.
12. GA. CODE ANN. §§ 14-9-206.6(b) and 14-9-206.7.
13. GA. CODE ANN. § 14-2-201.
14. GA. CODE ANN. § 14-2-122. Secretary of State Bulletin — Title 14, Fees and Charges.
15. GA. CODE ANN. §§ 14-2-202, 14-2-202(b)(5), and 14-2-856.
16. GA. CODE ANN. § 14-2-201.1.
17. GA. CODE ANN. § 14-2-402.
18. GA. CODE ANN. § 14-2-402(a).
19. GA. CODE ANN. § 14-2-902.
20. GA. CODE ANN. § 14-2-910.
21. GA. CODE ANN. §§ 14-2-911, 14-2-912, 14-2-914, and 14-2-627.
22. GA. CODE ANN. § 14-2-913.
23. GA. CODE ANN. § 14-2-630.
24. GA. CODE ANN. § 14-2-922.
25. GA. CODE ANN. § 48-7-21(b)(7)(B).
26. GA. CODE ANN. § 14-2-1501(a).
27. GA. CODE ANN. § 14-2-1503.
28. GA. CODE ANN. § 14-2-1503.
29. GA. CODE ANN. § 14-2-122.
30. GA. CODE ANN. § 14-2-1622.
31. GA. CODE ANN. § 14-2-122.
32. GA. CODE ANN. § 14-2-1622.
33. GA. CODE ANN. § 14-9-122.
34. GA. CODE ANN. § 14-2-1420.
35. GA. CODE ANN. § 48-8-9; GA. COMP. R. & REGS. chs. 560-7-8.32(5) and 506-12-3.02.
36. GA. CODE ANN. § 48-13-73.
37. GA. CODE ANN. § 48-7-21(a).
38. GA. CODE ANN. § 48-7-21(b).
39. GA. CODE ANN. § 48-7-31(b).
40. GA. CODE ANN. § 48-7-31(c).
41. GA. CODE ANN. §§ 48-7-56(a) and 48-7-31.
42. GA. CODE ANN. §§ 48-7-56(a) and 48-2-36.
43. GA. CODE ANN. § 48-2-40.
44. GA. CODE ANN. § 48-7-86(a)(1)(A).
45. GA. CODE ANN. §§ 48-7-57(a) and 48-7-86(e).
46. GA. CODE ANN. § 48-7-86(f).
47. GA. CODE ANN. § 48-7-40(h).
48. GA. CODE ANN. §§ 10-5-1–10-5-24.
49. GA. CODE ANN. § 10-5-9(13).
50. GA. COMP. R. & REGS. ch. 590-4-5-.01.
51. GA. CODE ANN. § 10-5-8.
52. GA. CODE ANN. §§ 10-5-12, 13, 14, and 24.
53. GA. CODE ANN. § 48-7-21.
54. GA. CODE ANN. § 11-6-101, *et seq.*
55. GA. CODE ANN. § 11-6-102(3).
56. GA. CODE ANN. § 11-6-102(1).
57. GA. CODE ANN. § 11-6-102.
58. GA. CODE ANN. § 11-6-104.
59. GA. CODE ANN. § 11-6-104.
60. GA. CODE ANN. § 11-6-104.
61. GA. CODE ANN. § 11-6-107.
62. GA. CODE ANN. § 11-6-104(1).
63. GA. CODE ANN. § 11-1-201(37).
64. GA. CODE ANN. § 11-9-101, *et seq.*
65. GA. CODE ANN. § 11-9-401.
66. GA. CODE ANN. § 11-9-305.
67. GA. CODE ANN. § 40-3-50.
68. GA. CODE ANN. § 34-8-153.
69. GA. COMP. R. & REGS. ch. 300-2-2-.02.
70. GA. CODE ANN. § 34-8-153; GA. COMP. R. & REGS. ch. 300-2-7-.02.
71. GA. CODE ANN. § 48-8-46; GA. COMP. R. & REGS. ch. 560-12-1-.31.
72. GA. CODE ANN. § 48-8-46; GA. COMP. R. & REGS. ch. 560-12-1-.31.
73. GA. CODE ANN. § 48-8-46.
74. GA. CODE ANN. § 48-13-70, *et seq.*
75. GA. CODE ANN. § 48-7-1, *et seq.*
76. GA. COMP. R. & REGS. ch. 560-12-1-.07.
77. GA. CODE ANN. § 48-7-116(a)(1).
78. GA. CODE ANN. § 48-7-120.
79. GA. CODE ANN. § 48-7-117.
80. GA. CODE ANN. § 48-8-30.

81. GA. CODE ANN. § 48-8-49.

82. GA. CODE ANN. § 48-8-50.

83. GA. CODE ANN. § 48-8-66.

84. GA. CODE ANN. § 48-8-2(6).

85. GA. CODE ANN. § 48-8-52.

86. GA. CODE ANN. § 48-8-3.

87. GA. CODE ANN. § 48-8-3 (34, 36, and 37).

88. GA. CODE ANN. § 48-5-3.

89. GA. CODE ANN. § 48-5-7.

90. GA. CODE ANN. §§ 48-5-7.2 and 48-5-7.3

91. GA. CODE ANN. §§ 48-5-7.1 and 48-5-7.5.

92. GA. CODE ANN. § 48-5-41.

93. GA. CODE ANN. § 48-5-2(i).

94. GA. CODE ANN. § 48-5-44.

95. GA. CODE ANN. § 48-5-48

96. GA. CODE ANN. § 48-6-23.

97. GA. CODE ANN. § 48-6-27(e)(2).

98. GA. CODE ANN. § 48-6-23.

99. GA. CODE ANN. § 48-6-22.

100. GA. CODE ANN. § 48-6-61.

101. GA. CODE ANN. § 48-10-8.

102. GA. CODE ANN. § 10-1-490.

103. GA. CODE ANN. § 15-6-77(d)(6).

104. GA. CODE ANN. § 10-1-492.

105. GA. CODE ANN. § 10-1-490.

106. GA. CODE ANN. § 10-1-491.

107. GA. CODE ANN. § 10-1-442(a).

108. See Georgia state form entitled *Application for Registration of Trademark or Service Mark* (available in the office of the Secretary of State).

109. GA. CODE ANN. § 10-1-441(6).

110. *Womble v. Parker*, 208 Ga. 378, 67 S.E.2d 133 (1951).

111. GA. CODE ANN. §§ 10-1-450 and 10-1-451(a).

112. GA. CODE ANN. §§ 48-7-20 and 47-7-101.

113. GA. CODE ANN. § 48-7-101.

114. GA. CODE ANN. § 48-7-103.

115. GA. CODE ANN. § 34-8-33.

116. GA. CODE ANN. §§ 34-8-151 and 34-8-49.

117. GA. CODE ANN. § 34-8-155.

118. GA. CODE ANN. § 34-9-1, *et seq.*

119. GA. CODE ANN. § 34-9-2.

120. GA. CODE ANN. § 34-9-1.

121. GA. CODE ANN. § 34-9-10.

122. GA. CODE ANN. § 34-9-2.1.

123. GA. CODE ANN. § 34-9-120.

124. GA. CODE ANN. §§ 34-9-19, 34-9-20, and 34-9-126.

125. *Samuel v. Baitcher*, 247 Ga. 71, 274 S.E.2d 327 (1981).

126. GA. CODE ANN. § 34-9-11.

127. GA. CODE ANN. § 34-4-3.

128. 29 U.S.C.A. Sec. 206.

129. 29 U.S.C.A. Sec. 207.

130. GA. CODE ANN. § 34-3-1.

131. GA. CODE ANN. § 39-2-9.

132. GA. CODE ANN. § 39-2-1.

133. GA. CODE ANN. § 39-2-3.

134. GA. CODE ANN. § 39-2-5.

135. GA. CODE ANN. § 39-2-6.

136. GA. CODE ANN. § 39-2-18.

137. GA. CODE ANN. § 39-2-4.

138. GA. CODE ANN. § 39-2-7.

139. GA. CODE ANN. § 39-2-7.

140. GA. CODE ANN. § 39-2-11.

141. *Georgia Power Co. v. Busbin*, 242 Ga. 612, 250 S.E.2d 442 (1978).

142. GA. CODE ANN. § 1-4-1.

143. GA. CODE ANN. § 34-1-2.

144. GA. CODE ANN. § 34-5-1.

145. GA. CODE ANN. § 34-5-3.

146. GA. CODE ANN. § 34-5-3.

147. GA. CODE ANN. § 34-5-5.

148. GA. CODE ANN. § 34-5-7.

149. GA. CODE ANN. § 34-6A-4(a).

150. GA. CODE ANN. § 34-6A-4(a).

151. GA. CODE ANN. § 43-1-2.

152. GA. CODE ANN. § 3-4-60.

153. GA. CODE ANN. § 3-4-80.

154. GA. CODE ANN. § 3-5-60.

155. GA. CODE ANN. § 3-5-80.

156. GA. CODE ANN. §§ 3-6-50 and 3-6-1.

157. GA. CODE ANN. § 12-4-100.

158. GA. CODE ANN. §§ 48-6-3 and 48-6-1.

159. GA. CODE ANN. § 48-6-1.

160. GA. CODE ANN. § 48-6-4.

161. GA. CODE ANN. § 48-9-3.

162. GA. CODE ANN. § 48-9-10(b).

163. GA. CODE ANN. § 48-9-10(c).

164. GA. CODE ANN. § 48-9-3.

165. GA. CODE ANN. § 48-9-14.

166. GA. CODE ANN. § 48-9-14.

167. GA. CODE ANN. § 48-9-14.

168. GA. CODE ANN. § 48-9-14.

169. GA. CODE ANN. § 48-11-2.

170. GA. CODE ANN. § 48-9-30.

171. GA. CODE ANN. § 48-9-31.

172. GA. CODE ANN. § 48-9-35.

173. GA. CODE ANN. § 48-9-33.

174. GA. CODE ANN. § 48-9-33.

175. GA. CODE ANN. § 48-12-2(b).

176. GA. CODE ANN. § 48-7-21(b)(9).

177. GA. CODE ANN. § 48-7-27(a)(3).

178. GA. CODE ANN. §§ 50-5-120–50-5-124.

179. GA. CODE ANN. § 50-5-122.

180. GA. CODE ANN. § 50-5-121(2).

181. GA. CODE ANN. § 7-4-2.

182. GA. CODE ANN. § 7-4-10.

Index

(continued)

Appendix

Checklist of Tax and Other Major Requirements for Nearly All Small Businesses

Requirement	None	1–4	5–10	11–14	15–19	20–99	100+	Chapter–Section Reference
Federal estimated taxes	√	√	√	√	√	√	√	Sec. 4.3, 11.4
Federal income tax returns	√	√	√	√	√	√	√	Sec. 4.12
Form SS-4, Application for Federal I.D. Number:								
Sole Proprietorships		√	√	√	√	√	√	Sec. 5.2
Partnerships	√	√	√	√	√	√	√	Sec. 5.2
Corporations	√	√	√	√	√	√	√	Sec. 5.2
Form 1099 returns	√	√	√	√	√	√	√	Sec. 4.7
Federal payroll tax returns		√	√	√	√	√	√	Sec. 5.2, 5.3
Provide and file W-2's to employees at year-end		√	√	√	√	√	√	Sec. 5.2
ERISA compliance:								
For unfunded or insured employees' welfare plan:								
Provide a Summary Plan Description to employees		√	√	√	√	√	√	Sec. 5.5
File a Summary Plan Description							√	Sec. 5.5
File *Form 5500, Annual Report*							√	Sec. 5.5
Provide a Summary Annual Report to employees							√	Sec. 5.5
File and provide to employees a Summary of Material Plan Modifications							√	Sec. 5.5
File a Terminal Report, if plan terminated							√	Sec. 5.5
For funded employee welfare plan:								
File and provide all items described in ERISA list		√	√	√	√	√	√	Sec. 5.5
For employees' pension or profit-sharing plan:								
Provide a Summary Plan Description to employees and file with U.S. Department of Labor		√	√	√	√	√	√	Sec. 5.5
File *Form 5500, Annual Report*							√	Sec. 5.5
File *Form 5500-C* or *Form 5500-R*		√	√	√	√	√	√	Sec. 5.5
Provide to employees and file a Summary of Material Modifications		√	√	√	√	√	√	Sec. 5.5
File a Terminal Report, if plan terminated		√	√	√	√	√	√	Sec. 5.5
Provide a Summary Annual Report to employees		√	√	√	√	√	√	Sec. 5.5
Bonding requirement for plan officials		√	√	√	√	√	√	Sec. 5.5
Federal Wage and Hour Laws and Regulations — coverage depends on nature of business and employee types not covered		√	√	√	√	√	√	Sec. 5.7
Federal Fair Employment Laws:								
Anti-discrimination laws regarding race, color, disability, religion, sex, etc.					√	√	√	Sec. 5.8
Equal Pay Act for women		√	√	√	√	√	√	Sec. 5.8
Anti-discrimination laws regarding age						√	√	Sec. 5.8
Anti-discrimination laws regarding federal contracts		√	√	√	√	√	√	Sec. 5.8

Requirement	Number of Employees of Business							Chapter–Section Reference
	None	1–4	5–10	11–14	15–19	20–99	100+	
Federal Fair Employment Laws: (continued)								
File *Form EEO-1*							√	Sec. 5.8
Post notice regarding discrimination: racial, sexual, etc.					√	√	√	Sec. 5.8
Post notice regarding age anti-discrimination laws						√	√	Sec. 5.8
Post other anti-discrimination notices by certain federal contractors		√	√	√	√	√	√	Sec. 5.8
Immigration Laws:								
Complete *INS Form I-9* for each new hire		√	√	√	√	√	√	Sec. 5.9
OSHA Job Safety Regulations:								
Health and safety		√	√	√	√	√	√	Sec. 5.6
Post *Job Safety and Health Notice*		√	√	√	√	√	√	Sec. 5.6
Post *Employee Rights Notice* regarding OSHA		√	√	√	√	√	√	Sec. 5.6
Record industrial injuries and illnesses				√	√	√	√	Sec. 5.6
Report job fatalities or multiple injuries to OSHA		√	√	√	√	√	√	Sec. 5.6
Federal and State Child Labor Laws		√	√	√	√	√	√	Sec. 5.7, 11.5
Local business licenses	√	√	√	√	√	√	√	Sec. 4.3, 11.4
Sales and use tax permit and returns, if selling tangible personal property	√	√	√	√	√	√	√	Sec. 11.4
Fictitious business name statement, if using fictitious business name	√	√	√	√	√	√	√	Sec. 11.4
State estimated taxes	√	√	√	√	√	√	√	Sec. 11.4
State income taxes	√	√	√	√	√	√	√	Sec. 11.2, 11.4
State Wage and Hour Laws and Regulations — most employees are covered, yet some types are not		√	√	√	√	√	√	Sec. 11.5
Workers' compensation insurance		√	√	√	√	√	√	Sec. 11.5
State Fair Employment Laws:								
General prohibition of discrimination		√	√	√	√	√	√	Sec. 11.5

Checklist of Official Government Posters and Notices Required to be Displayed by Businesses

Type of Poster or Notice	When required	Where to obtain
Local business license	Required to be obtained by nearly all businesses operating in a particular locality.	Local city hall or county courthouse
Sales tax permit	Required to be displayed at each place of business where tangible personal property is sold.	State tax office
OSHA poster regarding job safety and health	Required to be posted by all employers.	U.S. Department of Labor, Occupational Safety and Health Administration
OSHA poster regarding rights of employees	Required to be posted by all employers.	U.S. Department of Labor, Occupational Safety and Health Administration
U.S. Fair Labor Standards Act Wage and Hour poster, *Attention Employees*, *(WH Publication 1088)*	Required to be posted by employers with employees whose wages and working conditions are subject to the U.S. Fair Labor Standards Act.	U.S. Department of Labor, Employment Standards Administration, Wage and Hour Division offices
Federal Equal Employment Opportunity poster	Required to be posted by all employers with 15 or more employees 20 weeks of a calendar year or with federal contracts or subcontracts of $10,000 or more.	Federal Equal Employment Opportunity Commission offices
Federal Age Discrimination poster	Required to be posted by all employers with 20 or more employees, 20 or more weeks in a calendar year.	U.S. Department of Labor, Wage and Hour Division offices
Federal Rehabilitation Act poster regarding hiring of handicapped persons	Required to be posted by employers with federal contracts or subcontracts of $2,500 or more.	Assistant Secretary for Employment Standards, U.S. Department of Labor, Washington, D.C.
Poster regarding hiring of Vietnam-era veterans	Required to be posted by employers with federal contracts or subcontracts of $10,000 or more.	The government contracting officer on the federal contract

Quick Reference for Georgia Addresses

Secretary of State

The secretary of state's office will help you incorporate your business or direct you to the proper licensing board for your particular business.

Corporations Division
Georgia Secretary of State
West Tower, Suite 315
2 Martin Luther King, Jr. Drive
Atlanta, GA 30334
(404) 656-2817

Licensing Boards Division
Georgia Secretary of State
166 Pryor Street, SW
Atlanta, GA 30303
(404) 656-3900

Comptroller General

The Comptroller General oversees several offices and departments which issue various business licenses. See Section 11.6 for more information.

Commissioner's Office
Comptroller General
2 Martin Luther King, Jr. Drive
704 West Tower
Atlanta, GA 30334
(404) 656-2056
(404) 656-2078 (Industrial loan department)
(404) 656-2100 (Insurance department)
(404) 656-7087 (Safety fire department)

Department of Human Resources

The Georgia Department of Human Resources houses two agencies you may need to contact if your business is health care or food service-related. The Office of Regulatory Services licenses day care centers and health facilities, and the Public Health Division licenses food service establishments.

Office of Regulatory Services
Department of Human Resources
878 Peachtree Street, NE, Suite 800
Atlanta, GA 30309-3997
(404) 894-5144

Public Health Division
State Environmental Health Department
Department of Human Resources
878 Peachtree Street, Room 100
Atlanta, GA 30309
(404) 894-6644

Department of Industry, Trade and Tourism

The Georgia Department of Industry, Trade and Tourism assists industries in locating within the state and provides research information. Their main office is located in Atlanta.

Georgia Department of Industry, Trade and Tourism
285 Peachtree Center Avenue, NE
Atlanta, GA 30303
(404) 656-3545

Internal Revenue Service

When you need to file tax forms with the Internal Revenue Service (IRS), simply mail them to:
Internal Revenue Service
Atlanta, GA 39901

If you need to obtain forms from the IRS, write to:
Internal Revenue Service
Caller No. 848
Atlanta, GA 30370

For general tax questions and information, the IRS has a toll-free phone number you can use:
Federal Tax Information Hotline:
(800) 424-1040 or
(404) 522-0050 (in Atlanta)

Department of Natural Resources

The Georgia Department of Natural Resources has several branches and divisions which you may need to contact when starting and operating your business. These offices issue business licenses – refer to Section 11.6.

Department of Natural Resources
205 Butler Street SE, Suite 1258
Atlanta, GA 30334
(404) 656-3530 (General information)
(404) 656-3500 (Commissioner's office)
(404) 656-4713 (Environmental protection division)
(404) 656-6900 (Air protection branch)
(404) 656-3214 (Geologic survey branch)
(404) 656-2833 (Land protection branch)
(404) 656-0779 (Parks, recreation, and historic sites)
(404) 656-4708 (Water protection branch)
(404) 656-4807 (Water resources management)
(404) 656-3522 (Game and fish division)
(404) 656-3523 (Division director)

Georgia Department of Labor
148 International Boulevard, NE
Atlanta, GA 30303
(404) 656-3017

Department of Revenue

This Georgia Department of Revenue has many divisions which you will need to contact in regards to all state taxes.

Georgia Department of Revenue
Commissioner
270 Washington Street, SW, Room 410
Atlanta, GA 30334
(404) 656-4015

Alcohol and Tobacco Tax Unit
305 Trinity-Washington Building
270 Washington Street
Atlanta, GA 30334
(404) 656-4252

Income Tax Division
P.O. Box 38197
Atlanta, GA 30334
(404) 656-4165 (Corporate returns, license taxes)
(404) 656-4188 (Individual returns)
(404) 656-7043 (Trust and estates)
(404) 656-4181 (Withholding)

Motor Fuel Tax Division
421-C Trinity-Washington Building
270 Washington Street
Atlanta, GA 30334
(404) 656-4055 (Motor carrier fuel taxes)
(404) 656-4092 (Motor fuel licensing)
(404) 656-4050 (Motor fuel tax)
(404) 656-4058 (Truck permits)

Motor Vehicle Division
104 Trinity-Washington Building
270 Washington Street
Atlanta, GA 30334
(404) 656-4100 (Tags and titles)
(404) 362-6500 (Transfers)
(404) 656-4156 (Stolen tags and upgrades)

Property Tax Division
405 Trinity-Washington Building
270 Washington Street
Atlanta, GA 30334
(404) 656-4247 (Intangible property tax)
(404) 656-4246 (Real estate transfer tax)
(404) 656-4244 (Unclaimed property)

Sales and Use Tax Division
310 Trinity-Washington Building
270 Washington Street
Atlanta, GA 30334
(404) 656-4060

When trying to get assistance with tax problems or questions, you may find it more convenient to contact one of the Georgia Department of Revenue's 11 regional offices. Sales tax and income tax matters, in particular, can often be handled faster at the regional offices. Here are the locations of these regional offices:

Taxpayer Assistance
322 West Tower
Martin Luther King, Jr. Boulevard
Atlanta, GA 30334
(404) 656-4071 (Income tax)

Albany Regional Office
2700 Palmyra Road
P.O. Box 1357
Albany, GA 31703
(912) 430-4241 (General inquiries, sales, income, & motor fuel taxes)
(912) 430-4404 (Alcohol and tobacco tax)

Athens Regional Office
190 Ben Burton Circle   Mailing address: P.O. Box 1843
Bogart, GA 30622   Athens, GA 30603
(404) 542-6058 (General inquiries, sales, and motor fuel taxes)
(404) 542-6116 (Income, alcohol, and tobacco taxes)

Augusta Regional Office
1054 Claussen Road, Suite 310
Augusta, GA 30907
(404) 737-1870 (General inquiries)

Douglas Regional Office
P.O. Box 918
111 North Coffee Avenue
Douglas, GA 31533
(912) 384-1794 (General inquiries, sales, and motor fuel taxes)
(912) 384-4079 (Income, alcohol, and tobacco taxes)

Lithia Springs Regional Office
351 Thornton Road, Suite 101
Lithia Springs, GA 30057
(404) 732-1142 (General inquiries)

Macon Regional Office
2153 Vineville Avenue
Macon, GA 31208
(912) 751-6055 (General inquiries)

Rome Regional Office
1401 Dean Street, Suite E
P.O. Box 6004
Rome 30163-4101
(404) 295-6061 (General inquiries, income, and motor fuel taxes)
(404) 295-6061 (Sales, alcohol, and tobacco taxes)

Quick Reference for Georgia Addresses

Department of Revenue (continued)

Savannah Regional Office
6606 Abercorn Street
Savannah, GA 31405
(912) 356-2140 (General inquiries)

Tucker Regional Office
2082 East Exchange Place, Suite 120
Tucker, GA 30084
(404) 493-5600 (Sales tax and other inquiries)

Department of Labor

The Georgia Department of Labor issues employer unemployment tax numbers and provides information and assistance in areas such as unemployment insurance, experience tax ratings, labor and anti-discrimination laws, and employee safety and health regulations. You can contact the department's office in Atlanta or any one of the divisional offices located throughout the state.

Georgia Department of Labor
148 International Boulevard, NE,
  Suite 476
Atlanta, GA 30303
(404) 656-3017

Divisional Offices:

Albany Office:
1608 South Slappey Boulevard
P.O. Box 3450
Albany, GA 31708-6401
(912) 430-5010

Athens Office:
794 Prince Avenue
P.O. Box 1032
Athens, GA 30613-1699
(404) 542-8500

Atlanta Office:
2811 Lakewood Avenue, SW
Atlanta, GA 30315
(404) 669-3300

Augusta Office:
601 Green Street
P.O. Box 160
Augusta, GA 30913
(404) 721-3131

Blue Ridge Office:
East 2nd Street
P.O. Box 488
Blue Ridge, GA 30513
(404) 632-2033

Brunswick Office:
1321 Union Street
P.O. Box 1059
Brunswick, GA 31520
(912) 264-7373

Dalton Office:
417 West Crawford Street
P.O. Box 929
Dalton, GA 30722
(404) 272-2209

Douglas Office:
310 West Bryan
P.O. Box 1363
Douglas, GA 31533
(912) 383-4254

Dublin Office:
910 North Jefferson Street
P.O. Box 1226
Dublin, GA 31040
(912) 275-6525

Elberton Office:
5 Seaboard Street
P.O. Box 956
Elberton, GA 30625
(404) 213-2028

Gainesville Office:
2419 Corporate Drive, SW
P.O. Box 350
Gainesville, GA 30503
(404) 535-5491

Griffin Office:
1514 Highway 16 West
P.O. Box 79
Griffin, GA 30224
(404) 228-7240

LaGrange Office:
1002 Longley Place
P.O. Box 1225
LaGrange, GA 30240
(404) 845-4000

Macon Office:
744 Second Street
P.O. Box 6138
Macon, GA 31213
(912) 751-6022

Milledgeville Office:
156 Roberson Mill Road
P.O. Box 730
Milledgeville, GA 31061
(912) 453-5465

Rome Office:
462 Riverside Parkway
P.O. Box 5107
Rome, GA 30162
(404) 295-6051

Rossville Office:
One Sousa Drive
P.O. Box 309
Rossville, GA 30741
(404) 861-1990

Savannah Office:
5520 White Bluff Road
P.O. Box 22069
Savannah, GA 31403-2069
(912) 356-2773

Smyrna Office:
2972 Ask Kay Drive
P.O. Drawer 2597
Smyrna, GA 30081
(404) 319-3951

Statesboro Office:
62 Packing House Road
P.O. Box 558
Statesboro, GA 30458
(912) 764-9141

Thomasville Office:
120 North Crawford Street
P.O. Box 1340
Thomasville, GA 31799
(912) 225-4033

Toccoa Office:
112 North Alexander Street
P.O. Box 520
Toccoa, GA 30577
(404) 886-7461

Valdosta Office:
2808 North Oak Street
P.O. Box 1008
Valdosta, GA 31603-1008
(912) 333-5211

Vidalia Office:
Carter Center, Suite 16
P.O. Box 1106
Vidalia, GA 30474
(912) 537-9847

Waycross Office:
511 City Boulevard
P.O. Box 1609
Waycross, GA 31501
(912) 285-6105

Georgia County Seats

County	County Seat	Zip Code	Phone Number	County	County Seat	Zip Code	Phone Number
Appling	Baxley	31513	(912) 367-8126	Dade	Trenton	30752	(404) 657-4778
Atkinson	Pearson	31642	(912) 422-3343	Dawson	Dawsonville	30534	(404) 265-2525
Bacon	Alma	31510	(912) 632-4915	Decatur	Bainbridge	31717	(912) 248-3025
Baker	Newton	31770	(912) 734-3004	DeKalb	Decatur	30030	(404) 371-2762
Baldwin	Milledgeville	31061	(912) 453-4007	Dodge	Eastman	31023	(912) 374-2871
Banks	Homer	30547	(404) 677-2320 (ext. 240)	Dooly	Vienna	31092	(912) 268-4234
				Dougherty	Albany	31701	(912) 431-2198
Barrow	Winder	30680	(404) 307-3035	Douglas	Douglasville	31034	(404) 920-7252
Bartow	Cartersville	30120	(404) 382-2930	Early	Blakely	31723	(912) 723-3033
Ben Hill	Fitzgerald	31750	(912) 423-3736	Echols	Statenville	31648	(912) 559-5642
Berrien	Nashville	31639	(912) 686-5506	Effingham	Springfield	31329	(912) 754-6071
Bibb	Macon	31202	(912) 749-6527	Elbert	Elberton	30635	(404) 283-2005
Bleckley	Cochran	31014	(912) 934-3210	Emanuel	Swainsboro	30401	(912) 237-8911
Brantley	Nahunta	31553	(912) 462-5635	Evans	Claxton	30417	(912) 739-3868
Brooks	Quitman	31643	(912) 263-4747	Fannin	Blue Ridge	30513	(404) 632-2039
Bryan	Pembroke	31321	(912) 653-4681	Fayette	Fayetteville	30214	(404) 461-4703
Bulloch	Statesboro	30458	(912) 764-9009	Floyd	Rome	30161	(404) 291-5191
Burke	Waynesboro	30830	(404) 554-2279	Forsyth	Cumming	30130	(404) 781-2120
Butts	Jackson	30233	(404) 775-8215	Franklin	Carnesville	30521	(404) 384-2514
Calhoun	Morgan	31766	(912) 849-2715	Fulton	Atlanta	30303	(404) 730-5000
Camden	Woodbine	31569	(912) 576-5601 (ext. 210)	Gilmer	Elijay	30540	(404) 635-4462
				Glascock	Gilson	30810	(404) 598-2084
Candler	Metter	30439	(912) 685-5257	Glynn	Brunswick	31520	(912) 267-5610
Carroll	Carrollton	30117	(404) 830-5830	Gordon	Calhoun	30701	(404) 629-9533
Catoosa	Ringgold	30736	(404) 935-4231	Grady	Cairo	31728	(912) 377-2912
Charlton	Folkston	31537	(912) 496-2354	Greene	Greensboro	30642	(404) 453-3340
Chatham	Savannah	31402	(912) 652-7197	Gwinnett	Lawrenceville	30245	(404) 822-8100
Chattahoochee	Cusseta	31805	(404) 989-3424	Habersham	Clarkesville	30523	(404) 754-2923
Chattooga	Summerville	30747	(404) 857-2594	Hall	Gainesville	30501	(404) 531-7025
Cherokee	Canton	30114	(404) 479-0534	Hancock	Sparta	31087	(404) 444-6644
Clarke	Athens	30601	(404) 613-3233	Haralson	Buchanan	30113	(404) 646-2005
Clay	Ft. Gaines	31751	(912) 768-2631	Harris	Hamilton	31811	(404) 628-4944
Clayton	Jonesboro	30236	(404) 477-3398	Hart	Hartwell	30642	(404) 376-7189
Clinch	Homerville	31634	(912) 487-5854	Heard	Franklin	30217	(404) 675-3301
Cobb	Marietta	30060	(404) 528-1222	Henry	McDonough	30253	(404) 957-2121
Coffee	Douglas	31533	(912) 384-2865	Houston	Perry	31069	(912) 987-2170
Colquitt	Moultrie	31768	(912) 985-1324	Irwin	Ocilla	31774	(912) 468-5356
Columbia	Appling	30802	(404) 541-1139	Jackson	Jefferson	30549	(404) 367-1199 (ext. 251)
Cook	Adel	31620	(912) 896-7717				
Coweta	Newnan	30263	(404) 254-2695	Jasper	Monticello	31064	(404) 468-6651
Crawford	Knoxville	31050	(912) 836-3575	Jeff Davis	Hazelhurst	31539	(912) 375-6615
Crisp	Cordele	31015	(912) 276-2616	Jefferson	Louisville	30434	(912) 625-8834

County	County Seat	Zip Code	Phone Number	County	County Seat	Zip Code	Phone Number
Jenkins	Millen	30442	(912) 982-4683	Richmond	Augusta	30903	(404) 821-2447
Johnson	Wrightsville	31096	(912) 864-3484	Rockdale	Conyers	30207	(404) 929-4021
Jones	Gray	31032	(912) 986-6671	Schley	Ellaville	31806	(912) 937-5581
Lamar	Barnesville	30204	(404) 358-5145	Screven	Sylvania	30467	(912) 564-2614
Lanier	Lakeland	31635	(912) 482-3594	Seminole	Donalsonville	31745	(912) 524-2525
Laurens	Dublin	31021	(912) 272-3210	Spalding	Griffin	30223	(404) 228-9900 (ext. 308)
Lee	Leesburg	31763	(912) 759-6018				
Liberty	Hinesville	31313	(912) 876-3625	Stephens	Toccoa	30577	(404) 886-3598
Lincoln	Lincolnton	30817	(404) 359-4444 (ext. 24)	Stewart	Lumpkin	31815	(912) 838-6220
				Sumter	Americus	31709	(912) 924-5626
Long	Ludowici	31316	(912) 545-2123	Talbot	Talbotton	31827	(404) 665-3276
Lowndes	Valdosta	31601	(912) 333-5127	Taliaferro	Crawfordville	30631	(404) 456-2123
Lumpkin	Dahlonega	30533	(404) 864-3736	Tattnall	Reidsville	30453	(912) 557-6716
Macon	Oglethorpe	31068	(912) 472-7661	Taylor	Butler	31006	(912) 862-5594
Madison	Danielsville	30633	(404) 795-3351	Telfair	McRae	31055	(912) 868-6525
Marion	Buena Vista	31803	(912) 649-7321	Terrell	Dawson	31742	(912) 995-2631
McDuffie	Thomson	30824	(404) 595-2134	Thomas	Thomasville	31792	(912) 225-4108
McIntosh	Darien	31305	(912) 437-6641	Tift	Tifton	31794	(912) 386-7810
Meriwether	Greenville	30222	(404) 672-4416	Toombs	Lyons	30436	(912) 526-3501
Miller	Colquitt	31737	(912) 758-4102	Towns	Hiawassee	30546	(404) 896-2130
Mitchell	Camilla	31730	(912) 336-2000	Treutlen	Soperton	30457	(912) 529-4215
Monroe	Forsyth	31029	(912) 994-7022	Troup	LaGrange	30240	(404) 883-1740
Montgomery	Mt. Vernon	30445	(912) 583-4401	Turner	Ashburn	31714	(912) 567-2011
Morgan	Madison	30650	(404) 342-3605	Twiggs	Jeffersonville	31044	(912) 945-3350
Murray	Chatsworth	30705	(404) 695-2932	Union	Blairsville	30512	(404) 745-2611
Muscogee	Columbus	31902	(404) 571-4857	Upson	Thomaston	30286	(404) 647-5847
Newton	Covington	30209	(404) 784-2035	Walker	Lafayette	30728	(404) 638-1742
Oconee	Watkinsville	30677	(404) 769-3940	Walton	Monroe	30655	(404) 267-1307
Oglethorpe	Lexington	30648	(404) 743-5731	Ware	Waycross	31501	(912) 287-4340
Paulding	Dallas	30132	(404) 445-8871	Warren	Warrenton	30828	(404) 465-2262
Peach	Ft. Valley	31030	(912) 825-5331	Washington	Sandersville	31082	(912) 552-3186
Pickens	Jasper	30143	(404) 692-2014	Wayne	Jesup	31545	(912) 427-5930
Pierce	Blackshear	31516	(912) 449-2020	Webster	Preston	31824	(912) 828-3525
Pike	Zebulon	30295	(404) 567-8401	Wheeler	Alamo	30411	(912) 568-7137
Polk	Cedartown	30125	(404) 749-2114	White	Cleveland	30528	(404) 865-2613
Pulaski	Hawkinsville	31036	(912) 783-1911	Whitfield	Dalton	30720	(404) 275-7450
Putnam	Eatonton	31024	(404) 485-4501	Wilcox	Abbeville	31001	(912) 467-2442
Quitman	Georgetown	31754	(912) 334-2578	Wilkes	Washington	30673	(404) 678-2423
Rabun	Clayton	30525	(404) 782-3615	Wilkinson	Irwinton	31042	(912) 946-2221
Randolph	Cuthbert	31740	(912) 732-2216	Worth	Sylvester	31791	(912) 776-8205

INSTRUCTIONS FOR COMPLETION OF THE STATE TAX REGISTRATION APPLICATION

(PLEASE TYPE OR PRINT IN INK)

IDENTIFICATION SECTION

Line 1.   Enter your Georgia State Taxpayer Identifier Number. (If you do not have one, leave blank.)

Line 2.   Indicate the reason for this application as follows:

   a.   **CHANGE IN LOCATION ADDRESS** - If you are currently registered for Georgia Sales and Use, Withholding, Motor Carrier, Motor Fuel Distributor, and/or Alcohol Taxes and have changed the physical location of your business, check here.

   b.   **CHANGE IN ALCOHOL LICENSEE** - If you currently have a Georgia alcohol license and have changed your licensee, check here.

   c.   **NEW BUSINESS** - If you are starting a new business or you purchased an ongoing business, check here.

   d.   **CHANGE IN OWNERSHIP STRUCTURE** (Example: proprietorship to corporation) - If your business is currently registered under one form of ownership and will be operating under a different type of ownership structure, check here.

   e.   **ADDITIONAL TAX REGISTRATION** - If you are applying for an additional tax registration and are presently registered for another tax, check here.

   f.   **DIVIDED STORE** - If you are applying for alcohol licenses to operate as a divided store, check here. (NOTE: Two separate applications must be completed. Trade names must be different.)

Line 3.   Check all tax license and permit types for which you are applying. Complete CRF-002 and any of the following form(s) that apply to your registration.

Tax Type	Form #	Form Name
Sales and Use Tax	CRF-002	State Tax Registration Application
Withholding Tax	CRF-002	State Tax Registration Application
Motor Carrier Permit	CRF-006	Motor Carrier and Tanker Truck Permit Application
Motor Fuel Tanker Truck Permit	CRF-006	Motor Carrier and Tanker Truck Permit Application
Motor Fuel Distributor Tax	CRF-007	Motor Fuel Distributor Application
Tobacco License	CRF-008	Tobacco License Application
Alcohol License Retail	CRF-009	Alcohol License Application
Alcohol Wholesale	CRF-010	Schedule A - List of Brands
Alcohol Wholesale	CRF-011	Schedule B - Territory Designation

(See inside of back cover for phone numbers and locations of offices where forms and registration information may be obtained.)

Line 4.   If registered with the Secretary of State, enter the name under which your business is legally registered. If your business is not so registered, then enter the name under which you plan to operate.

Line 5.   Enter the trade name or doing-business-as (DBA) name of your business only if different from the Legal Business Name on Line 4.

Line 6.   Check the ownership structure under which your business is owned and operated. If "Corporation", enter the State and Date of Incorporation. (NOTE: If the ownership consists of a married couple, the ownership will be presumed to be a partnership.)

Line 7.   Enter your Federal Employer Identification (FEI) Number. If you have applied for an FEI number, write "APPLIED FOR." If you do not have an FEI number and you have not applied, leave blank.

Line 8.   If your business only operates seasonally, indicate the months you will conduct business, otherwise, disregard this line.

Line 9.   Enter the last month and day of your business' accounting year.

Line 10.   If you purchased an existing business, enter the following information regarding the former owner if known: legal business name, STI number, Georgia Sales Tax Number, Withholding Tax Number, and purchase price.

ADDRESS SECTION

Line 11.   Enter the physical location address of your business including suite/apartment number. (A post office box is not an acceptable location address. If you use a P.O. Box, your application will be rejected.)

Line 12.   Check "yes" or "no" if your location address is within the city limits. (Disregard this line if business is not located in Georgia.)

Line 13.   Enter the mailing address of your business if different from the location address listed on Line 11.

        Line a.   Check all tax type(s) for the address you are entering. (If you would like to have correspondence or reporting forms from any taxing unit sent to separate locations, please list these addresses on Lines 13 and/or 14, and indicate the tax related to each. Also, Form CRF-003 is available for additional addresses.)

        Line b.   If the addressee name is different from or in addition to the legal business name, enter the name as it should appear on a mailing label; otherwise, leave blank.

        Line c.   Enter the number and street address, P.O. Box or RFD Number.

        Line d.   Enter the city, state, zip code, county (only if address is located in Georgia), country, and telephone number.

Line 14.   List an additional mailing address if necessary. Please refer to the instructions on Line 13 in completing this Section. **Use Form CRF-003 to list further mailing addresses.**

OWNERSHIP/RELATIONSHIP SECTION

Line 15.   The Department of Revenue requires that the following information be furnished on all related individuals or businesses to determine the ownership of the applying business. **This Section MUST be completed for your application to be accepted.** Complete one Section for each related business or individual, check all relationships that apply, and enter the effective date of that relationship. For all applications, provide information for the following:

- **Owner** - If owner of the business, complete items C, D, and E.
- **Partner** - If the business is a partnership, complete a separate RELATIONSHIP Section (C, D, and E) for each partner.
- **Officer** - If the business is a corporation, complete a separate RELATIONSHIP Section (C, D, and E) for each corporate officer.
- **Parent Company** - If the business is a subsidiary, branch, or division of another business, complete a RELATIONSHIP Section (A, B, D, and E) for the parent company.
- **Shareholder** - If the business is a Subchapter S Corporation, complete a separate RELATIONSHIP Section (C, D, and E) for each shareholder.

For Alcohol License Applications:
- **Alcohol Licensee** - For the licensee of your business, complete a RELATIONSHIP Section (C, D, and E).
- **Manager** - For the manager of your business, complete a RELATIONSHIP Section (C, D, and E). If the licensee and manager are the same person, check "Alcohol Licensee" and "Manager" and complete only one Section.
- **Related Business** - If an owner, partner, or corporate officer has any financial interest in any other wholesale or retail alcohol business, for each such business, complete a separate RELATIONSHIP Section (A, B, D, and E).

For Motor Fuel Distributor License Applications:
- **Supplier** - For each supplier, complete a separate RELATIONSHIP Section (A, B, D, and E).

For All Relationships:

        Line a.   If the relationship checked is a business entity, enter the name of that business entity and the State Taxpayer Identifier (STI) number or license number (if known).

        Line b.   If this business is registered for Georgia Sales Tax and/or Withholding Tax, enter its Sales Tax and/or Withholding Tax numbers (if known).

        Line c.   If the relationship checked is an individual, enter the individual's full name, title, and Social Security Number (Social Insurance Number if Canadian). **Social Security Number is required by Revenue Regulation 560-1-1-.18.**

        Line d.   Enter the individual or business address here.

        Line e.   Enter the city, state, zip code, county (only if address is located in Georgia), country, and telephone number.

Line 16.   List any additional ownership/relationships. Please refer to the instructions on Line 15 in completing this Section. **Use Form CRF-004 to identify further ownership/relationship types.**

Sales and Use Tax Section

Line 17.   Identify the nature of your business. (If a combination of two or more, list percentages of receipts. Percentages must total 100%.)

Line 18.   Enter the kind of business you will operate, product(s) for sale, and/or service(s) to be provided. Examples of businesses are: grocery, restaurant, bakery, chain food store, department store, jewelry, hardware, service station, automobile dealership, furniture store, motel or hotel, warehouse, manufacturing plant, book store, etc. Specify if a combination of businesses.

Line 19.   Check appropriate yes or no answers as to whether you will or will not sell alcoholic beverages.

Line 20.   Check appropriate yes or no answers as to whether you will or will not sell tobacco products other than in a vending machine. Enter the date you actually started or will start selling tobacco products.

Line 21.   Check appropriate yes or no answers as to whether you will or will not sell gasoline and/or other motor fuels. If "yes", specify the dealer responsible for paying tax on the gasoline and/or motor fuel sales and enter its Sales Tax Number, if other than yourself.

Line 22.   Enter the date you actually started or will start selling or purchasing items subject to sales tax. (If an out-of-state business, enter the date of first such activity in Georgia.) Do not indicate your date of incorporation for the answer to this question. (Month/Day/Year required.)

Line 23.   Check the accounting method your business has elected to use to report Sales and Use Tax to the Department.
Cash Basis - The seller reports the sale and remits the tax in the month that the <u>tax is collected</u>.
Accrual Basis - The seller reports the sale and remits the tax in the month that the <u>sale is made</u>.

Line 24.   Check appropriate yes or no answers as to whether you will or will not have employees. If "yes", complete the Withholding Tax Section. If "no", proceed to Signature Section.

WITHHOLDING TAX SECTION

Line 25.   Check "Applicant or Payroll Service Bureau" or "Other" to identify the party responsible for filing and remitting the required payroll taxes. If "Applicant or Payroll Service Bureau", your business will be assigned a withholding number. If "Other", list the name and a Withholding Number of the business responsible for paying these taxes. The name and number listed will be verified on our Registration Files. If this information cannot be verified, a withholding number will be issued to the applicant.

Line 26.   Check "yes" if you expect to withhold more than $200 per month; otherwise, check "no".

Line 27.   Enter the number of employees hired or that you anticipate hiring once the business is started.

Line 28.   For Georgia Withholding Tax purposes, enter the date of the first payroll. (Month/Day/Year required.)

SIGNATURE SECTION

This application <u>must be signed by owner, partner, or corporate officer</u>. This form will not be accepted unless signed by someone listed in the Relationship Section or on Form CRF-004. **Stamped signature not acceptable.**

IF SALES AND USE TAX WAS COLLECTED OR GEORGIA WITHHOLDING TAX WAS WITHHELD AND DUE PRIOR TO THE FILING OF THIS APPLICATION, PLEASE COMPLETE AND ATTACH THE APPROPRIATE TAX RETURNS WITH **SEPARATE CHECKS** AND IDENTIFY EACH CHECK BY TAX TYPE. (COMBINED TAX PAYMENTS ARE NOT ACCEPTABLE AND WILL DELAY THE PROCESSING OF YOUR TAX PAYMENTS.)

THE PROCESSING OF THIS APPLICATION WILL BE DELAYED UNLESS ALL APPLICABLE QUESTIONS ARE ANSWERED, COMPLETE INFORMATION IS FURNISHED, AND IS PROPERLY SIGNED. PLEASE RETAIN A COPY OF THIS APPLICATION FOR YOUR FILE.

PLEASE ALLOW 4 TO 6 WEEKS FOR PROCESSING OF APPLICATION.

Notes

CRF-002 (Rev. 12/91)

GEORGIA DEPARTMENT OF REVENUE
REGISTRATION UNIT
P. O. BOX 740001
ATLANTA, GEORGIA 30374-0001

(PLEASE PRINT OR TYPE)

STATE TAX REGISTRATION APPLICATION
(Please Read Instructions Before Completing)

SAMPLE

FOR OFFICE USE ONLY

IDENTIFICATION SECTION

1	IF YOU HAVE A STATE TAXPAYER IDENTIFIER (STI), ENTER HERE:
2	REASON FOR APPLICATION [ ] Change in Location Address [ ] Change in Alcohol Licensee [ ] New Business [ ] Change in Ownership Structure [ ] Additional Tax Registration [ ] Divided Store (Alcohol Only - Separate Applications required.)
3	FOR WHICH OF THE FOLLOWING ARE YOU APPLYING? [ ] Sales and Use Tax [ ] Tobacco License [ ] Motor Fuel Distributor Tax [ ] Withholding Tax [ ] Motor Carrier Permit [ ] Motor Fuel Tanker Truck Permit [ ] Alcohol License
4	LEGAL BUSINESS NAME
5	TRADE NAME / DBA NAME
6	TYPE OF OWNERSHIP [ ] Sole Proprietorship [ ] County Government [ ] State Agency [ ] Estate [ ] Partnership [ ] Municipality [ ] Federal Agency [ ] Fiduciary [ ] Subchapter S Corp. [ ] Professional Association [ ] Other [ ] Corporation - State of Inc. _____ Date of Inc. ___ / ___ / ___
7	IF THE BUSINESS LISTED ABOVE HAS AN "FEI" NUMBER, ENTER HERE:
8	IF SEASONAL BUSINESS, STATE MONTHS BUSINESS WILL BE OPEN: Begin Thru
9	WHAT IS THE LAST MONTH AND DAY OF YOUR ACCOUNTING YEAR: Month Day
10	IF YOU CHECKED "NEW BUSINESS" ON LINE 2 AND YOU PURCHASED THAT BUSINESS, PROVIDE THE FOLLOWING INFORMATION REGARDING THE FORMER OWNER, IF KNOWN. LEGAL BUSINESS NAME STI NO. GA. SALES TAX NO. GA. WITHHOLDING TAX NO. PURCHASE PRICE OF BUSINESS $

ADDRESS SECTION

11	LOCATION ADDRESS, NUMBER AND STREET SUITE/APARTMENT NO.: (Enter physical location address of business. DO NOT use P. O. Box.) CITY STATE ZIP COUNTY COUNTRY PHONE ( )
12	IS THE ABOVE ADDRESS LOCATED WITHIN THE CITY LIMITS? [ ] Yes [ ] No

NOTE: To have correspondence and reporting forms sent to separate addresses, please complete Lines 13 and 14 and indicate the related tax type(s) for each. To list additional mailing addresses use Form CRF-003.

13		MAILING ADDRESS - IF DIFFERENT FROM THE LOCATION ADDRESS ON LINE 11 ABOVE. (Please identify tax type(s) to be mailed to the address below.)
	A	[ ] Sales and Use [ ] Withholding [ ] Alcohol [ ] Tobacco [ ] Motor Carrier / Tanker Truck [ ] Motor Fuel Distributor
	B	ADDRESSEE (c/o) (If different from or in addition to the Legal Business Name)
	C	NUMBER AND STREET, P. O. BOX or RFD NO.
	D	CITY STATE ZIP COUNTY COUNTRY PHONE ( )
14		ADDITIONAL MAILING ADDRESS (Please identify tax type(s) to be mailed to the address below.)
	A	[ ] Sales and Use [ ] Withholding [ ] Alcohol [ ] Tobacco [ ] Motor Carrier / Tanker Truck [ ] Motor Fuel Distributor
	B	ADDRESSEE (c/o) (If different from or in addition to the Legal Business Name)
	C	NUMBER AND STREET, P. O. BOX or RFD NO.
	D	CITY STATE ZIP COUNTY COUNTRY PHONE ( )

FOR OFFICE USE ONLY (left column boxes): L O C T | MAIL | MAIL

(Please Read Instructions Before Completing)

FOR OFFICE USE ONLY	OWNERSHIP / RELATIONSHIP SECTION
	(This section MUST be completed for your application to be accepted.)

SAMPLE

15 CHECK ALL THAT APPLY　　　　　　　　　　　　　　EFFECTIVE DATE: ___ / ___ / ___

[ ] Owner　　　[ ] Parent Company　　　[ ] Manager　　　[ ] Related Business
[ ] Partner　　　[ ] Shareholder　　　[ ] Tobacco Licensee　　　[ ] Motor Fuel Supplier
[ ] Officer　　　[ ] Alcohol Licensee　　　[ ] Tobacco Distributor

(For individuals, complete Lines C,D, and E. For businesses, complete Lines A, B, D, and E.)

A	BUSINESS NAME	STI or LICENSE NO.
B	GA. SALES TAX NO.	GA. WITHHOLDING TAX NO.
C	LAST NAME　　　FIRST　　　M.I.　　　TITLE　　　SOCIAL SECURITY NO.	
D	ADDRESS	
E	CITY　　　STATE　　　ZIP　　　COUNTY　　　COUNTRY　　　PHONE ( )	

16 CHECK ALL THAT APPLY　　　　　　　　　　　　　　EFFECTIVE DATE: ___ / ___ / ___

[ ] Owner　　　[ ] Parent Company　　　[ ] Manager　　　[ ] Related Business
[ ] Partner　　　[ ] Shareholder　　　[ ] Tobacco Licensee　　　[ ] Motor Fuel Supplier
[ ] Officer　　　[ ] Alcohol Licensee　　　[ ] Tobacco Distributor

(For individuals, complete Lines C,D, and E. For businesses, complete Lines A, B, D, and E.)

A	BUSINESS NAME	STI or LICENSE NO.
B	GA. SALES TAX NO.	GA. WITHHOLDING TAX NO.
C	LAST NAME　　　FIRST　　　M.I.　　　TITLE　　　SOCIAL SECURITY NO.	
D	ADDRESS	
E	CITY　　　STATE　　　ZIP　　　COUNTY　　　COUNTRY　　　PHONE ( )	

(TO REPORT ADDITIONAL RELATIONSHIPS, USE FORM CRF-004)

SALES AND USE TAX SECTION

17 NATURE OF BUSINESS (If combination of two or more, list approximate percentages of receipts. Must equal 100%.)
[ ] Retail ___%　　　[ ] Services ___%　　　[ ] Manufacturing ___%　　　[ ] Mining ___%
[ ] Wholesale ___%　　　[ ] Construction ___%　　　[ ] Processing ___%　　　[ ] Other ___%

18 WHAT KIND OF BUSINESS WILL YOU OPERATE? (Be specific as to the product sold or service provided.)

19 WILL YOU SELL ALCOHOLIC BEVERAGES?　　　[ ] Yes　　　[ ] No

20 WILL YOU SELL RETAIL TOBACCO OTHER THAN IN A VENDING MACHINE?　　　[ ] Yes　　　[ ] No　　　Date ___ / ___

21 WILL YOU SELL GASOLINE AND/OR MOTOR FUEL?　[ ] Yes　[ ] No　If "Yes", please specify the name and Sales Tax Number of the dealer responsible for paying the tax on gasoline and/or motor fuel sales, if other than yourself.
NAME　　　　　　　　　　　　　　SALES TAX NO.

22 WHEN DID OR WILL YOU START SELLING OR PURCHASING ITEMS SUBJECT TO SALES TAX?　　Date ___ / ___

23 WHAT ACCOUNTING METHOD WILL YOU USE?　　　[ ] Cash Basis　　　[ ] Accrual Basis

24 WILL YOU HAVE EMPLOYEES? [ ] Yes [ ] No　If "Yes", complete the following WITHHOLDING TAX SECTION. If "No", stop here and complete Signature Section.

WITHHOLDING TAX SECTION

25 WHO WILL BE RESPONSIBLE FOR FILING AND REMITTING THE PAYROLL TAXES FOR YOUR EMPLOYEES?
[ ] Applicant or Payroll Service Bureau　　　[ ] Other
If "Other", list the name and GA. Withholding No. of the business responsible for paying these taxes.
NAME　　　　　　　　　　　　　　GA. WITHHOLDING TAX NO.

26 DO YOU EXPECT TO WITHHOLD MORE THAN $200 PER MONTH?　　　[ ] Yes　　　[ ] No

27 HOW MANY EMPLOYEES DOES THIS BUSINESS HAVE OR WILL HAVE?

28 DATE ON WHICH WAGES WERE OR WILL FIRST BE PAID?　　Date ___ / ___

SIGNATURE SECTION

I HAVE EXAMINED THIS APPLICATION, AND TO THE BEST OF MY KNOWLEDGE IT IS TRUE AND CORRECT

_____　　_____　　_____
Signature　　　　　　　　　　Title　　　　　　　　　　Date

(MUST BE SIGNED BY OWNER, PARTNER, OR CORPORATE OFFICER AS LISTED IN THE RELATIONSHIP SECTION ABOVE.)

CRF-004 (Rev. 12/91)
GEORGIA DEPARTMENT OF REVENUE
REGISTRATION UNIT
P. O. BOX 740001
ATLANTA, GEORGIA 30374-0001

ADDITIONAL OWNERSHIP / RELATIONSHIP FORM
(Complete Only If Necessary)

(PLEASE PRINT OR TYPE)

FOR OFFICE USE ONLY

SAMPLE

LEGAL BUSINESS NAME:

CHECK ALL THAT APPLY   EFFECTIVE DATE   /   /

[ ] Owner   [ ] Parent Company   [ ] Manager   [ ] Related Business
[ ] Partner   [ ] Shareholder   [ ] Tobacco Licensee   [ ] Motor Fuel Supplier
[ ] Officer   [ ] Alcohol Licensee   [ ] Tobacco Distributor

(For individuals, complete Lines C, D, and E. For businesses, complete Lines A, B, D, and E.)

A   BUSINESS NAME   STI or LICENSE NO.

B   GA. SALES TAX NO.   GA. WITHHOLDING TAX NO.

C   LAST NAME   FIRST   M.I.   TITLE   SOCIAL SECURITY NO.

D   ADDRESS

E   CITY   STATE   ZIP   COUNTY   COUNTRY   PHONE ( )

CHECK ALL THAT APPLY   EFFECTIVE DATE   /   /

[ ] Owner   [ ] Parent Company   [ ] Manager   [ ] Related Business
[ ] Partner   [ ] Shareholder   [ ] Tobacco Licensee   [ ] Motor Fuel Supplier
[ ] Officer   [ ] Alcohol Licensee   [ ] Tobacco Distributor

(For individuals, complete Lines C, D, and E. For businesses, complete Lines A, B, D, and E.)

A   BUSINESS NAME   STI or LICENSE NO.

B   GA. SALES TAX NO.   GA. WITHHOLDING TAX NO.

C   LAST NAME   FIRST   M.I.   TITLE   SOCIAL SECURITY NO.

D   ADDRESS

E   CITY   STATE   ZIP   COUNTY   COUNTRY   PHONE ( )

CHECK ALL THAT APPLY   EFFECTIVE DATE   /   /

[ ] Owner   [ ] Parent Company   [ ] Manager   [ ] Related Business
[ ] Partner   [ ] Shareholder   [ ] Tobacco Licensee   [ ] Motor Fuel Supplier
[ ] Officer   [ ] Alcohol Licensee   [ ] Tobacco Distributor

(For individuals, complete Lines C, D, and E. For businesses, complete Lines A, B, D, and E.)

A   BUSINESS NAME   STI or LICENSE NO.

B   GA. SALES TAX NO.   GA. WITHHOLDING TAX NO.

C   LAST NAME   FIRST   M.I.   TITLE   SOCIAL SECURITY NO.

D   ADDRESS

E   CITY   STATE   ZIP   COUNTY   COUNTRY   PHONE ( )

SIGNATURE SECTION

I HAVE EXAMINED THIS FORM, AND TO THE BEST OF MY KNOWLEDGE IT IS TRUE AND CORRECT.

_____   _____   _____
Signature   Title   Date

(MUST BE SIGNED BY OWNER, PARTNER, OR CORPORATE OFFICER AS LISTED IN THE RELATIONSHIP SECTION ABOVE.)

CRF-004 (Rev. 12/91)
GEORGIA DEPARTMENT OF REVENUE
REGISTRATION UNIT
P. O. BOX 740001
ATLANTA, GEORGIA 30374-0001

ADDITIONAL OWNERSHIP / RELATIONSHIP FORM
(Complete Only If Necessary)

(PLEASE PRINT OR TYPE)

FOR OFFICE USE ONLY	LEGAL BUSINESS NAME:

SAMPLE

CHECK ALL THAT APPLY   EFFECTIVE DATE   /   /

[ ] Owner   [ ] Parent Company   [ ] Manager   [ ] Related Business
[ ] Partner   [ ] Shareholder   [ ] Tobacco Licensee   [ ] Motor Fuel Supplier
[ ] Officer   [ ] Alcohol Licensee   [ ] Tobacco Distributor

(For individuals, complete Lines C, D, and E. For businesses, complete Lines A, B, D, and E.)

A BUSINESS NAME   STI or LICENSE NO.

B GA. SALES TAX NO.   GA. WITHHOLDING TAX NO.

C LAST NAME   FIRST   M.I.   TITLE   SOCIAL SECURITY NO.

D ADDRESS

E CITY   STATE   ZIP   COUNTY   COUNTRY   PHONE
                                                                 (   )

CHECK ALL THAT APPLY   EFFECTIVE DATE   /   /

[ ] Owner   [ ] Parent Company   [ ] Manager   [ ] Related Business
[ ] Partner   [ ] Shareholder   [ ] Tobacco Licensee   [ ] Motor Fuel Supplier
[ ] Officer   [ ] Alcohol Licensee   [ ] Tobacco Distributor

(For individuals, complete Lines C, D, and E. For businesses, complete Lines A, B, D, and E.)

A BUSINESS NAME   STI or LICENSE NO.

B GA. SALES TAX NO.   GA. WITHHOLDING TAX NO.

C LAST NAME   FIRST   M.I.   TITLE   SOCIAL SECURITY NO.

D ADDRESS

E CITY   STATE   ZIP   COUNTY   COUNTRY   PHONE
                                                                 (   )

CHECK ALL THAT APPLY   EFFECTIVE DATE   /   /

[ ] Owner   [ ] Parent Company   [ ] Manager   [ ] Related Business
[ ] Partner   [ ] Shareholder   [ ] Tobacco Licensee   [ ] Motor Fuel Supplier
[ ] Officer   [ ] Alcohol Licensee   [ ] Tobacco Distributor

(For individuals, complete Lines C, D, and E. For businesses, complete Lines A, B, D, and E.)

A BUSINESS NAME   STI or LICENSE NO.

B GA. SALES TAX NO.   GA. WITHHOLDING TAX NO.

C LAST NAME   FIRST   M.I.   TITLE   SOCIAL SECURITY NO.

D ADDRESS

E CITY   STATE   ZIP   COUNTY   COUNTRY   PHONE
                                                                 (   )

SIGNATURE SECTION

I HAVE EXAMINED THIS FORM, AND TO THE BEST OF MY KNOWLEDGE IT IS TRUE AND CORRECT.

_____   _____   _____
Signature   Title   Date

(MUST BE SIGNED BY OWNER, PARTNER, OR CORPORATE OFFICER AS LISTED IN THE RELATIONSHIP SECTION ABOVE.)

STATE OF GEORGIA

DEPARTMENT OF REVENUE

INSTRUCTIONS FOR COMPLETION OF THE SALES & USE AND WITHHOLDING TAX APPLICATION (CRF-005)

Use this form to apply for a certificate of registration for Georgia Sales and Use Tax and/or to register for Georgia Withholding Tax Identification Number. Every person, firm, or corporation desiring to engage in or conduct business as a seller, user, distributor, manufacturer, or processor of tangible personal property in Georgia is required to file an application for a certificate of registration for Sales and Use Tax. Any business which is liable for withholding employee's state income tax must apply for a Georgia Withholding Tax Identification Number.

TYPE OR PRINT IN INK - DO NOT USE PENCIL

A: INSTRUCTIONS FOR COMPLETING:

Line 1 - Enter your Georgia State Taxpayer Identifier. (If you do not yet have one, leave blank).

Line 2 - Enter the name under which your business is legally registered with the Secretary of State. If your business is not registered, then enter the name under which your business owns property or acquires debt. If the business is a partnership the legal name is the partnership name. In the case of a sole proprietorship, the legal name is the name of the individual owner of the business.

Complete Lines 3 - 13 to register for Sales & Use Tax.
Line 3 - Identify the nature of your business. If a combination of two or more, list percentage of sales.

Line 4 - Enter the kind of business you operate or will operate. Examples are: grocery, bakery, restaurant, chain food store, department store, etc. Specify if a combination business. Specify products.

Line 5 - Check "yes" or "no" to answer as to whether you will sell alcoholic beverages, and/or tobacco products.

Line 6 - Check "yes" or "no" to answer as to whether you will sell motor fuels such as gasoline or diesel fuels.

Line 7 - Deleted

Line 8 - Enter the amount of anticipated sales per month OR per year; if you purchased this business, enter purchase price.

Line 9 - Enter the approximate total cost of the building OR the lease amount paid per month OR per year.

Line 10 - Enter the estimated cost for A) AND B).

Line 11 - Check "yes" or "no" if your business operates in a leased or rented department AND the lessor will report and remit the sales tax for you

Line 12 - Check the accounting method your business will use to report Sales and Use Tax to the Department.

Line 13 - Enter the date (MMDDYY) you actually started or will start selling or purchasing items subject to sales tax. (If an out-of-state business, enter the date of first activity in Georgia).

Complete lines 14-18 if applying for a Georgia Withholding Tax Identification Number.
Line 14 - Check "yes" or "no" in the spaces provided.

Line 15 - If "yes" in Line 14, check "yes" or "no" in the spaces provided.

Line 16 - If "no" in Line 15, check "yes" or "no" in the spaces provided.

Line 17 - Enter the number of employees hired or that you anticipate hiring.

Line 18 - Enter the date (MMDDYY) of the first payroll subject to Georgia withholding.

B: INSTRUCTIONS FOR SIGNING:

This application must be signed by the owner or a partners or an authorized officer of the corporation.

C: INSTRUCTIONS FOR MAILING AND REQUESTING INFORMATION:

If the applicant is a corporation, a Copy of the Corporate Charter must be attached to process this application.

The taxpayer should retain a copy of this application for his file and for inspection by the Revenue Commissioner or his Agents. Mail the original to the address shown below and call 404-656-4092 or write if you have any questions or need assistance in completing the Application.

Georgia Department of Revenue
Centralized Taxpayer Registration Unit
P.O. Box 740001
Atlanta, Georgia 30374-0001

THE PROCESSING OF THIS APPLICATION WILL BE DELAYED UNLESS IT IS PROPERLY SIGNED, COMPLETE INFORMATION IS FURNISHED, AND APPLICABLE QUESTIONS ARE ANSWERED.

CRF-005

SALES AND USE AND WITHHOLDING TAX APPLICATION
(Read Instructions Before Completing)

FOR OFFICE USE ONLY		IDENTIFICATION SECTION
	1	IF YOU HAVE A STATE TAXPAYER IDENTIFIER (STI), ENTER HERE:
	2	LEGAL BUSINESS NAME

SAMPLE

SALES TAX APPLICATION

3 NATURE OF BUSINESS (If combination of two or more, list percentages of sales)

[ ] RETAIL _____ %   [ ] SERVICES _____ %   [ ] MANUFACTURING _____ %   [ ] MINING _____ %
[ ] WHOLESALE _____ %   [ ] CONSTRUCTION _____ %   [ ] PROCESSING _____ % OTHER _____ ___ %

4 WHAT KIND OF BUSINESS WILL YOU OPERATE?

SPECIFY PRODUCTS PURCHASED OR SOLD

5 WILL YOU SELL ALCOHOLIC BEVERAGES ?   WILL YOU SELL TOBACCO PRODUCTS ?
[ ] YES   [ ] NO   [ ] YES   [ ] NO

6 WILL YOU SELL GASOLINE AND/OR MOTOR FUEL ?   IF "YES" SPECIFY THE PERSON OR COMPANY RESPONSIBLE FOR PAYING TAXES
[ ] YES   [ ] NO

7 Deleted

8 ANTICIPATED TOTAL SALES   PURCHASE PRICE
$ _____ per month OR $ _____ per year $ _____

9 IF BUILDING OCCUPIED BY THIS BUSINESS IS
(A) OWNED, APPROXIMATE COST $ _____
(B) LEASED, LEASE PAYMENT $ _____ per month OR $ _____ per year

10 ESTIMATED EXPENDITURES FOR
(A) FURNITURE AND FIXTURES $ _____ (B) MACHINERY AND EQUIPMENT $ _____

11 IF THIS BUSINESS OPERATES IN A LEASED DEPARTMENT, DOES THE LESSOR REPORT THE SALES TAX FOR YOU ?   [ ] YES   [ ] NO

12 WHAT ACCOUNTING METHOD WILL YOU USE ?
[ ] CASH BASIS   [ ] ACCRUAL BASIS

13 WHEN DID OR WILL YOU START SELLING OR PURCHASING ITEMS SUBJECT TO SALES TAX ? _____ _____ _____
Month   Day   Year

14 DO YOU HAVE EMPLOYEES ?   [ ] YES   [ ] NO (If "NO.. stop here and sign at bottom of this form; if "YES" proceed to fill out information in the following WITHHOLDING TAX APPLICATION)

WITHHOLDING TAX APPLICATION

15 IS YOUR BUSINESS OR PARENT BUSINESS CURRENTLY FILING GEORGIA WITHHOLDING TAXES FOR THESE EMPLOYEES ? [ ] YES   [ ] NO (If "YES", stop here and sign below)

16 DO YOU EXPECT TO WITHOLD $ 200 OR MORE PER MONTH ? [ ] YES   [ ] NO

17 HOW MANY EMPLOYEES DOES THIS BUSINESS HAVE ?

18 ON WHAT DATE WERE OR WILL WAGES FIRST BE PAID ?

19 IF SALES AND USE TAX WAS COLLECTED AND DUE PRIOR TO THIS APPLICATION, PLEASE REMIT PAYMENT WITH TAX REPORT FORM AND ATTACH TO THIS APPLICATION. IF GEORGIA TAX WAS WITHHELD AND DUE PRIOR TO THIS APPLICATION, PLEASE REMIT PAYMENT WITH TAX REPORT FORM AND ATTACH TO THIS APPLICATION. IF TAX REPORTS FORMS ARE NOT AVAILABLE, PLEASE ATTACH CHECK(S) AND INDICATE BELOW THE DISTRIBUTION OF THE TAX PAYMENTS.

[ ] SALES AND USE TAX PAYMENT $ _____
[ ] WITHHOLDING TAX PAYMENT $ _____
TOTAL $ _____

SIGNATURE SECTION

THIS APPLICATION HAS BEEN EXAMINED BY ME, AND TO THE BEST OF MY KNOWLEDGE IS TRUE AND CORRECT.

_____   _____   _____
Signature   Title   Date

(Must be signed by owner, partner, or authorized officer of corporation - Stamped signature not acceptable)

Notes

The book that will change for good the way you think about creating a business plan

We were impressed! In our world of business publishing, we sometimes see the unusual. A book so well conceived and well written that it gives you, the reader, value in ways you would never expect.

The Successful Business Plan by Rhonda M. Abrams is a great example. Frankly, it has more of what it *now* takes to get your idea or venture on paper in a way that sells.

More on marketing & sales. Better probe of target market. Tighter industry analysis. A new look at operations. Even a sharp new way for you to get the P&L and balance sheets on paper quickly. So simple it will bring sighs of relief. And there is something else here to make those reading your final plan sit up and take notice. It's the *look* of your plan. The logic of it. The way it presents itself clearly. *The Successful Business Plan* is strong on giving you ways to show your venture at its best. Proven ways. A needed aspect of business planning we found lacking until this book was written.

– The Editors at Oasis Press, PSI Research

About Rhonda M. Abrams

Educated at both UCLA and Harvard, Ms. Abrams heads a west coast management consulting firm. Her common-sense approach to problem solving has made *The Successful Business Plan* as readable as it is powerful. Over 11 months of writing, two hundred hours of interviews, and Ms. Abrams' years of experience make this new book the best for business planning today.

Her comment? *"No other work propels you as far forward in your enterprise as building your plan of action."*

© 1992 Publishing Services Inc.

1 You get expert help

Listen in, as Rhonda M. Abrams interviews some of today's most savvy business owners and venture financers. Bill Walsh, Nancy E. Glaser, Eugene Kleiner and a dozen more. 159 tips from 15 experts reveal what works in business plans, and what doesn't. What they have to say will help you write a plan that responds best to what people are looking for now. Straight talk by those who read business plans — about what should be in yours.

2 Worksheets to make it easy

You know plenty about your business. What you want now is your facts gathered and organized. You want the plan done fast, but complete, decisive. Get all that with the 72 worksheets in this book. They are packed with questions designed to draw out and organize all you know about your venture. The questions cover all the 11 critical plan sections and are clear on what to get and where it goes. You'll have the whole picture in front of you before you start writing the plan itself. No time wasted.

3 Sample plan to guide you

The sample plan is so interesting, you might forget it's there to guide you. Written in the actual wording and style used in plans already read and accepted. Section by section, the sample shows you how to put your facts & figures into a readable, compelling story. The story of your idea. To help present your idea there are specifics on retail, manufacturing, service and in-house corporate plans.

4 Get the binder and software combination

Give your plan a finished look. Use the 12 tabbed dividers to organize your final presentation. Also, a two-page planning checklist keeps you from missing even the smallest point. Extra copies of 28 critical worksheets give you plenty of room to work out details. IBM software includes a text editor program and prompts, as well as information taken directly from the book.

Proven tools and ideas to expand your business.

Marketing & Public Relations

Power Marketing

Book

A wealth of basic, how-to marketing information that easily takes a new or experienced business owner through the essentials of marketing and sales strategies, customer database marketing, advertising, public relations, budgeting, and follow-up marketing systems. Written in a friendly tone by a marketing educator, the book features worksheets with step-by-step instructions, a glossary of marketing terms, and a sample marketing plan.

How To Develop & Market Creative Business Ideas

Book

Step-by-step manual guides the inventor through all stages of new product development. Discusses patenting your invention, trademarks, copyrights, and how to construct your prototype. Gives information on financing, distribution, test marketing, and finding licensees. Plus, lists many useful sources for prototype resources, trade shows, funding, and more.

Marketing Your Products and Services Successfully

Book

Helps small businesses understand marketing concepts, then plan and follow through with the actions that will result in increased sales. Covers all aspects from identifying the target market, through market research, establishing pricing, creating a marketing plan, evaluating media alternatives, to launching a campaign. Discusses customer maintenance techniques and international marketing.

Customer Profile and Retrieval (CPR)

Software for IBM-PC & compatibles

Stores details of past activities plus future reminders on customers, clients, contacts, vendors, and employees, then gives instant access to that information when needed. "Tickler" fields keep reminders of dates for recontacts. "Type" fields categorize names for sorting as the user defines. "Other data" fields store information such as purchase and credit history, telephone call records, or interests.

Has massive storage capabilities. Holds up to 255 lines of comments for each name, plus unlimited time and date stamped notes. Features perpetual calendar, and automatic telephone dialing. Built-in word processing and merge gives the ability to pull in the information already keyed into the fields into form or individual letters. Prints mail labels, rotary file cards, and phone directories. *Requires a hard disk, 640K RAM and 80 column display. (Autodial feature requires modem.)*

Cost-Effective Market Analysis

Book

Workbook explains how a small business can conduct its own market research. Shows how to set objectives, determine which techniques to use, create a schedule, and then monitor expenses. Encompasses primary research (trade shows, telephone interviews, mail surveys), plus secondary research (using available information in print).

International Business

Export Now

Book

Prepares a business to enter the export market. Clearly explains the basics, then articulates specific requirements for export licensing, preparation of documents, payment methods, packaging, and shipping. Includes advice on evaluating foreign representatives, planning international marketing strategies, and discovering official U.S. policy for various countries and regions. Lists sources.

EXECARDS®

International Communication Cards

EXECARDS offer unique cards you can send to businesspeople of many nationalities to help build and maintain lasting relationships. One distinguished EXECARD choice is a richly textured and embossed white card of substantial quality that expresses thank you in thirteen languages; Japanese, Russian, French, Chinese, Arabic, German, Swahili, Italian, Polish, Spanish, Hebrew, and Swedish, as well as English. Another handsome option is an ivory card with thank you embossed in Russian and English. To each, you can add a personal note or order a custom printed message. *Please call for more information.*

Now – Find Out How Your Business Can Profit By Being Environmentally Aware

The Business Environmental Handbook

Book

Save your business while you are saving the planet. Here's your chance to learn about the hundreds of ways any business can help secure its future by starting to conserve resources now. This book reveals little-understood but simple techniques for recycling, precycling, and conservation that can save your business money now, and help preserve resources. Also gives tips on "green marketing" to customers .

Unique cards get you noticed. Books & software save you time.

Business Communications

Proposal Development: How to Respond and Win the Bid

 Book

Orchestrates a successful proposal from preliminary planning to clinching the deal. Shows by explanation and example how to: determine what to include; create text, illustrations, tables, exhibits, and appendices; how to format (using either traditional methods or desktop publishing); meet the special requirements of government proposals; set up and follow a schedule.

Write Your Own Business Contracts

 Book

Explains the "do's"and "don'ts" of contract writing so any person in business can do the preparatory work in drafting contracts before hiring an attorney for final review. Gives a working knowledge of the various types of business agreements, plus tips on how to prepare for the unexpected.

Complete Book of Business Forms

 Book

Over 200 reproducible forms for all types of business needs: personnel, employment, finance, production flow, operations, sales, marketing, order entry, and general administration. Time-saving, uniform, coordinated way to record and locate important business information.

EXECARDS®
Communication Tools

EXECARDS, business-to-business message cards, are an effective vehicle for maintaining personal contacts in this era of rushed, highly-technical communications. A card takes only seconds and a few cents to send, but can memorably tell customers, clients, prospects, or co-workers that their relationship is valued. Many styles and messages to choose from for thanking, acknowledging, inviting, reminding, prospecting, following up, etc. *Please call for complete catalog.*

PlanningTools™
Paper pads, 3-hole punched

Handsome PlanningTools help organize thoughts and record notes, actions, plans, and deadlines, so important information and responsibilities do not get lost or forgotten. Specific PlanningTools organize different needs, such as Calendar Notes, Progress/Activity Record, Project Plan/Record, Week's Priority Planner, Make-A-Month Calendar, and Milestone Chart. *Please call for catalog.*

Customer Profile & Retrieval (CPR)
Software for IBM-PC & compatibles

Easy computer database management program streamlines the process of communicating with clients, customers, vendors, contacts, and employees. While talking to your contact on the phone (or at any time), all notes of past activities and conversations can be viewed instantly, and new notes can be added at that time. *Please see description under "Marketing & Public Relations" section on previous page.*

Business Relocation

Company Relocation Handbook: Making the Right Move

 Book

Comprehensive guide to moving a business. Begins with defining objectives for moving and evaluating whether relocating will actually solve more problems than it creates. Worksheets compare prospective locations, using rating scales for physical plant, equipment, personnel, and geographic considerations. Sets up a schedule for dealing with logistics.

Retirement Planning

Retirement & Estate Planning Handbook

 Book

Do-it-yourself workbook for setting up a retirement plan that can easily be maintained and followed. Covers establishing net worth, retirement goals, budgets, and a plan for asset acquisition, preservation, and growth. Discusses realistic expectations for Social Security, Medicare, and health care alternatives. Features special sections for business owners.

Mail Order

Mail Order Legal Guide

 Book

For companies that use the mail to market their products or services, as well as for mail order businesses, this book clarifies complex regulations so penalties can be avoided. Gives state-by-state legal requirements, plus information on Federal Trade Commission guidelines and rules covering delivery dates, advertising, sales taxes, unfair trade practices, and consumer protection.

Need it tomorrow? In most cases that's possible if you order before noon, PST. Just give us a call at 800-228-2275.

Step-by-step techniques for generating more profit.

Financial Management

Financial Management Techniques for Small Business

Book and software for IBM

Clearly reveals the essential ingredients of sound financial management in detail. By monitoring trends in your financial activities, you will be able to uncover potential problems before they become crises. You'll understand why you can be making a profit and still not have the cash to meet expenses, and you'll learn the steps to change your business' cash behavior to get more return for your effort. Software makes your business' financial picture graphically clear, and lets you look at "what if" scenarios.

Risk Analysis: How to Reduce Insurance Costs

Book

Straightforward advice on shopping for insurance, understanding types of coverage, comparing proposals and premium rates. Worksheets help identify and weigh the risks a particular business is likely to face, then determine if any of those might be safely self-insured or eliminated. Request for proposal form helps businesses avoid over-paying for protection.

Debt Collection: Strategies for the Small Business

Book

Practical tips on how to turn receivables into cash. Worksheets and checklists help businesses establish credit policies, track accounts, and flag when it is necessary to bring in a collection agency, attorney, or go to court. This book advises how to deal with disputes, negotiate settlements, win in small claims court, and collect on judgments. Gives examples of telephone collection techniques and collection letters.

Negotiating the Purchase or Sale of a Business

Book

Prepares a business buyer or seller for negotiations that will achieve win-win results. Shows how to determine the real worth of a business, including intangible assets such as "goodwill." Over 36 checklists and worksheets on topics such as tax impact on buyers and sellers, escrow checklist, cash flow projections, evaluating potential buyers, financing options, and many others.

Business Owner's Guide to Accounting & Bookkeeping

Book

Makes understanding the economics of business simple. Explains the basic accounting principles that relate to any business. Step-by-step instructions for generating accounting statements and interpreting them, spotting errors, and recognizing warning signs. Discusses how banks and other creditors view financial statements.

Controlling Your Company's Freight Costs

Book

Shows how to increase company profits by trimming freight costs. Provides tips for comparing alternative methods and shippers, then negotiating contracts to receive the most favorable discounts. Tells how to package shipments for safe transport. Discusses freight insurance and dealing with claims for loss or damage. Appendices include directory of U.S. ports, shipper's guide, and sample bill of lading.

Accounting Software Analysis

Book

Presents successful step-by-step procedure for choosing the most appropriate software to handle the accounting for your business. Evaluation forms and worksheets create a custom software "shopping list" to match against features of various products, so facts, not sales hype, can determine the best fit for your company.

Financial Templates
Software for IBM-PC & Macintosh

Calculates and graphs many business "what-if" scenarios and financial reports. Forty financial templates such as income statements, cash flow, and balance sheet comparisons, break-even analyses, product contribution comparisons, market share, net present value, sales model, *pro formas*, loan payment projections, etc. *Requires 512K RAM hard disk or two floppy drives, plus Lotus 1-2-3 or compatible spreadsheet program.*

Yes, we accept credit cards — VISA, MasterCard, American Express, Discover, or your personal or business check.

Get business tips from over 157 seasoned experts.

Business Formation and Planning

The Successful Business Plan: Secrets & Strategies

Book and optional kit

Start-to-finish guide to creating a successful business plan. Includes tips from venture capitalists, bankers, and successful CEOs. Features worksheets for ease in planning and budgeting with the Abrams Method of Flow-Through Financials. Gives a sample business plan, plus specialized help for retailers, service companies, manufacturers, and in-house corporate plans. Also tells how to find funding sources.

Starting and Operating a Business In... series
Book available for each state in the United States, plus District of Columbia

One-stop resource to current federal and state laws and regulations that affect businesses. Clear "human language" explanations of complex issues, plus samples of government forms, and sources for additional help or information. Helps seasoned business owners keep up with changing legislation, and guides new entrepreneurs step-by-step to start and run the business. Includes many checklists and worksheets to organize ideas, create action plans, and project financial scenarios.

Starting and Operating a Business: U.S. Edition
Set of eleven binders

The complete encyclopedia of how to do business in the U.S. Describes laws and regulations for each state, plus Washington, D.C., as well as the federal government. Includes lists of sources of help, plus post cards for requesting materials from government agencies. This set is valuable for businesses with locations or marketing activities in several states, plus franchisors, attorneys, and other consultants.

The Essential Corporation Handbook

Book

This comprehensive reference for small business corporations in all 50 states and Washington, D.C. explains the legal requirements for maintaining a corporation in good standing. Features many sample corporate documents which are annotated by the author to show what to look for and what to look out for. Tells how to avoid personal liability as an officer, director, or shareholder.

Surviving and Prospering in a Business Partnership

Book

From evaluation of potential partners, through the drafting of agreements, to day-to-day management of working relationships, this book helps avoid classic partnership catastrophes. Discusses how to set up the partnership to reduce the financial and emotional consequences of unanticipated disputes, dishonesty, divorce, disability, or death of a partner.

California Corporation Formation Package and Minute Book

Book and software for IBM & Mac

Provides forms required for incorporating and maintaining closely held corporations, including: articles of incorporation; bylaws; stock certificates, stock transfer record sheets, bill of sale agreement; minutes form; plus many others. Addresses questions on fees, timing, notices, regulations, election of directors and other critical factors. Software has minutes, bylaws, and articles of incorporation already for you to edit and customize (using your own word processor).

Franchise Bible: A Comprehensive Guide

Book

Complete guide to franchising for prospective franchisees or for business owners considering franchising their business. Includes actual sample documents, such as a complete offering circular, plus worksheets for evaluating franchise companies, locations, and organizing information before seeing an attorney. This book is helpful for lawyers as well as their clients.

Home Business Made Easy

Book

Thinking of starting a business at home? This book is the easiest road to starting a home business. Shows you how to select and start a home business that fits your interests, lifestyle, and pocketbook. Walks you through 153 different businesses you could operate from home full or part time. Author David Hanania has boiled the process down to simple steps so you can get started now to realize your dreams.

The Small Business Expert
Software for IBM-PC & compatibles

Generates comprehensive custom checklist of the state and federal laws and regulations based on your type and size of business. Allows comparison of doing business in each of the 50 states. Built-in worksheets create outlines for personnel policies, marketing feasibility studies, and a business plan draft. *Requires 256K RAM and hard disk.*

To order these business tools, use the enclosed order form, FAX 503-476-1479 or call us toll-free at 800-228-2275

Gain the power of increased knowledge — Oasis is your source.

Acquiring Outside Capital

Financing Your Small Business

Book

Essential techniques to successfully identify, approach, attract, and manage sources of financing. Shows how to gain the full benefits of debt financing while minimizing its risks. Outlines all types of financing and walks you step by step through the process, from evaluating short-term credit options, through negotiating a long-term loan, to deciding whether to go public.

The Loan Package

Book

Preparatory package for a business loan proposal. Worksheets help analyze cash needs and articulate business focus. Includes sample forms for balance sheets, income statements, projections, and budget reports. Screening sheets rank potential lenders to shorten the time involved in getting the loan.

The Successful Business Plan: Secrets & Strategies
Book and software for IBM-PC

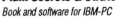

Now you can find out what venture capitalists and bankers really want to see before they will fund a company. This book gives you their personal tips and insights. The Abrams Method of Flow-Through Financials breaks down the chore into easy to manage steps, so you can end up with a fundable proposal. Requires a hard drive.

Financial Templates
Software for IBM-PC & Macintosh

Software speeds business calculations including those in PSI's workbooks, *The Loan Package, Venture Capital Proposal Package, Negotiating the Purchase or Sale of a Business, The Successful Business Plan: Secrets & Strategies*. Includes 40 financial templates including various projections, statements, ratios, histories, amortizations, and cash flows. *Requires Lotus 1-2-3, Microsoft Excel 2.0 or higher*

Business Planning System
Software for IBM-PC

Complete your business plan quickly and easily using this StandAlone program. Enjoy the flexibility of writing segments of the plan as you collect the information or as time allows. Examples of wording are included. Questions lead you through the development process.

Managing Employees

A Company Policy and Personnel Workbook

Book

Saves costly consultant or staff hours in creating company personnel policies. Provides model policies on topics such as employee safety, leave of absence, flextime, smoking, substance abuse, sexual harassment, performance improvement, grievance procedure. For each subject, practical and legal ramifications are explained, then a choice of alternate policies presented.

A Company Policy and Personnel Workbook
Software for IBM-PC & Macintosh

The policies in *A Company Policy and Personnel Workbook* are on disk so the company's name, specific information, and any desired changes or rewrites can be incorporated using your own word processor to tailor the model policies to suit your company's specific needs before printing out a complete manual for distribution to employees. *Requires a word processor and hard disk and floppy drive.*

Managing People: A Practical Guide

Book

Focuses on developing the art of working with people to maximize the productivity and satisfaction of both manager and employees. Discussions, exercises, and self-tests boost skills in communicating, delegating, motivating, developing teams, goal-setting, adapting to change, and coping with stress.

Safety Law Compliance Manual for California Businesses

Book

Now every California employer must have an Injury and Illness Prevention Program that meets the specific requirements of Senate Bill 198. Already, thousands of citations have been issued to companies who did not comply with all seven components of the complicated new law. Avoid fines by using this guide to set up a program that will meet Cal/OSHA standards. Includes forms.

Plus optional binder for

your company's safety program

Also available — Company Injury and Illness Prevention Program Binder — Pre-organized and ready-to-use with forms, tabs, logs and sample documents. Saves your company time, work, and worry.

People Investment

Book

Written for the business owner or manager who is not a personnel specialist. Explains what you must know to make your hiring decisions pay off for everyone. Learn more about the Americans With Disabilities Act (ADA), Medical and Family Leave, and more.

Why hesitate? If any product you order doesn't meet your needs, just return it for full refund or credit. 800-228-2275.

BOOKS FROM THE OASIS PRESS® Please check the edition (binder or paperback) of your choice

TITLE	BINDER	PAPERBACK	QUANTITY	COST
The Business Environmental Handbook		☐ $ 19.95		
Business Owner's Guide to Accounting & Bookkeeping		☐ $ 19.95		
California Corporation Formation Package and Minute Book	☐ $ 39.95	☐ $ 29.95		
A Company Policy and Personnel Workbook	☐ $ 49.95	☐ $ 29.95		
Company Relocation Handbook	☐ $ 49.95	☐ $ 19.95		
Complete Book of Business Forms	☐ $ 49.95	☐ $ 19.95		
Controlling Your Company's Freight Costs	☐ $ 39.95			
Cost-Effective Market Analysis	☐ $ 39.95			
Debt Collection: Strategies for the Small Business	☐ $ 39.95	☐ $ 17.95		
The Essential Corporation Handbook		☐ $ 19.95		
Export Now	☐ $ 39.95	☐ $ 19.95		
Financial Management Techniques For Small Business	☐ $ 39.95	☐ $ 19.95		
Financing Your Small Business		☐ $ 19.95		
Franchise Bible: A Comprehensive Guide	☐ $ 49.95	☐ $ 19.95		
Home Business Made Easy		☐ $ 19.95		
How to Develop & Market Creative Business Ideas		☐ $ 14.95		
The Loan Package	☐ $ 39.95			
Mail Order Legal Guide	☐ $ 45.00	☐ $ 29.95		
Managing People: A Practical Guide	☐ $ 49.95	☐ $ 19.95		
Marketing Your Products and Services Successfully	☐ $ 39.95	☐ $ 18.95		
People Investment	☐ $ 39.95	☐ $ 19.95		
Power Marketing for Small Business	☐ $ 39.95	☐ $ 19.95		
Proposal Development: How to Respond and Win the Bid (HARDBACK BOOK)	☐ $ 39.95	☐ $ 19.95		
Retirement & Estate Planning Handbook	☐ $ 49.95	☐ $ 19.95		
Safety Law Compliance Manual for California Businesses		☐ $ 24.95		
Company Illness & Injury Prevention Program Binder (OR GET KIT WITH BOOK AND BINDER $49.95)	☐ $ 34.95	☐ $ 49.95		
Starting and Operating A Business in... BOOK INCLUDES FEDERAL SECTION PLUS ONE STATE SECTION —	☐ $ 29.95	☐ $ 24.95		
PLEASE SPECIFY WHICH STATE(S) YOU WANT:				
STATE SECTION ONLY (BINDER NOT INCLUDED) — SPECIFY STATES:	☐ $ 8.95	BOOK & BINDER KIT		
U.S. EDITION (FEDERAL SECTION — 50 STATES AND WASHINGTON, D.C. IN 11-BINDER SET)	☐ $295.00			
Successful Business Plan: Secrets & Strategies (GET THE BINDER...IT'S A BUSINESS PLAN KIT)	☐ $ 49.95	☐ $ 21.95		
Surviving and Prospering in a Business Partnership	☐ $ 39.95	☐ $ 19.95		
Write Your Own Business Contracts (HARDBACK BOOK)	☐ $ 39.95	☐ $ 19.95		

BOOK TOTAL (Please enter on other side also for grand total)

SOFTWARE   Please check whether you use Macintosh or 5-1/4" or 3-1/2" Disk for IBM-PC & Compatibles

TITLE	5-1/4" IBM Disk	3-1/2" IBM Disk	MAC	PRICE	QUANTITY	COST
Business Planning System	☐	☐		☐ $129.95		
California Corporation Formation Package Software	☐	☐	☐	☐ $ 39.95		
★ California Corporation Formation Binderbook & Software	☐	☐	☐	☐ $ 69.95		
Company Policy & Personnel Software (Text Files)	☐	☐	☐	☐ $ 49.95		
★ Company Policy & Personnel Binderbook & Software (Text Files)	☐	☐	☐	☐ $ 89.95		
Customer Profile & Retrieval: Professional	☐	☐		☐ $119.95		
Financial Management Techniques		☐		☐ $ 99.95		
★Financial Management Techniques Binderbook & Software		☐		☐ $129.95		
Financial Templates	☐	☐	☐	☐ $ 69.95		
The Small Business Expert	☐	☐		☐ $ 34.95		
Successful Business Plan (Full Standalone)	☐	☐		☐ $ 99.95		
★ Successful Business Plan Binderbook & Software (Full Standalone)	☐	☐		☐ $125.95		

SOFTWARE TOTAL (Please enter on other side also for grand total)

Please add above totals on other side to complete your order. Thanks!

PSI Successful Business Library / Tools for Business Success Order Form (please see other side also)

Call, Mail or Fax to: PSI Research, 300 North Valley Drive, Grants Pass, OR 97526 USA
Order Phone USA (800) 228-2275   Inquiries and International Orders (503) 479-9464   FAX (503) 476-1479

Sold to: PLEASE GIVE STREET ADDRESS NOT P.O. BOX FOR SHIPPING

Name _____   Title: _____

Company _____   Daytime Telephone: _____

Street Address _____

City/State/Zip _____

❏   *YES, I want to receive the PREMIERE ISSUE of the PSI 1994 NEWSLETTER.*
     Be sure to include: Name, address, and telephone number above.

Ship to: (if different) **PLEASE GIVE STREET ADDRESS NOT P.O. BOX FOR SHIPPING**

Name _____

Title _____

Company _____

Street Address _____

City/State/Zip _____

Daytime Telephone _____

Payment Information:

☐ Check enclosed payable to PSI Research (When you enclose a check, UPS ground shipping is free within the Continental U.S.A.)

Charge - ☐ VISA ☐ MASTERCARD ☐ AMEX ☐ DISCOVER Card Number: _____ Expires _____

Signature: _____   Name on card: _____

EXECARDS — The Proven & Chosen Method of Personal Business Communications

ITEM	PRICE EACH	QUANTITY	COST
EXECARDS Thank You Assortment (12 assorted thank you cards)	$ 12.95		
EXECARDS Recognition Assortment (12 assorted appreciation cards)	$ 12.95		
EXECARDS Marketing Assortment (12 assorted marketing cards)	$ 12.95		
EXECARDS TOTAL (Please enter below also for grand total)			$

Many additional options available, including custom imprinting of your company's name, logo or message. Please request a complete catalog.

PLANNING TOOLS — Action Tracking Note Pads

ITEM		NUMBER OF PADS
Calendar Note Pad	☐ 1994	
	☐ 94/95	
	☐ 1995	
Total number of pads		
Multiply by unit price:	x	
PLANNING TOOLS TOTAL	$	

UNIT PRICE FOR ANY COMBINATION OF PLANNING TOOLS
1-9 pads $3.95 each
10-49 pads $3.49 each
50 or more pads $2.98 each

SAFETY PROGRAM FORMS

ITEM	PRICE EACH	QUANTITY
Employee Warning Notification (Package of 20)	$4.95	
Request for Safety Orientation (Package of 20)	$4.95	
Report of Potential Hazard (Package of 20)	$4.95	
SAFETY PROGRAM FORMS TOTAL	$	

YOUR GRAND TOTAL

BOOK TOTAL (from other side)	$
SOFTWARE TOTAL (from other side)	$
EXECARDS TOTAL	$
PLANNING TOOLS TOTAL	$
SAFETY PROGRAM FORMS TOTAL	$
TOTAL ORDER	$

Rush service is available. Please call us for details.

Please send me:

_____ **EXECARDS Catalog**

_____ **Oasis Press Software Information**

_____ **Oasis Press Book Information**

Use this form to register for advance notification of updates, new books and software releases, plus special customer discounts!

Please answer these questions to let us know how our products are working for you, and what we could do to serve you better.

Title of book or software purchased from us:_____

It is a:
- ☐ Binder book
- ☐ Paperback book
- ☐ Book/software combination
- ☐ Software only

Rate this product's overall quality of information:
- ☐ Excellent
- ☐ Good
- ☐ Fair
- ☐ Poor

Rate the quality of printed materials:
- ☐ Excellent
- ☐ Good
- ☐ Fair
- ☐ Poor

Rate the format:
- ☐ Excellent
- ☐ Good
- ☐ Fair
- ☐ Poor

Did the product provide what you needed?
- ☐ Yes ☐ No

If not, what should be added?_____
_____
_____
_____
_____
_____

This product is:
- ☐ Clear and easy to follow
- ☐ Too complicated
- ☐ Too elementary

Were the worksheets (if any) easy to use?
- ☐ Yes ☐ No ☐ N/A

Should we include:
- ☐ More worksheets
- ☐ Fewer worksheets
- ☐ No worksheets

How do you feel about the price?
- ☐ Lower than expected
- ☐ About right
- ☐ Too expensive

How many employees are in your company?
- ☐ Under 10 employees
- ☐ 10 – 50 employees
- ☐ 51 – 99 employees
- ☐ 100 – 250 employees
- ☐ Over 250 employees

How many people in the city your company is in?
- ☐ 50,000 – 100,000
- ☐ 100,000 – 500,000
- ☐ 500,000 – 1,000,000
- ☐ Over 1,000,000
- ☐ Rural (under 50,000)

What is your type of business?
- ☐ Retail
- ☐ Service
- ☐ Government
- ☐ Manufacturing
- ☐ Distributor
- ☐ Education

What types of products or services do you sell?
_____
_____
_____
_____

What is your position in the company?
(please check one)
- ☐ Owner
- ☐ Administration
- ☐ Sales/marketing
- ☐ Finance
- ☐ Human resources
- ☐ Production
- ☐ Operations
- ☐ Computer/MIS

How did you learn about this product?
- ☐ Recommended by a friend
- ☐ Used in a seminar or class
- ☐ Have used other PSI products
- ☐ Received a mailing
- ☐ Saw in bookstore
- ☐ Saw in library
- ☐ Saw review in:
  - ☐ Newspaper
  - ☐ Magazine
  - ☐ TV/Radio

Where did you buy this product?
- ☐ Catalog
- ☐ Bookstore
- ☐ Office supply
- ☐ Consultant
- ☐ Other_____

Would you purchase other business tools from us?
- ☐ Yes ☐ No

If so, which products interest you?
- ☐ EXECARDS® Communication Tools
- ☐ Books for business
- ☐ Software

Would you recommend this product to a friend?
- ☐ Yes ☐ No

If you'd like us to send associates or friends a catalog, just list names and addresses on back.

Do you use a personal computer for business?
- ☐ Yes ☐ No

If yes, which?
- ☐ IBM/compatible
- ☐ Macintosh

Check all the ways you use computers:
- ☐ Word processing
- ☐ Accounting
- ☐ Spreadsheet
- ☐ Inventory
- ☐ Order processing
- ☐ Design/graphics
- ☐ General data base
- ☐ Customer information
- ☐ Scheduling

May we call you to follow up on your comments?
- ☐ Yes ☐ No

May we add your name to our mailing list?
- ☐ Yes ☐ No

If there is anything you think we should do to improve this product, please describe:_____
_____
_____
_____

Thank you for your patience in answering the above questions.
Just fill in your name and address here, fold (see back) and mail.

Name_____
Title_____
Company_____
Phone_____
Address_____
City/State/Zip_____

PSI Research creates this family of fine products to help you more easily and effectively manage your business activities:

The Oasis Press®   PSI Successful Business Software
PSI Successful Business Library   EXECARDS® Communication Tools

If you have friends or associates who might appreciate receiving our catalogs, please list here. Thanks!

Name_____   Name_____

Title_____   Title_____

Company_____   Company_____

Phone_____   Phone_____

Address_____   Address_____

City/State/Zip_____   City/State/Zip_____

FOLD HERE FIRST

BUSINESS REPLY MAIL

FIRST CLASS MAIL PERMIT NO. 002 MERLIN, OREGON

POSTAGE WILL BE PAID BY ADDRESSEE

PSI Research
PO BOX 1414
Merlin OR 97532-9900

FOLD HERE SECOND, THEN TAPE TOGETHER

Please cut
along this
vertical line,
fold twice,
tape together
and mail.
Thanks!

✂ Cut out these post cards along the dashed lines. Just write in the information on reverse side, add your return address, then apply the proper postage and drop in the mail.

Affix
Stamp
Here

Name
Title
Company
Address
City
State & Zip

Sales and Use Tax Division
148 International Boulevard
P.O. Box 38136
Atlanta, GA 30334

Affix
Stamp
Here

Name
Title
Company
Address
City
State & Zip

Centralized Taxpayer Registration Unit
Georgia Department of Revenue
P.O. Box 740001
Atlanta, GA 30374-0001

Affix
Stamp
Here

Name
Title
Company
Address
City
State & Zip

Small and Minority Business Coordinator
Georgia Department of Administrative Services
West Tower, Suite 1602
200 Piedmont Avenue
Atlanta, GA 30334

Affix
Stamp
Here

Name
Title
Company
Address
City
State & Zip

U.S. Department of Labor – OSHA
1375 Peachtree Street, NE, Suite 587
Atlanta, GA 30367

Attn: Sales and Use Tax Division

Please send me:

☐ *Employer's Handbook*

☐ *Employment Security Booklet*

Name

Title

Company

Address

City   State   Zip

Post card provided by The Oasis Press, 300 North Valley Drive, Grants Pass, OR 97526   12/92

Attn: Centralized Taxpayer Registration Unit

Please send me:

☐ *The Taxpayer Registration booklet*

Name

Title

Company

Address

City   State   Zip

Post card provided by The Oasis Press, 300 North Valley Drive, Grants Pass, OR 97526   12/92

Attn: Small and Minority Business Coordinator

Please send me:

☐ *Yellow Pages for Small and Minority Businesses*

☐ *How to Do Business with the State of Georgia*

Name

Title

Company

Address

City   State   Zip

Post card provided by The Oasis Press, 300 North Valley Drive, Grants Pass, OR 97526   12/92

Attn: OSHA

Please send me:

☐ *OSHA Handbook for Small Businesses, OSHA 2209*

☐ *OSHA posters*

☐ *Your Workplace Rights in Action, OSHA 3035*

☐ *All About OSHA, OSHA 2056*

☐ *OSHA Inspections, OSHA 2098*

Name

Title

Company

Address

City   State   Zip

Post card provided by The Oasis Press, 300 North Valley Drive, Grants Pass, OR 97526   12/92